The Poverty Law Canon

The Poverty Law Canon

EXPLORING THE MAJOR CASES

Edited by
Marie A. Failinger and Ezra Rosser

University of Michigan Press
Ann Arbor

Published in the United States of America by the
University of Michigan Press
Manufactured in the United States of America
⊗ Printed on acid-free paper

2019   2018   2017   2016   4   3   2   1

A CIP catalog record for this book is available from the British Library.

Library of Congress Cataloging-in-Publication Data

Names: Failinger, Marie A., editor. | Rosser, Ezra, editor.
Title: The poverty law canon : exploring the major cases / edited by Marie A. Failinger
   and Ezra Rosser.
Description: Ann Arbor : University of Michigan Press, 2016. | Includes
   bibliographical references and index.
Identifiers: LCCN 2016005509| ISBN 9780472073153 (hardcover : alk.
   paper) | ISBN 9780472053155 (pbk. : alk. paper) | ISBN 9780472121977
   (e-book)
Subjects: LCSH: Legal assistance to the poor—United States—Cases. | Public
   welfare—Law and legislation—United States—Cases. | Law—Economic
   aspects—United States—Cases.
Classification: LCC KF390.5.P6 P68   2016 | DDC 349.73086/942—dc23
LC record available at http://lccn.loc.gov/2016005509

To my mother and father, Joan and Conard Failinger, and my grandparents, Nina and Harold Lang, and Emma and Conard Failinger Sr. Though you walked very different roads as homemaker, salesman, factory worker, carpenter, schoolteacher, and storekeeper, with as many political opinions to match, your generosity of spirit toward others has inspired this work.
    —M.F.

To my students and to my colleagues and mentors at American University Washington College of Law, especially Susan Bennett, Claudio Grossman, and Ira Robbins. It is a privilege to get to teach and write in your company.
    —E.R.

Contents

Part III • The Modern Era

Introduction

EZRA ROSSER

The poverty law cases presented here defy easy categorization. They do not fit comfortably into the study of either poverty or the law, and in fact are often excluded from both. That is not to say that the cases are not important. As the essays in this book show, poverty law cases offer scholars, activists, and students a great opportunity to see how the law impacts the lives of poor people and the ways poor people have challenged the practices and laws that arguably infringe upon their rights. Sometimes successful and sometimes unsuccessful, these challenges are grounded in the lived experiences of poor people, and it is by exploring their stories and the stories of their lawyers that we can see law's potential and its limits.

Poverty law is complex and amorphous, in much the same way that poverty is. Definitional issues abound: What is poverty? What is poverty law? The first question can be answered in a number of different ways. Some definitions of poverty focus on whether people have enough income to meet their basic needs. Other definitions focus on the relative status of people in their society. In the United States, the theoretical alternatives get reduced in practice to the poverty line (currently set by the Department of Health and Human Services at $24,250 for a family of four), which is used as a tool to measure poverty and to determine eligibility for a range of means-tested programs.

Poverty law also lacks a single definition. Generically, it is the law that impacts poor people or poor communities. But, of course, such a definition is arguably overbroad; defining poverty law has simply been inverted to a challenge to say what it is not. Poverty law can also be narrowly defined to be the law as it relates to antipoverty programs such as welfare and food stamps. While such a definition has the advantage of targeted simplicity, it is underinclusive, wrongfully excluding things like exploitation of poor consumers and systematic inequalities in the provision of public education from the umbrella of poverty law. While a satisfactory definition of poverty law remains elusive, for antipoverty advocates, lawyers, and community leaders, their work in poverty law, while it may cross fields, remains moored to the idea of improving the lives of poor people.

One of the recurring questions for those who study poverty in the United States is how much significance to place on the law and the poverty law canon of cases? We do not propose to answer that question. We leave that task to our readers, who will undoubtedly reach different conclusions regarding the relative significance of the law. Just as we believe it would be wrong to falsely elevate these cases, we also believe it is wrong to overly discount or neglect them. When the U.S. Supreme Court declares, as it did in *Edwards v. California*, that people cannot be barred from bringing the indigent into other states because such prohibitions violate a right to travel, that has real meaning to the poor whether they seek to cross state lines or not. Much the same can be said of a one-strike eviction policy that denies public housing residents the sort of tenancy rights that are expected outside the public housing context and that was upheld by the Supreme Court in *HUD v. Rucker*. The cases included here impact some of the most important areas of law and rights that relate to poor people, everything from consumer protection and equal education to access to justice and rights to privacy. So, at the most basic, these cases are important because of their coverage. But they also are part of the poverty law canon because collectively they speak to the way the rights of the poor have changed over time.

As with any effort to construct a canon, there is a risk that some cases will be missed and others may be included that perhaps should not have been. There is also the question of the canon's value: why attempt to bring together a canon of cases? What work is done by putting these stories and cases together? We welcome such discussions, but what does not seem debatable is the country's need to once again engage deeply on matters of poverty and on the rights of the poor. It has now been more than fifty years since President Lyndon Johnson announced the War on Poverty. Along with numerous social programs that continue to benefit poor people to this day, the War on Poverty brought legal resources to bear on issues of poverty that had and have a profound impact on the lives of those they represented directly and indirectly. The great recession of 2007–2009 narrowed the distance between the poor and the middle class by exposing the vulnerability that is common to most people in our society. It also helped underline the fact that we ignore at great peril the poor and their legal rights.

The chronological ordering of the essays in this book highlights the overall arc of how poverty law cases have fared in the courts through time. Martha Davis and others have observed this trajectory,[1] sometimes compared to a mountain of rights. Poor people and their advocates climbed the mountain through a string of victories at the United States Supreme Court in the late 1960s. As part of the War on Poverty, the newly created Office of Economic Opportunity supported legal aid attorneys and tasked them not only with assisting the poor on a direct services basis but also with law reform. The connection between the War on Poverty and legal aid attorneys was first articulated in an article published by the *Yale Law Journal*.[2] Edgar and Jean Cahn proposed the establishment of neighborhood law firms whose mission would include collateral and direct attacks on rules and regulations that harm the poor. They advocated "fostering and, where appropriate, subsidizing institutions and vehicles of dissent in slum communities." And with the financial support of the OEO and the Ford Foundation, that is exactly what young lawyers across the country began doing.

Using the law, they pushed for expanding the rights of the poor in everything from procedural due process and privacy in the context of welfare to consumer protections and rental housing standards. As Judge Patricia Wald recalls,

> It was a heady time: the first wave of poverty law reform coughed up big issue cases; the federal courts were hospitable, even eager to help us make new law for the poor and disadvantaged; a mildly benevolent Supreme Court smiled from on high. . . . We felt confident in "going for it," "doing the right thing," raising constitutional issues freely— almost profligately—seeking activist intervention from the courts, raising Cain with the welfare and the health care bureaucracies. We won the vast majority of issues we litigated.[3]

Given this friendly reception to lawsuits challenging rules and regulations that harmed the poor, it's no surprise that many of the biggest victories of the canonical poverty law cases come out of this era. The high water mark occurred in *Goldberg v. Kelly*, a 1970 decision in which the Supreme Court held that due process required pretermination hearings before an individual's welfare benefits could be cut. The case, citing Charles A. Reich's influential 1964 article *The New Property*, even hinted that welfare should be considered and protected as property akin to traditional real property.[4] The Court emphasized a structural understanding of poverty, noting that "forces not within the control of the poor contribute to their poverty." The Court went on to argue that "[w]elfare, by meeting the basic demands of subsistence, can help bring within the reach of the poor the same opportunities that are available to others to participate meaningfully in the life of the community." For those dedicated to using the law to further the rights of the poor, this was radical and exciting stuff, but the excitement was short lived.

Decided just two weeks after *Goldberg*, the Supreme Court's decision in *Dandridge v. Williams* ushered in a series of losses for those advocating for the poor. The Court was coming back down the mountain. Instead of recognizing the rights of the poor, the Court adopted a highly deferential stance toward policies that harmed poor individuals, families, and children. Just as quickly as the Court had expanded the rights of the poor in the late 1960s, it reversed course over the early years of the 1970s. In 1973, the Court sanctioned state-supported inequality in public education by refusing to apply strict scrutiny on the basis of wealth discrimination. *San Antonio Independent School District v. Rodriquez* put to rest any doubt that the courthouse doors of the Supreme Court were largely closed to the concerns of poor people. While there has been the occasional victory, the losses have continued in the modern era, though their significance is more debatable because the Court has avoided broad pronouncements on the rights of the poor. While the other branches of government have expanded some substantive rights (notably, for instance, the Affordable Care Act) and curtailed others (such as the welfare reform legislation of 1996), the Supreme Court's role has shrunk. This change reflects the deference the Court accords Congress and the states when it comes to social welfare policy and, on the other hand, the fact that antipoverty lawyers are avoiding the Supreme Court because of the likelihood of continued losses.

But it would be a mistake to treat the poverty law cases as simply a list of victories and losses devoid of context. The contributors to this volume demonstrate that the poverty law canon cannot be fully understood solely through the published opinions of courts, because doing so glosses over the stories behind the cases. Poverty law cases are based on the particular facts, life story, and claims of the parties, and because of this inherent grounding, they allow us to move beyond general statements regarding the rights we think poor people should have and actually consider how particular rules impact individuals and families. The cases presented here are not only grounded in the stories of individual poor people and families, they also emerge out of the litigation strategies pursued by their lawyers and by the lawyers on the other side of the case. The story behind each case also includes the story of the court dynamics and individual views of particular justices that formed the basis for the final published opinion. And finally, the decisions often reflect the forces in the larger society such as changes in the politics of poverty and the country's general willingness or unwillingness to support the poor.

The essays presented here are multidimensional; some include rich descriptions of the lives of the poor and their struggles, some include lengthy discussions of background history and relevant politics, and some delve deeply into the strategies pursued by the lawyers and the case itself. Each story is different and the emphasis placed on the story of the clients, the strategies of the lawyers, and the workings of the judicial system varies. One could write an entire book about any one of these individual cases, and such books exist. The contributors include many of the leading poverty law experts in the country, and they had to make difficult choices about what to emphasize, depending on the case. But read together the chapters show the complex history behind every published opinion and the importance of that history in understanding both the case and the place of poverty law cases in the larger antipoverty struggle.

Part I covers a period marked by a series of victories for poor people. The first essay in this section, "When Paupers Became People: *Edwards v. California* (1941)," by Clare Pastore, shows the prevalence and power of welfare residency statutes during the Great Depression. First giving the story behind the prosecution of Edwards for bringing his brother-in-law and pregnant sister-in-law to California from Texas, the chapter shows how the decision helped move the country away from simply continuing the isolation and removal goals inherited from Elizabethan poor laws. "Remaking the 'Law of the Poor': *Williams v. Walker-Thomas Furniture Co.* (1965)," by Anne Fleming, is grounded in the story of Ora Lee Williams, a single mother of eight on public assistance, and her relationship with a rent-to-own operation with a particularly harsh debt collection, repossession contract and practice. As Fleming shows, Judge Skelly Wright wrestled with how to draft an opinion that recognized the unconscionability of the contract Williams had signed. Ultimately, he only partially succeeded: the case led to legislative changes in support of consumer protection, yet Walker-Thomas was able to continue many of its problematic practices. The next essay, "Sylvester Smith, Unlikely Heroine: *King v. Smith* (1968)," by Henry Freedman, begins by describing how man-in-the-house rules served as a form of sexual regulation and punishment of welfare recipients, particularly minority recipients, and their children. It then shows how, by means of a careful briefing strategy, Columbia

University's Center on Social Welfare Policy and Law was able to convince the Supreme Court to recognize a statutory entitlement to receive aid unburdened by the substitute father rule. The case deservedly is understood as a high point in the poverty law canon.

The victories continue throughout the late 1960s. In "Legal Services Attorneys and Migrant Advocates Join Forces: *Shapiro v. Thompson* (1969)," Elisa Minoff relates an often overlooked element of *Shapiro*, a case frequently treated as limited to its holding. The Supreme Court in *Shapiro* struck down welfare residency requirements, but as the chapter shows, this positive outcome was not an isolated event. Instead it was the result of a concerted effort by lawyers and travelers aid organizations to increase the freedom of movement and migration in the United States. Melanie B. Abbott's chapter "Dignity and Passion: *Goldberg v. Kelly* (1970)" recounts the myriad hardships faced by the plaintiffs in this landmark case after their welfare benefits were cut off. The chapter ends by highlighting the Court's characterization of poverty as something that is not necessarily the fault of individuals in the society and of welfare as something more than mere charity. The final chapter in this section, "Litigating in the Zeitgeist: *Rosado v. Wyman* (1970)" by Wendy A. Bach, underscores that the victories of the 1960s were products of a particular brief moment, when the advocacy of antipoverty organizations, the economy, and the challenges of ordinary people aligned. The work of welfare rights organizations—getting people enrolled in welfare and helping them push for their special needs to be recognized—set the stage for the *Rosado* decision. Although the Supreme Court held in the case that New York, by eliminating special needs grants, was failing to meet the recognized needs of its citizens and could therefore lose federal welfare support, the victory was short-lived as the political moment quickly passed.

The focus in part II is on five cases in the 1970s in which poor people suffered losses in the courts. In "A Sweeping Refusal of Equal Protection: *Dandridge v. Williams* (1970)," Julie A. Nice shows how a rigorous defense of family caps by the Maryland attorney general's office managed to convince the Supreme Court to defer to the state despite the privations family cap policies can inflict on large families. The chapter's lengthy coverage of the legal strategy on both sides of the case showcases the importance of legal advocacy in convincing the Court to strike a new path when it is asked to review welfare policies. Michele Estrin Gilman's chapter, "Privacy as a Luxury Not for the Poor: *Wyman v. James* (1971)," focuses mainly on how the Court works through a poverty law case and the aftermath of the Court's decision to uphold New York's home visit policy against a privacy-based challenge.

After setting the scene by situating privacy in the welfare rights movement, Gilman delves into the inner workings of the Court and ends by connecting the case to ongoing policies of welfare surveillance. "A Tragedy of Two Americas: *Jefferson v. Hackney* (1972)," by Marie A. Failinger, connects the active involvement of antipoverty lawyers in dealing with a welfare protest by mothers and their children with a subsequent challenge to Texas's decision to reduce welfare benefits to a fixed percentage of recognized need. By tracing the case's progress through the courts to the Supreme Court, the chapter emphasizes the significant role that Justice Rehnquist (later Chief Justice Rehnquist) played in using the case to quash the welfare rights claims at the heart of the case.

The importance of the ideological shift in the Supreme Court and the work of the Court preceding the issuance of the final opinion are further developed in the last two chapters in this section. "Denying the Poor Access to Court: *United States v. Kras* (1973)," by Henry Rose, tells the story of how the case went from being framed as about access to the courts to being limited to bankruptcy. Skepticism about whether the plaintiff truly was unable to afford the bankruptcy filing fee together with a push from Justice Marshall's harsh dissent made a majority of the Court decide that there was not a constitutional issue with filing fee requirement. Finally, "'The Poor People Have Lost Again': *San Antonio Independent School District v. Rodriguez* (1973)," by Camille Walsh, focuses primarily on the paper history of this landmark defeat. She shows how the briefing strategy leading up to oral argument as well as the behind-the-scenes work processes of the justices contribute to the final result, which was the Court's signing off on a bifurcated system of education marked by striking inequality.

Part III, the final section of the book, looks at more recent cases and reflects on a group of outcomes that are mixed but that continue the trend of more losses than victories. The first chapter, "Reflecting and Foreshadowing: *Mathews v. Eldridge* (1976)," by John J. Capowski, combines elements of two previous cases: both the question presented in *Goldberg*, of the right to a pretermination hearing, and the Court's inability to understand the lives of the poor seen in *Kras*. The chapter describes how the Court came to hold that those on disability have no right to continue receiving payments until they have a chance to be heard. As Capowski recounts, changes in the makeup of the Court were coupled with changes in the larger society that made the Court unwilling to extend *Goldberg* beyond the welfare context. The next chapter, "Chronicle of a Debt Foretold: *Zablocki v. Red Hail* (1978)," by the trio of Tonya L. Brito, R. Kirk Anderson, and Monica Wedgewood, returns the reader's attention from the workings of lawyers and the Court to the background story of Roger Red Hail. Although the Red Hail opinion and briefs omit the fact that Red Hail was a member of the Oneida Tribe of Indians of Wisconsin, this chapter shows in rich detail the way his identity, the poverty of his community, and Indian activism eventually led all the way to the Supreme Court.

Part III ends with two more examples of losses from the perspective of antipoverty advocates. "The Movement for a Right to Counsel in Civil Cases: *Turner v. Rogers* (2011)," by Kelly Terry, is a particularly troubling reminder of how far the Court has withdrawn from the promise of the cases presented in part I. The chapter describes the combination of drug addiction and poor job prospects that led Michael Turner to fail to make child support payments and connects his subsequent imprisonment for contempt with the question of the case, whether individuals facing jail time for civil matters should have a right to counsel. Despite a movement to recognize a civil right to counsel, the Supreme Court found that there is no automatic right to legal assistance even though Turner's liberty was at stake. Finally, in "Public Housing as Housing of Last Resort: *Department of Housing and Urban Development v. Rucker* (2002)," Nestor M. Davidson places the one-strike rule, that public housing tenants could lose their housing for a single instance of drug-related activity, into its social and political context. As the chapter shows, the one-strike rule meant that tenants could be evicted for the actions of others supposedly under their control, such as children and grandchildren. Ultimately, the Court upheld the policy and in the process undermined the attachment public housing residents have to their homes. Considering the current makeup of the Supreme Court, it seems appropriate that these concluding chapters reflect pessimism that the rights of the poor will be recognized by the federal judiciary.

After reading these chapters, questions about how the poverty law cases should be understood in terms of more general antipoverty policy are likely to remain. But this book, by focusing on the lives of the poor, their legal representatives who sought to have their claims recognized, and on the workings of the Supreme Court, provides one possible way of integrating these cases into a broader understanding of U.S. policy regarding the poor. We do not claim that these poverty law cases are more important than understanding things like social movements and economics, but that any approach to the study of poverty that ignores the law is incomplete. By focusing on the stories behind the cases, the chapters that follow bring to life published opinions that on the surface can seem to be just about a single issue or rule. But behind the opinion are the stories of poor people, their lawyers, and of the judicial process. As the book illustrates, court decisions should not be seen as divorced from society and the experiences of the poor, for it is through the lives of the poor and the struggle to get their rights recognized that we can best understand the impact the law has on the poor and on society.

Notes

1. For perhaps the most significant scholarly treatment of the general arc of poverty law cases, see MARTHA DAVIS, BRUTAL NEED: LAWYERS AND THE WELFARE RIGHTS MOVEMENT, 1960–1973 (1993).

2. Edgar S. Cahn and Jean C. Cahn, *The War on Poverty: A Civilian Perspective*, 73 YALE L.J. 1317 (1964).

3. Judge Patricia M. Wald, *Ten Admonitions for Legal Services Advocates Contemplating Federal Litigation*, 27 CLEARINGHOUSE REV. 11, 12 (1993).

4. Charles Reich, *The New Property*, 73 YALE L.J. 733 (1964).

Part I

Victories

When Paupers Became People

Edwards v. California • (1941)

CLARE PASTORE

Fred F. Edwards left his home in Marysville, California, in late December 1939, headed for the tiny town of Spur, Texas. Edwards' brother-in-law, Frank Duncan, and Duncan's pregnant wife were destitute in Spur, and Edwards brought them in his car back home to Marysville, 40 miles north of Sacramento, where Mrs. Duncan gave birth just three weeks after leaving Texas. On January 3, 1940, when the family entered California, Edwards became a criminal in the eyes of the state. His offense: violation of Welfare and Institutions Code section 2615, which forbade any person from "bringing into the State any indigent person who is not a resident of the State." Edwards was convicted and sentenced to six months in the county jail.

Nearly two years later, the United States Supreme Court reversed the conviction, invalidating the California statute and similar ones in 27 other states.[1] The backdrop to *Edwards v. California* includes the Depression, the Dust Bowl migration to California, an armed blockade of the state briefly established by the Los Angeles Police Department, and a cast of colorful and historically significant figures.

Edwards is rich with significance for the circuitous doctrinal path of the constitutional right to travel, which has been thoroughly analyzed by many scholars. Here, I mean not to retrace those doctrinal steps but to suggest a different, additional enduring importance of the case. *Edwards* rejected a century of case law (which itself drew on hundreds of years of British common law and statutes) that affirmed states' police power to exclude "paupers, vagrants, and convicts" and reiterated that paupers were a "moral pestilence." *Edwards* thus marks a critical step in the journey of the most indigent Americans to citizenship. Although it would take decades more for the poor to approach real citizenship and for states to revise or repeal settlement and residence laws, prohibitions on voting or marrying, vagrancy laws, and other repressive measures against the poor, after *Edwards*, the term "pauper" evolved into what it is today: a mere synonym, albeit an antiquated one, for an indigent. *Edwards* is the case, therefore, that transformed the poorest Americans from "paupers"—a distinct legal category of those subject to universal opprobrium and with little claim to rights—into people.

Background: Westward Migration, Destitution, and Armed Deterrence

Migration and Destitution

Migration has been a part of life in California since the state's earliest days. The state's population grew 1,800 percent in 80 years, from less than 400,000 in 1860 to nearly 7 million by 1940. While significant portions of this growth came from migration in virtually every year, the pace of migration to California during the 1920s and 1930s dwarfed that of any other period and any other state.

The scale of this migration is difficult to comprehend today. According to a 1941 report by the U.S. House of Representatives' Select Committee to Investigate the Interstate Migration of Destitute Citizens (the Tolan Committee Report), "from 1920 to 1929, about 2,000,000 persons moved into California, the largest movement recorded for any State in any single decade of our history."[2] This number—which averaged nearly 4,000 per week—represented a 60 percent increase in the state's population in one decade. From 1930 to 1939, fully 40 percent of all migrants crossing state lines came to California, causing the state's population to grow by another 19 percent or 1.1 million people. By comparison, migration increased the population of neighboring Oregon by only 15 percent during the 1920s and 11 percent during the 1930s.

In addition to the sheer volume of migrants, the Depression and the Dust Bowl meant that huge numbers of these newcomers—like many of Americans everywhere—were broke. In his brief in the *Edwards* case, the California attorney general provided data from federal and state agencies concluding that more than 300,000 persons, or nearly a third of all those migrating to California between 1933 and 1939, received public assistance within a year of settling there, at a cost of approximately $13 million dollars ($220 million in 2015 dollars) in state and federal funds.

Many of the burdens of absorbing new migrants fell not on the state but on California cities and counties. For example, historian James N. Gregory notes that the federal Bureau of Agricultural Economics closely examined the budgets of two agricultural counties, Yuba and Kern, for public school, welfare, and health spending. The bureau estimated in 1940 that Kern County, home to Bakersfield, spent 28 percent of its entire budget on interstate migrants who had settled there over the previous decade, while Yuba (north of Sacramento) spent 21 percent of its 1940 budget on migrants.[3] As a journalist reporting stories that later formed the basis for his classic novel *The Grapes of Wrath*, John Steinbeck estimated in 1936 that there were at least 150,000 homeless migrants "wandering up and down the state."[4]

The influx of so many newcomers produced many tensions with longer-term residents. "Okies" now joined Japanese, Chinese, and Mexican immigrants as subjects of stereotyping and perceived unassimilability. As the Joad family is warned in Steinbeck's *The Grapes of Wrath*, "Okie use' ta mean you was from Oklahoma. Now it means you're a dirty son-of-a-bitch. Okie means you're scum."[5]

The social and economic effects of the mass internal migration of Americans in the 1930s led to a remarkable congressional inquiry, spanning 28 days of hearings in 1940 and 1941 in eight cities with more than three million words of testimony from nearly four hundred people. Those testifying included governors, mayors, state and federal relief officials, sociologists, economists, professors, scores of migrant citizens, and even Eleanor Roosevelt. The Select Committee to Investigate the Interstate Migration of Destitute Citizens came to be known as the Tolan Committee after its chair, congressman and social worker John Tolan of California. Its findings were collected in eight volumes of testimony and summarized in a seven-hundred-page report issued in April 1941.[6] Both the report and Congressman Tolan came to figure prominently in the *Edwards* litigation that same year.

Anti-Migrant Legislation

The statute at issue in *Edwards* was far from unique in America. Twenty-seven other states, including all of New England and several populous states such as New York and New Jersey, had similar statutes. Four southern states also had such laws, though no southwestern state did.

According to Congressman Tolan's Supreme Court amicus brief in *Edwards*, Florida and Mississippi's statutes applied only to restrain masters of vessels from bringing in indigents, while every other state broadly prohibited any person from doing so. Some states required knowledge of the migrant's indigent status or intent to render the migrant a public charge. Every statute included penalties, most commonly a misdemeanor conviction, fine, imprisonment, or civil penalty. Some barred only the bringing in of "paupers," the insane or disabled, or those likely to become a public charge, while 19 barred bringing persons who were "poor or indigent," "destitute," or simply "poor." All but a handful of the state statutes permitted the deportation or removal of the indigents, by court or administrative action.[7]

Importantly, the statutes barring the importation of paupers or poor persons were also part of an intricate web of "settlement laws" that defined and circumscribed state residence, permitted deportation or removal of destitute nonresidents, and defined eligibility for relief. For example, a "typical state settlement law," according to the Tolan Committee, did not permit a person to be considered a resident of a state until he or she had resided there continuously for three years with intent to remain. Time during which the migrant received "any public or private relief or support from friends, charitable organizations, or relatives other than legally responsible relatives," as well as time spent in a public institution or on parole, was excluded. Remaining away from the state for a period of a year for reasons other than employment could also result in the forfeiture of state citizenship.

The result of these settlement laws was that many thousands of persons found themselves without any state residence, ineligible for relief in any jurisdiction and subject to removal or being "passed on" to place after place. Women were particularly vulnerable since state law often provided that a wife's place of residence was that of her husband. Therefore, even a wife who remained in one place for the requisite period and avoided the disqualifying conditions of receipt of relief or institutionalization could lose residency if her husband left the state for an extended period. Representative Tolan noted at the San Francisco hearings that the Census report of 1940 was being delayed because there was so much difficulty in determining the states of residence of hundreds of thousands of Americans.

The Tolan Committee Report recounts in tragic detail the operation of many residency and removal statutes. For example:

Mrs. P was married to Mr. P in Pennsylvania on January 20, 1932, and, in the early part of 1933, Mrs. P deserted her husband in Pennsylvania, coming into New York. She had last heard from him November 18, 1938. Mrs. P had lived at the home of her father in Jamestown, New York, since she had deserted her husband. Decision: Since this woman had deserted her husband, she could not have established a settlement here and it would depend on the settlement laws of Pennsylvania as to whether or not she still retains settlement in that State.

In January 1935 a couple moved to Detroit, Mich., from New York City, where they had a settlement. In August 1935 the husband was sentenced to a 5-year term in a Michigan State prison and the woman returned to New York City. *Decision*: The settlement of this couple in New York City was lost because the husband was removed from the State for 1 full year. The wife could not acquire a separate settlement, not being legally divorced or separated. Since no new settlement was acquired, the couple are nonsettled persons.[8]

The Tolan Committee Report also documents litigation between states, and even between counties in the same state, over which jurisdiction bore responsibility for aiding indigents who had moved, or the costs of transporting them from one place to another. One case lays out in excruciating detail the brutal actions of two North Dakota counties that shuttled a paralyzed father and his ten children back and forth between the two counties and into and out of South Dakota (where the North Dakota counties claimed he was resident, despite a year's stay in their state following the promise of a job). The family was at one point ejected from a North Dakota county sheriff's car in another North Dakota county and left on the side of the road in early evening with no funds and no food; their goods were entrusted by the sheriffs to a stranger (whereupon "two dressers, a bed, and a table were broken and the woman's coat lost.") When officials in this second county drove the family to the state line, South Dakota officials promptly served them with an order to leave, and the South Dakota sheriff removed them back to North Dakota.

The case made its way to the North Dakota Supreme Court, which found that Burleigh County (North Dakota) was responsible for providing aid to the family until any eventual return to South Dakota. Justice Burr offered this commentary, evincing both compassion for the people involved and a firm commitment to the traditional principle that the poor "belonged" to some locality not necessarily of their own choosing:

[I]t may well be said few records show any such callousness toward human beings as this controversy between South Dakota and North

Dakota discloses. The case is an illustration of the extent to which "man's inhumanity to man" may be carried. Human beings are shifted around like so much cargo. Somewhere and somehow the well springs of humanity and brotherhood appeared to be dried up. Sick and impoverished creatures against whom there is no indication of crime, laziness, or willfulness, have no place to lay their weary heads, except such as the generosity of Adams County gives them as a mere subsistence in a situation not of its own making, and for which it is not responsible. The callous indifference of South Dakota seems scarcely credible in this age.[9]

Despite their harshness, however, California's section 2615 and the removal statutes were mild compared to some proposals urged upon legislatures at the time, or informally in use. For example, economist Paul Taylor, who with his wife, photographer Dorothea Lange, studied and documented migrant issues extensively during the 1930s and 1940s, obtained a 1936 document from the California State Board of Public Welfare directing county officials to seize the cars of migrants. That directive instructed, "A part of the plan for the stabilizing of migrants is that we take from them the easiest mode of transportation, which is the automobile," and that the proceeds from sales of these cars be used to finance the cost of transporting migrants out of California.[10] In 1935, the California Assembly passed the Jones-Redwine Bill, which proposed to prohibit the entry into the state of "all paupers, vagabonds, indigent persons, and persons likely to become public charges" and to create a special border patrol to enforce the measure.[11] (The measure failed in the state senate.) The same year, the Los Angeles Chamber of Commerce suggested that "undesirable indigent transients" should be sent to hard labor prison camps.[12]

Armed Deterrence: State Blockades in Florida, Colorado, and California[13]

Although the laws described above, following in the tradition of the Elizabethan poor laws, had long provided tools for counties and cities to resist aiding indigents who were not "their own," the governors of Florida and Colorado and the police chief of Los Angeles took matters to a new level in the mid-1930s. The Tolan Committee Report includes descriptions of the "bum blockades" in three states.

In Florida, Governor David Sholtz, a New Deal Democrat, declared a "winter blockade" in 1934, 1935, and 1936. The first year, according to the

Florida Times-Union, "Governor Sholtz telegraphed governors of all States east of the Mississippi River to 'serve notice' upon their people that no more transients could be accommodated" in Florida. In October 1936, the *New York Times* noted that Governor Sholtz had instituted his third annual blockade. "The border-patrol method is the most effective Florida has been able to devise for the protection of the better class of Winter visitors. It is sociological, not mercenary, but it obviously is not a complete success. Too many ingenious undesirables manage to slip past the guards." In November, the *Times* noted Florida's contention that by the end of the week, "it will have shunted from the State 2,000 hitch-hiking, rod-riding, and flivver-driving itinerants."[14]

Although controversial both in the state and nationally, Florida's seasonal blockade was not ended until a new governor took over in 1937. Announcing the abandonment of the blockade, Governor Fred P. Cone noted doubts about both the constitutionality and the efficacy of turning away the visibly indigent as a crime-fighting measure, noting that "[t]here are plenty of crooks in fine automobiles."

In Colorado, Governor Edwin C. Johnson proclaimed martial law by executive order in 1936 in a one-mile-wide area along the state's entire 360-mile southern border. The executive order directed the Colorado National Guard chief to "order out such troops as in his judgment may be necessary . . . to prevent and repel the further invasion of this State by . . . aliens, indigent persons, or invaders, and to repel and return all such persons" to the states from which they entered Colorado.[15] The first car halted at one checkpoint contained the University of Denver's new football coach and his wife, who "explained good-naturedly that they were on the way from their ranch in New Mexico to Denver and were waved on with a smile."

The measure caused an immediate uproar and was abandoned six days later after protests from (among others) beet growers anticipating the need for additional labor, both of Colorado's senators, and the governor of New Mexico, who threatened to bar Colorado goods from his state. Some of the *Denver News*' reporting of the situation bordered on the farcical. For example, one article began, "[k]haki-clad troops of the Colorado National Guard will move into Southern Colorado early Sunday to repulse a threatened invasion of alien beet laborers," and quoted the governor as saying "I have also learned that sheep shearers are coming into the state in large numbers."[16]

Meanwhile, back in California, in early February 1936 Los Angeles police chief John Edgar "Two-Gun" Davis announced that he had dispatched 126 city police to 16 checkpoints throughout the state (some as far as the Oregon border, 800 miles from the Los Angeles city limits) to turn away indigent transients. The action was supported by the mayor, the City Council, the Board of Supervisors, the Chamber of Commerce, and the railroads, which obligingly stopped incoming trains at the checkpoints. Those stopped were given the choice between turning back and thirty to eighty days at hard labor.[17] The measure provoked cries of outrage from civil libertarians. In response, the *Los Angeles Times* editorialized "Let's Have More Outrages" and opined that while the action might eventually be proven unlawful, "it will take some time to do it. In that interval a lot of undesirables can be turned back and a lot more discouraged from even starting in this direction."[18] The *Times* also excoriated the migrants as "two-legged locusts," "won't workers," criminal Bolsheviks, and unpatriotic undesirables.[19]

The blockade lasted only a little over two months, apparently because of a combination of cost, public outcry, and litigation. Although California governor Frank F. Merriam was quoted as saying mildly about the LAPD's action, "It's up to them if they can get away with it,"[20] California attorney general U. S. Webb termed it illegal, and a state senator who had engineered the defeat of the Jones-Redwine statewide blockade bill excoriated it as "damnable, absurd, and asinine." Historian Kevin Starr notes that "the illegality of this program, if not its outright fascism, soon aroused a chorus of protest from the American Civil Liberties Union, the American Association of Social Workers, the governor of Nevada, the attorneys general of Arizona and Oregon, the city commission of Phoenix, Oregon city officials . . . [and] even the chief of the California highway patrol, who resented the incursion of the LAPD into CHP jurisdiction."[21]

Prosecutions Under California's Anti-Migration Statute

California attorney general Earl Warren took a strikingly disingenuous tack regarding the number of people prosecuted under section 2615 in his defense of the measure in the Supreme Court. He asserted that although section 2615 and its predecessors had been in effect for more than 75 years, "California has resorted to its provisions, so far as our research has disclosed, only thirteen times in all those years."

There is room for skepticism about the attorney general's figures, however, because his brief explains that the methodology for determining the number of cases was simply to ask the state's Department of Social Welfare about its knowledge of prosecutions and then to contact the three counties identified by state welfare officials. It is unknown, therefore, whether other counties also prosecuted under Section 2615 without the knowledge of the Department of Social Welfare, much less whether the cases identified by this casual survey represent all prosecutions in the 75-year history of section 2615 and its predecessors, even in the three identified counties.

Moreover, 11 of the 13 identified cases, involving 16 defendants, arose in the same rural northern county (Tulare) and all were initiated in the five months between September 1939 and January 1940, with six in the month of November 1939 alone. Far from presenting a reassuring picture of the infrequency of resort to section 2615, therefore, the attorney general's own data appear to show a beleaguered county discovering a tool and dramatically accelerating its use over a recent period of time.

Additionally, the cases bluntly refute the state's attempt to convince the Court that the statute was primarily intended or used only to stop the "promotional bringing into the State" of persons to whom the defendant owed no legal duty of support.[22] Of the 13 cases identified (including that of Edwards himself), there is a close familial relationship between at least one of the defendants who "imported" the indigent unlawfully and at least one of the indigent migrants in 10 cases; one case includes no information about any relationship, and in two cases the attorney general reports a determination of no relationship.

The facts of the cases are often heartbreaking. In addition to the prosecution of Edwards himself for bringing his brother-in-law and pregnant sister-in-law to California, one Fred E. Woodward was charged in January 1940 with bringing in his own wife and their four children.[23] Another defendant, William Ensminger, traveled to Texas to pick up his ex-wife Minnie and their five children after learning that Minnie had been seriously injured in an accident while traveling with her new husband and Ensminger's children from Oklahoma to California. Her new husband had been "picked up on some charge" and sent to prison. Rather than leave his children and ex-wife stranded in Texas, Ensminger brought them to California, becoming a criminal in the process.

The eleven Tulare County cases are interesting for procedural reasons as well. In every one, the complaint was filed by A. H. Kincaid, special investigator to the district attorney, "whose duty it was to investigate cases wherein persons were unlawfully receiving assistance from the County Welfare Department." In some instances, prosecutions began when the migrants applied for aid at the County Welfare Department, while others were the result of "reports from various persons that a family of destitute people had recently arrived, which led to investigations." The attorney general's brief states that Mr. Kincaid "had no written memoranda but was able to recall from memory various facts that were involved in a number of the prosecutions."

The cases were all prosecuted in justice courts, a type of local tribunal presided over by justices of the peace, who were appointed by County Boards of Supervisors and were not required to be lawyers.[24] Appeal from justice court rulings could be taken to the superior court (as was done in *Edwards*), but no further appeal was available. The cases provide a sobering picture of the quality of justice available to the destitute.

In none of the cases does the attorney general's filing show any record of a defendant having a lawyer to contest the charge, although one defendant appeared with a lawyer at a subsequent proceeding for failure to comply with his sentence, and Fred Edwards was represented by ACLU lawyers seeking to challenge the law.[25] In the four cases where bail is mentioned, it was set at $500 or $1,000, astronomical sums to the indigent in 1939 and 1940. No trials seem to have occurred. Instead, guilty pleas followed rapidly after the filing of the complaint, sometimes on the same day.

In the six Tulare cases whose disposition is clear, defendants were sentenced to six months in the county jail or a work camp, with sentence suspended on conditions generally including that the defendant return the migrants to their home states and sometimes including what amounted to banishment: an order that the defendant not return to California for two years. In one case, the justice of the peace ordered the removal not only of the migrants and the defendant, but of the defendant's family as well. In another, the defendant was ordered to return the indigents "whence they came or to Arizona." Only two defendants, charged in the same case, seem to have pled not guilty, and perhaps as a result, their case appears to have been continued indefinitely. One defendant was returned to court after a guilty plea for failure to fulfill the conditions of his sentence and committed to the county jail.

In all, the 11 Tulare cases do nothing to support the attorney general's assurances to the Court that "the statute does not reflect the actual policy of the state of California with respect to indigents from other states" or that California has never practiced a policy "other than an attitude of warm friendship, especially for those who have little to bring to California except their health, and the character and hope that builds cities and states and nations."

Attorney General Warren's view of the law is also interestingly at odds with that of the sitting governor at the time, liberal Democrat Culbert L. Olson. Governor Olson (whom Warren would defeat resoundingly in the next gubernatorial election in 1942) testified before the Tolan Committee in San Francisco in September 1940, while Fred Edwards' case was pending. When Chairman Tolan mentioned laws criminalizing the transport of indigents in several states, Governor Olson predicted that when such laws reached the Supreme Court, "they will be nullified."

The Supreme Court Litigation

Section 2615 was defended by the Yuba County district attorney and (on re-argument) by attorney general Earl Warren. Later, of course, Warren became the famously liberal chief justice of the U.S. Supreme Court, although he dissented in the Court's second case upholding the rights of poor newcomers, *Shapiro v. Thompson*, in 1969. The lead lawyer actually litigating *Edwards* for the state was Warren protégé William Sweigert, later appointed to the U.S. District Court in San Francisco by President Eisenhower at Warren's urging, where he served 24 years. Also on the brief was Hiram Johnson III, grandson and namesake of California's 1911 reformist governor.

California had good reason to believe its statute would be upheld at the Supreme Court, and both the attorney general's and the Yuba County district attorney's briefs reflect that confidence. Both rely heavily on the Supreme Court's 1837 decision in *Mayor of New York. v. Miln*, 36 U.S. 102, a case frequently cited for the proposition that the police powers of states unquestionably extended to the ability to exclude paupers and other undesirables. This idea was well-rooted in the popular mind as well, as evidenced by its frequent repetition in, for example, newspaper articles supporting the "bum blockades" and the debate over the Jones-Redwine bill.

In *Miln*, the Supreme Court upheld a New York law imposing penalties upon any shipmaster who failed to provide a report to the mayor identifying all passengers on ships arriving in New York. The law also required payment of a bond to be used for repayment in the event a passenger, or even the later-born child of a passenger, became a public charge. While the Court's decision did not reach the bond provision since the defendant had been fined only for not filing a report, the following passage acquired, through frequent quotation, the status of well-settled doctrine:

> We think it as competent and as necessary for a State to provide precautionary measures against the moral pestilence of paupers, vagabonds, and possible convicts, as it is to guard against the physical

pestilence which may arise from unsound and infectious articles imported, or from a ship, the crew of which may be laboring under an infectious disease.[26]

As many scholars have noted, the term "pauper" was historically quite specific to those who received public assistance (and sometimes to the able-bodied who refused to work), rather than to anyone who was merely poor:

The stigma which clung to poor relief expressed the deep feelings of a people who understood that those who accepted relief must cross the road that separated the community of citizens from the outcast community of the destitute. . . . The stigma which attached to the Poor Law made "pauper" a derogatory term defining a class.[27]

Paupers were categorically excluded from many of the benefits of citizenship, often including the right to settle, marry, vote, and hold property. Indeed, the Articles of Confederation had explicitly excluded paupers from the rights of citizens: "[T]he free inhabitants of each of these states, *paupers, vagabonds and fugitives from Justice excepted*, shall be entitled to all privileges and immunities of free citizens in the several states."[28]

For more than a century, as Attorney General Warren noted in a 16-page exhibit of citations and quotations filed in the supplement to his brief, courts had cited the "moral pestilence" passage in *Miln* as authority for their laws, and the Supreme Court had many times reaffirmed its general principle.

Against this backdrop of assumed state power to exclude paupers, the question arose in *Edwards* of whether those who are merely poor (but not "paupers") were also covered by section 2615, which prohibited bringing into California "any indigent person" who was not a resident. The case was initially argued in April 1941 without the participation of the state, leading the justices to seek clarification of the statute's reach. According to the notes of Justices Douglas and Murphy from the Court's May 3, 1941, conference,[29] Justice Hughes urged that on the record before the court, there was no authority for the meaning of "indigent" and that

[T]here is nothing to show that [Mr. Duncan, the brother-in-law whom defendant Edwards was charged with bringing to California] is a pauper. A pauper is one who is on poor relief. It is also sometimes defined as a person who is likely to go on relief. The stipulation says that [Mr. Duncan] is an indigent person. There is nothing to show he was unemployable or impaired in body or mind. . . . It all comes down to the fact that this man has no money.

He urged the Court either to hold the statute unconstitutional or set it for reargument with participation by the California attorney general, noting that "I think the right here is a privilege or immunity of a citizen."

The case was reargued in October 1941 with both the attorney general and the Yuba County district attorney supporting the law. Samuel Slaff of the ACLU represented Mr. Edwards and Representative Tolan appeared as a "Friend of the Court."

The litigants urged several constitutional theories upon the Court. On behalf of Mr. Edwards, the ACLU principally argued that the statute violated the Commerce Clause, which grants Congress the power to regulate commerce among the states. Drawing heavily on the work of the Tolan Committee, Slaff's brief included a great deal of sociological and economic data about wages and migration. While never using the word "pauper," it squarely attacked the notion that migrants, even the poorest migrants, are categorically different in some legally relevant way from other Americans, pointing out that "by definition and cold economic fact *a goodly portion of even America's employed population* and a major portion of her migrants and unemployed are indigent."[30]

In opposition, the Yuba County district attorney placed all his eggs in the *Miln* basket, filing essentially a collection of statistical and economic data about the burden posed by migrants and a series of quotations from *Miln* and subsequent cases reciting the police power to exclude undesirables, with little real argument.

The attorney general took a more sophisticated tack. Urging a narrow interpretation of section 2615, he argued that by its terms the statute did not exclude any indigent person, but only prohibited others from bringing them into California. He suggested that in intent and operation the statute was aimed at the "promotion" of migration by persons not related to the migrants such as labor contractors, a theory sharply at odds with the facts of *Edwards*.

Congressman Tolan's amicus brief laid out systematically its arguments that the statute violated the Privileges and/or Immunities Clauses of the Fourth and Fourteenth Amendments, the Interstate Commerce Clause, and the Equal Protection Clause of the Fourteenth Amendment. It included an 84-page supplement of materials from the Tolan Committee Report highlighting the plight of migrants and urging rejection of the statute. Strikingly, however, Congressman Tolan's brief did not squarely attack the *Miln* doctrine. Instead, tacitly conceding that states have the authority to exclude paupers and the like, the brief addressed only the use of the *Miln* rationale against those who are merely unemployed:

> [I]n no case has [the *Miln*] doctrine been expanded to include persons who are not imbecilic, who are not drunkards, who are not vagrants or tramps; who are not diseased, who are not aged or infirm, nor as to persons who have always worked, persons who are willing to work, persons who are able to work and who are competent in every other respect, except that they are temporarily without work and without funds.[31]

The variety of legal theories raised in the briefs is reflected in the three *Edwards* opinions. The majority opinion was authored by Justice James F. "Jimmy" Byrnes. Byrnes, though little known today as a justice, was one of the most well-known and important "wise men" of the Roosevelt years, with a career unique in American history. Born in South Carolina and with a formal education extending only through the seventh grade (making him also the last Supreme Court justice not to have attended law school), Byrnes served in the highest echelons in all three branches of the federal government—as U.S. representative and senator, Supreme Court justice, and secretary of state—as well as governor of South Carolina. A close confidant and generally a staunch and powerful legislative ally of Franklin Roosevelt, Byrnes was confirmed within minutes of his formal nomination to the Court in 1941.[32]

As a justice, however, Byrnes was unremarkable. He served a single term and scarcely a year on the court, writing only sixteen opinions, of which *Edwards* was his first. By all accounts, Byrnes was restless and unhappy on the Court, missing the camaraderie and combat of the legislative process. Just two months into Byrnes' term on the Court, the Japanese bombed Pearl Harbor, and Byrnes once again immersed himself in politics. His biographer reports that throughout the early months of 1942, as Roosevelt sought to get war powers legislation through Congress and to centralize wartime political and economic authority, he turned to Justice Byrnes for political assistance, and Byrnes continued to grease the legislative wheels.[33] By early October 1942, Byrnes had resigned from the Court to become director of the Office of Economic Stabilization and later of the immensely powerful Office of War Mobilization, earning himself the nickname "the Assistant President." Although Byrnes' ambition to become Roosevelt's vice president and eventual successor was thwarted, President Truman named him secretary of state in 1945.

Despite his lack of enthusiasm for the life of a Supreme Court justice, Byrnes was an able craftsman of opinions and amenable to the coalition building often necessary to achieve a majority. *Edwards* was a prime example. Although he, along with Justices Jackson, Murphy, Douglas, and Black, was initially prepared to hold section 2615 unconstitutional as a violation of the Privileges or Immunities Clause of the Fourteenth Amendment,[34] Byrnes' eventual majority opinion struck the statute down under the Commerce Clause. The papers of the justices reveal that it was Justices Stone and Frankfurter who persuaded Byrnes that relying on the Privileges or Immunities Clause threatened to reopen the discredited *Lochner* line of cases in which anti–New Deal justices had struck down dozens of statutes based on substantive due process claims.[35] Stone warned that the "privileges and immunities" rationale could "expose our constitutional system to dangers to which it has been exposed in the last fifty years through the over-expansion and refinement of the due process and equal protection clauses."[36] The conference notes also reveal that Justice Owen Roberts initially voted to construe the statute as applying only to "paupers" and on that basis to uphold it.

Justice Byrnes' majority opinion spends but a single paragraph explaining its holding that California's statute violates the Commerce Clause. Citing a string of cases, he states that "it is settled beyond question that the transportation of persons is 'commerce' within the meaning of [the Commerce Clause]." Acknowledging that states nonetheless retain police powers over "matters of local concern" even when they touch on interstate commerce, he announces, "The issue presented in this case, therefore, is whether the prohibition embodied in Section 2615 against the 'bringing' or transportation of indigent persons into California is within the police power of that State. We think that it is not, and hold that it is an unconstitutional barrier to interstate commerce."[37]

The rest of the 2,400-word majority opinion, while not citing the Tolan brief or Tolan Committee Report, fully embraces the facts and the worldview they represent. First, the opinion asserts that ·the most important limit on state authority is "the prohibition against attempts on the part of any single State to isolate itself from difficulties common to all of them." Second, while noting that the issue of any obligation of states to aid newcomers was not before the Court, Byrnes states,

> We do, however, suggest that the theory of the Elizabethan poor laws no longer fits the facts. Recent years, and particularly the past decade, have been marked by a growing recognition that in an industrial soci-

ety the task of providing assistance to the needy has ceased to be local in character.

Finally, and most importantly, the majority dismisses the century-old *Miln* dicta:

> There remains to be noticed only the contention that the limitation upon State power to interfere with the interstate transportation of persons is subject to an exception in the case of "paupers." It is true that support for this contention may be found in early decisions of this Court. In [*Miln*], it was said that it is "as competent and as necessary for a state to provide precautionary measures against the moral pestilence of paupers, vagabonds, and possibly convicts; as it is to guard against the physical pestilence, which may arise from unsound and infectious articles imported." This language has been casually repeated in numerous later cases up to the turn of the century. In none of these cases, however, was the power of a State to exclude "paupers" actually involved.
>
> Whether an able-bodied but unemployed person like Duncan is a "pauper" within the historical meaning of the term is open to considerable doubt. . . . But assuming that the term is applicable to him and to persons similarly situated, we do not consider ourselves bound by the language referred to. *City of New York v. Miln* was decided in 1836. Whatever may have been the notion then prevailing, we do not think that it will now be seriously contended that because a person is without employment and without funds he constitutes a "moral pestilence." Poverty and immorality are not synonymous.[38]

Conclusion: Paupers to People

While it would take decades more for the poor to realize many of the rights of citizenship and for the vestiges of the Elizabethan poor laws to be swept entirely out of American law, the *Edwards* decision marked an end to the uncritical affirmation of the proposition that states enjoy the unquestioned right to exclude "paupers, vagabonds, criminals" and perhaps drunkards, lewd women, and those with certain disabilities from their territory and from the protection of their laws. Thus, while *Edwards* did not itself transform the poor into full citizens, it did turn them from paupers—a "moral pestilence"—into people in the eyes of the law.

Notes

1. Edwards v. California, 314 U.S. 160 (1941).

2. Except as otherwise noted, figures in this section are drawn from HOUSE OF REPRESENTATIVES, SELECT COMMITTEE TO INVESTIGATE THE INTERSTATE MIGRATION OF DESTITUTE CITIZENS, INTERSTATE MIGRATION 304–23 (1941) (hereinafter "Tolan Committee Report").

3. JAMES N. GREGORY, AMERICAN EXODUS 85 (1989).

4. JOHN STEINBECK, THE HARVEST GYPSIES 1 (1938) (originally published in seven parts in the SAN FRANCISCO NEWS, Oct. 5–12, 1936).

5. Historians have written extensively about the "racialization" of the perception of Okies. *See, e.g.*, PETER LA CHAPELLE, PROUD TO BE AN OKIE: CULTURAL POLITICS, COUNTRY MUSIC, AND MIGRATION TO SOUTHERN CALIFORNIA 25–29 (2007); WALTER J. STEIN, CALIFORNIA AND THE DUST BOWL MIGRATION 60 (1973).

6. In its second incarnation, beginning in March 1941, the Tolan Committee examined the growing number of migrants relocating to manufacturing centers seeking employment in the burgeoning defense industry. In 1942, emphasis shifted to the possible removal of Japanese Americans from the West Coast, following President Roosevelt's Executive Order No. 9066 authorizing exclusion from the coast of any person deemed a threat by the U.S. military. Records of all phases of the Tolan Committee, including its report and 10-part hearing transcript, are available in the National Archives. *See* GUIDE TO THE RECORDS OF THE U.S. HOUSE OF REPRESENTATIVES AT THE NATIONAL ARCHIVES 1789–1989 (Record Group 233), *available at* http://www.archives.gov/legislative/guide/house/chapter-22-select-migration-of-destitute-citizens.html, (last visited Nov. 12, 2013). Historian Kevin Starr has described the Tolan Committee Report as "sweeping and comprehensive in its detail, profoundly humanistic in its respect for testimony from the humble, with its details of day-to-day migrant life. . . . [It is] documentary art of the highest order." KEVIN STARR, ENDANGERED DREAMS: THE GREAT DEPRESSION IN CALIFORNIA 269–70 (1996).

7. Chart No. 1, Appendix to Tolan Amicus Brief, *available in* PHILLIP B. KURLAND AND GERHARD CASPER, LANDMARK BRIEFS AND ARGUMENTS OF THE SUPREME COURT OF THE UNITED STATES: CONSTITUTIONAL LAW 615 (1975).

8. Tolan Committee Report, *supra* note 2, at 619–20.

9. Adams County v. Burleigh County, 291 N.W. 281, 284–5 (N.D. 1940); reprinted in Tolan Committee Report, *supra* note 2, at 622. The criticism would seem equally applicable to the actions of the North Dakota officials.

10. Quoted in LINDA GORDON, DOROTHEA LANGE 257–58 (2009).

11. L.A. TIMES, May 17, 1935.

12. "Supplement to Brief of John H. Tolan" [hereinafter "Tolan Supp."], *available in* KURLAND AND CASPER, *supra* note 7, at 674.

13. Except as otherwise noted, facts in this section are drawn from the Tolan Supp., *supra* note 12, at 635 *et seq.*

14. *Florida Again Acts to Bar 'Drifters,'* N.Y. TIMES, Oct. 25, 1936, *Florida Bars*

Out 2,000, N.Y. Times, Nov. 20, 1936 (reprinted in Tolan Supp., *supra* note 12, at 683–84).

15. Executive Order of April 1936 (Tolan Supp., *supra* note 12, at 685).

16. *Troops Close State to Aliens, Jobless*, Denver News, Apr. 19, 1936 (Tolan Supp., *supra* note 12, at 686–87).

17. "The LAPD: 1926–1950," LAPD Official Website, http://www.lapdonline. org/history_of_the_lapd/content_basic_view/1109 (last visited Oct. 16, 2013). A Hearst Metrotone News clip discussing the "bum blockade" is available at http:// www.youtube.com/watch?v=zIZDMtRDCxI.

18. L.A. Times, Feb. 2, 1936.

19. L.A. Times, Feb. 4, Feb. 9, Mar. 23, 1936.

20. L.A. Times, Feb. 7, 1936.

21. Starr, *supra* note 6, at 178.

22. Brief of the Attorney General, 1941 WL 52965 at *28. Based on the material presented by the attorney general, only one of the cases might have exemplified the "promotional" activity the state argued was the target of the statute: according to the county district attorney's investigator, *People v. John Vaughn* involved a defendant who had completed four trips into California in a four-week period, bringing indigents unrelated to him each time.

23. Facts of the cases described here are drawn from Supplement to the Brief of the Attorney General, Exhibit 6 ("Record of Prosecutions in the Counties of the State of California Under Section 2615"), available in Kurland and Casper, *supra* note 7, at 461.

24. Three decades later, the California Supreme Court held that the federal due process clause prohibited nonattorney judges from presiding over criminal matters where incarceration was possible, unless the defendant consented. Gordon v. Justice Court, 12 Cal.3d. 323 (1974).

25. Scholar Elisa Minoff has written a dissertation on internal migration in America, including a detailed description of the ACLU's campaign to challenge California's law. *See* Elisa Martia Alvarez Minoff, Free to Move? The Law and Politics of Internal Migration in Twentieth-Century America (2013) (unpublished dissertation), *available at* http://dash.harvard.edu/bitstream/handle/1/11095954/Minoff_gsas.harvard_0084L_10957.pdf?sequence=1. She reports that the ACLU read of Mr. Edwards' arrest in the press and, not knowing his address, contacted him to offer representation by writing to "Fred Edwards, Marysville, CA." *Id.* at 212–13.

26. Mayor of New York v. Miln, 36 U.S. 102, 142 (1837).

27. T. H. Marshall, Class, Citizenship and Social Development, *quoted in* Chad Alan Goldberg, Citizens and Paupers: Relief, Rights, and Race, from the Freedmen's Bureau to Workfare 1 (2007).

28. Articles of Confederation, Art. IV (emphasis added).

29. As set forth in Del Dickson, The Supreme Court in Conference (1940–1985): The Private Discussions Behind Nearly 300 Supreme Court Decisions 782–83 (2001).

30. Brief of Appellant at 13, Edwards v. California, 1941 WL 53329 (U.S.), 2 (U.S., 2004) (emphasis in original).

31. Amicus Brief of John H. Tolan, *reprinted in* KURLAND AND CASPER, *supra* note 7, at 567.

32. DAVID ROBERTSON, SLY AND ABLE: A POLITICAL BIOGRAPHY OF JAMES F. BYRNES 299 (1994).

33. *Id.* at 312. Attorney General Francis Biddle reported to Roosevelt that "all defense legislation is being cleared by the departments and then through Jimmy Byrnes, who takes care of it on the Hill." *Id.*

34. DICKSON, *supra* note 29, at 783.

35. *See* Lochner v. New York, 198 U.S. 45 (1905).

36. Letter from Justice Stone to Justice Byrnes (Nov. 1, 1941), *quoted in* Michael J. Klarman, *An Interpretive History of Modern Equal Protection*, 90 MICH. L. REV. 213, 223 (1991).

37. 314 U.S. at 173. Though the Court was unanimous in finding the statute unconstitutional, several justices objected to the Commerce Clause rationale out of concern for the humanity of the persons involved. Justice Douglas, joined by Justices Black and Murphy, noted that "the right of persons to move freely from State to State occupies a more protected position in our constitutional system than does the movement of cattle, fruit, steel and coal across state lines" and that the freedom to travel is an "incident of national citizenship protected by the Fourteenth Amendment's Privileges and [*sic*] Immunities Clause." (314 U.S. at 169). (Justice Douglas likely meant to refer to the Fourteenth Amendment's Privileges *or* Immunities Clause; the Privileges *and* Immunities Clause is in Article Four of the Constitution.) Justice Jackson agreed that the Privileges or Immunities Clause was applicable, and noted that "the migrations of a human being . . . do not fit easily into my notions as to what is commerce. . . . [To so hold] is likely to result eventually either in distorting the commercial law or in denaturing human rights." *Id.* at 171.

38. *Id.* at 177.

Remaking the "Law of the Poor"

Williams v. Walker–Thomas Furniture Co. • (1965)

ANNE FLEMING

On August 11, 1965, the California Highway Patrol pulled over Marquette Frye in the Los Angeles neighborhood of Watts, setting off a chain of events that would lead to six days of civil disorder and leave millions in property damage and 34 dead. Contemporary observers could offer no singular explanation for what sparked and then fueled the fires that burned in Watts and other American cities in the mid-1960s, but they agreed that the credit practices of local merchants were contributing factors. In a subsequent study of the uprisings in Watts and other urban centers across the nation, a federal investigatory commission concluded that city residents had "[s]ignificant grievances concerning unfair commercial practices." "[M]any merchants in ghetto neighborhoods take advantage of their superior knowledge of credit buying by engaging in various exploitative tactics," including charging "exorbitant prices or credit charges."[1]

On the very same day in August 1965, in a quiet federal courthouse in downtown Washington, D.C., another story about law, debt, and urban poverty was unfolding. This dispute, between a low-income consumer and a retail merchant, had begun years before and took place thousands of miles away from Watts, in the nation's capital. It concerned a retail installment sales contract and the scope of a D.C. merchant's right to collect an outstanding debt from a poor African American mother. Yet the events in California and the District of Columbia were linked by more than just chronology. From

Watts to Washington, debt collection lawsuits were commonplace for poor families buying on credit in America's cities. They often ended in the loss of the household's furniture or the garnishment of the breadwinner's wages. No wonder, then, that participants in the uprisings in Watts and elsewhere targeted retailers' credit records. "These were destroyed before the place was burned," one witness recalled.[2]

The basic facts of the D.C. case were not in dispute. The defendant, Ora Lee Williams, a single mother of eight on public assistance, bought some household goods on credit from a local furniture store, Walker-Thomas Furniture Company (Walker-Thomas). When she defaulted, after paying off most of the debt, the store claimed the right to repossess everything Williams had purchased during the previous five years. With the aid of a volunteer lawyer, Williams contested the store's right to seize all her purchases. Both the trial judge and the intermediate appellate court ruled in favor of the store, finding no legal way to prevent the repossession. In 1965, more than two years after the store first sued Williams, the case finally reached highest court in the District of Columbia, the Court of Appeals for the D.C. Circuit. There, on August 11th, the case took an unexpected turn.

Hours before the uprising began in Watts, Judge Skelly Wright of the D.C. Circuit handed down his soon-to-be-famous opinion in the case, captioned *Williams v. Walker-Thomas Furniture Company*. Wright declared that courts in the District would not enforce a contract if the bargain was "unconscionable," meaning that there was "an absence of meaningful choice" for one party along with "terms which are unreasonably favorable to the other party." Wright found that the store's contract with Williams was potentially "unconscionable" and therefore unenforceable. He remanded the case to the trial court for further proceedings. The decision was among of the first in the country to apply the doctrine of unconscionability. Judge Wright later predicted that the doctrine would be part of "a growing area of the law—the law of the poor."[3]

Shopping in the "Other America"

By the time Ora Lee Williams' goods were seized, the problem of poverty was just beginning to garner national attention. Those on the economic margins of American society had never disappeared, but they had receded from view for those reaping the benefits of postwar prosperity. Historians often describe the 1960s as a moment when poverty was "rediscovered." Through popular works like Michael Harrington's *The Other America* (1962) and David Caplovitz's *The Poor Pay More* (1963), middle-class readers learned of the pockets of poverty lurking in rural West Virginia and the ghettos of inner cities. Bypassed by the new highways to suburban prosperity, poor urban households lived in what Harrington called the "Other America." As Caplovitz described, the poor also shopped in a world apart. They were "forced to live in a world of inflation that more well-to-do citizens are able to escape," paying high rates of interest for consumer goods bought on the installment plan. "Installment credit" was "the door" through which the poor "entered the mass consumption society."[4]

For Ora Lee Williams, her own front door became a portal into the postwar American consumer economy. At the time she began buying goods from Walker-Thomas, Williams lived in the 5500 block of Foote Street in the northeast quadrant of the District. She was separated from her husband and responsible for supporting herself and seven children. Between 1957 and 1962, the family got by on no more than $218 per month in public assistance. Williams' neighbors were almost all African American and more than a quarter also lived in poverty.[5]

Walker-Thomas employed a team of door-to-door salesmen who came to Williams' neighborhood hawking their wares, part of the "peddler economy" serving low-income consumers in cities across the nation. Agents traveled door-to-door offering a range of household goods on credit. The furniture store's salesmen doubled as collection agents, picking up monthly or biweekly payments while soliciting new sales. Williams eventually signed 16 separate contracts to purchase merchandise from Walker-Thomas, but went to the company's store only once.[6]

The Walker-Thomas storefront was located almost six miles from Williams' apartment, at 1031 Seventh Street in Northwest Washington. Merchants serving low-income consumers clustered in a row on Seventh Street, known as an "easy-credit" corridor. Walker-Thomas had occupied the same three-story retail space on Seventh Street since 1938, when it moved from its prior location down the block. The storefront was easily recognizable from a distance. A two-story-tall neon sign placed in the center of the yellow brick building advertised the store's name in vertically arranged characters spelling out "Walker-Thomas." From 1940 onwards, the neighborhood around the store was predominantly African American. By 1960, more than 90 percent of the residents were black and more than 40 percent of the families lived in poverty.[7]

Like other major American cities, the District of Columbia underwent significant demographic changes in the postwar period. By 1957, it was the first major city in the nation with a majority black population. Wealth clustered in particular quarters of the city, while others were marked by high rates of poverty. Poverty was disproportionately concentrated among the city's black population. Black and white, rich and poor lived and shopped in different places and spaces. One study of urban unrest in this period concluded that "[o]ur nation is moving toward two societies, one black, one white—separate and unequal."[8] Nowhere was this more apparent than in the nation's capital.[9]

Williams shopped and borrowed in a consumer landscape strikingly different from that of her white, middle-class, suburban counterparts. Poor consumers continued to finance new purchases through "installment" credit, which required regular payments at scheduled intervals. In contrast, retailers to the middle class offered their customers "revolving" credit, loans for goods purchased that were repayable in irregular amounts over time with no set payment schedule or end date. Revolving borrowers paid interest on their outstanding debt but had greater flexibility in deciding when and how much to pay each month, and their purchases were not subject to repossession by the seller. As one historian observed, "[e]ven as poor Americans evinced consumer desires of the 1960s, their credit experiences remained more akin to the world of the 1920s." In the two-tiered credit economy, Williams and her neighbors were trapped at the bottom.[10]

The Williams Purchases

Walker-Thomas Furniture arrived on Ora Lee Williams' doorstep in the form of agent #15, Mr. Wolfson. Williams made her first purchase from Wolfson on December 17, 1957. She bought a wallet, two pairs of solid-colored drapes, an apron set, a pot holder set, and a set of throw rugs. As Williams later testified, at the time she signed this and several subsequent contracts, "[t] here was no price, or anything filled in." Although the form contract was short—approximately six inches long—the salesman would fold over the contract before presenting it to Williams with the signature line visible and tell her, "Just sign your name down here." Williams explained that "[s]ometimes the salesman would say that he did not know the exact price of the merchandise, and that they would have to add their Sales Tax, and such as that. And he said that he could not fill it in because he wasn't sure." "He said that they would do that later at the store." In other words, the key term of the agreement—price—was missing when Williams executed the contract. Williams later learned that she owed Walker-Thomas $45.65, payable in $3.00 installments every other Saturday. Walker-Thomas collected the tax on the purchase (90 cents) from Williams the following Saturday, when the goods were delivered.[11]

Over the course of the next five years, Williams signed at least 13 additional contracts to buy various household goods. She paid Walker-Thomas approximately $1,056 over the course of five years, out of the total of $1,500 owed. Williams never received a copy of the contracts she signed. But even if she had, the significance of the terms would not have been immediately apparent. Buried in the middle of 22 lines of extremely fine print on the pre-printed form, the agreement stated that Williams' payments would be credited "pro rata" on all outstanding accounts. Walker-Thomas interpreted this provision, also known as an "add-on" clause, to mean that Williams' payments would be applied to all outstanding balances in proportion to the amount still owed on the purchases, rather than to retiring the oldest debts first or even pro rata in proportion to the original purchase price. In effect, Williams would never pay off any individual item until she paid off the entire debt owed to Walker-Thomas.

In the event she defaulted, Walker-Thomas would retain the right to seize all the items that Williams had purchased since 1957. The agreement further provided that the transaction was a "lease," rather than an outright sale; Williams agreed to "hire" the goods from Walker-Thomas. Williams would take actual possession of the items, but the company would retain title to the goods until Williams had paid off the total value of all the items she received and presented receipts to Walker-Thomas showing full payment.[12]

The balance owed on the items purchased in December 1957 decreased quickly at first, but , thanks to the obscure "pro rata" clause in Walker-Thomas' form agreement, it was never extinguished. According to Walker-Thomas's accounting scheme, by November 1962 Williams owed only 25¢ on the original purchase of $45.65. She also owed $2.34 on a folding bed and chest of drawers, both purchased in August 1958 for $127.40, 3¢ on another 1957 purchase (price $13.21), and amounts ranging from 96¢ to $10.32 on other sales from 1958 through 1960. None of these debts would be fully paid until Williams paid off every item purchased. Most of her payments were applied toward the outstanding balances on her more recent purchases. Each payment made was spread over the balances owed on all her contracts, in proportion to the amount still owed on each.[13]

By late 1962, Williams was teetering on the edge of default. Her payments had increased from $6.00 to $36.00 per month. She paid regularly from May through August of 1962. Then she faltered, paying $102 total from September through November. Walker-Thomas stopped accepting her payments when she could not pay the full monthly amount due. The furniture company then filed a lawsuit against Williams, demanding that the U.S. Marshal seize all the items Williams had purchased since 1957. On the same day the lawsuit was filed, the clerk of the court signed off on Walker-Thomas's demand and ordered the U.S. Marshals to seize the 22 items listed in the complaint. They took a bed and chest purchased in 1958, along with a more recently acquired washing machine and stereo. The remaining goods "were not recovered," either because the marshals could not locate them or because they declined to seize them. At the time, Williams owed $444.40 in total, less than the cost of her last purchase, an Admiral stereo. Without the fine print in the Walker-Thomas contract, only the stereo could have been repossessed. After seizing the property, the U.S. Marshals appraised the items taken. They deemed the washing machine to be worthless and valued the remaining items at $91.50.[14]

Debt Collection Before *Williams*

Absent the intervention of the Legal Assistance Office of the Bar Association of the District of Columbia, Ora Lee Williams' case might have ended with the loss of her furniture. Repossession through court action was a standard business practice for Walker-Thomas. In the years leading up to Williams' case, the company rarely filed fewer than one hundred seizure requests (called "writs of replevin") in the local court. Most cases did not go to trial; those that did usually resulted in a verdict for the furniture company. Williams' case was unusual in that she had an attorney who not only tried the case but also represented her through multiple appeals.[15]

Walker-Thomas's collection methods were common among retailers to the poor. One study of District retailers found that 11 "low-income market retailers" similar to Walker-Thomas filed 2,690 cases against delinquent customers in one year alone. In contrast, the mainstream retailers studied reported only 70 filed actions. Low-income market retailers averaged one lawsuit for every $2,599 in net sales; mainstream retailers averaged one for every $232,299 in net sales. These figures suggest that low-income retailers employed "a marketing technique which includes actions against default as a normal matter of business rather than as a matter of last resort." Most cases ended in judgment for the merchant because the buyer never appeared, in some cases because he never received notice of the lawsuit.[16]

Even when such cases reached a judge, the law did not often favor poor borrowers seeking relief from their contracts. In cases where D.C. courts refused to enforce one-sided credit agreements, they grounded their decisions in traditional contract defenses, such as fraud, mistake, lack of mutual assent, or violation of public policy. To prevail on such defenses, borrowers generally needed a lawyer. Without an attorney to make the borrower's case, courts usually enforced credit contracts as written, as in the 1954 case of *Elizabeth Coates v. Walker-Thomas Furniture.*[17]

In *Coates*, a local D.C. court reluctantly found in favor of the lender, Walker-Thomas Furniture, in a case involving an installment sales contract. The furniture company sold various items on credit to defendant Elizabeth Coates between 1949 and 1952. Coates paid $1,482 out of $1,687.56 charged before she defaulted. Citing the "pro rata" provision of the conditional sales contract, Walker-Thomas demanded seizure of all the items Coates had purchased since 1949. Coates appeared without a lawyer. "Unable to satisfactorily ascertain any legal way in which the law could be of aid in solving the inequities in this situation," the court found for Walker-Thomas. It suggested that the problem required legislative intervention.[18]

District borrowers won when they could raise other contract defenses and, perhaps more importantly, had the benefit of legal representation. For example, in a 1963 case, the D.C. Court of Appeals refused to enforce a sales contract on the grounds of fraud and lack of mutual assent. The borrower bought a television set on credit for the quoted price of $189 from Hollywood Credit Clothing Company, located just down the Seventh Street shopping corridor from Walker-Thomas. When the buyer returned home, he noticed that the contract he had signed stated the price as $289, plus carrying charges; he owed $345.35 in all. Evidence admitted at trial showed that the suggested retail price of the set was $169.95. The borrower returned the television immediately and the store sued for recovery of the contract price.

Pierre Dostert of the Bar Association's Legal Assistance Office, who would later take up Williams' case, represented the borrower. The trial and appellate courts ruled in favor of the borrower, finding that there was no meeting of the minds as to the contract terms and that the borrowers' agreement was obtained by fraud or misrepresentation. In another case from 1963, the buyer prevailed on a procedural defense raised by her attorney.[19]

The Rediscovery of Unconscionability

After Walker-Thomas seized her belongings in March 1963, Williams found her way to the D.C. Bar Association's Legal Assistance Office housed in the D.C. trial court, then called the Court of General Sessions. Federally funded legal services for the poor were not yet up and running in the District.

The Legal Assistance Office had received other complaints against Walker-Thomas, but the borrowers were not poor enough to qualify for free legal assistance. The office agreed to defend Williams against Walker-Thomas. Williams' attorneys also represented two married codefendants, William and Ruth Thorne, in a separate collection action filed by the furniture company. The two cases were later consolidated on appeal.[20]

The lawyer who would argue the case before Judge Wright, Pierre Dostert, "decided to take the two cases as far as necessary to achieve a precedent which would afford some protection to the lesser members of the community." Meeting that goal would end up requiring two appeals and 210 hours of legal work.[21] Paying for hundreds of hours of legal work would have been prohibitively expensive for Williams, a poor debtor who could not even afford to pay $36 a month to stave off repossession of her belongings. Without free legal representation, Williams would surely have joined the hundreds of borrowers whose cases ended either in default or in a verdict for Walker-Thomas. Instead, her case proceeded from the trial court to the D.C. Court of Appeals and finally to the D.C. Circuit. Then, at the eleventh hour of the litigation, the case took a surprising and quite fortuitous turn: for the very first time, the parties briefed the issue of unconscionability.

Although *Williams* is now famous as a case about unconscionability, the parties almost failed to brief the defense. Williams did not raise unconscionability at trial or during her initial appeal. It arose in the D.C. Circuit largely by luck of timing. After Williams submitted her brief in the initial appeal but before she petitioned for review to the D.C. Circuit, Congress adopted the Uniform Commercial Code for the District of Columbia. The Uniform Commercial Code, a model set of state laws governing commercial transactions, included a provision that allowed courts to refuse to enforce "unconscionable" sales contracts as written.

The adoption of the Uniform Commercial Code in the District of Columbia altered the subsequent course of the litigation. Williams raised the newly enacted U.C.C. provision on unconscionability, U.C.C. § 2-302, in her petition for review to the D.C. Circuit. Although the D.C. Circuit rarely granted discretionary requests for review, a three-judge panel voted to hear both cases and consolidated them for purposes of briefing and argument.

The panel of judges left no record of their reasoning for deciding to hear the case. Perhaps the first sentence of Williams' statement of the case grabbed the judges' attention: "Appellant, a person of limited education and separated from her husband, is maintaining herself and her seven children by means of public assistance." Two of the three judges who granted review, Judge Skelly

Wright and Chief Judge David Bazelon, were concerned about the plight of the poor. Bazelon maintained a folder of clippings from the *Washington Post* and reports on the subject of poverty. Judge Wright chaired the special committee of the Judicial Council that reviewed a grant proposal to the Ford Foundation seeking funding to establish a neighborhood legal services program for the poor. Years later, he published a forceful editorial in the *New York Times* titled *The Courts Have Failed the Poor* (1969), critiquing the legal treatment of low-income people.[22]

The court also issued an unusual order when it granted Williams' petition for review. It appointed a local lawyer as amicus curiae. The amicus brief ended up focusing almost exclusively on unconscionability and its impact on the case. As a result of this unlikely chain of events, unconscionability became the major issue in *Williams* just as the case reached the D.C. Circuit.[23]

Wright Wrestles With Unconscionability

Williams and the companion case, *Thorne v. Walker-Thomas Furniture Co.*, came up for oral argument before the three-judge panel of Skelly Wright, David Bazelon, and John Danaher in April 1965. The case was argued on a Friday morning. By the following Monday, Wright had written a first draft of the opinion, vacating the judgment for Walker-Thomas and ordering that the case be remanded to the trial court for further proceedings. Wright would write several drafts of the decision over the coming months, shifting his reasoning in response to comments from the panel.[24]

Wright's early drafts began with a discussion of Walker-Thomas's business practices, rather than Williams' knowledge and capacity to understand the terms of the deal. On remand, Wright suggested, the trial court should investigate if the store stood to profit from the repossession. Wright wrote, "It might be shown" that the company sold high-priced items to the defendants with the knowledge that they would likely default and repossession of all items purchased would "inevitably ensue." The company could then resell the items to the next customer, perhaps recouping an "amount greater than the debt secured by the items" and "greater than the valuation given the items at the time of repossession."[25]

The sales scheme Wright imagined was not prohibited under then-existing D.C. law. Under a conditional sales agreement, a seller in the District could sue a defaulting buyer either for the amount owed or could "treat the sale as a nullity" and recover the goods. Unlike many other states, the District had not adopted the Uniform Conditional Sales Act, which required a creditor to return to the debtor any surplus received from the seizure and sale of its collateral. The District's law concerning conditional sales did not change until the passage of the U.C.C.[26]

For Wright, the backgrounds and education levels of the borrowers—Williams and the Thornes—were less important than the tyranny of the lender-seller or, as Wright later dubbed it, the "manufacturer-seller-financier complex." In early drafts of the opinion, Wright concluded that "the conscionability" of the contracts "might certainly be questioned" if his predictions of Walker-Thomas's business practices were accurate and if, "as a matter of practice," the company made no effort to return any surplus funds recovered to the borrower. He also instructed the trial court to admit evidence showing the value of the items Walker-Thomas sold, to determine if Williams' stereo "was new or repossessed" and if it had "a market value anywhere near $514."[27]

Yet Wright did not publish that version of the decision. The final decision laid out a two-part test for unconscionability. It required "an absence of meaningful choice" for one party along with "contract terms which are unreasonably favorable to the other party." The opinion identified a few facts relevant to "choice," such as "gross inequality of bargaining power," and whether each party, "considering his obvious education or lack of it," had a "reasonable opportunity to understand the terms of the contract." Wright noted that consent might be negated if the "important terms" were "hidden in a maze of fine print and minimized by deceptive sales practices." Unlike Wright's early drafts, the final decision did not identify what findings might be relevant to the second requirement: terms "unreasonably favorable" to the other party. After conferring with Judge Bazelon and learning that Judge Danaher planned to dissent, Wright deleted the section concerning Walker-Thomas's knowledge of defendants' likelihood of default and opportunity to profit from repossession. He also omitted reference to the possible value-price disparity of the goods Walker-Thomas sold.[28]

In other words, the final opinion did not convey many of Wright's concerns about the contract terms and Walker-Thomas's business practices. In identifying facts relevant to the trial court's inquiry, it focused more on contract formation than on the substance of the bargain. It allowed the court to avoid affirming the decision below in favor of the store, without casting too much doubt on the many thousands of similar deals that Walker-Thomas had transacted with borrowers like Williams. Wright circulated the opinion and Danaher's dissent to the full court. Bazelon concurred in the decision; three other judges (not on the panel) noted minor corrections and their agreement with the majority's disposition. With a few revisions, the text went off to the printer.[29]

The *Williams* Litigation Spurs Statutory Reform

Meanwhile, as Williams was seeking a legal victory through the D.C. courts, a coalition of reformers had gathered in the District of Columbia to draft new consumer credit legislation. They mobilized in reaction to the *Williams* litigation, getting down to work shortly after the D.C. Court of Appeals affirmed the trial court's judgment in favor of Walker-Thomas. In denying Williams relief, the Court of Appeals faulted the legislature: D.C. had no Retail Installment Sales Act to protect installment buyers like Williams. The D.C. Board of Commissioners took note of the ruling. On the board's instruction, the Corporation Counsel set to work assembling a committee to "draft legislation to deal with the problem." One member of the committee described the proposed legislation as "the direct result of the factual situation in the *Williams* case."[30]

References to the *Williams* decision recur throughout the debates and studies that led up to passage of consumer protection measures in the District. In 1967, Professor Egon Guttman of Howard Law School testified before Congress in favor of installment sales regulations, on behalf of a coalition of organizations involved in drafting the proposed legislation. The consumer coalition members agreed that protective legislation must include an "Ora Lee Williams clause" to limit installment sellers' right to repossess. (Guttman was quite familiar with the *Williams* situation; he had assisted in drafting the amicus brief filed with the D.C. Circuit.) Another witness at the same hearing applauded the proposed legislation for attacking "the Ora Lee Williams situation." In its statement in support of the bill, the D.C. Bar Association likewise referenced the facts of *Williams*, arguing that the law offered protection without overreaching. It would "discourage installment sellers" from offering a "combination hi-fi-TV set costing $500.00" to "a person living on welfare," without outright barring "such sales to such persons." Committee reports similarly noted that the legislation would help "eliminate the type of abuse illustrated by the celebrated case of *Williams*."[31]

Unrest in the streets of D.C. heightened public awareness of the issue but failed to provoke congressional adoption of the proposed measures. In April 1968, the District erupted in the wake of the assassination of Martin Luther King. Uprisings occurred in more than a hundred other American cities as well. In the streets of D.C., rioters targeted "buy now, pay later" stores. Several buildings on the Seventh Street "easy-credit" corridor, just down the block from Walker-Thomas, burned to the ground. Angry customers sought out merchants' credit records, "the books," which recorded their debts and symbolized their perceived exploitation by retailers like Walker-Thomas. A woman yelled at looters in the Walker-Thomas store, "Get the books! Get the books!" A man watching a clothing store burn shouted, "Burn those damn records!" "Don't grab the groceries," a woman rummaging through a delicatessen near 7th and S Streets advised her son to "grab the book."[32] In response, Congress did not enact local installment sales legislation for the District. Instead, it adopted the Truth in Lending Act, federal consumer credit legislation requiring lenders to disclose loan terms.

Installment sales regulation for D.C. took a while longer, but in 1971, Congress finally passed the D.C. Consumer Credit Protection Act. The law took aim at "overreaching and unconscionable commercial practices," specifically outlawing "pro rata" loan provisions like the one in Ora Lee Williams' contract. Lenders were now required to apply payments to retiring the oldest debts first. The new law also expressly gave courts the power to refuse enforcement of "unconscionable" loans. The D.C. Council also later enacted an unfair and deceptive acts and practices law, known as a "UDAP" statute, which prohibited specified unfair trade practices and, more generally, "unconscionable contracts." Under the now-required accounting method, Williams would have paid off everything except for the stereo before she defaulted.[33]

The Aftermath: Walker-Thomas Settles and Adapts

For Williams and Walker-Thomas, the litigation ended in a stalemate of sorts. Neither side had won a judgment. After the D.C. Circuit's decision, Walker-Thomas's right to seize Williams' furniture was still in doubt. To obtain a ruling on the issue, the parties would have to undergo a second trial. So in 1965, Williams and Walker-Thomas returned to the trial court, where the case had begun more than two years earlier. The lawsuit dragged on for a few months longer, but Walker-Thomas finally settled, paying Williams $200 for the goods seized from her home three years earlier.[34]

Williams' lawyer, Pierre Dostert, later remarked that Walker-Thomas should never have permitted the case to reach the appeals court. But he did not view the opinion as a clear victory. Instead, it created "a degree of uncertainty" and "a dormant threat to unconscionable conduct which could become very active with little or no notice." He observed that local lawyers had begun to make use of the decision in defending the poor clients against repossession actions. He also predicted that lenders would be more likely to settle at trial, rather than risk a finding of unconscionability.[35]

Indeed, unconscionability had several drawbacks as a device for policing the low-income marketplace. First and foremost, the majority of poor consumers were unlikely to raise unconscionability as a defense, or even to appear in debt collection suits. The federal War on Poverty had increased the availability of free legal assistance nationwide, but poverty lawyers could not represent more than a fraction of needy borrowers. Moreover, after *Williams*, lenders were more likely to settle with borrowers who had viable unconscionability claims, rather than risking costly litigation and an adverse court decision. Given that few consumers had the resources or legal acumen to raise unconscionability as a defense, creditors like Walker-Thomas likely realized that they would be better off dropping or settling their claims against the few "squeaky wheels" like Williams who put up a fuss. Finally, procedural rules restricted the ability of poor consumers to assert the defense to challenge the price term of consumer contracts. After *Williams*, the Court of Appeals affirmed that a contract might be found unconscionable based on price. Yet courts required buyers to set out the factual basis for the defense in their complaint, while limiting their ability to get necessary information from the seller through discovery. As a result, few consumers prevailed in challenging contracts based on price.[36]

Walker-Thomas did change its contracts to comply with the installment sales regulations Congress adopted in 1971. By 1977, the furniture company had deleted the "pro rata" clause from its form contract, instead applying payments to the oldest purchase first. Future District borrowers faced with "pro rata" clauses could defend based on statutory protections, not the doctrine of unconscionability.[37]

Walker-Thomas did not fundamentally alter its business practices, however. By the mid-1970s, most Walker-Thomas clients were still working poor, and many received government assistance. The company continued to solicit business and collect payments through door-to-door salesmen and to sell used and repossessed merchandise as "new." In many cases, customers did not learn of the cost of the merchandise they had purchased until after it was delivered. Collection agents would time their visits to coincide with the arrival of customers' welfare or social security checks. Salespersons cleverly provided check-cashing services for their customers, thereby allowing the company to deduct the monthly installment payment before handing over the remaining cash to the customer.[38]

If a customer failed to pay, the store would send threatening letters, make early morning and late evening collection calls, contact the borrower's relatives and friends, and—if necessary—repossess the merchandise. Often Walker-Thomas would repossess goods by removing them from the customer's home when no adults were present or would intimidate the customer into turning over the goods without a court order. When necessary, the company would sue to recover the balance owed, either through judicially sanctioned repossession or an order for a money judgment. To dissuade a customer from complaining to outside authorities, a salesperson might threaten to withhold credit in the future or to notify the authorities about unreported income. Walker-Thomas employed six men, known as "pimps," who investigated customers to obtain information that might be used to intimidate customers into not complaining. For women on welfare, this might include the whereabouts of an estranged spouse whose income could disqualify the family from receiving relief. The Federal Trade Commission investigated Walker-Thomas in 1975; the company later entered into a consent decree to halt its unfair, false, misleading and deceptive trade practices. By the end of the twentieth century, the Walker-Thomas storefront on Seventh Street was shuttered.[39]

Conclusion: Ora Lee Williams Sparks Legislative Change

Within a few decades after the D.C. Circuit issued its decision in *Williams*, the "law of the poor" no longer appeared to be a "growing area of the law" as Wright had forecast in 1967. "The poor," as a category of analysis, had found little traction in the courts in the late 1960s and early 1970s. Yet Judge Wright's prediction did not entirely miss the mark. The *Williams* litigation played an important role in creating a "law of the poor" consumer, just not the part that Wright had envisioned. In this instance, a long and winding court battle brought limited relief to the defendant, Ora Lee Williams, who eventually settled rather than continue her years-long fight to reclaim her furniture. Her case did, however, help change the rules that governed lending to the poor in Washington, D.C. By raising public consciousness of problems in the low-income marketplace and alerting District lawmakers to a recurring problem in need of a legislative fix, the *Williams* litigation fueled the drive for substantive reforms on the local level.[40]

The history of the case thus highlights the role of litigation in catalyzing a movement for legislative change and also helps situate Wright's decision within the context of its historical moment. Although some modern commentators have criticized the decision on policy grounds, this history shows that Wright's opinion resonated with an emerging policy consensus of his time, in favor of substantive limits on installment sales to poor borrowers like Ora Lee Williams. The legislation that followed endorsed Wright's view of the problem in *Williams*, putting in place a new set of rules to govern "installment" sales contracts and banning outright the "pro rata" allocation of payments.[41] In the future, poor borrowers in the District would be protected by these statutory rules, rather than needing to invoke the doctrine of unconscionability.

Notes

Material from this chapter also appears in Anne Fleming, *The Rise and Fall of Unconscionability as the "Law of the Poor,"* 102 GEO. L.J. 1383–1441 (2014). For research help, I thank the staff and librarians of the Library of Congress, the National Archives and Records Administration, the Ford Foundation, the Archives of the Biddle Law Library, and the Clerk's Office of the D.C. Court of Appeals.

1. UNITED STATES KERNER COMMISSION, REPORT OF THE NATIONAL ADVISORY COMMISSION ON CIVIL DISORDERS 274, 276 (1968).

2. GERALD HORNE, FIRE THIS TIME 65 (1995) (quoting observer John Buggs of the Los Angeles Human Relations Commission).

3. Williams v. Walker-Thomas Furniture Co., 350 F.2d 445 (D.C. Cir. 1965); J. Skelly Wright to William E. Shipley of the Lawyers Cooperative Publishing Company, July 12, 1967, Library of Congress, Washington, D.C., Manuscript Division, J. Skelly Wright papers [hereinafter "Wright Papers"], box 77, "Williams v. Walker-Thomas Furniture Co. S.T. 1965" folder.

4. JAMES T. PATTERSON, AMERICA'S STRUGGLE AGAINST POVERTY 97–111 (1994); DAVID CAPLOVITZ, THE POOR PAY MORE xv–vii (1967).

5. Data for D.C. census tract 786 (1960), Social Explorer Professional, http://www.socialexplorer.com (last visited Nov. 25, 2013); COUNCIL OF ECONOMIC ADVISORS, ANNUAL REPORT 58 (1964), *available at* http://fraser.stlouisfed.org/publications/erp/issue/1208/download/5639/ERP_ARCEA_1964.pdf (setting the poverty line at $3,000 in 1962 dollars for all families, regardless of size); Blake D. Morant, *The Relevance of Race and Disparity in Discussions of Contract Law,* 31 NEW ENG. L. REV. 889, 926 n.208 (1997) (Williams' race); Williams v. Walker-Thomas Furniture Co., 198 A.2d at 916 (D.C. 1964).

6. *Hearings on Consumer Credit Labeling Bill, Before Senate Comm. on Banking and Currency,* 86th Cong. 101 (1960) (statement of William Kirk, Union Settlement Association, New York, N.Y., describing "peddler economy"); David Greenberg, *Easy Terms, Hard Times: Complaint Handling in the Ghetto, in* NO ACCESS TO LAW: ALTERNATIVES TO THE AMERICAN JUDICIAL SYSTEM 379, 381 (Laura Nader ed., 1980). Some information concerning Walker-Thomas's sales and collection practices is drawn in part from Greenberg's 1975 field research on the furniture store. The practices he observed are in keeping with those described in the *Williams* records. Transcript of Record at 39, 45, 47, 54 Williams v. Walker-Thomas Furniture Co., 198 A.2d 914 (D.C. 1964) (No. 3389) (available at District of Columbia Court of Appeals) [hereinafter "*Williams* Record"].

7. Warren Grant Magnuson, THE DARK SIDE OF THE MARKETPLACE: THE PLIGHT OF THE AMERICAN CONSUMER 36 (1968); National Register of Historic

Places Nomination Form for the East Side of the 1000 Block of Seventh-Street N.W., Record No. 84000861, National Parks Service (1984) (manuscript at 8, 14), *available at* http://pdfhost.focus.nps.gov/docs/NRHP/Text/84000861.pdf; data for District census tracts 48 and 49 (1940–70), Social Explorer Professional, http://www.socialexplorer.com (last visited Nov. 25, 2013).

8. UNITED STATES KERNER COMMISSION, *supra* note 1, at 1.

9. HOWARD GILLETTE, BETWEEN JUSTICE AND BEAUTY 153–54 (1995); FEDERAL TRADE COMMISSION, ECONOMIC REPORT ON INSTALLMENT CREDIT AND RETAIL SALES PRACTICES OF DISTRICT OF COLUMBIA RETAILERS (1968), *reprinted in Consumer Protection Legislation for the District of Columbia: Hearing on S. 316, 2589, 2590 and 2592 Before Subcomm. on Business and Commerce of the S. Comm. on the District of Columbia*, 90th Cong. 257 (1967–68) [hereinafter "1968 FTC REPORT"]; Frank Porter, *District Poverty Rate Lower Than Average of Other City Areas*, WASH. POST, Mar. 4, 1964, at E1.

10. 1968 FTC REPORT, *supra* note 9, at 251; Louis Hyman, *Ending Discrimination, Legitimating Debt*, 12 ENTER. & SOC'Y 200, 201, 208–9 (2011).

11. *Williams* Record at 47–50, 114, 116–24, 126–28, 133 (Pl. Ex. 1, 3–8, 10–11, 13–15, Def. Ex. 5).

12. Robert H. Skilton and Orrin L. Helstad, *Protection of the Installment Buyer of Goods Under the Uniform Commercial Code*, 65 MICH. L. REV. 1465, 1476 (1966); *Williams* Record at 107 (Writ of Replevin); Brief for Respondent Walker-Thomas Furniture at Exhibit B, *Williams*, 350 F.2d 445 (D.C. Cir. 1965) (No. 18604) (available at Records of U.S. Courts of Appeals, Record Group 276, National Archives Building, Washington, D.C. [hereinafter "NARA"], Record Group 276); Wright's opinion misstated the amount charged and paid as $1,800 and $1,400, respectively. *Williams*, 350 F.2d at 447 n.1. *E.g., Williams* Record at 114 (Pl. Ex. 1).

13. The figures on Williams' payments, cited in this and following paragraph, appear in Brief for Respondent, *supra* note 12, and *Williams* Record at 129 (Def. Ex. 1) (payment receipt).

14. *Williams* Record at 53–54, 61, 103–4, 106–7; Brief for Respondent, *supra* note 12, at 6.

15. Pierre E. Dostert, *Appellate Restatement of Unconscionability*, 54 A.B.A. J. 1183, 1184 (1968).

16. 1968 FTC REPORT, *supra* note 9, at 255, 278; *Abuse of Process*, 3 COLUM. J.L. & Soc. PROBS. 17 (1967); J. Skelly Wright, *The Courts Have Failed the Poor*, N.Y. TIMES, Mar. 9, 1969, at Magazine 26.

17. *An Ounce of Discretion for a Pound of Flesh*, 65 YALE L.J. 105, 108 n.19 & 20 (1955) (citing cases in which courts have granted relief to a "victimized party" by invoking fraud, lack of mutuality, etc. rather than labeling the contract unconscionable); *Unconscionable Sales Contracts and the Uniform Commercial Code, Section 2-302*, 45 VA. L. REV. 583, 584 n.4 (1959) (same).

18. The unpublished 1954 decision was appended to the Walker-Thomas Brief in the *Thorne* case. Transcript of Record at 11 (Brief of Plaintiff, Appendix), Walker-Thomas Furniture v. Thorne, 198 A.2d 914 (D.C. 1964) (No 3412) (available at District of Columbia Court of Appeals) [hereinafter "*Thorne* Record"].

19. Hollywood Credit Clothing Co. v. Gibson, 188 A.2d 348 (D.C. 1963); Hollywood Credit Clothing Co., 77 F.T.C. 1594 (1970) (noting location of store); Becton v. Walker-Thomas Furniture Co., 192 A.2d 125, 126 (D.C. 1963) (prevailing on procedural defense on appeal); The *Becton* case was later dismissed for failure to prosecute. Walker-Thomas Furniture Co. v. Becton, 200 A.2d 190 (D.C. 1964).

20. Brian Gilmore, *Love You Madly: The Life and Times of the Neighborhood Legal Services Program of Washington, D.C.*, 10 U. D.C. L. Rev. 69 (2007); Dostert, *supra* note 15, at 1184.

21. Skilton and Helstad, *supra* note 12, at 1480.

22. Williams Petition for Allowance of Appeal at 1, *Williams*, 350 F.2d 445 (D.C. Cir. 1965) (No. 18604); David L. Bazelon Papers, MSS 003, Biddle Law Library, University of Pennsylvania Law School [hereinafter "Bazelon Papers"], box 179, "Subject Files Poverty Rpts. 1958–1962" folder and "Subject Files Poverty Rpts. 1963–65" folder; Bazelon Papers, box 180; "Subject Files Poverty Rpts. 1966–75" folder and "Subject Files Poverty Clippings" folder; Earl Johnson, Justice and Reform; the Formative Years of the OEO Legal Services Program 28–29 (1974). Wright, *supra* note 16.

23. On the frequency that the court granted requests for review, see Dostert, *supra* note 15, at 1185. The third member of the review panel was Judge Fahy. Brief for Respondent, *Williams*, 198 A.2d 914 (D.C. 1964) (No. 3389) (available at District of Columbia Court of Appeals); Williams Petition for Allowance of Appeal at 1 (May 22, 1964), Order granting appeal (July 22, 1964), Brief of Williams/Thorne, and Brief of Amicus Curiae (January 13, 1965), *Williams*, 350 F.2d 445 (D.C. Cir. 1965) (No. 18604) (available at District of Columbia Court of Appeals, file for Case No. 3389).

24. Brief for Williams, 198 A.2d 914 (D.C. 1964) (No. 3389) (available at District of Columbia Court of Appeals); Williams Petition for Allowance of Appeal at 1 (May 22, 1964), Order granting appeal (July 22, 1964), Brief of Williams/Thorne, and Brief of Amicus Curiae (January 13, 1965), 350 F.2d 445 (D.C. Cir. 1965) (No. 18604) (available at District of Columbia Court of Appeals, file for Case No. 3389).

25. Draft Opinion at 6–8 (June 29, 1965), Wright Papers, box 77, "Williams v. Walker-Thomas Furniture Co. S.T. 1965" folder.

26. Marvins Credit, Inc. v. Morgan, 87 A.2d 530, 531 (D.C. 1952) (describing creditor remedies under conditional sales agreement); D.C. Code § 28:9–504(2) (1963) ("If the security interest secures an indebtedness, the secured party must account to the debtor for any surplus . . .") (modern provision at D.C. Code § 28:9–615(d)).

27. Draft Opinion at 6–8 (June 29, 1965), Wright Papers, box 77, "Williams v. Walker-Thomas Furniture Co. S.T. 1965" folder; Wright, *supra* note 16.

28. 350 F.2d 445 (D.C. Cir. 1965).

29. Memo from Bazelon to Wright (July 15, 1965); memo from Bazelon to Wright (July 23, 1965); memo from Edgerton to Wright (July 28, 1965); memo from Fahy to Wright (July 27, 1965); memo from McGowan to Wright (July 26, 1965), Wright Papers, box 77, "Williams v. Walker-Thomas Furniture Co. S.T. 1965" folder.

30. 198 A.2d 915, 916 (D.C. 1964); *Consumer Protection Legislation for the District*

of Columbia: Hearing on S. 316, S. 2589, S. 2590, and S. 2592 Before the Subcomm. on Business and Commerce of the S. Comm. on the District of Columbia, 90th Cong. 29–30 (1967) (letter from D.C. Commissioner Walter E. Washington); Benny L. Kass, *More Than Case Law Needed,* A.B.A. J. 316 (1969).

31. *Consumer Protection Legislation for the District of Columbia: Hearing on S. 316, S. 2589, S. 2590, and S. 2592 Before the Subcomm. on Business and Commerce of the S. Comm. on the District of Columbia,* 90th Cong. 60 (1967) (testimony of Egon Guttman); *id.* at 119 (testimony of Stephen M. Nassau, representing the Consumer Protection Committee of the Greater Washington Chapter of Americans for Democratic Action); *id.* at 28 (Report of the Bar Association of the District of Columbia). S. REP. NO. 90-1519, at 15 (1968).

32. Willard Clopton Washington, *Curfew Imposed As Roving Bands Plunder and Burn,* WASH. POST, Apr. 6, 1968, at A1. Photograph: "D.C. Riot. April '68. Aftermath" (Warren K. Leffler) (photograph of the Intersection of Seventh and N St, NW, April. 8, 1968, on file with the Library of Congress, Prints and Photographs Division, Washington, D.C.), *available at* http://hdl.loc.gov/loc.pnp/ppm sca.04301; William Raspberry, *The Day the City's Fury Was Unleashed,* WASH. POST, Apr. 13, 1988, at A1; Willard Clopton Jr. and Robert G. Kaisar, *11,500 Troops Confront Rioters; Three-Day Arrest Total at 2686,* WASH. POST, Apr. 7, 1968, at A1; Ward Just, *Generation Gap In the Ghetto,* WASH. POST, Apr. 7, 1968, at B6; the federal Truth in Lending Act passed in 1968 as Title I of the Consumer Credit Protection Act.

33. D.C. Consumer Credit Protection Act of 1971, Pub. L. No. 92-200, § 4, 85 Stat. 665, 670 (codified as amended at D.C. Code § 28-3805 (West 2012)); D.C. Consumer Protection Practices Act of 1976, D.C. Law 1-76 (codified as amended at D.C. Code §§ 28-3901 to 28-3913 (West 2012)).

34. Paul Richard, *Installment-Plan Law Will Shield the Needy,* WASH. POST, Mar. 28, 1966, at B1.

35. Skilton and Helstad, *supra* note 12, at 1479–80 (quoting letter from Dostert to authors); Dostert, *supra* note 15, at 1186.

36. Arthur Allen Leff, *Unconscionability and the Crowd—Consumers and the Common Law Tradition,* 31 U. PITT. L. REV. 349, 356 (1969); Patterson v. Walker-Thomas Furniture Co., 277 A.2d 111, 113–14 (D.C. 1971) (on price unconscionability); to get discovery related to the unconscionability of the price term, a consumer first had to plead a "sufficient factual predicate for the defense." *Id.* at 114; Patterson's claim failed, as did the price unconscionability claim in *Morris v. Capitol Furniture & Appliance Co.,* 280 A.2d 775 (D.C. 1971); on the "squeaky wheel" problem, see Amy Schmitz, *Access to Consumer Remedies in the Squeaky Wheel System,* 39 PEPP. L. REV. 279 (2012).

37. Blackmond v. Walker-Thomas Furniture Co., 428 F. Supp. 344, 345 (D.D.C. 1977).

38. For a longer discussion of the effects of the decision on Walker-Thomas, see Eben Colby, *What Did the Doctrine of Unconscionability Do to the Walker-Thomas Furniture Company,* 34 CONN. L. REV. 625, 646–60 (2002); Greenberg, *supra* note 6, at 381–90.

39. Greenberg, *supra* note 6, at 381–82, 385–90; In re Walker-Thomas Furniture

Co., 87 F.T.C. 26 (1976); Walker-Thomas remained in business at least through the late 1980s. *Morris Levin Obituary*, WASH. POST, Jun. 30, 2007, at Metro B5 (noting that Levin, a Walker-Thomas executive, retired from the firm in 1987).

40. *See* San Antonio Indep. School Dist. v. Rodriguez, 411 U.S. 1 (1973); Lindsey v. Normet, 405 U.S. 56 (1972); Dandridge v. Williams, 397 U.S. 471 (1970); other scholars have also observed the "salience-raising effect" of high-profile court cases. *See, e.g.,* Nathaniel Persily et al., *Gay Rights, in* PUBLIC OPINION AND CONSTITUTIONAL CONTROVERSY 234, 256 (2008) (arguing that gay-marriage litigation raised the salience of the issue and created a short-term backlash against gay rights); Michael J. Klarman, *Brown and Lawrence (and Goodridge)*, 104 MICH. L. REV. 431, 453 (2005) (arguing that *Brown v. Board of Education* "dramatically raised the salience of the segregation issue").

41. *E.g.*, Richard A. Epstein, *Unconscionability*, 18 J.L. & ECON. 293, 306 n.36, 307 (1975).

Sylvester Smith, Unlikely Heroine

King v. Smith • (1968)

HENRY FREEDMAN

Sylvester Smith, a 34-year-old Selma, Alabama, African American widow with four children, was unaware of a press conference held in Washington, D.C., in February 1966. At that conference, the NAACP Legal Defense and Education Fund lawyers urged the federal government to stop state welfare agencies from refusing to help children of a woman who had a steady male friend:

> The needy mother without a husband is caught in an impossible dilemma. She may try to conduct a secret relationship, endanger her grant, and live as if she were a criminal, or she may abandon her effort to develop male friendships altogether, or she may strip herself of every last vestige of dignity by reporting constantly on the intimacies of her friendship.

Edward Sparer, who had just founded the Center on Social Welfare Policy and Law (now the National Center for Law and Economic Justice), said this was "one of the most important and most significant issues in welfare."[1] A few months later, Sylvester Smith's battle to keep her benefits launched a struggle that went to the Supreme Court, revolutionized our understanding of the welfare law, and resulted in hundreds of thousands of poor families getting desperately needed help.

Background: Sylvester Smith's Dilemma

Sylvester Smith and William Williams grew up in Tyler, a country town 15 miles south of Selma. Their parents were friends. As children, they visited each other's homes. As adults, they and Mrs. Williams were good friends and visited each other's homes with their children.

When Mrs. Smith was 23 years old, her husband and the father of her three children died "in a fight over a woman."[2] A few months later, she began to receive Aid to Dependent Children (ADC) welfare benefits for their three children. She had a fourth child, and when his father left town several years later, she also began receiving ADC for him.

Mrs. Smith, now 34 years old, moved into Selma in the summer of 1966. She worked from 3:30 a.m. to noon in a cafe, starting at $16 a week, which later rose to $20 a week. She had a new welfare caseworker, a "young bull-dogged woman named Miss Jacqueline Stancil,"[3] who poked around and learned that Mr. Williams was visiting Mrs. Smith.[4]

On October 1, 1966, Stancil told Smith that an undisclosed third party had told the department that Smith was "going with" Williams, and un-less she could prove otherwise, he would be considered a "substitute father," which would disqualify the family from aid.[5] Smith conceded that Williams on occasion stayed overnight at her house. When Stancil told Smith she had to terminate the relationship, Smith responded that she was still young, that "If I end with him, I'm gonna make a relationship with somebody. If God had intended for me to be a nun I'd be a nun."[6]

Mr. Williams had to work to support nine children of his own. He was not the father of any of Mrs. Smith's children and was not providing any sup-port to them. Nonetheless, Alabama pronounced him the "substitute father" for all of Mrs. Smith's children.[7]

Origins of Alabama's Substitute Father Rule

Much of welfare administration had been about race and sex long before Sylvester Smith came on the scene. In the early part of the past century, many states and localities operated "Mothers' Pension" programs, which were generally limited to widows. Determinations were discretionary and often infused with concern about perceived moral character of participants. Race discrimination was rife.[8]

The Social Security Act of 1935 (the "Act"), enacted in the midst of the Great Depression and best known for the Social Security retirement program, also created the ADC program to help states assist needy families who did not have a breadwinner. ADC was a "grant-in-aid" program, under which states were reimbursed generously if they complied with federal guidelines.

In tune with the times, the 1935 Congress was determined to assure that states would continue to have free rein in running their programs. The debate was dominated in particular by powerful southern senators insisting upon enormous state discretion to assure that no federal bureaucrat could tell states how to deal with "their Negro problem."[9]

Nonetheless, there were two provisions in the ADC statute that turned out to be key in Sylvester Smith's case. The first was Section 406 in the original 1935 Act, which said that a "dependent child" who might get benefits was a child who had been "deprived of parental support or care by reason of the death, continued absence from the home, or incapacity of a parent." The second was Section 402(a)(9) (renumbered 10 at the time of the Supreme Court decision), which provided that aid "shall be furnished with reasonable promptness to all eligible individuals." It had been added in 1950 for the purpose of eliminating waiting lists.

The United States Department of Health, Education, and Welfare (HEW), the agency that oversaw the administration of the ADC program, understood the Act to mean that states could pick and choose which needy dependent children were eligible for benefits so long as the state used classifications that "rest[ed] upon some clearly evident difference bearing a reasonable and just relation to the Act" and did not "carry out a purpose prohibited under the Constitution."[10] HEW said that "states [had] been advised [that excluding] children from eligibility on the ground that they are illegitimate raised grave constitutional questions and enforcement of such legislation would result in the loss of federal financial participation."[11] Indeed, loss of all federal funding was the only weapon HEW had in its arsenal. HEW was loathe to use that weapon both because it would deprive thousands of needy children of benefits and because the state's congressional delegation could put such pressure on HEW that it would have to back down. So the agency resorted to letters of exhortation.

By the 1950s, states were developing policies to reduce participation, in particular black participation, in ADC. Many of these policies relied on the presence of a child born out of wedlock to disqualify the family on the ground that the home was not "suitable" or that the child had a "substitute father." These requirements did not gain much public attention until July 1960, when Louisiana implemented a "suitable home" policy, informing 5,991 families with 22,501 children that they would no longer get benefits because the family home was unsuitable. This drew wide press attention, with gifts of money and clothing arriving from England and from school children and churches across the country.[12]

Under great public pressure and days before leaving office in January 1961, HEW secretary Arthur Flemming issued the "Flemming Ruling," which provided that states could no longer deny aid on the ground that a home was unsuitable unless the child was moved to a suitable home. Congress confirmed this policy and created the foster care program to make federal funds available to states so they could provide an alternate foster home for any children the state determined were living in an unsuitable home. Also about this time, Congress changed the name of the program to Aid to Families with Dependent Children (AFDC), but Alabama continued to call its program ADC.[13]

Alabama continued, unsuccessfully, to seek HEW approval of suitable home and substitute father policies, as detailed in the decisions in this case. Under the Alabama regulation, an able-bodied man, married or single, was considered a substitute father of all the children of the applicant mother in three different situations: (1) if "he live[d] in the home with the child's natural or adoptive mother for the purpose of cohabitation," (2) if "he visit[ed] [the home] frequently for the purpose of cohabiting with the child's natural or adoptive mother," or (3) if "he [did] not frequent the home but cohabit[ed] with the child's natural or adoptive mother elsewhere."[14]

Meanwhile, Back in New York: The Center Gears Up

Edward Sparer, the "father of welfare law," created the legal services office of Mobilization for Youth on New York's Lower East Side in the early 1960s. Appalled at the lawlessness he found in the welfare system, in 1965 he established the Center on Social Welfare Policy and Law ("Center") at Columbia University to study, analyze, train, and litigate. He identified possible legal challenges relying on federal constitutional rights of equal protection, due process, and privacy, and he proselytized lawyers joining the growing legal services movement.[15]

In support of his determination to have the Center lead a systematic, incremental strategy to convince the courts to expand the provision of basic support to all needy people, Sparer hired Martin Garbus, an experienced litigator, as codirector to focus on litigation. Sparer believed it would be best to litigate these cases in the South, where the courts had become accustomed to finding discrimination and entering orders against state officials. The Center worked with civil rights attorneys in the NAACP Legal Defense Fund and other organizations to seek out cases. One of the first was *Anderson v. Burson*,[16] which stopped Georgia counties from cutting off all aid at the time of the okra harvest.

And then a call came in from Alabama.

Sylvester Smith Goes to Court

While the hardships that the substitute father policy was causing were clear and legal arguments had been developed, a case could not be filed unless a brave person stepped forward—a recipient currently being harmed by the policy who was willing to face a media storm, public scorn, difficulty for her children in school, and hostility from the agency that provided her very means of subsistence. Sylvester Smith was that person.

Civil rights workers in Selma relayed the information about Smith to the Center. To Garbus, the facts were perfect. Alabama had no proof that Mr. Williams was the father of any of the children, was living in their home, or was performing any of a father's duties, including providing support. The policy itself "disqualified all families in which the mother was *thought* [emphasis in original] to have any relationship with a man, with or without income and in or out of the house." Smith worked full-time and still needed benefits. HEW had raised concerns with the state over the years, but had never approved or disapproved the regulation, although it had approved similar regulations in other states.[17]

The Center had to move quickly. The complaint against Commissioner King and other Alabama officials, filed in December 1966 in federal court, was modeled on the Center's papers in *Anderson v. Burson*. The complaint said plaintiffs were suing on behalf of a class consisting of Alabama's "needy Negro mothers and dependent Negro children." For Equal Protection Clause purposes, discrimination on the basis of race calls for the higher "strict scrutiny" level of review. Martha Davis writes that Center lawyers used this language in their haste to file the case and without thinking through "the messy factual issues that this allegation raised: whether more 'Negro' applicants cohabited and whether the ratio of blacks to whites [who] were cut off matched the ratios of those receiving welfare."[18]

After setting out the facts of the case, the complaint asserted several constitutional legal claims: the policy violated the Equal Protection Clause by treating children with a "substitute father" differently from other children, it was a classification not consistent with the purposes of the ADC statute, its arbitrary determinations violated the Due Process Clause, and its intrusions into intimate personal life violated the plaintiffs' constitutional liberty rights.

Surprisingly, certainly in hindsight, the complaint did not make the claim that a unanimous Supreme Court relied upon: that denying aid to Smith and her children violated the statute itself. Rather, in the course of making the equal protection claim, the complaint asserted that the family was deprived of benefits *to which they were entitled under the statute* by a classification that violated the Equal Protection Clause.

There were compelling reasons for presenting a constitutional claim in any event, both for federal jurisdiction and to invoke the opportunity—no longer available today—to secure appointment of a three-judge federal panel because the case challenged a state law or policy on federal constitutional grounds.[19] Securing a three-judge panel both increased the possibility of getting at least one favorable judge and provided a right of direct appeal (not just certiorari) to the Supreme Court.

But a statutory claim could have been made as well. Was it thought just too daring? HEW, presumably the expert in interpreting the law, had never talked of statutory entitlement. And Sparer's original analysis, and incremental strategy toward universal coverage, focused on constitutional claims.

Fortunately for the plaintiffs, the case was assigned to Judge Frank M. Johnson Jr., one of the leading federal judges in the South on civil rights cases. He referred the case to the chief judge of the Fifth Circuit for appointment of a three-judge panel. In the interim, he ordered that HEW be designated to appear as amicus curiae and as a party "to accord this Court the benefit of its views and recommendations, with the right to participate actively as a party in every phase of said proceedings." To Judge Johnson's frustration, HEW was virtually absent throughout the case, despite his repeated requests.[20]

Meanwhile, life continued to be hard for Sylvester Smith. After she brought suit, some stores refused to extend credit to her, and some days her children went hungry.[21]

The Lawyers Dig Out the Facts and Argue the Law

Plaintiffs set up the next step in the case—"discovery," or interrogating witnesses under oath and reviewing documents—very well. Garbus first questioned Commissioner King, who responded:

> You don't understand, Mr. Garbus. We're not interested in the mother's fooling around. We are not in the business to judge people morally.

The regulation has nothing to do with sex. We're interested in getting the men to support the children. Any mother whose aid was stopped could always choose "to give up her pleasure or to act like a woman ought to act."

King continued that the question is "does the man have the privileges of a husband" but denied that he meant sexual relations.[22] Yet his denial was belied at many other stages of the case. For example, the attorney for Alabama advised the three-judge court that "[w]ith Mrs. Smith's permission, an investigator would have gone to her favorite policeman or grocer to inquire whether she was still enjoying sexual relations with Williams and, if so, where and how often."[23]

King also strongly denied that the regulation was aimed at Negroes. He asserted that since two-thirds of the rolls were black, about two-thirds of those cut off would be black. He would not provide data on the composition of the class, however, and eventually the parties agreed that seven county commissioners would testify about terminations. Their testimony established that every terminated recipient in their counties was Negro.

The commissioners, all women, also expressed pride that they were now social welfare professionals helping their clients. One raised her voice: "The ladies want our help in getting rid of the men who live off their welfare checks and this does it. They really do. Many times I tell them, 'You shouldn't go with Mr. Jones or Mr. Washington because he's no good,' and they appreciate it."[24]

The discovery process was so effective at establishing the facts that the parties agreed there was no need for testimony at the trial, since the court had so much material from the document discovery and depositions. The parties submitted their evidence and arguments to the three-judge court on May 15, 1967.

Martha Davis writes that the lawyers and a sociologist at the Center prepared a "Brandeis brief" to present the court with social science data as well as legal argument.[25] Indeed, plaintiffs submitted a 99-page brief, of which more than 40 pages were devoted to background and facts: Alabama's earlier attempts to use a suitable home policy to reduce the number of Negroes on the rolls; the background of the substitute father policy and how effective it had been in reducing the number of Negroes on the rolls; the communications between the state and federal officials in which the federal officials kept turning down variants of Alabama's policy; the arbitrary and vague standards used to implement the policy; the complete absence of any state efforts to collect support for the AFDC recipients despite the state's purported interest in securing support for the children; and the facts surrounding the application of the regulation to Sylvester Smith.

In the brief, deposition testimony was used to demonstrate how arbitrary the policy was. For example, some officials said there was no specific standard for how frequently cohabitation had to have occurred. Commissioner King said the regulation should be applied if the parties had weekly sex. One county director testified that the regulation should be applied if the parties had sex once every three months; another said once every six months would be enough.[26]

The next 50 pages of plaintiffs' brief were devoted to the legal claims, with extensive citation to case law. Notably, the first sentence captured what the Supreme Court would ultimately conclude, though for plaintiffs it was meant only as an introduction to the equal protection claim: "ADC financial assistance is a statutory entitlement under both the laws of Alabama, and the Federal Social Security Act, and where the child meets the statutory eligibility requirements, he has a right to receive benefits."

The brief went on to contend that "it is perfectly clear that this regulation is directed at the ADC mother's sexual relations with men, and not the parental support and care of her children." Ms. Stancil, the caseworker, never asked Mrs. Smith about support that Mr. Williams might be providing, and Mr. Williams was in fact living with his own wife and supporting his own children.

The legal section of the brief argued that the regulation violated due process, equal protection, and the Fifth Amendment right against self-incrimination; more specifically, it complained about the lack of adequate notice and a hearing for plaintiffs before benefits were terminated, vague standards for applying the policy, and unreasonable procedures, including imposing the burden of proof on the recipients. The language was strong:

> We may begin by recalling the obvious fact, which the audacity of this policy tends to obscure: the conduct which the policy regulates is by its nature as private as any human activity within the cognizance of an administrative agency. The administrative action in question here is to be placed on a finding of the occurrence of intimacies between a man and a woman, which, in all but extraordinary circumstances other people cannot know of their own knowledge. The allegations of a forbidden relationship between a client and an unrelated man . . . are, as the depositions show, always in the nature of rumor, gossip, and innuendo.

The final claim, that the regulation unconstitutionally invaded the privacy of mothers receiving aid, was the shortest. To prove that she is not having a sexual relationship with a man, the brief argued, "the mother will have to persuade local welfare officials that each man who visits her—or whom she sees outside of her home—is not interested in her sexually." If she failed, she would have to open her relationship to neighbors, law enforcement officials, and grocers, which would surely drive the man away in any event.

After the case was submitted to the three-judge panel, Garbus left the Center to become associate director of the American Civil Liberties Union (ACLU), and he took the case with him.[27]

The Three-Judge Court Says the Substitute Father Policy Violates the Equal Protection Clause

The three-judge court assigned to the case, including Johnson, Circuit Judge John C. Godbold of Montgomery, and District Judge Virgil Pittman of Mobile, issued its unanimous *per curiam* decision on November 8, 1967, almost a year after the case had been filed.[28] The opinion first set out the relevant provisions of the Social Security Act and Alabama policy, gave a straightforward account of the facts of Sylvester Smith's case, and reviewed the history of HEW policy including the Flemming Ruling. The court quoted extensively from the correspondence between HEW and Alabama over suitable home policies and the move to the substitute father policy. The court said it would not rest its decision upon racial considerations and held that the policy was unconstitutional under the Equal Protection Clause.

While the opinion acknowledged that ADC "is a statutory entitlement under both the laws of Alabama and the federal Social Security Act, and where the child meets the statutory eligibility requirements he has a right to received financial benefits," that statutory fact was treated only as the basis for determining that a state-imposed eligibility classification—"the alleged sexual behavior of the mother"—was arbitrary and inconsistent with the purposes of the Act was therefore invalid under the Equal Protection Clause. The court noted that a state could be concerned about an ADC mother's immorality, but it could not demonstrate its concern by denying children their ADC benefits. The court did not reach the other claims raised. It then ordered Alabama to immediately reinstate each otherwise eligible child who had been declared ineligible because of the "man in the house" policy and to file a list with the names and addresses of those who had been restored.

Supreme Court justice Hugo Black granted the state's request to stay the order pending appeal, ostensibly because the state claimed it did not have funds to pay about $645,000 a year for benefits and add caseworkers. But new federal legislation designed to limit federal AFDC expenditures became law on January 2, 1968, to take effect July 1, 1968, that would cap the AFDC rolls at their level during the first three months of 1968. Garbus asked Justice Black to lift the stay so Alabama could add the cases to the rolls and not be subject to the cap. On January 30, Justice Black directed the state to restore some 15,000 to 20,000 children to the rolls.[29]

The State's Brief Fails to Establish
That the Case Is Not about Morality

Since Alabama was appealing the decision below, it submitted its brief first. It certainly did not help the Supreme Court understand the ramifications of the case. The brief's discussion of the equal protection claim rambled for 30 pages over centuries of philosophy and anthropology to claim that disqualifying families where there was a sexual relationship outside marriage served the rational and legitimate purpose of discouraging further out-of-wedlock childbirth. The brief emphasized the state's concerns about what conduct the public, and more particularly legislators, would tolerate from ADC recipients. To rebut "another fallacy" in the three-judge court's opinion about the means the state had available to discourage the birth of children out of wedlock, the brief riffed: "Whereas Scripturally the great requirement for releasing from condemnation a woman taken in adultery was 'go and sin no more (John 18:11),' the Alabama regulation goes considerably further in its no condemnation concept. Thus the mother is given up to sixty days to present her evidence." (Alabama's reply brief continued in similar fashion: "Unbridled sex in this country recently has become more stylish," and, "There appears to be a belief held among many that sexual relations are necessary to health. [Appellants] assert that chastity does accord with good health."[30])

The state next argued that the entire regulation should not have been struck down, since there were three different ways a person could be determined to be a substitute father, and not all of them were addressed by the three-judge court. But the discussion drifted off: "Monogyny is found in all African societies, but polygyny is found in most. In . . . the Belgian Congo a specialized form of polyandry, or the marriage of one woman to two or more men, sometimes occurs concurrently with the predominating polygynous marriage."

The remainder of the brief addressed such matters as the alleged failure to exhaust administrative remedies and argued that Smith's privacy was not invaded since the intimate relationship with à man is related to an ADC eligibility condition.[31]

Sylvester Smith's Brief Focuses Entirely on Constitutional Claims Once More

As in the lower court, Garbus presented an extensive factual history of HEW's correspondence with the state, followed by plaintiffs' legal arguments: First, once again mentioning but not remarking on the plaintiffs' statutory entitlement, he reiterated the equal protection arguments that challenged classifications based on the recipient's alleged sexual behavior, race, and their children's illegitimacy, suggesting that heightened scrutiny was warranted under equal protection precedent. Next, he covered the due process arguments, addressing the state's arbitrary procedures and vague standards, including the imposition of the burden of proof on the ADC mother, and argued that these mothers had the right to be heard on the validity of the state's action before termination of their benefits. Finally, he argued that the policy was an unwarranted invasion of privacy.

Finally, the Center's Amicus Brief Presents the Statutory Entitlement Argument

Ed Sparer, who had left the Center for Yale Law School in the middle of 1967, and the staff at the Center believed that *King v. Smith* offered an opportunity to secure a transformative interpretation of the Social Security Act: that there was an enforceable statutory entitlement to aid for anyone who met the federal definition of dependent child. Indeed, Martha Davis writes that Garbus's colleagues at the Center felt that he "was throwing away the recipients' strongest claim in the brash hope of garnering an important constitutional victory."[32] As a result, Paul Dodyk, the brilliant young Columbia Law School professor serving as faculty director of the Center after Sparer left, Brian Glick, associate director, and Sparer submitted an amicus brief with the NAACP Legal Defense and Education Fund to present the statutory entitlement argument directly.

The argument rested upon the two statutory provisions: First, the Act says AFDC is to be provided to children deprived by reason of the death, absence, or incapacity of a "parent." The brief contends that this provision meant a "parent" who could normally be expected to provide economic support. That could only be a natural or adoptive parent, or a stepparent required by law to provide support. It would not include a stepparent or any other person not legally obligated to support the child. (Of course, if that person was in fact providing support, that might affect the child's financial eligibility because of the income received, clearly not the case here). The brief reviewed the legislative history of the ADC program, showing that during the Great Depression Congress was concerned that children without a breadwinner parent would not benefit from unemployment insurance or the work programs that were being created.

But winning on that point would only mean Alabama could not treat Mr. Williams as a parent. It would not assure that Mrs. Smith's children would get benefits. To support the claim that anyone who meets the eligibility definition has a legally enforceable right to receive aid, the brief pointed to Section 402(a)(9), which said aid had to be provided promptly to all eligible individuals.

After making its primary statutory pitch, the Center's amicus brief then turned to equal protection, rebutting Alabama's argument that the purpose of the policy was to shift the burden of support to the individual responsible for the child's existence. The brief showed how the policy did not accomplish that goal at all, but was rather an expression of moral disapproval running afoul of the Flemming Ruling.

Moreover, special scrutiny was required because of the policy's drastic impact on the ability of the poorest and most helpless children to maintain life itself. The brief evoked the possibility that these children would starve because of the state's policy. One can wonder whether this "right to life" equal protection argument could have alarmed the Court, leading to the *Dandridge v. Williams* decision two years later, which put to rest any hope of an incremental expansion of equal protection and due process to secure a "right to life."

The Oral Argument Portends a Victory

Mary Stapp, the attorney for Alabama, led off. After an easy opening, she ran into trouble. Justices Warren and Fortas were concerned that no support was actually being provided by the so-called "substitute fathers." Justices Marshall and Douglas were alarmed that the child was suffering for the acts of its mother. Justice Stewart disliked the notion that the state said it could help some children more by taking away benefits from other children. Justice White asked what would happen to the Alabama policy if the federal law clearly stated that parent meant only a natural parent and whether that would eliminate the need to reach the constitutional question. Stapp repeatedly failed to understand Justice White's question, to his clear consternation, and said she would save the balance of her time for rebuttal.

When Garbus rose to argue, he had already become convinced that he wanted to stress the statutory argument that had not been addressed explicitly in his brief.[33] He was delighted when Justice White asked if the case could be decided by finding the Alabama policy contrary to the federal statute. Justices Fortas, Black, and Stewart seemed to agree, but later Justice Harlan expressed puzzlement about the statutory argument. Justices Stewart and White came to Garbus's aid by responding to Justice Harlan. Most critically, the thrust of the half-hour allotted to Garbus was on the irrational hardship caused by the regulation. Equal protection and the other constitutional claims were hardly mentioned.

In her rebuttal, Stapp confirmed the importance of the statutory claim: "If you construed the statute like Mr. Garbus suggests, then HEW would never have had authority to permit any State to carve out lesser classifications." She then unwisely let herself get into a discussion of "informal polygamy" with Justice Marshall.

Toward the end of her rebuttal, Justice Black tried to give her a hypothetical fact pattern to see how the suitable parent rule would apply, and she kept confounding him with her answers until he replied "Never mind" with obvious annoyance. She then said she wanted to quote language that Justice (then Senator) Black had used in 1935 when the Act was adopted, which had not been included in her brief but apparently supported the idea that states would have discretion. She could not find the piece of paper she had written it on, and her argument ended with Justice Harlan suggesting she "just put it on a piece of paper and give it to me." But there is no mention of that language in the Court's decision.[34]

Unanimous Decision: A Statutory Entitlement to AFDC

On June 17, Garbus received a telegram from the Supreme Court informing him Smith had won.[35] The unanimous opinion, written by Chief Justice Warren, his last decision before he retired, was a complete affirmation of the statutory entitlement argument.[36] The opinion quickly disposed of preliminary questions: the court below had federal jurisdiction, the constitutional claim meant that a three-judge court was proper, and there was no need to exhaust administrative remedies in this type of case.

Then, the opinion noted that under the Alabama policy it was irrelevant whether the "substitute father" was legally obligated to support the children or even whether he supported them. The arbitrariness in the policy and its uneven enforcement was confirmed by the testimony from three Alabama officials who said "frequent" or "continuing" sexual relations meant, for them, at least once a week, every three months, or every six months. Then the Court gave a statement of the facts of Mrs. Smith's case.

Turning to the law, the Court said that the Act required that AFDC "shall be furnished with reasonable promptness to all eligible individuals" and that a "dependent child" was one that has been deprived of "parental" support or care. With no acknowledgment that it was upending decades of understanding of the Act by HEW and the states, the Court held that "In combination, these two provisions of the Act clearly require participating States to furnish aid to families with children who have a parent absent from the home, if such families are in other respects eligible."

The Court stressed that it was not directing state expenditures or abridging the right of states to set their own standard of need and level of benefits. Nor was the Court questioning Alabama's general power to deal with illegitimacy or conduct it considered immoral. But, the Court held, the state could not address these moral concerns "by flatly denying AFDC assistance to otherwise eligible dependent children." It acknowledged that these morality interests were once relevant and summarized the developments in welfare administration from the nineteenth century up to the Flemming Ruling, the congressional affirmation of that policy and creation of the foster care program, followed by amendments emphasizing the importance of providing social services for troubled families. In light of these developments since 1960, the Court held that "it is simply inconceivable . . . that Alabama is free to discourage immorality and illegitimacy by the device of absolute disqualification of needy children."

The Court also rejected Alabama's argument that the state was attempting to be fair to two-parent families by treating families with substitute parents the same, pointing out that the substitute parent had no obligation to support the children. When Congress created the program in 1935, the Court said, it had in mind a breadwinner parent who was legally obligated to provide support and provided other programs to help unemployed breadwinners.

The Court then noted that it did not need to consider the equal protection claim in light of the statutory holding and concluded, "We hold today only that Congress has made at least this one determination: that destitute children who are legally fatherless cannot be flatly denied federally funded assistance on the transparent fiction that they have a substitute father."

Aftermath: The Fruits of Victory

The *King v. Smith* decision affected 21,000 children in Alabama and 400,000 throughout the country.[37] As for Sylvester Smith, she met Mr. Garbus for the first time some weeks after the decision came down. She told him of people she knew who had been restored to the rolls. She herself was still destitute; she was being denied ADC by the new worker at the welfare agency, and she could not come up with the $15 to purchase food stamps, a barrier to access that was later eliminated. After Garbus threatened to sue the state once again, her aid was restored.[38]

On June 21—four days after the decision came down—HEW sent a letter to the states attaching the decision and a proposed regulation that was being sent to the Federal Register with a 30-day comment period. On July 10 Lee Albert, the executive director of the Center, sent a letter to the legal services community, reporting that the Center, representing the National Welfare Rights Organization (NWRO), had been successfully negotiating with staff at HEW to secure improvements in the draft regulation. In response to the NWRO's request that the welfare agency rely primarily on the mother's declaration about the facts establishing eligibility, Albert reported that HEW secretary Wilbur Cohen had assured Rev. Ralph Abernathy of the Poor Peoples Campaign that a regulation requiring the states to rely on the applicant's word on all matters relating to eligibility would be published shortly. And while the NWRO's recommendation that HEW order that retroactive benefits be paid to the plaintiff class was not accepted, Albert pointed out that recipients could now sue the state for those benefits.[39]

The *Washington Post* later reported that George Wiley, who headed NWRO, said that the new regulations met most of the organization's demands.[40] A biography of Wiley reports:

> When Wiley met with HEW officials to discuss guidelines for implementing the court rulings he was an amiable negotiator, calm and articulate. But he could also chase HEW Secretary Wilbur Cohen outside the Capitol shouting, "Are you going to enforce the Supreme Court ruling?" Press microphones were shoved in Cohen's face. "I am," the secretary answered, tight-lipped, and pushed the microphones away.[41]

The Center's negotiations to implement the decision in *King* also achieved a federal regulation barring any state from assuming that income of a man living in the house with AFDC parents and their children was provided to the children unless the agency had proof that it was. This regulation was upheld by the Supreme Court in *Lewis v. Martin*, 397 U.S. 572 (1970). The Center participated as amicus in *Lewis* and asserted that the resulting change in policy provided many more millions of dollars of benefits to children in need each year.

For the next three years, Center attorneys and recipient leaders and staff from NWRO met regularly with HEW policy staff and negotiated a number of important ADC regulations. After Richard Nixon's re-election in 1972, however, HEW staff members from the Lyndon Johnson years who had negotiated these provisions were removed in the most sweeping presidential transition to that time. Nixon installed people from Governor Ronald Reagan's staff who had chafed under years of legal services welfare litigation in California and who immediately set about repealing or eviscerating many of those hard-won regulations protecting AFDC families.

Although the Center and its allies had achieved a positive working relationship with the policy staff at HEW, the HEW Office of General Counsel was aghast at the decision in *King*. Throughout the course of the litigation, the HEW lawyers had said little, hoping that these young legal services lawyers would succeed in getting the substitute father policy struck down on constitutional grounds. Instead, they had been told by the Supreme Court that their entire understanding of Title IV of the Social Security Act—that it only set the outer bounds for federal matching but still permitted states to pick and choose which categories of families would be covered so long as that choice was rational—was wrong. Instead, the "outer bounds" for eligibility defined who had to be covered.

The lawyers in the HEW General Counsel's office could not believe that was what the Supreme Court meant. With two more important cases involving categorical eligibility in the pipeline, they set out to convince the Court that it had gone too far. In the first case, *Townsend v. Swank*, the Social Security Act gave states the option of covering children between the ages of 18 and 21 if they were in high school, college, or vocational school. Illinois chose to cover children in high school or vocational school only. HEW submitted an amicus brief asserting that the Court should rule that the Act intended to set an outer limit for eligibility under the federal program, not to mandate coverage of all three categories. But Justice Brennan, in a unanimous decision for the Court, found that there was no basis for the exercise of state discretion in the statute or legislative history and that AFDC eligibility must be determined using federal standards unless evidence of a contrary congressional intent was clearly shown.[42]

The second case, *Carleson v. Remillard*, addressed a California regulation that said a parent absent due to military service was not continually absent. HEW filed an amicus brief trying to distinguish *Townsend* on the ground that in that case Congress had identified a clear category—a high school, college, or vocational school student—as the intended recipient of the benefits. In Carleson, by contrast, the federal law did not define "absent," which gave the states flexibility to define the term to exclude the children of military parents. Indeed, they noted, HEW had approved other states' provisions denying aid under similar circumstances. If states had "to extend AFDC coverage to all classes of persons for whom federal matching funds are available . . . nearly every state plan will be invalid," they claimed.

In response to HEW's argument, the Center filed an amicus brief, noting in a footnote that:

> The Solicitor General has taken what has become his usual posture before this Court . . . namely, that prior decisions of the Court with which it does not agree, could not possibly have been intended by the Court. . . . [T]he Townsend decision and its explicit repudiation of HEW's position, is wished away by the Government.

In *Carleson*, HEW's argument was rejected in a unanimous decision written by Justice Douglas.[43]

It soon became clear to the Center that HEW would not adopt sweeping regulatory changes to implement these decisions. Yet there was much that lawyers in each state could do to challenge categorical limitations in state programs. In 1972 the Center distributed an extensive analysis of the possibilities for litigation in a three-volume *Materials on Welfare Law*.[44] Between *King* and *Townsend*, however, the Court had decided in *Dandridge v. Williams* that constitutional welfare litigation would be subject only to rational basis scrutiny, thereby cutting off any avenue for plaintiffs to claim special protection for a "right to life" or "right to welfare." Chastened by *Dandridge*, the Center staff writers concluded that they "would encourage lawyers and welfare rights groups to focus on ways to expand eligibility under the federal statute rather than outside that statute." But in a footnote, they acknowledged that an equal protection claim, if not foreclosed by a Supreme Court decision like *Dandridge*, might nonetheless be needed to confer federal court jurisdiction over the case.[45]

The manual most prominently stressed the importance of attacking "collateral eligibility conditions," such as a requirement that the mother cooperate in pursuing child support from the father of the child. Indeed, the Supreme Court had already summarily affirmed a lower court decision finding such a requirement contrary to the Act as it existed at that time.[46] Other requirements noted as susceptible to challenge were disqualifications based on the transfer of property, failure to pursue medical treatment, refusal to sign a loyalty oath, and work requirements.[47]

In August 1972, in my capacity as executive director of the Center, I reported to the Center's Board of Directors that in addition to providing the *Materials* to the field, we were training incoming Reginald Heber Smith Fellows at four regional training conferences and had presented these issues to an enthusiastic session at the NWRO Convention. Center lawyers were also active in a variety of cases across the country, including two cases in the Fifth Circuit.[48]

The next year, however, the Supreme Court upended the Center's strategy to attack collateral eligibility requirements for AFDC by allowing New York to adopt work requirements clearly more onerous than those imposed under the Act. The plaintiffs' counsel in that case had unfortunately chosen to rely entirely on the theory that federal law pre-empted state law, rather than building upon the statutory entitlement victory the Center had achieved in the *King-Townsend-Remillard* trilogy. The Center submitted an amicus brief pressing the *King* argument, but it was not to be. The new more conservative Supreme Court majority, in *New York Dept. of Social Services v. Dublino*, upheld New York's work requirement as not pre-empted by federal law. Even worse, it dismissed the relevance of the *King* trilogy in one paragraph at the end, saying, "In those cases, it was clear that state law excluded people from AFDC benefits who the Social Security Act expressly provided would be eligible," whereas in this case, "the Act allows for complementary state work incentive programs and procedures incident thereto—even if they become conditions for continued assistance."[49]

Justices Marshall and Brennan disagreed strongly in *Dublino*, saying there was no such authority in the Act for more onerous work requirements than the federal statute delineated.[50] But the message was clear: work requirements were a potent political issue, and the Supreme Court simply did not want to interfere with efforts to impose them. Since so many of the remaining limitations on AFDC eligibility were based on various types of cooperation requirements, the power of the *King-Townsend-Carleson* trilogy to secure protections for AFDC recipients proved to be less than had been hoped. Nonetheless, the trilogy continued to govern many aspects of state administration of the AFDC program until it was repealed in 1996, with a major impact on the lives of many families.

Conclusion: Repealed But Not Dead

The Personal Responsibility and Work Opportunity Reconciliation Act of 1996 replaced AFDC with Temporary Assistance to Needy Families (TANF), which provided a block grant to the states rather than matching funds as under AFDC. The law stated explicitly that it "shall not be interpreted to entitle any individual or family to assistance under any State program funded under this part."[51] While this language, and the block grant nature of the TANF program, intentionally eliminated the impact of *King v. Smith* on cash assistance administration, it could not eliminate recipients' constitutional due process notice and prior hearing rights under *Goldberg v. Kelly*.[52] Where a statute sets out mandatory eligibility standards, a "statutory entitlement" is created and can be enforced in litigation.[53] And, most importantly, since the Medicaid program is a grant-in-aid program paralleling the structure of AFDC, *King* and its progeny can still be—and are—cited to prevent states from denying eligibility to those Congress intended to cover in the program.[54]

While the three-judge court and Supreme Court found it unnecessary to address race discrimination in *King*, there is no question that racial stereotyping and incorrect perceptions that families on the welfare rolls were overwhelmingly people of color were central in promoting public hostility to welfare programs over the ensuing decades, and they greatly influence TANF administration today.[55] Yet brave plaintiffs who have much to lose are still willing to stand up to make powerful impact litigation possible.[56]

Notes

1. Fred P. Graham, *Denial of Welfare for Children of Unwed Mothers Is Assailed*, N.Y. Times, Feb. 4, 1966.

2. Walter Goodman, *The Case of Mrs. Sylvester Smith: A Victory for 400,000 Children*, N.Y. Times Magazine, Aug. 25, 1968, at 29.

3. Martin Garbus, Ready for the Defense 144 (1971).

4. Smith v. King, 277 F. Supp. 31, 35 (M. D. Ala. 1967).

5. Brief for Appellees at 11, King v. Smith, 392 U.S. 309 (1968).

6. Goodman, *supra* note 2, at 29.

7. King v. Smith, 392 U.S. 309, 316–17 (1968).

8. Henry Freedman, *The Welfare Advocate's Challenge: Fighting Historic Racism in the New Welfare System*, 36 Clearinghouse Rev. 31 (2002).

9. *Id.*

10. Garbus, *supra* note 3, at 9.

11. HEW, Illegitimacy and Its Impact on the Aid to Dependent Children Program 9, 54 (1960).

12. Winifred Bell, Aid to Dependent Children 137, 140 (1965).

13. 392 U.S. 309, 313, n.1. Alabama continued to call its program ADC, so both terms appear in this discussion.

14. 392 U.S. 309, 313–314.

15. See, e.g., Edward V. Sparer, Social Welfare Law Testing, 12 Prac. Law. 13 (1966).

16. 300 F. Supp. 401 (N. D. Ga. 1968).

17. Garbus, supra note 3, at 150–52.

18. Martha F. Davis, Brutal Need: Lawyers and the Welfare Rights Movement, 1960–1973, 62 (1993).

19. 22 U.S.C. § 2281, repealed Pub. L. 91-384, § 7 (1976).

20. Garbus, supra note 3, at 171.

21. Id. at 150.

22. Id. at 157–58.

23. Id. at 163.

24. Id. at 159–60.

25. Davis, supra note 18, at 64.

26. The information in this paragraph and the next four paragraphs comes from Plaintiffs' Trial Brief of Fact and Law, King v. Smith, 392 U.S. 309 (1968).

27. Garbus, supra note 3, at 166.

28. 277 F. Supp. 31 (M. D. Ala. 1967).

29. See Fred P. Graham, Alabama Warns of Welfare Cut; Says it May Slash Payments if High Court Voids Purge, N.Y. Times, Nov. 22, 1967; UPI, Alabama Wins Stay of Court's Order on Welfare Rolls, N.Y. Times, Nov. 28, 1967; AP, Alabama Set Back on Welfare Issue: 15,000 Children Must Get Aid Pending Final Edict, N.Y. Times, Jan. 31, 1968.

30. Garbus, supra note 3, at 186, 188.

31. Brief for Appellants, King v. Smith, 392 U.S. 309 (1968).

32. Davis, supra note 18, at 66.

33. Garbus, supra note 3, at 194.

34. A recording and transcript of the argument can be found at www.oyez.org.

35. Davis, supra note 18, at 68.

36. The discussion that follows is based on the Supreme Court's decision at 392 U.S. 309 (1968).

37. Goodman, supra note 2, at 28–29.

38. Garbus, supra note 3, at 150, 206.

39. Letter on file with author.

40. Welfare Rule Explained by HEW Chief, Wash. Post, Aug. 6, 1988.

41. Nick Kotz and Mary Lynn Kotz, A Passion for Equality: George Wiley and the Movement 259 (1977).

42. 404 U.S. 282 (1971).

43. 406 U.S. 598 (1972).

44. An earlier version of these materials had been prepared in 1967 by Edward Sparer for training of the first class of the Reginald Heber Smith Fellowship. The Center's 1972 edition was funded by the Office of Economic Opportunity for distribution to all local legal services programs.

45. CENTER ON SOCIAL WELFARE POLICY AND LAW, MATERIALS ON WELFARE LAW II-93 (1972).

46. Meyers v. Juras, 404 U.S. 803 (1971).

47. CENTER ON SOCIAL WELFARE POLICY AND LAW, *supra* note 45, at III:171–73.

48. Memorandum to Board, August 8, 1972, on file at the National Center for Law and Economic Justice.

49. New York Dept. of Social Svcs. v. Dublino, 413 U.S. 405, 421–22 (1973).

50. *Id.* at 425–32.

51. 42 U.S.C. § 601(b).

52. 397 U.S. 254 (1970).

53. *See* Weston v. Cassata, 37 P.3d 469 (Colo. Ct. of App. Div. I, 2001).

54. *See* Camacho et al. v. Texas Workforce Commission et al., 408 F. 3d 229, 235, *citing* Carleson v. Remillard. *Camacho* and *Carleson* are invoked in an October 4, 2013, publication from the National Health Law Program discussing improper work requirements being considered by state Medicaid programs.

55. Mary Mannix and Henry Freedman, *TANF and Racial Justice*, 47 CLEARINGHOUSE REV. 221 (2013); Freedman, *supra* note 8.

56. Many of their names appear in the case names reported throughout the web site of the National Center for Law and Economic Justice; *see* www.nclej.org. Apart from the citations provided above, the facts of *King v. Smith* as recited here can be found in a variety of sources, including the case complaint, the briefs, the two court decisions, the Martin Garbus book, and the Walter Goodman article cited previously. Legal papers in the case and newspaper clippings cited here are on file with the author.

Legal Services Attorneys and Migrant Advocates Join Forces

Shapiro v. Thompson • (1969)

ELISA MINOFF

In December 1966, Juanita Smith moved to Philadelphia from Lincoln, Delaware, with her partner and five children: Johnny Smith (age six), Tabitha Miller (age four), Sophia Paynter (age three), William Paynter Jr. (age one and a half), and Voncell Paynter (nine months). Smith was not new to the city. Born in 1943 at an army hospital in Petersburg, Virginia, she moved to Philadelphia with her mother when she was one month old. After completing his service, her father joined them. Smith spent her childhood and adolescence in Philadelphia. It was only in 1959, at the age of 17, that she moved to Delaware. But she did not find the opportunities in Delaware that she had hoped for.

After seven years, Smith was living with her growing family in a two-bedroom trailer that lacked running water and electricity. Her partner had a low-paying job at a country club, while she worked seasonally in a cannery. Smith had wanted to work as a nurse's aide, but she found that "well, down here, if you are colored you can't. . . . Well, they just don't have any colored nurses here. I mean I could get a job in the kitchen, you know, or cleaning up, but not as a nurse's aid [sic]."[1] When Smith's father visited the family in the fall of 1966, he urged them to return to Philadelphia, where jobs were better and family was close. At age 24, pregnant with her sixth child, and with "terrible vericosities" requiring medical attention, Smith took her father's advice.

When Smith and her family returned to Philadelphia, however, things did not work out as planned. Her partner could not find work in the city and he soon left the family, moving back to Delaware. Meanwhile Smith's father, who had promised to support them as they settled, was laid off from his job at United Parcel. Two months after arriving, with nowhere else to turn, Smith applied for Aid to Families with Dependent Children. She received two checks before the Department of Public Welfare realized that she had not satisfied Pennsylvania's one-year residence requirement for public assistance and denied her further assistance.[2]

Durational residence requirements had made life difficult for poor people on the move since the colonial era. Descended from Elizabethan-era poor laws that required "settlement" in a community in order to be eligible for relief, residence requirements limited public assistance to those who had lived in a state or locality for the length of time stipulated by the state's statute, often one year. When Juanita Smith returned to Philadelphia in 1966, 40 states, including Pennsylvania, required a period of residence to be eligible for general assistance, which was entirely state-funded, or for categorical assistance—such as Aid to Families with Dependent Children, Old Age Assistance, Aid to the Disabled, and Aid to the Blind—which was partially federally funded. Every year thousands of families were denied assistance for failing to meet their state's residence requirements.[3] In early 1967, Smith's family was one of many in similar straits. But that year, Smith and dozens of others who lacked residence for welfare refused to accept their fate. They lawyered up.

Smith and her fellow plaintiffs found representation at neighborhood legal services offices. Their attorneys, fresh out of law school, hoped to use the law as a tool for social reform.[4] Some hoped to establish a right to welfare. Smith's case eventually reached the Supreme Court, consolidated with two other challenges to residence requirements in *Shapiro v. Thompson* (1969). *Shapiro v. Thompson* was very much of its moment. It was made possible by the new federal funding disbursed by the Office of Economic Opportunity as part of the War on Poverty and by the law review articles, conferences, strategy-focused "back up centers," and storefront legal services offices that funding supported. When the Supreme Court held residence requirements unconstitutional in 1969, the decision quickly became a landmark in the new area of social welfare law. Many contemporaries saw it as a step toward establishing a right to welfare.

But *Shapiro v. Thompson* was not just about welfare and welfare rights. It was also about migration and the right to move. Social workers, public welfare officials, and social welfare leaders who worked with migrants had agitated against residence laws since the Great Depression. These migrant advocates understood that residence laws were drafted to detract poor or otherwise undesirable migrants. They hoped that reforming the laws would allow migrants not only to receive the support they needed, but also to move about freely and to be treated as full citizens. A decade before *Shapiro* reached the Supreme Court, a broad coalition of these critics launched a national campaign to urge Congress to reform residence requirements. They mobilized social service organizations as well as public welfare departments to demand a new federal program of public assistance that would provide relief to all in need, newcomers and long-time residents alike. These critics played a crucial, if forgotten, role in the cases consolidated in *Shapiro v. Thompson*. They were the ones who first came up with the political and legal arguments against residence laws and who provided financial support to the plaintiffs and testified to the problems caused by the laws as the cases wound their way through the courts.

Shapiro v. Thompson bore the imprint of both longtime critics of the laws and of legal services attorneys who had only recently realized the harm the laws caused. Justice Brennan's majority opinion in *Shapiro* was not only notable for establishing new equal protection doctrine requiring strict scrutiny of laws that restricted fundamental rights, as many legal scholars have noted. It was also notable for its discussion of the right to travel, or freedom of movement. The language of the decision made it clear that the Court understood the case to be about migration.

The newspaper coverage of *Shapiro* indicated that most politicians and members of the public followed the Court's logic. The coverage also suggested, however, that this case about migration made top-to-bottom reforms of the welfare system necessary, even inevitable. That such reforms did not take place had something to do with the politics of welfare and something to do with the politics of migration.[5]

Early Critiques of Residence Laws

As the Depression worsened in the early 1930s, newspapers warned that hordes of unemployed migrants were commandeering freight cars and thumbing rides on the nation's roads. Aware of these reports, public officials took action, deputizing police officers to patrol their states' borders and sweeping migrants into city jails with the help of vagrancy laws. To the same end, state legislators lengthened their residence requirements in the hopes that denying migrants relief would deter them from coming in the first place.[6] In 1937, the

Pennsylvania state legislature passed the law that thwarted Juanita Smith. When the state's attorney general was asked to interpret the new residence law a year later, he argued that it needed to be construed strictly because any other understanding would "attract dependents of other states to our Commonwealth."[7]

A group of social welfare experts leading private social service organizations and New Deal agencies recognized the turn against migrants during these years and worked to aid migrants, devoting particular attention to reforming residence laws. These migrant advocates included leaders of organizations that worked with migrants, such as the National Travelers Aid Association, the Salvation Army, and the National Urban League, as well as staffers of the short-lived Federal Transient Program, which provided direct relief to migrants in the first two years of the New Deal. By the mid-1930s, these social welfare leaders were gathering at regional and national conferences to discuss how states could amend their settlement laws to decrease or eliminate residence requirements for general assistance. In Chicago, local public welfare officials and social reformers organized to challenge Illinois's new three-year residence law on constitutional grounds. In Washington, members of a national lobby group for migrants and New Deal administrators convinced sympathetic congressmen to introduce legislation creating a new category of federally funded general assistance, to be available to all impoverished persons, migrants included.[8]

Social welfare leaders' agitation against residence laws did not lead to significant reforms before World War II. The constitutional challenge to Illinois's residence law failed, and Congress never passed legislation establishing a new category of federally funded general assistance.[9] But the organizations, and indeed some of the individuals, who had criticized residence laws during the Depression continued the fight in the postwar period. As they did, the problems the laws posed for migrants were foremost on their minds.

A Legislative Campaign Against Residence Laws

In the mid-1950s, after more than a decade of contending with the migration problems resulting from war, veterans of the Depression-era attempts to aid migrants once again turned their attention to the migration of the poor. These social welfare leaders, like urban policy experts at the time, were becoming aware of the influx of migrants into the nation's cities. They observed that many of these migrants were fleeing rural poverty in the South and many (though far from all) were African American.[10] These social welfare leaders once again began calling for reforms to the nation's system of public assistance to help migrants. As before, they understood residence requirements to be the major obstacle to migrants' access to public assistance, and they launched a legislative campaign against the laws.

The National Travelers Aid Association led the campaign against residence laws in the late 1950s, guided by social welfare consultant Elizabeth Wickenden. Travelers Aid had participated in the incipient action against residence laws in the 1930s and liked to describe itself as the only social agency devoted exclusively to helping people on the move. It placed caseworkers and volunteers in bus depots and train stations across the country to help marooned vacationers as well as more troubled migrants. Wickenden had worked to reform residence laws from within the New Deal apparatus in the 1930s, first as acting director of the Federal Transient Program and later as an aide in the Works Progress Administration. As a Washington liaison and consultant to major social welfare organizations since the war, Wickenden was widely respected for her knowledge of Capitol Hill.

Together, Wickenden and the staff at Travelers Aid built a large coalition against the laws. As during the Depression, voluntary agencies that worked with migrants were the most vocal critics of the laws and the most active members of the coalition. Public welfare officials, who found residence laws difficult to administer and costly to enforce, also enthusiastically supported the campaign. Organized labor, religious social service agencies, and even a few traditionally conservative organizations such as the American Legion rounded out the coalition.

Travelers Aid supplied the material for the campaign, printing and distributing articles outlining the reasons for eliminating residence requirements, leaflets providing state-by-state information on the length of residence required to qualify for different benefits, as well as testimonials from prominent social agencies and social welfare leaders against the laws. They convinced national reporters to write articles on the problems caused by residence requirements, and even commissioned a play to "stimulate discussion" on the subject.[11] Travelers Aid distributed these materials to its local chapters, which then lobbied for reforms in statehouses.

Two of the most widely distributed articles of the campaign, which laid out themes that critics of the laws took up in states, were transcripts of speeches by Elizabeth Wickenden and constitutional law expert Jacobus tenBroek. They both argued that the laws were anachronistic and did not make sense in a modern economy. After briefly charting the history of residence laws, Wickenden suggested that they were based on the feudal concept that people, like serfs, "belonged" to a place. Residence requirements were unfit for modern living, Wickenden maintained, since they punished "the very Americans who have fulfilled one of the prime social duties of our time: the obligation of mobility."[12] Wickenden and tenBroek also argued the laws violated migrants' rights. Wickenden charged that residence laws made migrants "second class citizens," since "measures of common protection, established as socially necessary for others living in the community, are not available to them."[13] TenBroek elaborated on this point. He argued that residence laws violated the right of free movement, which he asserted was an "aspect of the personal liberty guaranteed by the Fifth and Fourteenth Amendments, to be inseparably appertinent to national citizenship and to be sheltered by the equal protection concepts implicit in the Fifth Amendment and explicit in the Fourteenth Amendment." An important element of the right of free movement, he argued was the right "to be upon an equal footing with those already in the community to which you go." TenBroek believed that residence requirements, by denying migrants opportunities and resources granted others who lived in a community, denied them this right.[14]

The message of the campaign against residence laws that these and other articles laid out was simple. Residence requirements restricted migration, which was important to the national economy and to economic mobility. They hurt everyday Americans, who moved to be closer to family, to find work, to better their health, or otherwise improve their circumstances. And finally, that the laws violated the rights of migrants, including their "right to move freely," a right sometimes described as a human right, but more often described as a right of citizenship.

While the campaign against residence laws stimulated reforms in a few states, it floundered in others. Juanita Smith's home state of Pennsylvania was one in which the campaign met resistance. From the late 1950s through the 1960s the Pennsylvania Department of Public Welfare had asked the legislature to liberalize its residence requirement for welfare, and voluntary organizations in the state had rallied behind its proposals. The department had not asked for the laws to be eliminated entirely, but only that the one-year residence requirement be amended to "one year's residence out of five years." The proposal sometimes passed the Pennsylvania House but was invariably held up by the Senate. The director of the division within the Department of Public Welfare in charge of enforcing the statutory residence requirement explained the failure to achieve reform: "The Department doesn't get its proposals enacted by the Legislature, because there is a pool of opinion that the residence requirements result in an influx of people into the Commonwealth."[15]

The politics of migration frustrated the campaign against residence laws. In the early 1960s, state and local politicians were awakening to the migration of low-income, often minority Americans that social welfare and urban experts had begun to observe a few years earlier. To many politicians and to some more established residents, this migration was a problem, and residence requirements seemed like a useful tool to stem the migrant tide. In 1961, the city manager of the economically struggling Hudson Valley city of Newburgh, New York, made national headlines when he blamed migrants for the city's problems. The manager claimed that his city's generous public assistance was attracting "the dregs of humanity into this city . . . [in a] never ending pilgrimage from North Carolina," and he issued a new welfare code that made it almost impossible for migrants to receive relief.[16] Many state legislators shared the city manager's diagnosis of urban problems and attempted to strengthen their residence laws even as Travelers Aid and its allies sought to liberalize them.

As inhospitable politicians obstructed reform at the state level, leaders of the campaign against residence laws increasingly pushed for federal reform, but there too they encountered resistance. Though the Democratic Party platform endorsed eliminating residence requirements in 1960, and President Kennedy proposed legislation to encourage states to reduce and eliminate residence requirements, Congress balked. Witnesses at public hearings testified that reducing or eliminating residence laws would lead poor migrants to flood their states.[17] Kennedy signed the Public Welfare Amendments of 1962 without the incentives to eliminate residence requirements that he had originally proposed.

After this defeat in Washington, Travelers Aid, Wickenden, and the broad coalition against residence requirements put the legislative campaign on hold. In the six years since they had launched the campaign, the reforms enacted were limited. But the arguments they generated were not forgotten. They were repurposed.

Turning to the Courts

In the 1960s, one longtime migrant advocate and critic of residence requirements became a leading proponent of legal services for the disadvantaged. Elizabeth Wickenden saw in the legal process the potential, as she put it, "not only for promoting the rights of this peculiarly disadvantaged group of people but more significantly for effecting a more equitable and protective application of welfare law and policy."[18] Largely because of her contributions, the early strategizing in the new area of social welfare law recognized the need to challenge residence requirements.

Wickenden had begun theorizing about how the law could be used to help the poor in the wake of the Public Welfare Amendments of 1962. She did so with the help of a group she called her "legal brain trust," including welfare rights theorist Charles Reich, family law judge Justine Wise Polier, and Polier's husband, civil rights lawyer Shad Polier.[19] With their help, Wickenden drafted two memos in 1963 and in 1965 that helped shape the field of welfare law. Both recognized the need to challenge residence requirements and settlement laws. In the 1963 memo, Wickenden denounced the laws in some states allowing public welfare officials to forcibly remove migrants who had not met the state's residence requirement. The removal policy, Wickenden suggested, denied persons "primarily distinguished by their poverty" the "constitutional guarantee" of "freedom of movement among the states."[20] In the 1965 memo, Wickenden included residence laws in a list of practices that she thought were legally suspect. She suggested that residence laws might be attacked by citing the precedent of *Edwards v. California* (1940), which had declared state laws barring the transportation of indigents unconstitutional.[21] Wickenden distributed both memos widely.

In addition to drafting influential memos, Wickenden helped establish one of the first support centers to aid legal services lawyers opening up offices across the country. The Project on Social Welfare Law at New York University opened its doors in 1965 and began immediately to focus on residence requirements. In the first issue of the project's informational bulletin, the staff explained that the project was dedicated to considering the violation of constitutional and statutory rights of public assistance applicants, including "arbitrary or unreasonable eligibility requirements, inequitable distribution of benefits, use of 'midnight' and other unreasonable searches, release of privileged information, and *restrictions on freedom of movement*" (emphasis added). The legal director of the Project, Bernard Harvith, spent a substantial portion of his first year on the job drafting a law review article on "The Constitutionality of Residence Tests for General and Categorical Assistance Programs."[22]

Wickenden also worked closely with "welfare law guru" Ed Sparer, who was one of the first practitioners of this new type of legal aid and was simultaneously developing similar critiques of residence laws.[23] In the mid-1960s, Sparer penned influential law review articles laying out how legal services attorneys might go about challenging laws that discriminated against the poor. In one of these articles, he, like Wickenden, tenBroek, and others involved in the legislative campaign against residence laws, described the laws as infringing "the welfare recipient's right to freedom of movement and choice of residence."[24] In another, Sparer listed residence requirements as among the top ten areas of public assistance law that he believed legal services attorneys should address.[25] The legal services support center he founded, the Center on Social Welfare Policy and Law at Columbia's School of Social Work, began distributing information to neighborhood lawyers on how to bring test cases against residence requirements.[26]

When legal services attorneys opened their doors, they quickly began preparations to challenge residence laws. But first they needed to find clients; or, rather, clients needed to find them.

Bringing Suit

In order for migrants who had failed residence tests to walk through a door at a neighborhood legal services organization, and in order for those migrants to successfully become clients, they needed the support of a wide range of community agencies. Young legal services attorneys were only able to bring challenges to residence laws because of their close relationship with these agencies, some of which had been involved in the legislative campaign against residence laws.

Juanita Smith, for example, learned about the resources funded by the War on Poverty from the nurse at her son's school, who told her to go to the "Anti-Poverty Program" when the Department of Public Welfare stopped offering assistance. The Philadelphia Anti-Poverty Action Committee in turn sent Smith to attorney Thomas Gilhool of Community Legal Services, one of the first OEO-funded neighborhood legal services organizations.[27] Gilhool agreed to represent Smith and challenge the state's residence requirement and suggested that she seek help from Travelers Aid while her case was being argued. In March 1967, Juanita Smith approached social worker Reba Haimowitz at the Travelers Aid booth in 30th Street Station. Haimowitz helped Smith with her rent, gave her money to pay for food stamps, and covered some of the family's other costs in the ensuing months. Just as Smith's case was being heard by a three-judge panel of the U.S. District Court of the Eastern District of Pennsylvania, Haimowitz declared that Travelers Aid would only be able to support Smith for another week or two.[28] This declaration helped prove that Smith suffered "immediate and irreparable injury" and therefore justified the preliminary injunction her lawyers sought. The executive director of the Travelers Aid Society of Philadelphia later submitted an affidavit supporting her case.[29]

The second case consolidated with Smith's in *Shapiro v. Thompson* was also made possible by the collaboration of Travelers Aid officials, who had long criticized the laws. Plaintiff Minnie Harrell and her three daughters—Yvonne, Virginia, and Gwendolyn—had been denied public assistance in Washington, D.C., for failing to meet the city's residence requirement in 1967. They had moved to the district from the eastern edge of Long Island, New York, after Harrell had separated from her husband and been diagnosed with cancer. Harrell wanted to be closer to her siblings, who lived in the capital, so that they could care for her daughters as she underwent treatment. That fall, Harrell was hospitalized three times a week for radiation treatments. She picked up the occasional day job as a domestic, but because of her health she was largely unable to work.[30] When she was denied assistance, the Travelers Aid Society of Washington offered some aid but told her lawyer, in a letter that was later submitted to the court, that they could not assume the long-term costs of the family.[31] Meanwhile Catherine Hiatt, the executive director of the Travelers Aid Society, who had testified against residence laws before Congress, submitted an affidavit in Harrell's case.[32]

Finally, *Shapiro v. Thompson* itself was made possible by the collaboration of public welfare officials who had long criticized the laws. Nineteen-year-old Vivian Marie Thompson was pregnant when she moved to Hartford, Connecticut, from Dorchester, Massachusetts, in June of 1966 with her five-month-old son. Thompson's mother, who lived in Hartford, had encouraged the two to relocate and promised to support them once they did. When Thompson's mother's income proved insufficient and Thompson was denied assistance for failing to meet Connecticut's residence requirement, Brian Hollander at Neighborhood Legal Services of Hartford took up her case.[33] Hartford's Department of Welfare ensured that Thompson's case made it to court. The department normally tried to circumvent the state's residence requirement for welfare and place applicants who could not satisfy the requirement in education and training programs. But when the state legislature passed a new residence law in the early 1960s, the director and his colleagues had agreed that when the appropriate case appeared they "should test out" the law. Thompson's, they thought, was that case, and instead of circumventing the residence law, they enforced it and convinced a private agency that had long since abandoned supporting migrants to aid Thompson so that her case could be brought to court.[34]

Constructing Constitutional Arguments

Longtime critics of residence requirements did not only suggest that the laws should be challenged and facilitate the cases logistically. Their ideas also shaped the constitutional arguments the legal services attorneys made, thanks in part to the careful shepherding of the cases by the support centers founded by Wickenden and Sparer.

Staff members at the backup centers helped some of the legal services attorneys when they first filed complaints and became even more involved as the cases were appealed and legal services attorneys prepared to argue before the Supreme Court. The summer before the residence cases reached the Court, the Project on Social Welfare Law hosted a conference on residence laws for the young legal services attorneys. At the conference, they were advised by Jacobus tenBroek, who had first outlined a constitutional critique of the requirements in a speech that Travelers Aid transcribed and distributed during its legislative campaign; Bernard Harvith, who had written the law review article on residence laws in his first year as director of the Project on Social Welfare Law; and other staff members of the NYU Project on Social Welfare Law and the Columbia Center on Social Welfare Policy and Law.[35] Each of the briefs that legal services attorneys filed in Court several months later was cosigned by a lawyer associated with either NYU or Columbia.

The legal services attorneys for Smith, Harrell, and Thompson rested their arguments on different constitutional provisions, but they each emphasized that residence laws harmed their clients as migrants and violated their freedom of movement, a point Wickenden and tenBroek had helped make a recurrent theme of the legislative campaign against residence requirements. In their brief to the Supreme Court, Smith's lawyers argued that the true purpose of the Pennsylvania law was to deter the migration of poor citizens to the state, and they explicitly refuted the idea that their case relied on the assumption that public assistance was a fundamental right.[36] Instead, they argued that residence laws violated the Equal Protection Clause and unreasonably burdened the right to move freely from state to state and to settle, a right that, they suggested vaguely, derived from several clauses in the Constitution.[37] Harrell's lawyers, by contrast, did rest their case in part on a right to assistance—or, as it was framed at the time, "a right to life"—but in the main the argument paralleled that of Smith's brief. They asserted that the D.C. law impinged on the "fundamental personal freedoms" of a "voiceless minority," including the right to life, freedom of movement, and the right of association, denying migrants like Harrell equal protection.[38] Thompson's attorneys likewise asserted that the residence law violated the Equal Protection Clause, while also emphasizing that the law abridged the right to establish residence in Connecticut and infringed on the right to travel in violation of the Privileges and Immunities Clause of the Fourteenth Amendment.[39]

Lawyers for Smith, Harrell, and Thompson also highlighted the harm the laws caused their clients as migrants. In each of the cases, the affidavits and complaints plaintiffs filed in lower courts and then refiled in the Supreme Court recounted their life histories, from their place of birth to their elementary and high school attendance to their work, their marriages, their relocations, their pregnancies, and their current circumstances. In each case, the plaintiff's movement was portrayed as rational and necessary. For Thompson, it allowed her to be closer to her mother as she gave birth to her second child. For Harrell, it allowed her siblings to care for her children while she underwent treatment for cancer. For Smith, it allowed her to escape the Jim Crowism of southern Delaware and access a better job market while being closer to family.

These same themes also wove through the amici briefs filed on behalf of Smith, Harrell, and Thompson, many of which cited publications of the long campaign against residence laws and were signed by organizations that had participated in the campaign. The National Travelers Aid Association and the National Association of Social Workers signed on to the Center on Social Welfare Policy and Law's amici brief. The Council of Jewish Federations and Welfare Funds and the National Council of Churches of Christ in the USA, two other organizations that had participated in the legislative campaign against residence laws, signed on to an amici brief along with several other religious organizations. Jacobus tenBroek had corralled these social agencies to join the court battle.[40]

Elizabeth Wickenden sat in the Supreme Court as the lawyers for Smith, Thompson, and Harrell argued their cases. Though she did not think the legal services lawyers presented an especially clear and convincing case against residence laws, she later noted in her diary, "it was impressive to see the array of extremely young, bright and dedicated OEO lawyers arguing the case."[41]

Deliberation and Decision

Shapiro was a difficult case for the Warren Court. Initially, Chief Justice Earl Warren seemed to have enough votes to uphold the law, and he circulated a draft majority opinion in May 1968. But Justice Abe Fortas, an old friend and confidant of Wickenden's, circulated a draft dissent arguing that the laws' purpose was to discourage the poor from entering states. The laws burdened the right to travel, he wrote, while also creating unreasonable classifications in violation of the Equal Protection Clause. After Fortas's draft was circulated, justices switched and withheld their votes, and the Court became deadlocked. They set the case for reargument.[42]

Strategists at the backup centers convinced the legal services attorneys to allow Archibald Cox to reargue their cases. Cox, who had been solicitor general during the Kennedy and Johnson administrations, was as experienced arguing before the Supreme Court as the legal services attorneys were inexperienced. Cox emphasized the same themes as the legal services attorneys, but the brief he composed for reargument was more elegant and his oral argument more compelling. Cox maintained, simply, that residence requirements violated the Equal Protection and Due Process Clauses by "discriminating, without justification, between persons identically situated in relation to fundamental human needs, solely because of the exercise of liberty of geographic mobility."[43] For Cox, as for the legal services attorneys, the harm that residence laws caused migrants was at the heart of the case. In his oral argument, Cox repeatedly emphasized that residence requirements violated a right to move. As Cox put it, "I don't like to call it the right to travel, because it's the right to migrate and settle in a new place, to seek new advantages, not just to move around." And again later, he clarified, "I have sought to stress the right to live where you please—the right to journey raises different problems and is a lesser right—our case deals with the right to live where you please, the right to seek better opportunities." Cox drove home this point by telling the stories of the plaintiffs, including Juanita Smith.[44]

The presentation was enough to convince six justices to cast their votes to strike down residence requirements. Justice Brennan's decision on April 21, 1969, echoed the analysis of longtime critics of the laws, as it had been restated by legal services attorneys and streamlined by Cox. Citing the legislative history of the laws at bar, Brennan emphasized that there was "weighty evidence" that the true purpose of the laws was to exclude the poor from the states.[45] Brennan expounded at length on the constitutional right to travel, arguing not only that the purpose of excluding the indigent was impermissible because it infringed on the right to travel, but also that the laws needed to be judged by a stricter standard of whether they promoted a compelling government interest because the classification created by the laws *touched* on the right to travel, which was a "fundamental right."[46] In his estimation, and that of five other justices, the laws did not meet this test. They denied the plaintiffs equal protection.

The Public Response

In the wake of the Supreme Court decision, articles in national newspapers and magazines predicted that welfare recipients, now freed from the shackles of residence requirements, would flee to high-benefit states, especially from the low-benefit states of the South. The press coverage recognized, as had critics of the laws and the Court, that residence requirements were designed to limit migration, and they quoted policymakers and social welfare experts who expected migration to increase once the laws were lifted. Many were concerned about this eventuality, especially politicians in receiving states like California. Governor Ronald Reagan warned of a "mass migration" to the state, while the Los Angeles County Supervisor declared that the state would become "a welfare bonanza and fair game for recipients who will holler, 'Come one, come all!'"[47]

The only solution to this expected surge of migration, politicians and social welfare experts agreed, was federal intervention, either through increased federal funding, "national standards" or uniform benefit levels across states, or complete federal administration. Democratic senator Walter Mondale told reporters that the decision should lead to nationwide standards for welfare.[48] Robert Finch, President Nixon's secretary of health, education, and welfare, said that the ruling made national standards "inevitable."[49] The *New York Times* editorialized, a day after the ruling, "Now that the Supreme Court has struck down these unworthy attempts to fence out the poor, it is up to Congress and the Nixon Administration to make welfare a Federal responsibility and establish uniform standards of assistance."[50]

Five days after the Supreme Court's decision in *Shapiro*, Nixon met with his advisors to discuss welfare reform proposals. His domestic policy staff, led by Daniel Patrick Moynihan, had been considering reforms for months, but it was at that meeting that they agreed the administration should propose a guaranteed minimum income for families with children. In a televised speech four months later, Nixon announced his Family Assistance Plan (FAP) to the public. It would correct the current problems of the welfare system, including that it "breaks up homes," "penalizes work," and "robs recipients of dignity." It would also correct the problem of the "grossly unequal" benefit levels that varied from one state to another. As Nixon told his television audience, "one result of this inequality is to lure thousands more into already overcrowded inner cities, as unprepared for city life as they are for city jobs."[51] FAP, in other words, would help solve the migration problem that had preoccupied state and local proponents of residence laws for the past decade.

Immediately following Nixon's speech, FAP seemed untouchable. The White House was inundated with telegrams approving Nixon's proposal.[52] As a solution to both the dependency problem and the migration problem in the wake of the abolition of residence requirements, commentators expected FAP to sail through Congress. Elizabeth Wickenden agreed: "[T]he Supreme Court decision proscribing residence requirements made virtually inevitable the ultimate federalization and standardization of welfare payments."[53]

While in the late 1950s and early 1960s, the politics of migration had made residence laws almost impossible to reform through the legislative process, once the Supreme Court struck down residence requirements, the politics of migration seemed to necessitate a major overhaul of the nation's public welfare system.

Conclusion

FAP, however, did not become law despite the air of inevitability that surrounded it in the early 1970s. The complicated politics of welfare seemed to doom the plan, as it proved too conservative for Congress's liberals and too liberal for Congress's conservatives.[54] But it did not help that by the mid-1970s, the politics of migration had changed. Migrants had not taken to the roads in the wake of *Shapiro* and flooded high-benefit states, as commentators had predicted. Moreover, the urbanward migration that had defined the postwar period and concerned so many state and local politicians had come to an abrupt halt. Cities were as troubled as ever, but politicians no longer blamed migrants. As the politics of migration changed, the need to overhaul the system of public assistance in the United States seemed less pressing.

Longtime migrant advocates and legal services attorneys had won a major victory in *Shapiro v. Thompson*. By striking down residence laws, *Shapiro* ended the centuries-long practice of discriminating against migrants in public assistance. But because the politics of migration changed quickly in the years immediately following the decision, *Shapiro* did not force the fundamental reforms to the nation's system of public assistance that some had assumed it would in the summer of 1969.

Notes

1. Appendix for Reynolds v. Smith in Shapiro v. Thompson, 394 U.S. 618 (1969), File Date 4/4/1968, 169 pp., Term Year: 1968, *U.S. Supreme Court Records and*

Briefs, 1832–1978, Gale, Cengage Learning, Harvard University [hereinafter *U.S. Supreme Court Records and Briefs*], 36a.

2. *Id.*

3. All residence requirements referred to in this chapter are durational residence requirements, but the term durational has been omitted for simplicity's sake.

4. Smith's lawyer, Thomas Gilhool, graduated from Yale Law School in 1964. *See* Interview with Thomas Gilhool, Visionary Voices, Institute on Disabilities, Temple University, *available at* http://disabilities.temple.edu/voices/detailVideo.asp?mediaCode=006-01 (last visited Nov. 8, 2013). Brian Hollander, who represented the named plaintiff in *Shapiro v. Thompson*, had been practicing less than three years and needed to get special permission to argue before the Supreme Court because he had not been practicing long enough to be admitted to the Supreme Court bar. See Shapiro v. Thompson, National Archives and Records Administration, Washington, D.C. [hereinafter NARA I], RG 267, box 8535, file 2 of 4.

5. For a full accounting of the politics of migration in the mid-twentieth century and the debates over residence laws, see Elisa Minoff, Free to Move? The Law and Politics of Internal Migration in Twentieth-Century America (April 2013) (unpublished PhD dissertation, Harvard University) (*available at* http://gradworks.umi.com/35/67/3567004.html).

6. See testimony of Dorothy de la Pole, Staff, National Travelers Aid Association, *Interstate Migration, Hearings Before the Select Committee to Investigate the Interstate Migration of Destitute Citizens*, 76th Cong., 3rd Sess., Part 3, Chicago Hearings (Aug. 19–21, 1940).

7. Shapiro v. Thompson, 394 U.S. 618, 629 (1969).

8. Minoff, *supra* note 5 (see chapter 4 on conferences and congressional legislation, chapter 5 on constitutional challenges). Congressman Jerry Voorhis of California introduced legislation in the 75th and 76th Congresses to make public assistance available to migrants, and then on April 12, 1939, he introduced legislation to establish a general relief category of the Social Security Act. See H.R. 5736, 76th Cong., 1st Sess.

9. For the challenge to the Illinois statute, *see Heydenreich v. Lyons*, 374 Ill. 557 (1940).

10. James N. Gregory, Southern Diaspora: How the Great Migrations of Black and White Southerners Transformed America (2007).

11. Sid Ross and Ed Kiester, *The Family Nobody Wants*, Parade, Sept. 29, 1957, and *The Family Nobody Wants-Part II*, Parade, Oct. 6, 1957; Basil Beyea, *The Uprooted*, Plays for Living, written for the National Travelers Aid Association, 1963.

12. Elizabeth Wickenden, Address at National Travelers Aid Association Biennial Convention: The Social Costs of Residence Laws (Mar. 22, 1956).

13. *Id.*

14. Jacobus tenBroek, *The Constitution and the Right of Free Movement* (1955) (New York: National Travelers Aid Association), Jacobus tenBroek Library, Baltimore, Md., Jacobus tenBroek Papers, Series 1L Law Review Articles, FC-25 D3, F69 Subcollection 3: Writings.

15. *Reynolds* Appendix, *supra* note 1, at 97a.

16. Meg Greenfield, *The 'Welfare Chiselers' of Newburgh, New York*, THE RE-PORTER, Aug. 17, 1961.

17. *Public Welfare Amendments of 1962: Hearings Before the Committee on Ways and Means on H.R. 10032*, 87th Cong., 2nd Sess., 309–310, 644 (Feb. 7, 9 & 13, 1962).

18. Elizabeth Wickenden, Address at the Conference on the Extension of Legal Services to the Poor: The Legal Needs of the Poor: From the Point of View of Public Welfare Policy (Nov. 12, 1964) (on file with author).

19. Wickenden used the phrase "legal brain trust" in a letter to Charles Reich, January 5, 1965, National Social Welfare Assembly Papers [hereinafter NSWA Papers] (on file with the University of Minnesota Social Welfare History Archive), SIP Wickenden Public Social Policy Correspondence and Memoranda 1965 folder, box 57.

20. Elizabeth Wickenden, Poverty and the Law: The Constitutional Rights of Assistance Recipients (Mar. 25, 1963), NSWA Papers, Committee Social Issues and Policies, Jan–March 1963 folder, box 52.

21. *See* drafts of "Check List of Legal and Constitutional Issues Affecting the Rights of Individuals Seeking or Receiving Welfare and Related Public Benefits," NSWA Papers, SIP, Wickenden, Project on Social Welfare Law, Correspondence, Memoranda 1964–1965 folder, box 20.

22. On Wickenden's first attempts to find funding for the center, *see* NSWA Papers, SIP Wickenden Public Social Policy Activity Summaries 1963–71 folder, box 55; *Welfare Law Bulletin* 1 (Dec. 1965), New York School of Law, Project on Social Welfare Law, courtesy of Norman Dorsen, New York University; and Bernard Evans Harvith, *The Constitutionality of Residence Tests for General and Categorical Assistance Programs*, 54 CAL. L. REV. 567 (1966).

23. MARTHA F. DAVIS, BRUTAL NEED: LAWYERS AND THE WELFARE RIGHTS MOVEMENT, 1960–1973 (1993).

24. Quoted in Edward V. Sparer, *The Role of the Welfare Client's Lawyer*, 12 U.C.L.A. L. REV. 368 (1964–1965).

25. Edward V. Sparer, *Social Welfare Law Testing*, 12 PRAC. LAW 13 (April 1966). *See also* Edward V. Sparer, *The New Legal Aid as an Instrument of Social Change*, U. ILL. L. F. 57 (1965).

26. On Sparer's preparation of residence briefs, *see* letter from Wickenden to Homer Sloane, September 15, 1964, NSWA Papers, SIP Wickenden Public Social Policy Correspondence, May–December 1964 folder, box 57.

27. For the history of Community Legal Services of Philadelphia, see the organization's website: http://www.clsphila.org/Content.aspx?section=about%20cls (last visited March 27, 2010).

28. *Reynolds* Appendix, *supra* note 1 at 46a.

29. *See* Aff. of Catherine M. Kerner, Executive Director of the Travelers Aid Society of Philadelphia, in *id.* at 12a–13a.

30. Casefile, Harrell v. Board of Commissioners, No. 1497-67 Civil, D.C. District Court, NARA I, RG 21, box 3529.

31. Letter from Ruth Rosenhouse, caseworker, Travelers Aid to L. Silver in *id.*

32. *USDC DC*, Affidavit in Support of Counter-motion for Summary Judgment, Catherine Hiatt, Exec. Director, Travelers Aid, filed Aug. 25, 1968, Harrell v. Board of Commissioners of the District of Columbia et al., 33 OT 1968, NARA I, RG 267, box 8543.

33. Complaint, Vivian Marie Thompson v. Bernard Shapiro, U.S. District Court for the District of Connecticut, Civil Action No. 11821, filed February 15, 1967, Shapiro v. Thompson, NARA I, RG 267, box 8535, file 3 of 4.

34. Transcript of Trial, Civil Action No. 11821, Thompson v. Shapiro, May 19, 1967 (filed June 30, 1967); testimony of Richard F. Mastronarde, director of welfare, City of Hartford, in *id.*

35. List of persons who attended the Conference on Residency held on July 26, 1967, at New York University, letter from Lois P. Sheinfeld, associate legal director of the Project on Social Welfare Law to "Johnny" dated August 10, 1967, in the possession of Henry Freedman, National Center for Law and Economic Justice.

36. Brief for the Appellees, Reynolds v. Smith, October Term 1967, No 1138. For refutation of public assistance as a fundamental right, see 17–18.

37. *Id.* at 34.

38. Brief for Appellees, Washington v. Harrell, Shapiro v. Thompson, 394 U.S, 618, Appellees Brief, File Date 4.26.1968, 84pp., 30, *U.S. Supreme Court Records and Briefs.*

39. Brief for Appellees, Shapiro v. Thompson, 394 U.S. 618, Appellees Brief, File Date 4.12.1968, 43pp., *U.S. Supreme Court Records and Briefs.*

40. See letters between tenBroek and Brian Hollander, tenBroek Papers, Folder, Thompson Case—Connecticut Residence, FC-2, D1, F 10 Subcollection 4: Case Files.

41. Diary entry for May 7, 1968, Wisconsin Historical Society, Elizabeth Wickenden Papers, folder 17, box 10.

42. Davis, *supra* note 23, at 78–79.

43. Supplemental Briefs for Appellees on Reargument, Shapiro v. Thompson, 394 U.S. 618 (1969), File Date 9.19.1969, 54 pp., *U.S. Supreme Court Records and Briefs.*

44. Shapiro v. Thompson, The Oyez Project at IIT Chicago-Kent College of Law, http://www.oyez.org/cases/1960-1969/1967/1967_9 (last visited Oct. 11, 2013).

45. 394 U.S. at 628.

46. *Id.* at 638.

47. Earl Behrens, *Unruh Backs Pleas to U.S. to Pay All Welfare Costs*, S. F. Chron., Apr. 26, 1969; *State Open to Mass Invasion of Poor*, Oakland Tribune, Apr. 23, 1969; *Reagan Riles at Welfare Ruling*, S. F. Chron., Apr. 23, 1969.

48. Welfare Proposal by Murphy in Oakland Tribune, Apr. 22, 1969, Shapiro v. Thompson, Residence April 21, 1969, USSC Decision and notes, dip ps. Etc., tenBroek Papers, FC-30, D1, F69, Subcollection 2: Records of the National Federation of the Blind, Series 8: NFB Legal Files.

49. Fred P. Graham, *Residency Rules for Relief Invalidated by High Court*, N.Y. TIMES, April 22, 1969; *State Residency Regulations for Welfare are Ruled Unconstitutional by Justices*, WALL ST. J., April 22, 1969.

50. *Landmark for the Poor*, N.Y. TIMES, Apr. 22, 1969.

51. Richard Nixon, *Address to the Nation on Domestic Programs* (Aug. 8, 1969), *available at* Gerhard Peters and John T. Woolley, The American Presidency Project.

52. Memo from Moynihan to Council for Urban Affairs, 8/25/69, Library of Congress, Daniel Patrick Moynihan Papers, folder: Council for Urban Affairs Meetings, August 25, 1969, box I 266.

53. Elizabeth Wickenden, *Problems in Federalization of Assistance*, March 17, 1971, Wickenden Papers, folder 17, box 15.

54. For an analysis of FAP's failure, see Alice O'Connor, *False Dawn of Poor-Law Reform: Nixon, Carter, and the Quest for a Guaranteed Income*, 10 J. POL'Y HIST. 99 (1998) (especially note discussion on 116).

Dignity and Passion

Goldberg v. Kelly • (1970)

MELANIE B. ABBOTT

[T]he due process clause is not simply the blueprint for an empire of reason. . . . Whether the government treats its citizens with dignity is a question whose answer must lie in the intricate texture of daily life.
—*Justice William J. Brennan Jr.*[1]

Daily life for people living in poverty in New York City in the late 1960s was daunting. Families ensnared in poverty's web faced an overabundance of insufficiency—of food, of security, of convenience, of opportunity, of dignity. Thomas Johnson, a *New York Times* reporter, spent some time in 1966 living with welfare recipients in an apartment house in Harlem and in single-room-occupancy hotels.[2] He chronicled their daily struggles, from the constant losing battle with cockroaches, to the children's disappointment at their inability to eat what they wanted or to share in activities with their friends, to the difficult choices some women made to earn money to feed their children when the welfare benefits ran out. Johnson's story gave a face to the hardship of those in New York's poorest communities, the same areas from which the named plaintiffs in welfare rights cases a year or so later would emerge.

The reporter visited the Pressley family, a mother and six children ranging in age from 3 to 16. Mrs. Pressley received welfare benefits totaling $406 per month (cash assistance from which the $30 per week she earned working for a local community agency was subtracted, but to which employment expenses were added). Her monthly expenses totaled $403 per month, including costs for food, rent, transportation, child care, school expenses, and roach killer.

The Pressleys were renters, sharing the six-room apartment of 76-year-old Addie Paden, a retired nurse who remembered when the apartment building was a luxurious space. After Mrs. Paden's husband died, she had begun to take in boarders, including some who had attacked or beaten her.

Despite the crowded rooms and the war with the roaches, the accommodations shared by Paden and the Pressleys were safer and more comfortable than those of other welfare recipients living in single-room-occupancy housing in the city. According to Johnson, the SRO residents, many of them elderly or disabled, lived "in their cell-like cubicles in constant, and often justified fear of marauding drug addicts, drunks and petty criminals. Facilities at many of these buildings are dehumanizing at best. In many cases they are unhealthy and unsafe."

A recurring theme for Johnson was the difficult relationship between benefits recipients and the caseworkers and investigators charged with administering the welfare programs for the city and state agencies. Pressley reported that she had lost a job when her caseworker had contacted her employer directly after Pressley had asked him not to. Pressley provided information verifying her employment, but the caseworker called anyway, causing her employer to fire her. "I was fired the same day," she said. "Many people don't want [welfare] clients working for them." Pressley also revealed that her benefits had been terminated after she had worked for another employer and her welfare caseworker failed to record the income. Pressley said she was "indicted for grand larceny for concealing my income, but the judge threw the case out of court." In desperation and seeking funds to feed her family, Pressley admitted that she dressed up and went to a bar, seeking work as a prostitute. The bartender gave her money and urged her to go to the local police station, where she received a box of donated food.

Poverty in New York City, Late 1960s

Johnson's story on the Pressleys, their landlady, and the other welfare recipients in New York City shared the grim details of life on welfare in the mid-1960s. It painted a bleak picture of the challenges facing the city's poor, highlighting themes that would re-emerge in the arguments and opinions in the *Goldberg* litigation a short time later. The barriers confronting Kelly and his fellow plaintiffs were in no way unique; the plaintiffs represented hundreds, even thousands of others who had fought similar battles simply to survive in the city.

A snapshot of the welfare picture in 1967–68 reveals that the city's welfare rolls were increasing at the rate of 14,000 people per month in early 1968. At the end of 1967, there were 780,000 city residents receiving assistance from the welfare fund, costing the city more than $1 billion for the fiscal year.[3] Sixty percent were children and 18 percent were mothers. The city administrator responsible for managing the welfare rolls blamed the increase in welfare receipt on an influx of low-income people seeking economic opportunities unavailable in their former states, along with a loss of manufacturing jobs and the lack of jobs suitable for those with limited job skills. Though the city had closed 99,000 welfare cases in 1967, it had opened 161,000 new ones.

The growth in the welfare rolls in 1968 was a reflection of both local and national trends in the approach to poverty over the preceding decade. A *New York Times* story at the end of 1970 reported that the number of people enrolled in welfare programs in New York City had nearly tripled since 1966, from 500,000 to 1.4 million.[4] About one in seven New Yorkers was receiving assistance, with the budget of the Department of Social Services representing about one-fourth of the city budget.[5] The national trend followed the same path. In 1959, there were 39.5 million people in the United States classified as poor, of whom 17 percent received some sort of aid. By 1968, only 25.4 million people were reported to be living in poverty, though 40 percent were receiving some government assistance. The *Times* noted that while the cost of assistance programs had continued to rise, it nonetheless fell far short of meeting the need.[6] The benefits provided by the states were not intended to satisfy the needs of those receiving them; poverty programs were not intended to eliminate poverty.[7] Some states, for example, chose not to accept all the federal funding available so that they would not be forced to come up with matching state funds. And only half of the states providing aid to dependent children provided the amount of assistance sufficient to meet the need they themselves had identified as minimal.[8] The tension among cities, states, and the federal government was constant, reflecting financial, political, and moral dilemmas. In the midst of this ongoing struggle, the lawsuit that would eventually come to be known as *Goldberg v. Kelly* was born.

Welfare Programs, Procedural Challenges

Lawyers representing the poor in New York City and throughout the country had been working for years to improve the quality of life for benefits recipients. Though some attention was being paid to efforts nationally to institute a "guaranteed minimum income" or a "negative income tax," advocates recognized that there was little likelihood that such programs could really happen.

Lawyers dealt on a daily basis with welfare recipients whose benefits had been cut off or who had suffered as a result of caseworkers' arbitrary actions. They knew that no matter how strongly they believed that litigation could play a role in implementing a more widespread solution to the problems of those in poverty, they needed to try to help their clients first. And they also acknowledged that efforts to achieve broad social change through litigation would likely put off even the most sympathetic judges.[9]

By early 1968, lawyers at the Legal Unit of Mobilization for Youth, Inc. (MFY), with the assistance of colleagues at the Center on Social Welfare Policy and Law, decided to tackle the issue of the termination of welfare benefits without a predeprivation hearing. Benefits recipients experienced terminations of their benefits as an expression of the power that city and state officials had over them; their inability to challenge a termination until after it had occurred meant that they would endure extended periods of time without any means to provide for their daily needs. A lawyer at MFY said, "Termination was the device that the welfare department used to shake people up. The feeling that you can get terminated any time for anything makes you much more subservient and pliable to whatever caseworkers want."[10]

The First Plaintiffs Challenge Their Cutoffs

Kelly v. Wyman, the action originally filed by MFY, began with six plaintiffs: John Kelly, Randolph Young, Juan DeJesus, Pearl McKinney, Pearl Frye, and Altagracia Guzman. The District Court for the Southern District of New York consolidated a case called *Sheafe v. Wyman* with *Kelly* because of the similarity of the issues. That case included two additional plaintiffs, Ruby Sheafe and Esther Lett. Twelve more plaintiffs eventually joined the case as intervenors, ten enrolled in AFDC and two receiving Home Relief.[11]

The lawyers arguing for the plaintiffs in the consolidated cases recognized that their greatest chance for success rested in their ability to present to the courts the obstacles and challenges faced by the individuals they represented. They illustrated "the day-to-day realities of the lives of poor people— struggling to provide a bare minimum of basic necessities for themselves and their children, while confronting an inefficient, unpredictable, and often hostile welfare bureaucracy."[12] Once the case reached the Supreme Court, Justice Brennan would get the message: "The brief for the recipient told the human stories that the state's administrative regime seemed unable to hear."[13]

The stories of the individual plaintiffs demonstrate the breadth of the challenges and indignities of life for benefits recipients in late 1960s New

York City. In June of 1966, John Kelly, a 27-year-old African American man, was struck by a hit-and-run driver and injured so seriously that he was unable to work.[14] He was enrolled in the state's Home Relief cash assistance program and received $80.05 every two weeks, the only income he had to pay his living expenses.

In December 1967, Kelly had a regularly scheduled meeting with his welfare caseworker. The caseworker told Kelly to move out of the Broadway Central Hotel and into the Barbara Hotel. Kelly was concerned that the Barbara Hotel was a home base for people he "knew to be drug addicts and drunkards";[15] he didn't want to live there. He was more concerned, however, that if he refused to move he would lose his benefits. He followed orders and moved in.

Kelly spent only a few days at the Barbara Hotel before, fearful for his safety, he moved to a friend's apartment. He maintained the Barbara Hotel as his mailing address, hoping that the caseworker would not realize he had disobeyed the order. When he went to the hotel to claim his mail, hoping to find his Home Relief check, the desk clerk told him that his checks had been terminated because he had left the hotel. Kelly then understood that the desk clerk was in contact with the caseworker and had shared information about Kelly's actions. He subsequently learned that an additional check, intended to pay for a winter coat, had also been returned to the welfare agency.

Concerned about the termination of his benefits and in need of funds, Kelly attempted twice in January 1968 to meet with his caseworker at the Gramercy Welfare Center. She refused to meet with him both times. Kelly was told on both occasions that the case had been terminated because he had disobeyed the caseworker's instructions to move to the Barbara Hotel and to remain there or risk immediate termination of the case. Subsequent efforts by caseworkers at MFY were similarly unsuccessful. Following termination of his Home Relief benefits, Kelly was left, according to the complaint filed on his behalf, with "no assets, no means of support" and unable to work.

Randolph Young was another recipient of Home Relief aid, receiving $57 twice a month until his aid was terminated in January 1968.[16] Young, age 40, had been receiving assistance off and on since 1957. He suffered from numerous health problems and was frequently hospitalized. During his hospitalization in January 1968, he received no cash assistance; his case was placed on "Hospital Suspension." Young left the hospital on January 8, 1968, and received $20 to cover his rent and food for a week. Soon after he received those funds, he was beaten and robbed. The NY Department of Social Services (DSS) replaced the money that had been stolen. Young, who had been searching for work, found a job and DSS advanced him $5 for lunches and carfare. He lost the job, however, because he was unable to perform the heavy labor required.

On January 12, 1968, Young was told by his caseworker that his assistance had been terminated and that he would receive no further aid. Lawyers with MFY eventually learned that DSS's reason for closing his case was "mismanagement of funds," apparently relating to the theft of the $20. Young was left completely without support and at the mercy of his friends.

Juan DeJesus also received Home Relief assistance, in the amount of $56.80 twice a month.[17] DeJesus did not receive the check he expected on January 3, 1968. He had no notice of the cancellation of his benefits. His caseworker told him that his case was terminated because DeJesus drank and took drugs and because DeJesus had failed to provide sufficient verification of previous employment. DeJesus neither drank nor took drugs and had already presented the employment verification in response to a previous request. Efforts by social workers and lawyers at MFY were unsuccessful in getting the benefits reinstated, and DeJesus was left completely without support and dependent on a friend who was also a recipient of state assistance.

Home Relief recipients were not the only ones affected by the DSS terminations of benefits. Pearl McKinney, age 37, received help through Aid to Families with Dependent Children (AFDC), funded by the federal government but administered by the states. To support herself and four of her five children, McKinney received $155 semimonthly.[18] In 1967, McKinney's rent in a New York City Housing Authority apartment had been increased by more than 20 percent without a corresponding increase in her benefits. She was served with eviction papers and avoided eviction only because of the intervention of an attorney with MFY, who spent months battling the City Department of Social Services to stop the eviction and obtain an increase in her rental allowance to cover the increase in her rent payments.[19] Eventually, after failing to appear for scheduled hearings, representatives of the city finally announced that the rental allowance would be increased and that she would receive a payment to cover the back rent that had been assessed since the increase took effect.

McKinney's problems didn't end there, however. Her oldest child, Marvin, was 19 in 1967. He was removed from her AFDC budget in July or August of that year because he was deemed able to care for himself. At the end of that year, McKinney's caseworker requested that Marvin meet with her to discuss his financial situation. Marvin went to the meeting and shared a statement of his earnings. Late in December 1967 the caseworker again requested information about Marvin's earnings; the information was forwarded by MFY in a certified letter. Marvin was earning $55 a week; he did not contribute to the family's expenses because he was soon to be married and he was saving for his future home. MFY attorneys believed that Marvin was not legally required to contribute to the family's upkeep.

McKinney's benefits were terminated as of January 23, 1968. The caseworker's letter indicated that the reason for the termination was McKinney's failure to provide information requested about Marvin's earnings. At the time of filing of the complaint, McKinney had no funds available to pay for food for her family.

Pearl Frye received funds under AFDC to help her to support her eight children, ranging in age from 3 to 15.[20] Her semimonthly benefit of $126 was terminated on December 1, 1967. Her benefits did not include a subsidy for rent because her family lived rent-free in a house owned by the father of some of her children. The father and his wife, Minnie, owned the house; Pearl Frye was not married to the owner of the house and had no financial interest in it.

Shortly before she would have received her December 16, 1967, check, she received notice from DSS that her benefits were being terminated for failure to cooperate and for failure to explain the ownership of the house. Mrs. Frye talked with DSS caseworkers about the closing of her case. They told her that DSS would reopen the case if she would bring the father of the children with her to their office. She did so, but the case was not reopened.

After the case was closed, her caseworker told Frye to place her children into a day care center and find a job. She visited a day care center but was told that she had too many children for them to accept; they suggested she obtain public assistance. When she applied for jobs, employers told her she belonged at home with her children.

Through the efforts of a non-DSS social worker, Frye was able to obtain a one-time emergency grant for food on January 16, 1968. Despite the scheduling and adjournment of two fair hearings throughout December 1967 and January 1968, Frye had been unable to challenge the termination of her benefits. She had numerous and significant health problems, some possibly related to the stress of her financial situation, and had no prospects for additional resources to support herself and her children.

The sixth of the original plaintiffs, Altagracia Guzman, had not yet had her benefits terminated when the complaint was filed, but repeated threats of termination by DSS sent her to MFY for help.[21] Guzman, 29, was receiving $170 each month in AFDC benefits for her four children, aged one month to nine years. She was married but separated from her husband, who gave her

$20 per week to help in supporting the children. He also bought gifts and furniture for their household and "act[ed] as a father" to the children. He did not, however, live with the family.

On repeated occasions DSS tried to force Guzman to sue her husband for support. She refused, believing that court-ordered support would be less than she was already receiving and that the suit would discourage her husband from being involved in the children's lives. Eventually DSS decided to file suit itself and then tried to force Guzman to sign a document concerning the eventual support payments. Guzman refused to sign despite threats from DSS that they would close her benefits case if she did not cooperate. Her lawyers determined that the cooperation of the benefits recipient was not required under state law in such cases, but DSS continued to exert pressure on her. At the time the case was filed, DSS had threatened to close her case within the next month. If that happened, she would be unable to provide for her children.

Esther Lett was one of the two plaintiffs in *Sheafe v. Wyman*, consolidated with *Kelly* by the district court. In an affidavit filed in support of the complaint in that case, Lett stated that she and her four dependents, nieces and nephews ages three months, 7, 12 and 15 years, had received public assistance until it was terminated on February 1, 1968, and that they were "absolutely destitute" and "on the verge of starvation" as of the end of that month.[22] Lett and the children had been treated at a local hospital for illness caused by eating spoiled food given to them by a neighbor.

Lett's problems with the Department of Social Services began when the agency decided that she had concealed assets, in the form of earnings from work they insisted she had done as a teacher's aide for the Board of Education. The Department claimed that she had earned $1,982 for work done from July 1967 through February 1968. Lett stated that she had worked for the board in the Head Start program for six weeks during the summer of 1967, but that she had completed her work on August 20, 1967, and had earned only $350 during that period. She asserted that DSS was aware of those earnings and that there had been a fair hearing on that subject during that time.[23] Lett asserted that she had earned only an additional $300, working as a day care substitute, since the end of her term with Head Start.

Lett's affidavit described her ordeal on February 27, 1968, when she went to a DSS office seeking emergency aid for herself and her dependents. Because she hadn't eaten that day, she passed out while waiting for her case to be processed. After a total of eight hours of waiting, including some time after she had been revived, she was given "a single issue emergency grant" of

$15 and told to return on Friday, three days later, though without any assurance that she would receive any additional help. She concluded her plea for assistance by stating:

> I have no money, and have been living these past three weeks from what little food my neighbors could spare for myself and my four dependent children. We will all starve without being restored to full public assistance. I have told the Department of Social Services the truth, but they have erroneously decided that I am earning a lot of money and concealing it. . . . I do not know who is making the mistake. But someone will have to correct the mistake, because we are all so much in need of aid. This is an awful thing to happen right here in New York City in 1968.[24]

The Defendants Weigh In

The defendants in the consolidated case included George Wyman, New York State welfare commissioner, Jack Goldberg, the New York City welfare commissioner, and members of the State Board of Welfare.[25] Lawyers for the plaintiffs considered suing federal officials in the Department of Health, Education, and Welfare (HEW), but ultimately concluded that fighting the federal authorities directly would be too risky. They did not know what position the federal agency would take on the pretermination hearing issue, and they feared that if HEW opined that the hearings provided in the regulations were adequate, the court would defer to that position. A better approach, they concluded, was to sue the state and city agencies responsible for administering the federal program, allowing a more indirect attack on the regulatory scheme.[26] Ten months after the case was filed, and after oral arguments had taken place, HEW filed an amicus brief in response to a request from the presiding judge. The brief took no position on the substantive issues, but instead merely explained the operation of certain federal regulations.[27]

The District Court Case

The six original plaintiffs filed suit in the U.S. District Court for the Southern District of New York seeking the appointment of a three-judge panel to consider their request for an injunction preventing the state and city welfare officials from terminating or suspending welfare benefits without a predeprivation hearing. The complaint asserted that the enforcement of state statutes and regulations by those officials deprived the plaintiffs of property without due process under the Fourteenth Amendment and violated their statutory hearing rights under the Social Security Act.[28]

The three-judge panel, headed by Judge Wilfred Feinberg of the U.S. Court of Appeals for the Second Circuit, held hearings in the summer of 1968. In an opinion issued in November, the court noted that the hearing provisions under both the AFDC and New York Home Relief programs had changed while the suit was pending. When the suit was filed, the state agency responsible for administering both types of welfare assistance did not require any notice or any hearing prior to the termination of benefits. A state procedure called a "fair hearing" had only recently been implemented to provide for a hearing after benefits had been suspended.[29] After the suit was filed, the New York Department of Social Services first amended its regulation to provide for notice and a hearing before termination of benefits, then repealed that new regulation, and finally adopted yet another regulation.

The final product of this administrative juggling was a choice for local agencies between two options, both of which provided for notice and some form of hearing. Option (a), in effect in New York State outside of New York City, provided a welfare recipient whose benefits were threatened with termination with seven days' written notice, including an explanation of the reasons for the threatened action and the opportunity to have an in-person hearing at which the recipient would be permitted to present oral or written evidence to an official with a rank higher than that of the official who had approved the termination. Option (b), adopted by the city welfare officials, provided the same notice as in option (a) but after that it provided only the opportunity for the recipient to request a review of the threatened action. For that review, the recipient could choose to submit a written statement or other evidence of his objections to the threatened termination of his benefits.[30] The court also noted that a recipient whose benefits were found to have been wrongfully terminated after a hearing was, at the time the suit was filed, entitled only to two months of retroactive benefits for repayment of debts which he had incurred for necessities. Because the duration of a benefit termination was apparently longer than two months, the court said that the limited retroactivity imposed hardships on the recipients. The court noted that the federal government had since imposed a requirement that benefits found to have been terminated improperly would be fully reimbursed.[31]

After addressing the current administrative landscape, the court dealt with the critical issue of the constitutional protection of welfare benefits in only a few sentences:

Defendants do not deny plaintiffs' general propositions that the terminations here under attack amount to "state action" and that the protections of the due process clause apply. Nor do defendants attempt to argue that welfare benefits are a "privilege," rather than a right, and that therefore they may fix the procedures of the termination as they see fit.[32]

In support of its conclusion, the district court cited the work of influential Yale scholar Charles Reich, who had applied the understanding he gleaned about treatment of benefits granted by the government to corporations and other wealthy parties to his work on behalf of lawyers representing welfare recipients. Reich declared that property should be redefined and that the government granting benefits should not be characterized as gratuities but rather as entitlements. He argued that although entitlements flowed freely to wealthy citizens in the form of licenses, franchises, contracts, pension rights, and union memberships, "[i]t is only the poor whose entitlements . . . have not been effectively enforced."[33] Importantly for the broader impact of the analysis in *Goldberg*, Reich insisted that the poor were not responsible for their predicament: "today we see poverty as the consequence of large impersonal forces in a complex industrial society—forces like automation, lack of jobs and changing technologies that are beyond the control of individuals."[34] His work was one of the foundations of the litigation strategy of the advocates working on a range of welfare-rights issues, including *Goldberg v. Kelly*.

After briefly addressing the definition of the protected right, the court went on to consider the particular characteristics of pretermination hearings that should be provided to welfare recipients whose benefits were threatened. The court focused its analysis on the need for pretermination review, stating its concern in bleak terms: "While post-termination review is relevant, there is one overpowering fact which controls here. By hypothesis, a welfare recipient is destitute, without funds or assets."[35] The opinion then recited the facts involving two of the plaintiffs, Angela Velez and Esther Lett, highlighting the hunger and deprivation that had been suffered by both women and their families. The court noted that though neither plaintiff had been able to clearly establish the facts in her case, it seemed clear that the impact of the termination of benefits was dramatic: "[T]o cut off a welfare recipient in the face of this kind of 'brutal need' without a prior hearing of some sort is unconscionable, unless overwhelming considerations justify it."[36]

The state and the city argued that their actions were justified by their need to protect the public treasury. While acknowledging that the necessity to protect public funds was important, the court nonetheless found that protective measures were available, including expediting hearings and providing additional hearing officers. "While the problem of additional expense must be kept in mind, it does not justify denying a hearing meeting the ordinary standards of due process."[37]

The court then devoted considerable attention to the elements of the hearing that would satisfy the mandates of the Due Process Clause.[38] Addressing both the nature of the issues presented in the termination cases and the limitations likely experienced by many welfare recipients, the court held that an in-person hearing was necessary rather than merely an opportunity for the recipient to challenge benefits deprivations in writing. The court also criticized the sufficiency of the notice, stating that the vague "reasons for the intended action" was not adequate to fully inform the welfare recipient of the reasons for the proposed termination:

> We do not hold that the welfare recipient about to be terminated must be accorded the opportunity for confrontation and cross-examination in a formal manner, with the full panoply of a trial-type hearing, including testimony under oath. The right to face those providing harmful information and have them interrogated may be substantially achieved in an informal way, and we use the term "cross-examination" here in that less formal sense.[39]

Thus, the court enjoined the city's use of option (b), finding it constitutionally inadequate. The court denied the request for an injunction against the use of option (a), though it discussed the arguments plaintiffs had made against that option, both on its face and as applied. Though the court expressed some concern with the amount of detail provided about the source of the evidence against the recipient, the opportunity for the recipient to challenge the source in person, and the impartiality of the final decision maker, the court chose not to enjoin the use of option (a) in light of "the newness of the regulation and the paucity of information given us on its use outside of New York City."[40]

Less than two months after the opinion was issued, the city was forced to begin complying with the court's ruling in *Goldberg v. Kelly* when Justice Harlan rejected the city's request that it not be required to comply with the ruling until after the Supreme Court had reviewed the case. The state then dropped out of the case, leaving the city to appeal the court's ruling concerning option (b).

The Supreme Court accepted the case, consolidating it with *Wheeler v. Montgomery*,[41] a California case in which a three-judge district court panel had upheld California's hearing procedure in response to a challenge from a recipient of Old-Age Assistance whose benefits had been terminated following her receipt of money from her son's estate. The court in *Wheeler* had found that the hearing process available there—arguably a more fair process than that at issue in *Goldberg*—was adequate. Though *Wheeler* had reached the Supreme Court first, the Court accepted the filing by the New York attorneys of an amicus brief in *Wheeler* urging the Court to accept *Goldberg* and to consolidate the two cases.[42] Ultimately, the Court found *Goldberg* to be the more significant case, issuing the opinion in that case and relegating *Wheeler* to "companion case" status, issuing a one-paragraph opinion reversing "on the authority of *Goldberg*."[43]

The Supreme Court Case

Justice Brennan, writing for the Court majority in *Goldberg*, began his opinion by summarizing the statutory changes made in New York's procedures since the suit was filed. The Court then defined the issue as whether due process required that a benefits recipient whose benefits were to be terminated be given a pretermination hearing.

After summarizing the three-judge court's analysis, the Court began by addressing the right/privilege distinction. The Court stated that the defendants had not challenged the constitutional nature of welfare benefits. "Such benefits are a matter of statutory entitlement for persons qualified to receive them. Their termination involves state action that adjudicates important rights. The constitutional challenge cannot be answered by an argument that public assistance benefits are 'a "privilege" and not a "right."'"[44] As authority, the Court cited the work of Charles Reich, though it did not elaborate in the opinion's text. In a footnote, however, the Court quoted a portion of Reich's discussion of entitlements benefiting the wealthy as contrasted with those for the poor.[45] The Court agreed with the district court's conclusion that welfare benefits were essential for daily living, thus making a pretermination hearing necessary:

> [W]hen welfare is discontinued, only a pre-termination evidentiary hearing provides the recipient with procedural due process. . . . For qualified recipients, welfare provides the means to obtain essential food, clothing, housing, and medical care. . . . Thus the crucial fac-

tor in this context . . . is that termination of aid pending resolution of a controversy over eligibility may deprive an eligible recipient of the very means by which to live while he waits. Since he lacks independent resources, his situation becomes immediately desperate. His need to concentrate upon finding the means for daily subsistence, in turn, adversely affects his ability to seek redress from the welfare bureaucracy.[46]

The Court's analysis of the nature of the pretermination hearing that was necessary tracked that of the three-judge district court. The Court concluded that neither a complete record nor a comprehensive opinion was required at the pretermination stage. Instead, the Court said that "minimum procedural safeguards, adapted to the particular characteristics of welfare recipients" would be sufficient.[47] To that end, the Court agreed that written submissions would likely be inadequate for a welfare recipient, both because of the nature of the information involved and because of the skills required to prepare a written argument. "Timely and adequate notice" was required, along with oral presentation, though a formal trial-type proceeding was not required. Cross-examination or confrontation of adverse witnesses was also necessary. And finally, the Court concluded that the decision maker must be impartial and must base his or her ruling solely on the information presented at the hearing. Though a formal statement of findings of fact and conclusions of law was not necessary, the Court thought it essential that the decision maker explain his or her conclusion and indicate the evidence on which the decision was based.[48]

The most significant part of the Court's opinion, though, may have been Justice Brennan's statement about the causes and effects of poverty. In his description of the "important governmental interests" reflected by the administrative procedures at issue, he wrote:

From its founding the Nation's basic commitment has been to foster the dignity and well-being of all persons within its borders. We have come to realize that forces not within the control of the poor contribute to their poverty. This perception, against the background of our traditions, has significantly influenced the development of the contemporary public assistance system. Welfare, by meeting the basic demands of subsistence, can help bring within the reach of the poor the same opportunities that are available to others to participate meaningfully in the life of the community. . . . Public assistance . . .

is not mere charity, but a means to 'promote the general Welfare, and secure the Blessings of Liberty to ourselves and our Posterity.'[49]

This statement reflects a clear sense of Justice Brennan's view of the importance of welfare programs in easing the plight of those living in poverty. Rather than accepting the defendants' arguments about the fiscal impact of pretermination hearings for benefits recipients subject to termination of their benefits, Justice Brennan highlighted the importance of treating people living in poverty as if they were potential contributors to society rather than merely a drain on it.

In dissent, Justice Black argued that the Court's holding exceeded the Court's constitutional powers and impermissibly broadened the construction of the Fourteenth Amendment. Black believed that Brennan's opinion was based on a conclusion that it was unconscionable to deprive a benefits recipient of his benefits without a hearing, and that it was therefore unconstitutional. Black contended that the result of the imposition of a hearing requirement would be an increasing level of caution on the part of state and city officials before they determined that an applicant was eligible for benefits.[50]

Conclusion: Justice Brennan Looks Back

Justice Black's concerns did not dampen the power of Justice Brennan's rhetoric. His statements for the Court about the dignity of all individuals and the desire of those living in poverty to participate meaningfully in community life are stirring even more than 40 years later.

Justice Brennan's view of *Goldberg* as one of his most important opinions gives additional credence to that view. In a speech in 1987, Justice Brennan talked about "Reason and Passion," reflecting specifically on *Goldberg*. He suggested that though the welfare system under review was a rational one, the Court's rejection of the lack of a pretermination hearing was an indication that the system lacked passion. The administrative process, "a product of formal reason, . . . did not comport with due process. It did not do so because it lacked that dimension of passion, of empathy, necessary for a full understanding of the human beings affected by those procedures." Brennan went on to say that, in his view, the Due Process Clause required ongoing attention to the "passion that understands the pulse of life beneath the official version of events."[51]

In this time of widening inequality between rich and poor, ever-increasing intolerance and aggressive indifference to those who have the least, Brennan's call for understanding of the human lives touched by government actions is powerful. Though decisions in subsequent cases may have diminished the precedential value of *Goldberg v. Kelly*, we can only hope for a resurgence of attention to his most humane call for passion. The need has never been greater.

> You remember when you felt each person mattered
> When we all had to care or all was lost
> But now you see believers turn to cynics
> And you wonder was the struggle worth the cost
>
> ———
>
> Carry on, my sweet survivor, carry on my lonely friend
> Don't give up on the dream, and don't you let it end . . .[52]

Notes

1. William J. Brennan Jr., *Reason, Passion, and "The Progress of the Law,"* 10 CARDOZO L. REV. 3, 21–22 (1988) [hereinafter Brennan, *Reason*]. The text of the article is from a speech delivered as the Forty-Second Annual Benjamin N. Cardozo Lecture to the Association of the Bar of the City of New York (Sept. 17, 1987).

2. Thomas A. Johnson, *Life on Welfare: A Daily Struggle for Existence*, N.Y. TIMES, Dec. 19, 1966, at 1. All references to the Pressleys, their landlady, and other welfare recipients in this and the next four paragraphs come from Johnson's article.

3. The city paid approximately 30 percent of the annual welfare budget, with the state and the federal government paying the remaining 70 percent. Peter Kihss, *Welfare Budget Asks $1.4-Billion, Biggest City Item*, N.Y. TIMES, Jan. 6, 1968, at A1. All information in this paragraph on the details of the welfare scheme in 1967–68 comes from this article.

4. Francis X. Clines, *Welfare: A Patchwork of Federal and State Programs*, N.Y. TIMES, Dec. 31, 1970, at 33.

5. Richard Rogin, *Now It's Welfare Lib*, N.Y. TIMES, Sept. 27, 1970, at SM 16.

6. *Id.*

7. Clines, *supra* note 4.

8. *Id.*

9. MARTHA F. DAVIS, BRUTAL NEED: LAWYERS AND THE WELFARE RIGHTS MOVEMENT, 1960–1973 71–72 (1993). Davis's book is the seminal work on this case, providing a thorough and fascinating analysis of the litigation that framed the welfare rights movement.

10. *Id.* at 86, *citing to* Davis's interview with former MFY attorney David Diamond.

11. *Id.* at 93.

12. Stephen Wizner, *Passion in Legal Argument and Judicial Decision Making: A Comment on Goldberg v. Kelly*, 10 Cardozo L. Rev. 179, 180 (1988). Wizner was one of the lawyers representing the plaintiffs in *Goldberg*.

13. Brennan, *Reason, supra* note 1, at 21.

14. Descriptions of the plaintiffs are based in part on Davis, *supra* note 9. Some of the litigation materials, including the Complaint for Three-Judge Court, Declaratory Judgment, Injunctive Relief, United States District Court for the Southern District of New York, Civ. No. 394-1968, Kelly v. Wyman (Jan. 26, 1968), [hereinafter Complaint] are included in Robert M. Cover, Owen M. Fiss & Judith Resnik, Procedure 61–72 (1988) [hereinafter Cover].

15. *See* Complaint, *supra* note 14, at IX, par. 3.

16. *See id.* at X.

17. *Id.* at XI.

18. *Id.* at XII.

19. *See* Cover, *supra* note 14, Aff. of Stephen Wizner in Support of Foregoing Complaint, at 73–74.

20. *See* Complaint, *supra* note 14, at XIII.

21. *Id.* at XIV.

22. Cover; *supra* note 14, at 77, Affidavit of Esther Lett in Support of Foregoing Complaint.

23. *Id.*

24. *Id.*

25. *See* Davis, *supra* note 9, at 89–90.

26. *Id.*

27. *Id.* at 97.

28. *See* Complaint, *supra* note 14, at I-III.

29. Kelly v. Wyman, 294 F. Supp. 893, 896 (S.D.N.Y. 1968) (*aff'd sub nom.* Goldberg v. Kelly, 397 U.S. 254 (1970)).

30. *Id.* at 896–98 & n.7.

31. *Id.* at 896.

32. *Id.* at 898.

33. Charles A. Reich, *Individual Rights and Social Welfare: The Emerging Legal Issues*, 74 Yale L.J. 1245, 1255 (1965).

34. *Id.*

35. Kelly v. Wyman, *supra* note 29, at 899.

36. *Id.* at 900 (footnote omitted).

37. *Id.* at 901.

38. The court noted that an analysis avoiding the constitutional question might have sufficed to address at least part of the issue in the case, but because that analysis (noting the hearing rights provided under the Social Security Act) would not have applied to the terminations of benefits under state and city programs, it was appropriate to tackle the constitutional question directly. *Id.* at 902.

39. *Id.* at 905.

40. *Id.* at 906, *see also* 907.

41. 296 F. Supp. 138 (N.D. Cal. 1968).

42. *See* DAVIS, *supra* note 9, at 100–102.

43. Wheeler v. Montgomery, 397 U.S. 280 (1970).

44. Goldberg v. Kelly, 397 U.S. 254, 262 (1970) (citations omitted).

45. *Id.* at 261–262 & note 8, *quoting from* Reich, *supra* note 33. The court also cited Reich's *The New Property*, 73 YALE L.J. 733 (1964) in the footnote.

46. *Goldberg*, 397 U.S. at 264 (citations and footnotes omitted).

47. *Id.* at 267.

48. *Id.* at 269–71.

49. *Id.* at 265 (footnote omitted).

50. *Id.* at 271–80.

51. Quotes in this paragraph are from Brennan, *Reason*, *supra* note 1 at 21, 22.

52. PETER YARROW, BARRY MANN & CYNTHIA WEIL, SWEET SURVIVOR (Silver Dawn, 1978).

Litigating in the Zeitgeist

Rosado v. Wyman • (1970)

WENDY A. BACH

The Zeitgeist creates the parenthesis within which law moves.
—*Burt Neuborne, 2013*

The political world that gave rise to *Rosado v. Wyman* is almost unimaginable today. Today welfare recipients are stigmatized, targeted, criminalized, and blamed for a wide range of social ills. Depending on welfare to meet basic needs is, in today's political world, the moral equivalent of a crime. But *Rosado v. Wyman* was not filed in 2013 or even in the early 1970s. It was filed in 1969, at the apex of the welfare rights movement and in response to drastic grant cuts that were a direct attack by the State of New York on one of the most potent tools of that movement. It was filed at a political moment when actors across the political spectrum believed that the nation was on the verge of instituting a national guaranteed minimum income. By 1970, it appeared that the plaintiffs had achieved a modest win. In response to the Supreme Court opinion in *Rosado*, the state reversed course and raised benefit levels. But that victory would not hold. Just a year later, citing the very same opinion, the state lowered benefit levels.

This strange reversal in the state's position on welfare benefit levels between 1970 and 1971 was possible and indeed legal because ultimately the win in *Rosado* relied not on the strength of federal welfare law but on the strength of the welfare rights movement and the political consensus about whether or not the state had a moral obligation to meet the needs of women and children on welfare. In New York State, the politics of that question shifted dramatically between 1969 and 1971. And *Rosado*'s fate shifted with it. In this sense, the story of *Rosado* is an object lesson in the way political context defines the parameters within which lawyers work for social change. As Professor Burt Neuborne, then a lawyer at the New York Civil Liberties Union and author of an amicus brief in *Rosado* so aptly put it, "the zeitgest creates the parenthesis in which law moves. . . . The movement of the zeitgeist makes it impossible to understand what was happening in *Rosado* because it's outside the current parentheses."[1] Understanding *Rosado* thus offers an opportunity to look closely at the political parenthesis that framed conversations about poverty and welfare at the time.

The story begins a few years before *Rosado*, with striking optimism among some elites that the nation should and could meet the economic needs of those in poverty. That earlier story focuses too on the extraordinary tale of the welfare rights movement in New York City. The case begins, and the story continues, in 1969 as the plaintiffs' lawyers faced a frontal attack on the welfare rights movement. And the story ends in 1971 as the movement faltered, the idea of a national guaranteed annual income (GAI) faded, and Rockefeller turned rightward, joining a growing chorus of those who would scapegoat and stigmatize poor women, poor children, and poor communities.

Background: Welfare Reform and the Guaranteed Annual Income

In March 1967, Governor Nelson A. Rockefeller invited "100 of the nation's leaders in industry, labor, news media, philanthropic foundations and government . . . to help plan new approaches to public welfare in the United States."[2] Participants at the November 1967 conference included, among many others, senators, the heads of major foundations, the chairman of the New York Stock Exchange, and the leaders of many major corporations and public organizations. The conference attendees were charged with finding "possible approaches to deal more effectively with the persistence of welfare dependency in a nation of plenty."

At the conclusion of the Arden House conference, a steering committee was appointed to summarize the recommendations to the group as a whole. The chair of that group was Joseph C. Wilson, chairman of the board and CEO of Xerox Corporation. In the view of the steering committee, the current system of public welfare was inadequate for a variety of reasons. Perhaps most importantly, the system did not provide assistance to the vast majority of those in poverty. According to the committee's report, while 30 million Americans were living in poverty, only 8 million received assistance. The system was also, in the view of the committee, "inefficient, inadequate, and has so many disincentives that it encourages continued dependency."[3]

In response to these problems, the committee called not for the destruction of economic support that would be put in place in 1996 but instead for replacing Aid to Families with Dependent Children ("AFDC") "with an income maintenance system, possibly a negative income tax, which would bring all 30-million Americans up to at least the official poverty line."[4] The system they envisioned would "provide a Federal floor below which no state would be permitted to fall and no person would be expected to live."[5] Short of a GAI, the committee called for drastic revisions of AFDC that sought to destigmatize the program, provide support for work, and remove administrative barriers to receipt of assistance. The proposed changes included elimination of "man in the house" rules, expansion of day care, childcare, and work supports, and the replacement of "the costly, demeaning and inefficient investigations now used almost universally" with an "affidavit system to determine eligibility with spot checks similar to those used by the Internal Revenue Service."[6] The system committee members envisioned was a far cry from the system that the 1996 reform left in its wake.

The Arden House report is far from an anomaly for the period. Nationally, both the Johnson and the Nixon administrations pushed for federalization and expansion of economic support. As early as 1965, the Office of Economic Opportunity (OEO), the department within the Johnson administration that was charged with implementing the War on Poverty, proposed a GAI.[7] GAI proposals within OEO included an incremental approach to reforming AFDC that would have provided a national floor in that program, a negative income tax proposal, and a family allowance.[8]

By the early years of the Nixon administration, the GAI looked nearly inevitable. Nixon's Task Force on Public Welfare, headed by Richard P. Nathan, advocated for a $1.4 billion plan to nationalize welfare.[9] In 1969 Nixon called publicly for the creation of the Family Assistance Program, or FAP, which would have provided a basic income guarantee of $1,600 for a family of four, and a broad coalition supported that effort.[10]

Governor Rockefeller of New York was at the forefront of support for FAP. He chaired a Committee on Human Resources for the National Association of Governors, and in the late summer of 1968, 43 of the 48 governors assembled for the 61st annual National Governor's Conference supported the

FAP.[11] At that meeting, Rockefeller authored a policy statement, endorsed by the association, urging the federal government to assume the full cost of welfare programs within five years.[12]

GAI ideas within the Nixon administration were also buoyed by large-scale support from the political left and significant support from the center. The GAI was supported by a wide range of organizations and coalitions, including the Citizen's Crusade Against Poverty, founded in 1963 by United Auto Workers president Walter Reuther; the 1968 Poor People's Campaign; the National Urban League; and the NAACP. The GAI was a central component of the Freedom Budget, "a program endorsed by hundreds of liberal organizations."[13] Support also came from numerous commissions and agencies: "The Council of Economic Advisors, the White House Conference on Civil Rights, the National Commission on Technology, Automation and Economic Progress . . . the White House Conference on Food, Nutrition and Health, the Kerner Commission, and President Nixon's Task Force on Urban Affairs."[14] One particularly telling sign of the far reach of this support was the discussion at the 1966 U.S. Chamber of Commerce Symposium on the GAI.[15] While the symposium certainly included opponents, the very fact that the Chamber of Commerce held a national symposium on the issue gives some sense of its political viability at the time.[16] As Marisa Chappell has observed, "[i]n 1968 *Time* magazine could legitimately write about a 'Considerable Consensus' behind a guaranteed income."[17]

This support for the GAI did not, of course, originate out of pure generosity from those in power. As Marisa Chappell describes it, "[b]y the late 1960s, entrenched poverty, soaring welfare costs, mounting impatience on the part of poor black urban residents, and civil rights leaders' increasing attention to the economic foundations of racial oppression put tremendous pressure on urban mayors, who lobbied Congress for financial aid."[18] The welfare rights organizing that came under attack in 1969 and that gave rise to *Rosado* had created much of this pressure.

1965 to 1968: Welfare Rights Organizing and the Growth of New York's Welfare Program

In the years leading up to the filing of *Rosado*, welfare rights organizing and legal representation were extraordinarily effective both in building a movement and in bringing significant funds into the hands of welfare recipients. In New York City, not only had the number of people receiving welfare grown, but due to the special needs and fair hearing campaigns, the size of grants and the total funds given to poor families had grown exponentially.

This growth in the size of AFDC was in large part a product of several deliberate pressures exerted on the welfare system. In 1965, Frances Fox Piven and Richard Cloward published "A Strategy to End Poverty,"[19] which quickly became a crucial resource for the movement. The strategy proposed a wide-scale mobilization in poor communities to flood the welfare system with applications. As Piven and Cloward described it:

> If hundreds of thousands of families could be induced to demand relief . . . we thought it likely that a huge increase in the relief rolls would set off fiscal and political crisis in the cities, the reverberations of which might lead national political leaders to federalize the relief system and establish a minimum income system.[20]

George Wiley, who had developed his political organizing skills when he founded the Syracuse chapter of the Congress of Racial Equality, played a central role in the founding of the National Welfare Rights Organization ("NWRO"). Wiley embraced Piven and Cloward's ideas and developed an organizing strategy based on their theory.[21] Lawyers, largely funded by federal War on Poverty funds and working at the Center for Social Welfare Policy, the Legal Aid Society, and MFY Legal Services, supported and augmented this campaign by flooding the centers not only with applications but also with requests for fair hearings when applications were denied. While the welfare department had the authority to issue special needs grants for things like furniture, clothing, school supplies, dishes, and many other households items, the availability of these grants was largely unknown to recipients. Lawyers and organizers created request forms and flooded the local centers with requests for these grants. When requests were denied, organizers staged sit-ins in the welfare centers to demand that the grants be paid, and lawyers filed fair hearings to contest the adverse determinations. The scale of these efforts was enormous. By the end of 1967, 4,322 fair hearing requests had been filed with the welfare administration. "At the same time, the city's welfare rolls rose to 746,000 relief recipients, an increase of more than 28% over the previous year."[22] By the summer of 1968 the city funds spent on special needs alone reached $10 million to $12 million per month.[23]

During the height of the special needs campaigns, Sylvia Law, who would later be a driving force behind the filing of *Rosado*, was a law student at New

York University School of Law. She had spent most of her law school semesters at MFY Legal Services doing welfare work, primarily on the special needs campaigns. Her favorite campaign involved telephones. Families were entitled to a special needs grant to pay for a telephone if they needed it for "health or family welfare."[24] In Law's view, "everyone [had] reasons" under that standard. She spent her time doing surveys of broken public phones to establish that they weren't available in poor communities, and going to meetings in the evenings helping people fill out forms to request telephones. She filed fair hearings and "almost never lost."[25]

Piven and Cloward's theory that such a campaign would create a crisis was borne out. By 1968 the city was reaching a fiscal breaking point in the welfare program, and the state's response was twofold. They tried to stop the bleeding by cutting grants and eliminating special needs. In addition, and crucially, Rockefeller led the nation's governors in demanding federalization of welfare. Ultimately, the second strategy would fail, leaving only the attack on the state welfare program and welfare organizing in place.[26]

1968: The New York State Grant Cut

By letter dated August 14, 1968, George Chesbro, the acting commissioner of the New York City Department of Social Services, requested federal approval of a demonstration project for its AFDC program. Under the demonstration project, New York City would eliminate special needs grants and replace them with "a cyclical series of grants which will be expected to meet the preponderance of what have traditionally been defined as 'special' needs for clothing and household replacements. The payment would be based on family size at the level of $100 per person per year."[27] The next year, after a series of hearings around the state on the issue of welfare, during which professional after professional testified to the administrative burden of administering special needs grants, the idea of the flat grant was brought to scale. New York State revised Section 131-a of its Social Services Law to institute a flat grant payment system throughout the state. The legislature found that "'the spiraling rise of public assistance rolls and the expenditures therefore,' and the 'economic concerns of the people of the state of New York,' justified the move to a flat grant."[28] The statewide grant structure revision was enacted on March 31, 1969, and was to go into effect on July 1st. *Rosado v. Wyman* was filed on April 10, 1969, to stop the state from implementing this provision.

The repeated assertions by Chesbro and the state that the flat grant would meet the preponderance of needs that were formerly covered by the basic and special needs grants was far from accurate. In fact, the move to the flat grant meant vast reductions both in overall aid and in the amount many families would receive. The reason for this reduction lay within the complexity of the budgeting methodologies at issue. Prior to the demonstration project, recipient families received a regular grant for food and a few other basic necessities (rent grants were separate). For example, in 1967, a family of five would have received a basic grant of $235.80 per month.[29] In addition, all recipients were eligible for special needs grants.[30] As detailed above, due to the extraordinary success of the organizing campaign, the actual dollar amounts received by any particular family could, and in fact did, often far exceed the basic grant. By June 1968, each individual person receiving special needs grants was receiving an average of $16 per month.[31] For a family of five, that meant an additional $80 in average aid. So that same family of five would be receiving on average $315.80 per month. The revision of state law would mean elimination of this system, so even though the basic grants for the same family of five went from $235.80 in 1967 to $254 in the statute,[32] the elimination of special needs grants made this seeming increase a net loss.

According to the plaintiffs' filings, the named plaintiffs faced, on average, a 19 percent reduction in their monthly budgets.[33] As Judge Weinstein held in the early stages of the litigation, "[t]he change to a flat grant system—long favored by some as a more enlightened method of public assistance—has been used as a subterfuge to enact drastic cuts in both standards of need and levels of benefits."[34] So whatever the rhetoric, the move to a flat grant was devastating both because the effect was a drastic cut in already meager benefits and because it entirely destabilized a primary organizing tool. There was no question in the minds of lawyers supporting the movement that they had to respond.

1969: The Litigation

At the time *Rosado* was filed, Sylvia Law had just become a lawyer. She was, like many other central figures in the welfare rights litigation world, a Reginald Heber Smith (or "Reggie,") Fellow. She worked at Columbia University's Center for Social Welfare Law and Policy. While her new role at the center was to bring impact litigation, she remained strongly tied to movement work. While she spent her days at the center litigating, she spent her evenings supporting the movement directly, "going to police stations with women who'd been arrested for sitting down in the Commissioner's office."[35] Law understood as well as anybody that the New York State move to the flat grant was disastrous for the movement and the people she cared about. *Rosado* was, then, all about challenging the budgeting cuts and, as much as possible, saving the special needs campaign. She was, in her words, "ready to quit if we weren't willing to challenge the New York reforms."[36]

For the litigation team, though, there were no perfect claims and certainly no claims that would enable them to force a return to special needs. While the special needs campaign had been extraordinarily effective in building the movement and raising the effective level of grants, the special needs grants were, even in the eyes of their most fervent defenders, "obviously irrational from an [administrative] fairness point of view."[37] As Frances Fox Piven explains it, while the loss of special needs grants was strategically devastating, the move to a flat grant was actually a small victory:

> I used to say to my colleagues including the welfare rights women, listen the flat grant is actually a victory. Before the flat grant you didn't get any special needs. They were just there on the book and nobody got them. So the flat grant was a victory. . . . The trouble was that this little organizing tactic ran smack into the face of what was a small but nevertheless transparently good reform.[38]

While it was clear that special needs grants could not ultimately be saved, it was also clear that the budget cuts were a disaster and the lawyers had to respond.

The complaint in *Rosado* challenged the New York State move to a flat grant on two separate grounds, one constitutional and one statutory. The moving papers were skillfully crafted to lay bare the extraordinary hardship that resulted from the grant cut and to frame this hardship as morally unacceptable. The affidavit of Dr. Robert Dorsen, deputy director of OBGYN at Lincoln Hospital, filed in support of plaintiffs' motion for a preliminary injunction, is exemplary of these filings. In it, Dr. Dorsen spoke clearly, using terms of progress and moral outrage. In regards to the welfare budget reductions at issue in *Rosado*, he stated:

> [i]t is inconceivable to me that at a time when the medical and allied health services professions have begun to make inroads into the health problems of the poverty population of our City that we could anticipate a retrogression of our progress. The possible harm inflicted upon pregnant mothers and newborn children as a result of the cutback of public assistance grants is incalculable.[39]

Numerous professionals echoed Dorsen's sentiments. Joseph Vigilante, who was the dean of the Social Work School at Adelphi University, described a study focusing on the lives of five New York City welfare recipients. He described current conditions as "deplorable" and stated that "[i]t is inconceivable to me that these reductions, coupled with termination of special grants will permit maintenance of life with any degree of dignity and without great harm to the physical, mental, emotional and moral health of these families, and of families similarly affected by this legislation."[40]

Affidavits submitted by the named plaintiffs laid bare the specific hardships they were suffering as a result of the grant cuts. The plaintiffs reported an inability to feed their families and detailed a host of specific needs that would go unaddressed should the grant cuts be enacted. Louise Lowman needed money to buy clothes for her son. Sophia Abrom needed chairs, a bed, a washing machine, sufficient clothing and better food. The plaintiffs also talked about the difficulties they faced even under the prior system. As Annie Lou Philips described it:

> It has been very difficult for me to feed and clothe my children while we receive $274.00 per month. It will be impossible for me to do so when, and if, our total income is reduced to $224.00. . . . Since we, at the present time, have nothing more than the bare necessities of life, we [will] have to subsist on less if our welfare budget is reduced.[41]

While the stories told by the plaintiffs' lawyers were extraordinarily compelling and spoke in terms of moral outrage, their claims were more technical and not as strong as they might have hoped. First, the complaint alleged an equal protection violation based on a discrepancy between the value of grants in Nassau County, just east of New York City, and the grants in the city itself. The equal protection claim was weak from the start and would quickly drop out of the litigation as a result of a statutory amendment by the state.[42]

The *Rosado* suit went forward on the second claim, alleging that New York's legislation violated the recently passed section 402(a)(23) of the Social Security Act, which required that the states adjust their standard of need "to reflect fully changes in living costs since such amounts were established" and to proportionately adjust "any maximums that the state imposes on the amount of aid paid to families."[43] To understand this claim, one has to know a bit about AFDC requirements and budgeting methodologies at the time.

Pursuant to federal law, states participating in the AFDC program had to make a determination as to the needs of individuals. This determination resulted in a calculation called the "standard of need." Although it rarely was realistic in terms of the actual cost of these items, it was theoretically supposed to be a real assessment of basic necessities. It also set the levels that would determine who was eligible for aid. After making that determination, the states were required to make a separate determination about grant levels. Some states, like New York, paid benefits at 100 percent of the standard of need, some set "maximums" or caps above which the state would not pay even when family size increased, and some paid some percentage of the standard of need. Focusing on the more technical meaning of "maximum," the Court would ultimately hold that section 402(a)(23) did not require states either to pay benefits at the standard of need or, in fact, to pay any particular amount of benefits. As the federal administering agency made clear during the litigation, "[i]n the event the State is not able to meet need in full under the adjusted standard the State may make ratable reductions."[44] In other words, at least in the view of the Department of Health, Education and Welfare, nothing in federal law would stop any state from recalculating the standard of need upwards as required by federal law and then deciding to pay only 80 percent or 20 percent of that need.

But this relationship between the requirement to update the standard of need and the level of benefits the state would pay was not entirely clear at the beginning. The lawyers in *Rosado* initially claimed that section 402(a)(23) compelled New York both to redetermine need and to proportionately adjust the prior "maximum" grant levels up to reflect any increase in need. Since New York purported to pay 100 percent of need, that would mean that, absent a state statutory change, New York would have to recalculate the standard of need and then pay at that level. The plaintiffs argued that the 1968 legislation, which moved to a flat grant without any redetermination of need, violated section 402(a)(23).

Section 402(a)(23) was the best legal hook available to the plaintiffs' lawyers, but it was a far weaker provision than the Johnson administration had sought in 1967. The administration had originally proposed a provision that would not federalize welfare benefits but would compel states to recalculate their standards of need upward and then pay benefits at 100 percent of those levels, rather than applying ratable reductions or maximums to the higher standard of need. During the 1967 federal legislative debates, the administration pushed hard for its proposal, but it ultimately lost. The watered-down and decidedly more ambiguous version became law.[45]

The use of section 402(a)(23) was also borne of a purposeful litigation strategy designed by Ed Sparer and the other lawyers to make progress in the courts on the issues of poverty and economic need. While the focus of much of the litigation campaign was on constitutional claims, federally statutory claims were equally important. As Sylvia Law described it, the first goal was "to create a vibrant statutory entitlement so that whatever Congress said you shall receive, that was enforceable."[46] Section 402(a)(23) might not have been tremendously strong, but it was a federal rule about grant levels and the plaintiffs lawyers were committed to making as much of it as they possibly could.

In the initial battles in district court, the fight between the plaintiffs and defendants was about whether section 402(a)(23) required the state to actually raise benefits. The defendants maintained that the provision focused only on the standard of need and not on the benefit levels. Federal officials at the U.S. Department of Health, Education and Welfare (HEW) supported the defendants' position. District Court Judge Jack Weinstein, however, agreed with the plaintiffs that while 402(a)(23) did not require the state to pay full need, it did require states both to recalculate the standard of need and to "increase its levels of payment by an amount sufficient to offset the rise in the cost of living."[47] In the context of New York's statutory provision requiring benefits at 100 percent of the standard of need, this position would result in precisely what the Johnson administration had wanted: benefits being paid at the level the state found necessary to meet need.

When the case went up on appeal the Second Circuit disagreed. Not only did the Court of Appeals hold that the district court should have declined to exercise jurisdiction pending review by HEW, but it stated that Congress expressed "an intent not to impose controls on the levels of benefits set by the states."[48] As the case rushed feverishly toward the Supreme Court, the battle lines were set.

The Supreme Court opinion took a different tack. While the Court made clear that New York would not be compelled to pay any particular benefit level, it did take seriously the congressional mandate that the state recalculate the standard of need. The Court found that, in moving to a flat grant, "New York [had] in effect, impermissibly lowered its standard of need by eliminating items that were included prior to the enactment of 402(a)(23)."[49] In other words, by eliminating the special needs grants, New York had violated federal law. Unless New York could establish that the eliminated special needs "no longer constituted part of *the reality of existence* for the majority for welfare recipients"[50] this elimination violated federal law. The state was ordered to recalculate its standard, and the penalty for failure to do so was extreme: "petitioners [would be] entitled to declaratory relief and appropriate injunction by the District Court against the payment of federal monies."[51] In other words, if New York State did not appropriately recalculate its standard of need, it would lose all its federal AFDC funds.

The Supreme Court's focus on "the reality of existence" in *Rosado* is telling. As Harlan read it, while 402(a)(23) did not actually force a change in benefit levels, it had, at least potentially, important political consequences: it required "states to face up realistically to the magnitude of the public assistance requirement and lay bare the extent to which their programs fall short of fulfilling actual need."[52] In addition, "while it [left] the States free to effect downward adjustments in the level of benefits paid, it accomplish[ed] within that framework the goal, however modest, of forcing a State to accept the political consequences of such a cutback and [brought] to light the true extent to which actual assistance falls short."[53] The import of this warning was clear. *Rosado* would only succeed in holding off grant decreases if, as a matter of politics, New York remained committed to paying benefits at 100 percent of the standard of need.

1970: The Immediate Aftermath— The Political Consensus Holds

The *Rosado* case was remanded to the District Court in April of 1970. At that point, if not far earlier, it was clear that New York State had a practical option that would have ended the litigation. The Supreme Court had made it clear that the state could recalculate the standard of need and then pay benefits at some percentage of need below 100 percent. Passing such legislation would have avoided months of additional litigation as well as the very real possibility that the state might lose all of its federal AFDC funds. It also would have allowed the state to maintain or even lower welfare expenditures.

Instead, Harlan's observations proved astute. Despite the Supreme Court's clear invitation to do so, in 1970 New York was apparently unwilling to set benefit levels at a pro rata share of need. In fact, at oral argument before the Supreme Court, the fact that New York paid at the standard of need was asserted as a point of pride. As Philip Weinberg, who argued for New York before the Court, stated, "New York simply doesn't do that. We've never indulged in that. We pay 100% of the standard of need."[54] Jack Weinstein agreed. As he remembers the state's position in the litigation, "the State wasn't willing to say we're giving less than we think people need."[55] In reaction to the Supreme Court opinion, the legislature amended the Social Services Law and raised the grants. The legislature increased the flat grant and included provision for several additional special needs grants.[56] To return to the example of a family of five, the 1968 legislation challenged in *Rosado* would have given that family $254 per month and would have allowed for a special needs grant for the replacement of furniture or clothing destroyed as a the result of "fire, flood, or like catastrophe." The 1970 legislation was slightly more generous. That same family of five received $284 in monthly assistance and could receive special needs grants not only to replace furniture or clothing destroyed by catastrophe but also grants for "furniture required for the establishment of a home," "essential repair of heating equipment, cooking stoves and refrigerators," "day care . . . homemaker services . . . camp fees . . . [and] life insurance premiums."[57]

The wider political consensus operating when New York agreed to raise its benefit levels gives us some sense of why the New York State legislature might have reacted to *Rosado* by raising grant levels. Recall that this was just three years after the Arden House report had strongly endorsed the idea of a guaranteed minimum income. In 1969, Nixon had proposed the Family Assistance Plan (FAP), which was for all intents and purposes a guaranteed annual income program. Rockefeller, largely in response to the extraordinary budget pressures created by the growing welfare rolls, led the National Governors Association in pushing the federal government to institute this program. In 1970, FAP passed through the House of Representatives and headed to the Senate. At that moment, it still seemed possible that the federal government might assume full fiscal responsibility for the welfare program and might well go further, providing a guaranteed minimum income to a far broader set of people. Perhaps at that moment, for New York State, continuing to purport to pay benefits at 100 percent of the standard of need remained possible and perhaps even morally compelled. But that moment did not last.

1971: The GAI Effort Falters and New York State Shifts to the Right

By 1971 the hopes of welfare reform advocates lay in ruins. The battle for the GAI was nearly lost, felled by the ascendancy of conservative politics. In response to these developments, Governor Rockefeller would shift, joining the increasingly popular Ronald Reagan by talking tough on welfare.[58] Rockefeller stopped making the case that there was some moral obligation to meet the needs of the poor, gave up his previous demands that the federal government respond, and moved toward rhetoric that sounds similar to that which supported the evisceration in 1996 of AFDC. In 1971, *The Nation* published an article describing a Rockefeller welfare reform proposal. The article opens with a quotation from a Rockefeller aide: "He's convinced that we're going right down the road to disaster if we don't do something about the welfare problem." In that particular moment Rockefeller was proposing a thinly veiled version of the durational residency requirements struck down in *Shapiro v. Thompson*.[59] But for *Rosado*'s benefits question, what was clear, at least to those writing for *The Nation*, was that the failure of FAP combined with the lack of substantial opposition from the left to the attack on welfare had driven Rockefeller to switch course. "It was . . . a conviction that the federal Government was not about to take over welfare costs that spurred Mr. Rockefeller to action. . . . Five years ago, the Governor would not have risked the wrath of the liberal establishment with such a proposal."[60]

Rosado's fate was ultimately tied to these shifting political realities. The 1970 victory in fact proved fleeting. In 1971, just months after the final Second Circuit decision in *Rosado*, the New York State legislature reversed course and took up the Court's invitation to pay benefits at less than 100 percent of the standard of need. As the legislature explained:

> New York is presently one of only fourteen states which pay one hundred percent of the established standard of need. . . . The Supreme Court . . . in Rosado v. Wyman . . . ruled that a state may reduce payment levels to accommodated budgetary realities . . . In order to accommodate present budgetary realities it will be necessary for the state of New York to pay no more than ninety percent of the standard of need.[61]

The brief victory in 1970 faltered on the rightward turn in welfare politics. The lawyers who filed *Rosado*, and the New York State officials who responded, worked in a political context in which the idea of a national guaranteed income was palpable, realizable, and, at least for a time, virtually inevitable. In this context the idea of desperate need in the midst of plenty was, at least in some quarters, morally unacceptable.

For a moment, the state was forced to "face up realistically to the magnitude of the public assistance requirement and lay bare the extent to which their programs fall short of fulfilling actual need."[62] For a moment, the political consequences of publicly refusing to meet need were apparently too steep. As Frances Fox Piven sees it, the power of the movements in 1970 perhaps left the politicians with few alternatives.

> At that moment in time the Court is right that movement associated groups could have made a lot of hay over the fact that New York

(or any urban state at least) would only pay 80, 70, 50 percent of the standard of need. . . . I am not sure that in some deep way people's attitudes are different but there was at least a veneer of opinion created by propaganda that [would have made it impossible for New York to pay less than the standard of need].[63]

Yet it is important to remember that even in that moment, New York fought behind the scenes throughout the final phases of the litigation to eliminate particular needs from the standard, thereby enabling them to in effect lower grant levels without publicly acknowledging that they were doing so. As Jack Weinstein views it, "[New York was] claiming they were giving a hundred percent . . . [but] their actual grants were less than a hundred percent."[64] But in 1970 the state did briefly maintain its public position that it was providing benefits that met the economic needs of women and children in poverty.

Over forty years later, the idea of welfare has traveled a long and horrific journey. By 1971 New York State paid benefits at 90 percent of the standard of need. By 1972, FAP was dead in committee. By 1986, the nation would see the rise of the image of the welfare queen, with all its extraordinary racism. These ideas would take hold and gain ascendance, surrounded by a veritable storm of right-leaning organizations that would scapegoat welfare for virtually every conceivable evil befalling the middle class. Today, not only have Americans lost any notion that we have some moral responsibility to meet need, but, as Kaaryn Gustafson has recently and disturbingly observed, today's "[w]elfare rules assume the criminality of the poor, [and] . . . the logics of crime control now reign supreme over efforts to reduce poverty or to ameliorate its effects."[65]

But 1969 and 1970 were different. The lawyers and activists who fought for economic support were wise wielders of their own political zeitgeist. Ultimately *Rosado* tells an extraordinary story both about what was possible at a particular moment in time and about the extraordinary importance of political context on the parenthesis in which movement lawyering functions.

Notes

Thanks to Sylvia Law, Burt Neuborne, Judge Jack Weinstein, Stephen Cole, and Frances Fox Piven, who all graciously agreed to be interviewed for this project. Thanks also to Henry Freedman for agreeing to an interview and for providing access to the *Rosado* files housed at the National Center for Law and Economic Justice. Transcripts and recordings of these interviews are on file with the author.

Finally thanks to Joseph Prestia, PhD, who provided invaluable research assistance in this project.

1. Interview with Burt Neuborne, Inez Milholland Professor of Civil Liberties, New York University School of Law, Aug. 1, 2013 (transcript on file with author).

2. The Steering Committee of the Arden House Conference on Public Welfare, appointed by Governor Nelson A. Rockefeller, Report 9 (1967).

3. *Id.* at 12.

4. *Id.*

5. *Id.*

6. *Id.* at 13.

7. Brian Steensland, The Failed Welfare Revolution: America's Struggle over Guaranteed Income Policy 49–50 (2008).

8. *Id.* at 62.

9. Marisa Chappell, The War on Welfare: Family, Poverty and Politics in Modern America 71 (2010).

10. *Id.* at 115.

11. UPI, *Federal Funding on Welfare Urged: Rockefeller Asks Governors to Demand National Action*, N.Y. Times, Aug. 31, 1969.

12. James Naughton, *Governors Laud Plan on Welfare*, N.Y. Times, Sep. 1, 1969.

13. Chappell, *supra* note 9, at 59.

14. *Id.*

15. Steensland, *supra* note 7, at 64–67.

16. Chappell, *supra* note 9, at 61–63.

17. *Id.* at 59.

18. *Id.* at 68.

19. Frances Fox Piven & Richard Cloward, Poor People's Movements: Why They Succeed, How They Fail 276 (1978).

20. *Id.*

21. Martha Davis, Brutal Need: Lawyers and the Welfare Rights Movement, 1960–1973 44–45 (1995).

22. *Id.* at 50.

23. *Id.* at 53.

24. Interview with Sylvia Law, Elizabeth K. Dollard Professor of Law, Medicine and Psychiatry, New York University School of Law, July 29, 2013 (transcript on file with author).

25. *Id.*

26. *See generally* Davis, *supra* note 21, at 40–58.

27. Letter from George W. Chesbro, acting commissioner of the New York City Department of Social Services, to James Callison, regional commissioner, Department of Health, Education, and Welfare, Aug. 14, 1968 (on file with author).

28. Complaint at 2, Rosado v. Wyman, 304 F. Supp. 1356 (1969) (on file with author).

29. Plaintiffs Memorandum of Law in Support of Motion for a Preliminary Injunction at 25, Rosado v. Wyman, 304 F. Supp. 1356 (1969) (on file with author).

30. Complaint at 4, Rosado v. Wyman, 304 F. Supp. 1356 (1969) (on file with author).

31. Memorandum of Law in Support of Motion for Preliminary Injunction at 27 n.15, Rosado v. Wyman, 304 F. Supp. 1356 (1969) (on file with author).

32. 1969 N.Y. Sess. Laws c. 184.

33. Plaintiffs Memorandum of Law in Support of Motion for a Preliminary Injunction at 25, Rosado v. Wyman, 304 F. Supp. 1356 (1969) (on file with author). Calculation based on figures asserted in Plaintiffs' Memorandum of Law in Support of Motion for Preliminary Injunction at 27, Rosado v. Wyman, 304 F. Supp. 1356 (1969) (on file with author).

34. Rosado v. Wyman, 304 F. Supp. 1356, 1381 (1969).

35. Law interview, *supra* note 24.

36. *Id.*

37. *Id.*

38. Interview with Frances Fox Piven, Distinguished Professor, City University of New York Graduate Center, Oct. 3, 2013 (transcript on file with author).

39. Affidavit of Robert Dorsen, deputy director of obstetrics and gynecology at Lincoln Hospital, in support of Plaintiffs Motion for a Preliminary Injunction, Rosado v. Wyman, 304 F. Supp. 1356 (1969) (on file with author).

40. Affidavit of Joseph Vigilante, dean of the Social Work School at Adelphi University, in support of Plaintiffs Motion for a Preliminary Injunction, Rosado v. Wyman, 304 F. Supp. 1356 (1969) (on file with author).

41. All quotations and references to the initial filing are contained with the Order to Show Cause, Rosado v. Wyman, 304 F. Supp. 1356 (1969) (on file with author).

42. Rosado v. Wyman, 304 F. Supp. 1354 (1969).

43. Rosado v. Wyman, 304 F. Supp. 1356 (1969).

44. 45 CFR 233.20(a)(2)(ii) § 4 F.R. (1969), quoted from Memorandum of Law in Support of Motion for Preliminary Injunction at 29.

45. Rosado v. Wyman, 397 U.S. 397, 409–413 (1970).

46. Law interview, *supra* note 24.

47. 304 F. Supp 1356, 1376 (1969).

48. 414 F. 2d 170, 179 (1969).

49. 397 U.S. 397, 416 (1970).

50. *Id.* at 419 (emphasis added).

51. *Id.* at 420.

52. *Id.* at 413.

53. *Id.*

54. Rosado v. Wyman, Supreme Court oral argument transcript, available at http://www.oyez.org/cases/1960-1969/1969/1969_540 (last visited Dec. 17, 2013).

55. Interview with Jack B. Weinstein, United States District Court Judge, Aug. 1, 2013 (transcript on file with author).

56. 1970 N.Y. Laws chap. 516, 2039–2042. On remand, the plaintiffs did seek

to challenge the 1970 grant levels, and they won this claim as to the northern and western upstate counties but lost as to New York City. Rosado v. Wyman, 437 F. 2d at 621. Although the Second Circuit upheld the preliminary injunction, the issue of grant levels in the northern and western counties of New York were litigated in another case. *Rosado* was effectively over at that point.

57. 1970 N.Y. Laws chap. 516, 2039–2042.

58. James E. Underwood & William J. Daniels, Governor Rockefeller in New York: The Apex of Pragmatic Liberalism in the United States 209 (1982).

59. 394 U.S. 618 (1969).

60. Frank Lynn, *Rockefeller Talk Tough and Aide Says 'It's No Baloney'*, N.Y. Times, Mar. 14, 1971.

61. 1971 N.Y. Laws chap. 133, 725–26.

62. 397 U.S. at 413.

63. Piven interview, *supra* note 38.

64. Weinstein interview, *supra* note 55.

65. Kaaryn Gustafson, Cheating Welfare: Public Assistance and the Criminalization of Poverty 1 (2011).

Part II

Losses

A Sweeping Refusal of Equal Protection

Dandridge v. Williams • (1970)

JULIE A. NICE

The Supreme Court's decision in *Dandridge v. Williams* is one of the most significant cases not only in poverty law but also in constitutional law.[1] *Dandridge* stands primarily for the proposition that courts should defer to the choices made by the political branches of government regarding how to allocate scarce resources spent on social welfare programs. In the lasting language of Justice Potter Stewart's opinion for the *Dandridge* majority, "the intractable economic, social, and even philosophical problems presented by public welfare assistance programs are not the business of this Court."[2]

Prior to the *Dandridge* decision, the Supreme Court had ruled in favor of poor people in several significant cases, dismissing popular stereotypes and going so far as to suggest that government classifications burdening poor people might be sufficiently "suspect" to warrant heightened judicial scrutiny. Most importantly, the Court unanimously pronounced that California could not could treat poverty as synonymous with morality by fencing out impoverished newcomers;[3] rejected Illinois's "squalid discrimination" against indigent criminal defendants;[4] invalidated Virginia's poll tax because "lines drawn on the basis of wealth or property, like those of race, are traditionally disfavored";[5] ruled that California could not rely on "the saving of welfare costs" to justify "an otherwise invidious discrimination" against new residents;[6] and held New York could not deny recipients "the very means by which to live" without a hearing prior to termination of welfare benefits.[7]

Dandridge abruptly ended this momentum toward equal constitutional protection of poor people. Since the *Dandridge* decision in 1970, courts have applied minimal rational basis review to public welfare programs, accepting merely conceivable governmental purposes while ignoring actual purposes and disregarding the grossly overinclusive and underinclusive fit between the government's purposes and where it draws exclusionary lines. This prompted Justice Thurgood Marshall to describe this minimal rational basis review as requiring "no scrutiny whatsoever."[8] Litigants and courts now routinely invoke *Dandridge* to justify reflexive rubber-stamp review, which has effectively immunized social welfare regulation from review and deconstitutionalized poverty law.[9]

But *Dandridge* is about much more than the application of minimal rational basis review for equal protection challenges of social welfare programs. The *Dandridge* litigation directly presented the federal courts with an opportunity to evaluate Elizabethan-era assumptions about poor people and welfare programs within the American constitutional system. Behind *Dandridge* is the story of the struggle of impoverished families to survive on welfare benefit amounts far below what was needed for minimal subsistence. *Dandridge* is also about the grave difficulty of keeping a large poor family intact, let alone thriving. Because Maryland, like other states, paid a substantially higher benefit amount for any dependent child who was placed outside of the home, the perverse effect of the maximum family grant was to incentivize the "farming out" of children and the breakup of the family unit.

To explore the societal aspect, this chapter tells the story of the Gary family, one of two families that served as named plaintiffs in *Dandridge*.[10] It also recounts the litigation's twists and turns, from the state's initial perfunctory federalism defense to its lawyer's assertion of an ideologically conservative position far beyond official policymakers' views.

The Gary Family Struggles to Survive Together

When Junius Gary met his future wife Jeanette, he was a bright and hardworking young man with an engineering bent and a job constructing Ferris wheels for the circus.[11] Junius and Jeanette were married in Baltimore, Maryland, in 1952. Jeanette was particularly religious and believed marriage was for life. Shortly after their wedding, Junius served in the army, but he suffered serious injuries and was decorated and honorably discharged in 1955. During the early years of their marriage, Jeanette lost several babies and was told she couldn't have children. To everyone's surprise, she eventually gave birth to eight children over a span of less than seven years between early 1957 and late 1963. But the close proximity of these pregnancies took a heavy toll on Jeanette's health, which was compromised by high blood pressure, arthritis, and possibly diabetes. After his stint in the army, Junius worked as a truck driver and chauffeur until he suffered an automobile accident. Due to dizzy spells, blackouts, and seizures that plagued him for the rest of his life, Junius was no longer able to hold down a steady job, and the family began receiving public assistance under the Aid to Families with Dependent Children (AFDC) program.

By all accounts, Junius and Jeanette shared one overriding goal: to keep the family together at any cost. The state of Maryland didn't make it easy for the large Gary family to stay together. Like other states participating in the AFDC program, Maryland had established schedules for determining a family's standard of need based on cost of living estimates. These schedules for 1968 showed that the Gary family would need $331.50 per month to meet subsistence expenses.[12] Due to budget constraints, however, Maryland had implemented a maximum family grant of $250 per month for AFDC families living in the Baltimore area. But if Junius and Jeanette sent any of their children to live outside the home, each child would be entitled to $65 per month, regardless of the family maximum.

The family of ten was not able to survive on the maximum grant of $250 per month. Their monthly rent was $75. Their home had no central heating system, so they had to heat each room separately with gas space heaters, resulting in gas and electric bills as high as $50 per month. Because they were constantly behind in paying their utility bills, they suffered frequent shutoffs of their gas and electricity. Junius and Jeanette simply didn't have enough money left from their AFDC grant to feed, clothe, and provide all the other necessities for raising their eight children. They frequently couldn't even afford to spend the required $86 per month to participate in the food stamp program.

As their son Junius Jr. explains, "Life was a constant struggle to make ends meet. There were hungry days. We had to ration. We sometimes only ate once or twice a day."[13] In a good month, they would take a wagon and load up on cheese and canned welfare food. Their daughter Cathy reports that their mother was very resourceful in cooking meals from the welfare food because she knew how to cook from scratch. Sometimes their father killed chickens for a poultry farm and he was allowed to bring home the chicken feet, which served as the foundation for many creative family meals. Both their father and mother were forced to work "under the table" to supplement their public assistance. Junius was always looking to make money from odds and ends jobs, and Jeanette did domestic cleaning.

Their daughter Cathy explains that her parents were family-oriented and "they would have done anything just to keep all of us together." Junius took his children fishing and Jeanette took them to church. These influences lasted, as the Gary children remain religious and enjoy fishing to this day. The family spent quite a bit of time together and their son, Anthony, remembers that they seemed to grow up much closer than the families of their friends. Their father was a strict disciplinarian who enforced a curfew and kept close tabs on the whereabouts of his children. Anthony thinks his father was worried about "the way the world was heading and he wanted to keep us from being part of that."

Their mother was proud of her work cleaning the homes of professional baseball players such as Brooks Robinson, the star third baseman for the Baltimore Orioles. Jeanette occasionally took each of her children with her to work, and her children saw firsthand how the Caucasians she worked for lived. But Jeanette made sure her children's exposure to such wealth was tempered by the recognition that "there is good in people." During the 1968 riots following the assassination of Dr. Martin Luther King Jr., Brooks Robinson and his wife gave Jeanette extra money to help the Gary family get through until stores in the black neighborhoods reopened. Junius Jr. remembers being inspired with hopefulness by that small act of kindness. Once when some of his friends were harassing white people, Junius Jr. intervened because their hostility simply didn't make any sense to him. He wasn't raised that way. As Junius Jr. explains, the Gary family was "rooted in spiritualism. No matter what adversity we met, the spiritual principle kept us grounded."

The family's primary adversary was unrelenting poverty. As Anthony saw it, "a lack of jobs was the main problem," which was exacerbated by the fact that families receiving public assistance were not allowed to work much then. He remembers welfare caseworkers coming to do home inspections: "We knew that, when they were coming to the house, they were looking for things. My mother and father made sure we kept our house as clean as possible. They made sure we did the best to keep it up, even if the place itself was run down." Junius Jr. saw his parents persevere and do everything they could. But watching his father "run on a treadmill to nowhere," he recalls, "kind of made me wonder what were my chances."

The biggest break the family received was getting approved for subsidized housing in 1973. Junius Jr. remembers moving into a newly remodeled house, which seemed like "a palace." This was a turning point. After they moved into public housing, hunger was no longer the constant problem it had been before.

But the hardship and stress of the family's poverty had already taken a heavy toll, especially on their father. To his children, Junius was a contradiction in terms. He was very intelligent, with an engineer's mind. He could be resourceful, versatile, and adaptable. He was always trying to teach his children how to get along in the world, for example making sure each child knew how to ground electrical wires. Once when the family was living in a three-story house, he placed a ladder out of the third-floor window onto the adjoining building and showed the children how to use this as an escape route in case of fire. On a social level, their father was outgoing and had many friends. Junius was active in the civil rights movement, particularly the Congress of Racial Equality (CORE), and he sometimes let his children tag along when he went to CORE headquarters. But his inability to work frustrated him, and his behavior was erratic and sometimes violent. When he drank too much, he could be physically and verbally abusive to Jeanette and the children. Anthony laments that he doesn't think his father "ever reached a point where he was happy."

The children also watched their father suffer unpredictable seizures from time to time. But Junius wasn't expressive with his children, and they didn't understand what was wrong with him. Junius died unexpectedly at the age of 45. Long after their father's death, Anthony and his siblings learned that Junius had been blown off a train when it was bombed during the war, and they suspect he had suffered from undiagnosed posttraumatic stress disorder. Now, for the most part, they simply believe their father did the best he could.

Although Jeanette "went through so much" with their father, Cathy remembers how her mother "always held everything together." After her husband's death, Jeanette took courses and became certified as a medical technician, but she wasn't able to find a job using her training. Jeanette cleaned houses for most of her life, and her economic situation "pretty much stayed the same" until her death at the age of 75.

Against all odds, Junius and Jeanette accomplished their goal of keeping their family together. But without sufficient funds to make ends meet each month, the family suffered enormous hardship. On a positive note, their three oldest children—Junius Jr., Cathy, and Anthony—express deep appreciation today for the closeness the eight siblings still share. But the downside is that the lives of the Gary children, like those of their parents, have been a constant struggle, with one brother in prison, several battling substance abuse, and most of them needing support from social services at one point or another.

Until his untimely death just five years after the *Dandridge* decision, Junius Gary despaired the enormous price his family paid for the combination of disadvantages they suffered based on race, disability, and poverty.

The Gary and Williams Families Challenge Maryland's Maximum Family Grant

The children of Junius and Jeanette Gary surmise that their parents became involved in the lawsuit to challenge Maryland's maximum family grant due to their father's active participation in the Baltimore chapter of CORE. Junius Jr. specifically remembers many occasions on which he accompanied his father to gatherings at local CORE headquarters, where his father spent time with local CORE director Danny Gant.

For several decades, CORE had been at the vanguard of civil rights, leading the organization of direct action tactics such as sit-ins and the freedom rides. It seems likely that local CORE leaders in Baltimore were tied to the national leadership of both the civil rights and welfare rights movements, which had become inextricably linked. After President Lyndon Baines Johnson launched the War on Poverty in 1964 with the establishment of the federal Office of Economic Opportunity and its Community Action Program, Baltimore was one of the major "collision sites" where African American activists challenged the white political infrastructure and demanded the promised "maximum feasible participation" of their impoverished community members.[14]

Nearby in Washington, D.C., George Wiley, a chemistry professor and former national leader of CORE, established the Poverty/Rights Action Center in the spring of 1966, which quickly evolved into the National Welfare Rights Organization (NWRO).[15] Wiley collaborated closely with theorist-activists Frances Fox Piven and Richard Cloward, adopting their strategy of creating major economic pressure by encouraging people to pursue rights in the welfare system.[16] The national welfare rights movement quickly emerged onto the national scene in 1966,[17] and 99 percent of the NWRO's membership were poor, black, female recipients of AFDC.[18]

In Maryland, an organization of welfare mothers knows as "The Rescuers from Poverty" lobbied state welfare officials in 1965 and 1966 for increased housing allowances, special clothing allowances, food stamps for the purchase of fresh food, job training, and increased grant levels to allow larger families in urban areas such as Baltimore to meet their actual needs.[19] By the time the *Dandridge* lawsuit was making its way through the court system during the summer of 1968, national community organizers had taken notice of the activity in Baltimore and had persuaded Junius Gary's friend and local CORE director Danny Gant to bring Baltimore-style tactics to CORE's national headquarters in New York.[20]

Whatever the extent of CORE's involvement in the specific decision to challenge Maryland's maximum family grant, there is no question that such a test case had been on the radar screen of Ed Sparer. As legal director of the Center on Social Welfare Policy and Law at Columbia University ("the Center"), Sparer was the primary architect of the national strategy of using constitutional litigation to pursue welfare rights. In April 1966, Sparer published an article listing the top ten issues ripe for "social welfare law testing" and offered the Center's "maximum aid" to attorneys bringing such challenges.[21] Number four on Sparer's wish list was to challenge maximum family grants. In encouraging such challenges, Sparer noted that more than one-third of the states imposed maximum family grants regardless of the number of eligible children, and that the maximums ranged from a high of $250 to a low of $81. As Sparer understood, "the effect is that children of a family of six children or more could receive maximum payments only by living outside their mother's home."

Sparer's optimism about the prospect for such a lawsuit was buoyed by a successful challenge before the Iowa Supreme Court, which found the state's maximum family grant discriminated based on the number of children in the family "with no consideration as to need" and thus was "disconnected" from the purpose of aiding dependent children in the home.[22] Sparer's conclusion was short and direct: "It is recommended that such statutes in other states be tested on grounds of both state and federal constitutional provisions, as well as possible conflict with the purpose and provisions of the federal Social Security Act and state welfare law."[23]

Whether they arrived at the same conclusion independently or as a result of Sparer's encouragement, local legal services attorneys in Baltimore apparently agreed with Sparer that the maximum family grant was ripe for challenge. The Gary and Williams families were represented by Joseph A. Matera of the Legal Aid Bureau. On February 28, 1968, Matera filed a class action complaint with the federal district court in Maryland, requesting review by a three-judge panel and an order declaring that Maryland's maximum family grant contravened the Equal Protection and Due Process Clauses of the Fourteenth Amendment as well as the purposes of the federal and state AFDC program. Matera also asked for temporary and permanent injunctions prohibiting state and local welfare officials, including Edmund Dandridge, chairman of Maryland's State Board of Public Welfare, from applying the maximum grant regulation.[24]

The complaint relied primarily on an alleged violation of equal protection based on the maximum grant regulation's "effect of treating needy children differently based on an arbitrary standard not related to the purpose of AFDC—the size of their family."[25] The only fundamental right mentioned in the complaint was the guarantee of marital privacy mentioned in a brief paragraph at the end. Nowhere does the initial complaint assert any claim to a level of judicial scrutiny higher than rational basis review, nor does the complaint mention any fundamental right to welfare benefits or any right to life.

In his opening legal brief on the merits before a three-judge panel of the federal district court for Maryland in June 1968, Matera invoked the classic understanding of rational basis review, asserting that courts are required to "determine the question whether the classifications drawn in a statute are reasonable in light of its purpose" and that the government may not classify people on arbitrary or irrational grounds.[26] Effectively conceding that rational basis review was the proper judicial standard, Matera argued the maximum grant arbitrarily created two classes of AFDC families based solely on the size of the family unit, the first class of families of six persons or less who were granted AFDC benefits equal to actual need and the second class of families of seven persons or more who received an amount which was both unrelated to actual need and insufficient to meet actual need. In this brief, Matera repeated his allegation that the maximum grant violated the right of marital privacy protected by due process and recognized in *Griswold v. Connecticut*. He also added an assertion that the maximum grant violated the "right to life," which he asserted was "the most basic right of all."[27]

Little Attention to Fundamental Rights

This brief appearance of a "right to life" was the closest Matera came to an argument for a fundamental right to subsistence. He grounded this "right to life" on a dissent in a case associated with the natural law philosophical foundation for the Supreme Court's *Lochner*-era of laissez-faire deference to economic regulation, a philosophy that had been repudiated when the Supreme Court began upholding economic legislation associated with the New Deal.[28] This citation to *Lochner*-era reasoning has been criticized as both ironic and possibly fatal to Matera's claims.[29] But this framing of a right to life was not far from Ed Sparer's own writing on the subject. Blending natural-law principles with the foundational social contract, Sparer had described the issue quite simply: "Upon what moral premise must the starving man or woman accept the majority's vote on whether he or she shall live or not?" Sparer's answer was clear: "The right to live is a *sine qua non* of the social contract."[30]

The District Court Rejects the State's Perfunctory Defense

Frank DeCosta, an assistant attorney general for the state of Maryland, was assigned to represent Edmund Dandridge and the other welfare officials named as defendants. DeCosta's answer admitted that the maximum grant regulation gave less assistance per person to large families than to small families and he separately agreed to a stipulation admitting all the complaint's allegations regarding the economic circumstances of the Gary and Williams families, including the incapacity of the parents to work. But DeCosta's answer denied any constitutional or statutory violation and invoked a federalism defense, simply asserting that "[p]oor relief is a state not a federal question."[31]

DeCosta then filed a motion to dismiss the lawsuit, alleging various technical deficiencies and denying that the complaint raised a substantial constitutional question or any claim upon which relief could be granted.[32] In his brief, DeCosta quoted extensively from a recent federal district court opinion in *Snell v. Wyman* that had rejected both due process and equal protection challenges to New York's laws requiring welfare recipients to repay the cost of their benefits from any proceeds received from interests in real property, personal injuries, and life insurance policies. DeCosta relied primarily on the *Snell* decision's synthesis of classic boilerplate language repudiating *Lochner*-era judicial activism in matters of social policy, which invoked the "minimum rationality" test for due process claims and the "reasonable basis" test for equal protection claims, even if the classification was "not made with mathematical nicety" and resulted in "some inequality" and "rough," "illogical," or "unscientific" accommodations. This very same synthesis of quotations would loom large in the Supreme Court's ultimate decision in *Dandridge*.

In June 1968, a three-judge panel held proceedings in open court; the only witness called was Thomas Schmidt, the state's chief of the Division of Fiscal and Statistical Management. Schmidt testified that the state relied on economic analyses to determine the standard of need for food and housing and that his office had requested the maximum grant be eliminated. The governor's budget, however, had disallowed this elimination due to the state's deficit in AFDC funding.[33] Schmidt also explained that the federal government provided AFDC funds for each eligible individual, but that Maryland determined grant levels and distributed funds on a family basis. Judge Harrison Winter, one of the federal judges on the panel, interjected to ask Schmidt whether the maximum grant had the effect of "shifting a greater proportion of burden of those welfare payments to federal funds," and Schmidt answered, "Yes, sir." On cross-examination, Matera asked the witness, "But, in effect, each individual in that family would receive less than the Department of Welfare computes to be their minimal need because of their maximum grant regulation, isn't that so?" Schmidt answered, "That is correct."

The following day, June 25, 1968, the three-judge panel issued a ruling from the bench, rejecting the state's various technical defenses (including abstention, Eleventh Amendment immunity, and lack of indispensable party defendants who controlled the state's budget) and denying the motion to dismiss based primarily on their finding that the constitutional claim was "not insubstantial."[34] On December 13, 1968, the three-judge panel issued its initial written opinion, concluding that "if Maryland has appropriated insufficient funds to meet the total need under AFDC, as measured by the standards for determining need that Maryland has prescribed, Maryland may not, consistent with the Social Security Act or the equal protection clause, correct the imbalance by application of the maximum grant regulation."[35] With this panel decision invalidating the maximum grant regulation—the same conclusion reached by all other state and federal courts that had considered the question—Matera appeared to be sailing to an easy victory on behalf of the Gary and Williams families and the class they represented.[36] But all of this was before attorney George Liebmann became involved.

The State Demands a Do-Over

George Liebmann was counsel to the Department of Social Services in the Maryland attorney general's office. Upon reviewing the case, Liebmann found DeCosta's brief for the state to be "very inadequate" and considered the "very liberal" Judge Harrison Winter's opinion for the three-judge panel to be "an incredible piece of nonsense."[37] Liebmann was especially distressed that the three-judge panel seemed to treat Maryland's maximum grant as novel when his own research found that "about thirty other states had about ten different variations of the Maryland regulation." He frankly didn't think the regulation would be adequately defended if he didn't do it himself. So Liebmann simply took over the state's defense.

Under "great stress" to submit a proposed order within 10 days of the three-judge panel's written opinion, Liebmann filed an unusual motion "to amend findings of fact and judgment or in the alternative to take additional testimony, or for a new trial, or in the alternative to alter or amend the judgment."[38] In support of this motion, Liebmann filed a memorandum supplementing the record with nine new exhibits covering nearly 100 pages. They offered detailed explanations of the historical, legislative, budgetary, and regulatory contexts for the maximum grant regulation. Key exhibits included documents showing the history of the maximum grant; statements from Maryland Department of Social Services directors explaining that the maximum grant had been in continuous effect since the implementation of statewide welfare standards in 1944; charts tracking increased state spending on public assistance between 1957 and 1967; Department of Health, Education, and Welfare documents showing that federal officials were well aware of the state maximum grants and had acknowledged as much in issuing a policy requiring cost-of-living adjustments to the AFDC standards and specifying that "any maximums that the State imposes on the amount of aid paid to families will have been proportionately adjusted"; memoranda from the state Department of Public Welfare related to the administration of the maximum grants; a 1966 report of a state Legislative Council Committee titled "Public Welfare Cost"; and a 1948 governmental efficiency commission report on the Department of Public Welfare.

As these documents made clear, Liebmann intended to mount a vigorous and more "ideological" defense of the regulation.[39] The exhibits included troubling assumptions regarding welfare recipients. For example, one 1948 statewide study of the public welfare system found "some evidence tending to confirm" the "widespread" belief among local county welfare officials that the maximum grant was "excessive" in some areas and should remain sufficiently meager to serve "successfully as an incentive for recipients' regaining self-support." This study also recommended better coordination to prosecute "desirable" cases of "desertion, non-support, bastardy and the occasional overpayments," which, although they typically involve "very small sums," could "have some deterring effect upon would-be offenders, provided sufficient publicity is given them." The state also demonstrated it had the highest rise in welfare spending among states between 1957 and 1967, and it reported a 232.6 percent increase in the number of children receiving AFDC benefits, from 19,841 in 1956 to 65,984 in 1965. Nonetheless, Liebmann's exhibits also confirmed that state welfare officials had repeatedly proposed abandonment of the maximum grant restriction to no avail, due to limited funds.

Ten days after Liebmann submitted this voluminous filing, the three-judge district court panel held another hearing. Judge Winter pressed Liebmann on the fact that the state previously had presented "the sworn testimony of a representative of the state that they wanted to repeal the regulation" and that the "only reason" they did not repeal it was because the governor failed to budget it and the legislature failed to appropriate it.[40] Liebman openly conceded that the state's official policy position favored a repeal of the maximum family grant, but he asserted that the state's then-current position could not bind past and future executive and legislative policymakers and that "there are other grounds which gave rise to this regulation, which can be urged in support of it." Liebmann further urged the national importance of the panel's reconsideration. He described the welfare rights movement as furthering not only "constructive" but also "frankly, destructive" purposes, and argued that the impact of the *Dandridge* decision would be "very, very profound" because it could establish "that the states, in framing their welfare structures, have to completely disregard the impact of the level of welfare payments on the labor market, on the wage structure. From that, the implications which flow," he surmised, were "considerable."

Not to be outdone, Judge Winter quarreled, "why isn't it totally irrational?" He doubted that tying the maximum grant to current wage levels to encourage work made any sense as applied to these families. As he put it, "How can this chain of reasoning apply when it is the child who is eligible because the parent is physically or mentally incapable of working, is dead or is absent?" Judge Winter further reminded Liebmann that the state had stipulated to the facts that Mr. and Mrs. Gary were physically incapable of working and that Mrs. Williams' husband had left her and that she too was incapable of working. Liebmann paused before he suggested, "there undoubtedly is a feeling on the part of at least some legislators that . . . there is some—perhaps some tendency to overstate the extent of disability."[41]

Liebmann argued further that the state was entitled to consider factors other than need, such as "the real difficulty of limiting abuse of a welfare program, when you had total payments that were significantly higher than the wage rate." To this, Liebmann added a responsible-procreation justification, arguing that the maximum "was designed to assure that persons of limited resources did not have an incentive to bear children that persons of less limited resources do not have." He emphasized that the "average wage-earner" does not receive increased income "by reason of additional children."[42]

Liebmann then tied this back to the welfare rights movement, arguing that the movement was "perhaps more highly organized, at least at its center, than this court may realize, that, really, these welfare rights cases are, in a sense, only the opening wedge." He proceeded to claim that what welfare rights activists "really want and need is a system of family allowances, a system in which the objection that a wage-earner's compensation does not vary with the number of children is obviated by providing it for them, as well as for everyone else."[43]

Pulling no punches, Liebmann directly invoked the laissez-faire principle that "very harsh market forces" operate "as a form of economic discipline." If the courts did not allow the state to impose limits on welfare payments, then the "deep concern" to ensure that welfare payments do not detract from the "incentive to work" would require "some even more direct form of coercion or compulsion of labor." These "ideological" justifications were sufficient to demonstrate that the maximum grant was reasonable and not irrational, which was all that was required. Finally, Liebmann rebutted the importance of the stipulated facts about the Gary and Williams cases, conjecturing that they were "extreme cases," given his certainty that Matera "did not choose his weakest cases when he brought this suit."[44]

What followed was a prolonged skirmish regarding the question whether the federal government had approved the state's maximum family grant. After additional research and evidentiary wrangling, Matera and Liebmann entered into a second stipulation of facts concluding that no statement of federal approval or disapproval of the state's maximum grant regulation had come to their attention. Their stipulations put the ball back in the court of the three-judge panel. The judges analyzed the legislative record in considerable detail and concluded that Congress had not endorsed the maximum grant with "unmistakable clarity." But, rather than order additional presentation of evidence, the panel simply withdrew its prior conclusion that the maximum grant violated federal law.[45]

Liebmann considered the three-judge panel's second opinion to have been written in "bad grace," in part because it criticized the state's lawyers for filing a multifaceted motion asking for the consideration of newly discovered evidence with no compelling excuse as to why these exhibits were not previously brought to the court's attention. Liebmann was upset that the second opinion was not clear "about which lawyer it was chastising." As Liebmann recalls, this second opinion prompted the Maryland attorney general and deputy attorney general to demand a hearing with the three-judge panel in chambers, during which they "read out the judges in such a way that one rarely hears federal judges read out."[46]

No matter, the three-judge panel unequivocally rejected the state's new defense to the constitutional challenge, finding "no merit" in Liebmann's ideological justification for the maximum grant based on the Elizabethan-era "principle of less benefit."[47] The judges painstakingly restated Liebmann's arguments, noting that each applied, at best, to subcategories of AFDC recipients, and that "alone or in combination," they had no logical connection with the group of recipients as a whole and therefore the regulation was "invalid on its face for overreaching." The goal of discouraging desertion had no application to situations involving dependency because of death, unemployment, or incapacity of the wage earner, as in the case of Junius and Jeanette Gary. Because Maryland allowed benefits in excess of the maximum if children were placed outside the family, the panel found this had the effect of subverting the statutory goal of preserving the family unit intact. Similarly, they found that the goal of encouraging employment was irrelevant to AFDC beneficiaries, such as Junius and Jeanette Gary, who were not employable. Acknowledging the possible legitimate interest in encouraging employment, the court concluded this goal could be advanced by work incentives aimed at employable beneficiaries. Moreover, the panel found that the goal of encouraging limitation of family size was "diffidently pressed" and irrelevant to families like the Gary and Williams families whose children were all born before they became eligible for AFDC benefits. Finding the maximum grant "either totally inapplicable or patently ineffective" to the claimed purposes, the panel concluded the regulation violated equal protection because it cut "too broad a swatch on an indiscriminate basis as applied to the entire group" of those eligible for AFDC.

The Battle Moves to the Supreme Court

The briefs before the Supreme Court largely reprised the ideological battle waged during the district court hearings between Liebmann and Judge Winter. Liebmann's brief for the state invoked the "fear of a cycle of dependency" inherited from the philosophy underlying the British poor laws and detailed the extensive pedigree of maximum grants in Maryland and other states. Liebmann also quoted extensively from several exhibits he submitted before the district court, especially the 1948 state commission report noting a concern "to keep the public assistance grant from exceeding the earnings available to a comparable family which is self-supporting" and the 1967 state legislative committee report expressing concern that the high benefit level is "partly responsible" for discouraging employment.[48] Liebmann again asserted that Maryland's maximum bore "a clear relationship to the minimum wage rate," and he framed the district court's decision as having found the maximum void under equal protection "only for 'overbreadth.'"

Liebmann's brief for the state then turned to four major arguments. First,

Liebmann argued that the overbreadth doctrine, presumably borrowed from First Amendment jurisprudence, was inapplicable to state economic legislation. Second, he argued that the record did not support the district court's assumption that the maximum would subvert the goal of preserving intact families, given that "sociological treatises" and "newspaper accounts" had claimed that the availability of welfare benefits was to blame for encouraging fathers to desert families. Third, Liebmann argued that the traditional "reasonable basis" standard governed, quoting at length from the *Snell* decision. Finally, he argued that the maximum grant was supported by four rational bases: encouraging employment, maintaining equity between welfare and wage earning families, encouraging responsible procreation, and avoiding the harm of across-the-board cuts to welfare benefits. Liebmann noted that "certain groups" prefer welfare to work, necessitating some semblance of an "economic whip."

On behalf of the Gary and Williams families and the class they represented, Matera responded that the maximum grant bore "no rational relation to a valid state objective" and was "arbitrary and unreasonable discrimination invalid under traditional concepts of equal protection." He contended that the record established that the regulation "neither encourages employable recipients to seek employment nor promotes family unity by discouraging desertion." Matera also contended that the court should apply more demanding scrutiny because the maximum grant infringed fundamental rights to marital privacy, procreation, and the right to life, and created a "suspect classification" based on the status of dependent children in a large family.[49]

Matera countered the state's brief with his own list of famous rational basis cases going as far back as the late nineteenth century, emphasizing that the government's classification "must always rest upon some difference which bears a reasonable and just relation to the act in respect to which the classification is proposed, and can never be made arbitrarily and without any such basis."[50] He then argued that the maximum grant was irrational and counterproductive to some of these purposes, noting that the federal Social Security Act directly incentivizes and compels AFDC beneficiaries to seek employment, which rendered the state's maximum grant "unrelated" to this objective. Conceding that welfare classifications need not be made with "mathematical nicety," Matera nonetheless argued that the maximum was grossly overinclusive because it applied to beneficiaries like the Gary and Williams families, which contained no employable adult, and defectively underinclusive because all AFDC families, not merely large families, should be encouraged to work.[51]

Matera conceded the legitimacy of increasing family stability and cohesiveness, but argued that the maximum grant created pressures to fragment families by incentivizing placing children outside the home. Matera also countered the state's claim that welfare benefits encouraged fathers to desert their families with a 1966 legislative report showing that only 15.2 percent of AFDC families were eligible due to parental desertion. He contended it would be unreasonable for the state to penalize 85 percent of beneficiaries, including Junius and Jeanette Gary, to reach this small fraction.

Matera then argued that even if discouraging procreation were a permissible state objective, the maximum grant was not reasonably related to discouraging child bearing because it penalized large families, such as the Gary and Williams families, that had borne all of their children prior to making application for AFDC. He suggested, however, that if discouraging child bearing was the basis for the regulation, then more demanding special scrutiny should be applied because the regulation would infringe the fundamental rights of procreation and marital privacy. Moreover, it would be invidious discrimination to discourage child bearing only of families poor enough to qualify for public assistance, and would punish innocent children for the acts of their parents. Further, he asserted that saving welfare costs is not a sufficient or independent ground for an invidious classification.[52]

But Matera did not take the state's bait to frame the case as about a fundamental right to welfare: "The State's cryptic suggestion that it may withhold benefits from large families to discourage procreation because there is no general right to public assistance is the same tired assertion of arbitrary power condemned by this Court in a long line of cases." In support, Matera cited numerous cases in which the Supreme Court had ruled that even though there was no independent constitutional right to public assistance, the state could not condition public assistance upon the surrender of constitutional rights.[53]

Matera also argued for heightened scrutiny, not only because of fundamental liberty rights affected, but also because it contained a suspect classification of children in large families. He concluded with a lengthy section explaining that the maximum grant violated the AFDC program's primary purposes of strengthening family life and providing assistance to all eligible individuals, and he denied that the federal government had approved Maryland's maximum grant regulation.[54]

In the state's reply brief, Liebmann rehearsed his primary ideological claim that the case involved the power of the government to design welfare programs with an eye toward the effects upon "the labor force, family solidarity, and the growth of population." As he put it, "Enough has been said to show that reasonable men can believe that the principle of less benefit can play a part in the design of public assistance programs in a society in which the private sector of the economy remains paramount."[55]

California filed a short amicus curiae brief supporting Maryland, but its argument seemed to lend support to Matera's claim that the primary reason behind the maximum grant was saving welfare costs: "California and its counties are facing a taxpayer's revolt largely due to soaring costs of the health and welfare programs."[56] At oral argument, Matera again emphasized this point, noting that the only witness the state called testified that the purpose of the maximum grant was to conserve state funds.

The Center Weighs In

Although Ed Sparer had moved on to teach at the University of Pennsylvania, lawyers for the Center on Social Welfare Policy and Law made sure to weigh in with an amicus brief.[57] The Center reminded the justices that its lawyers had argued both *Goldberg v. Kelly* and *Rosado v. Wyman* during the same 1969–1970 term of the Court.[58] Emphasizing the regulation's lack of a rational justification, the Center also urged that a "searching appraisal" is required "because of the fundamental importance of public assistance, the powerlessness of AFDC children, the effect of the maximum on the maintenance of an intact family unit and the classification of children based on parental conduct over which they have no control." Underscoring the right to life, the Center did not refer to older natural-law sources but instead cited language from recent lower federal courts regarding the "brutal need" for public assistance, and argued that the ability to obtain food, clothing and shelter was "fundamental to the very existence and survival of the race," even more than the right to procreation recognized in *Skinner v. Oklahoma.*[59] The Center added an intriguing new argument that the "elemental importance" of public assistance benefits produced their status as "fundamental human rights."[60]

The Lawyers Get Their Day Before the Supreme Court

At oral argument, both Liebmann and Matera tracked the arguments they made in their briefs. Liebmann explained that any additional money required by elimination of the maximum would have to come from state funds, and he emphasized the importance of the work incentive, the undesirability of establishing benefit levels higher than prevailing wage rates in the community, and the incentive for the male head of the family to remain at home to provide sufficient support.[61]

Matera focused on the two classes created by the maximum grant regulation, claiming that a state could not treat needy children in a large family differently than needy children of a small family on the arbitrary basis of family size. He emphasized that the children of the Gary and Williams families each would have been entitled to receive $65 per month if they were placed outside the home, which undermined the AFDC program's purpose of keeping families together and ensuring that all eligible individuals receive assistance. Re-emphasizing the poor fit of the regulation, he noted that less onerous alternatives of achieving the state's interests were available, such as the federal government's new work incentive program. He made no mention, however, of any right to life claim or any right to welfare or any heightened scrutiny based on poverty itself.[62]

But one troubling exchange occurred when Justice Thurgood Marshall struggled to understand the equal protection argument. He noted that the younger children in families with maximums would "eat along with the rest; it just means that everybody would eat less." Matera agreed, but emphasized that a welfare parent might send one or more children to be placed elsewhere rather than live on meager rations. Justice Marshall replied that Matera would "have to establish that this is basic subsistence and nothing else will do. Otherwise, I have trouble with the equal protection argument."[63] As Martha Davis has noted, Matera and his colleagues "were naturally disturbed by this dialogue." If their equal protection argument "did not even convince Marshall, one of their staunchest supporters on the Court, would any of the justices accept the argument that life and death subsistence issues were at stake?"[64]

The Supreme Court Decides

From the first sentence of the majority opinion, it was clear that the state had won the day. Justice Potter Stewart framed the case as involving "the validity of a method used by Maryland, in the administration of an aspect of its public welfare program, to reconcile the demands of its needy citizens with the finite resources available to meet those demands." After describing the operation of the maximum family grant, Justice Stewart considered whether the "per capita diminution" violated federal law governing the AFDC program. The majority saw "nothing in the federal statute that forbids a State to balance the stresses that uniform insufficiency of payments would impose on all families against the greater ability of large families—because of the inherent economies of scale—to accommodate their needs to diminished per capita payments." While the majority found that farming out of children might attenuate the family tie, it could not be destroyed. Noting plaintiffs' concession that the state could proportionately reduce benefits for all families, which would reduce aid below the standard of need for all Maryland recipients, Justice Stewart concluded that providing at least some aid to all eligible children in large families satisfied the AFDC requirement of furnishing aid "with reasonable promptness to all eligible individuals."[65]

Justice Stewart dispatched a spare equal protection analysis in short course. Conceding that a state may not "impose a regime of invidious discrimination," and that the maximum grant regulation resulted in "some disparity in grants of welfare payments to the largest AFDC families," he squarely rejected the district court's use of the First Amendment's doctrine of "overreaching," which had no place in a case dealing with "state regulation in the social and economic field, not affecting freedoms guaranteed by the Bill of Rights."[66]

With a series of quotations and citations from well-known rational basis cases mostly tracking the district court opinion in *Snell v. Wyman*, Stewart noted: (1) that invalidation for overreaching would be "far too reminiscent" of the judicial activism of the *Lochner* era, which had "long ago passed into history"; (2) that a classification would not be invalidated because it was "not made with mathematical nicety or because in practice it results in some inequality"; (3) that the practical problems of government allow "rough accommodations—illogical, it may be, and unscientific"; and (4) that a "statutory discrimination will not be set aside if any state of facts reasonably may be conceived to justify it."[67]

Justice Stewart conceded that these cited cases involved state regulation of business or industry while *Dandridge* involved "the dramatically real factual difference" of "the most basic economic needs of impoverished human beings."[68] But he noted that the majority could "find no basis for applying a different constitutional standard," given no claim of "racially discriminatory purpose or effect" that might have made the maximum family grant "inherently suspect."[69]

Turning to the case, Stewart found it "enough that a solid foundation for the regulation can be found in the State's legitimate interest in encouraging employment and in avoiding discrimination between welfare families and the families of the working poor."[70] Two features of Maryland's program were noteworthy: first, the combination of the maximum grant "with permission to retain money earned, without reduction in the amount of the grant," provided an employment incentive, and second, the state's "keying of the maximum family AFDC grants to the minimum wage a steadily employed head of a household receives" maintained "some semblance of an equitable balance" between welfare and bread-winning families.[71] To the claims of overinclusion and underinclusion, Stewart replied that equal protection does not require states to "choose between attacking every aspect of a problem or not attacking the problem at all," so long as the maximum grant regulation was "rationally based and free from invidious discrimination."[72]

In his final paragraph, Justice Stewart wrote his most far-reaching words. No matter whether the maximum grant program was wise, he opined, "the intractable economic, social, and even philosophical problems presented by public welfare assistance programs are not the business of this Court." He concluded that "the Constitution does not empower this Court to second-guess state officials charged with the difficult responsibility of allocating limited public welfare funds among the myriad of potential recipients."[73] These were ironic words, given that Maryland's welfare officials actually didn't support the maximum grant restriction or Liebmann's justification of it, and all the state's first lawyer had asked was to let state officials decide what was good public policy.

Conclusion

Reflecting on his victory in *Dandridge*, George Liebmann believes that "[m]ost people didn't understand [the case's] significance" and laments that the maximum grant regulations were repealed after the New Deal–era social workers "were replaced by neophytes."[74] The only "backlash" he encountered was from the plaintiffs' lawyers: they "glared daggers" at him because he had "snatched" victory from them. He had been "reasonably confident they would decide for the state" because he couldn't see Justices Douglas, Black, and White, "who had so prominently defended New Deal legislation," invalidating state economic laws on constitutional grounds.[75] With these three plus the Republicans, he thought he "had a good chance, even though the decision came as a surprise to many." He is glad he won because a different outcome could have been used by "any sympathetic judge" to overturn the will of the people and because "power of the purse must be a legislative function." "Even if the plaintiffs had been successful," he claims, "the political action against forced appropriations would have been strong, because they were providing welfare funds for relatively unpopular groups."[76]

On the other hand, three years after the loss in *Dandridge*, Ed Sparer pointedly criticized those who brought this lawsuit:

> A far better case would have been one from Mississippi where the grant was only $108 and the state was well known as racist. But the Maryland case was brought by lawyers who appeared to want nothing to do with the Center and after they had won in the trial court, the decision to go on to the Supreme Court of the United States was in the hands of Maryland, not the plaintiffs.[77]

Some have argued that this litigation was not ripe because the constitutional claim was undertheorized. But during the 1940s, 1950s, and 1960s, Professor Jacobus tenBroek had provided the theoretical framework to justify heightened scrutiny for governmental regulation of poor people.[78] And because *Dandridge* was such a decisive defeat, it is easy to assume the Court decided that poor people are not a suspect class or that poverty is not a suspect classification. But a close reading of the record does not support this assertion. Nowhere in the decision did the Court address the questions of whether the government's classification based on poverty or treatment of poor people might be suspect or whether there was a right to basic subsistence. Indeed the Court went so far as to note that lawyers for plaintiffs were not arguing for any such right.

In his *Dandridge* dissent, Justice Marshall decried "the Court's sweeping refusal to accord the Equal Protection Clause any role in this entire area of the law."[79] We are left to wonder whether Ed Sparer was right when, in his critique of the litigation, he suggested that "affirmative judicial scrutiny to guarantee equal protection could have led to a different America."[80] Perhaps that other America could have required a better fit between the welfare program's ends and its means, with the simple goal of reducing the government's rough treatment of the Gary family and so many like them, who otherwise endure under the heavy yoke of grinding poverty.

Notes

The author thanks USF law graduate Sarah Schulze for her research assistance and USF law librarian John Shafer for his sleuthing skills.

1. Susan E. Lawrence, The Poor in Court: The Legal Services Program and Supreme Court Decision Making 128–32 (1990).

2. Dandridge v. Williams, 397 U.S. 471, 487 (1970).

3. Edwards v. California, 314 U.S. 160, 174–77 (1941).

4. Griffin v. Illinois, 351 U.S. 12, 23–24 (1956) (Frankfurter, J., concurring).

5. Harper v. Va. Bd. of Elections, 383 U.S. 663, 668 (1966).

6. Shapiro v. Thompson, 394 U.S. 618, 633 (1969).

7. Goldberg v. Kelly, 397 U.S. 254, 264–65 (1970).

8. James v. Valtierra, 402 U.S. 137, 145 (1971) (Marshall, J., dissenting).

9. Julie A. Nice, *No Scrutiny Whatsoever: Deconstitutionalization of Poverty Law, Dual Rules of Law, & Dialogic Default*, 35 FORDHAM URBAN L.J. 629 (2008).

10. The first named plaintiff in the litigation was Linda Williams, the mother of eight children who became dependent on Aid to Families with Dependent Children after her husband deserted the family following the birth of their last child. Many details about plaintiffs were included in documents compiled in the appendix filed on May 19, 1969, with the United States Supreme Court (hereafter "Appendix"). *See* Appendix at 5–16, 71–75.

11. The three oldest children of Junius and Jeanette Gary graciously shared the information about their family that was not part of the record in the litigation. Interviews of Anthony Gary (November 21, 2013) and Junius Jr., Cathy, and Anthony Gary (November 22, 2013) are on file with me, and I am sincerely grateful to each of them for their assistance.

12. Appendix at 71–75.

13. The quotations from the Gary family are taken from the interviews described, *supra* note 11.

14. Rhonda Y. Williams, *"To Challenge the Status Quo by Any Means": Community Action and Representational Politics in 1960s Baltimore, in* THE WAR ON POVERTY: A NEW GRASSROOTS HISTORY, 1964–1980, at 63–64 (Annelise Orleck & Lisa Gayle Hazirjian eds., 2011).

15. FRANCES FOX PIVEN & RICHARD A. CLOWARD, REGULATING THE POOR: THE FUNCTIONS OF PUBLIC WELFARE 321–22 (1971, 1993 paperback edition).

16. FRANCES FOX PIVEN & RICHARD A. CLOWARD, POOR PEOPLE'S MOVEMENTS: WHY THEY SUCCEED, HOW THEY FAIL 276–78 (1977, 1979 paperback edition).

17. FELICIA KORNBLUH, THE BATTLE FOR WELFARE RIGHTS: POLITICS AND POVERTY IN MODERN AMERICA 33–38 (2007).

18. ELIZABETH BUSSIERE, (DIS)ENTITLING THE POOR: THE WARREN COURT, WELFARE RIGHTS, AND THE AMERICAN POLITICAL TRADITION 84 (1997).

19. Appendix at 148–49.

20. George W. Collins, *Danny Gant Is Leaving CORE's Target City*, BALTIMORE AFRO-AMERICAN, Aug. 6, 1968, at 1.

21. Edward V. Sparer, *Social Welfare Law Testing*, THE PRACTICAL LAWYER 13 (April 1966).

22. *Id.* at 21–22, quoting Collins v. State Bd. of Social Welfare, 81 N.W.2d 4, 9 (Iowa 1957).

23. *Id.* at 22.

24. *Id.* at 5–24.

25. *Id.* at 10.

26. *Id.* at 31 (quoting McLaughlin v. Florida, 379 U.S. 184, 189 (1964) and citing Yick Wo v. Hopkins, 118 U.S. 356 (1886)).

27. Matera's argument is available at Appendix 31–45, citing Griswold v. Connecticut, 381 U.S. 479 (1965).

28. BUSSIERE, *supra* note 18, at 147–48.

29. *Id.*at 109.

30. *Id.* at 95.

31. Appendix at 70–71.

32. For DeCosta's memorandum, see *id.* at 55–56, 67–69 (quoting from Snell v. Wyman, 281 F. Supp. 853 (S.D.N.Y. 1968)).

33. These references to Schmidt's testimony can be found at Appendix at 76–79, 82–83.

34. *Id.* at 83–87.

35. *Id.* at 99.

36. Brief for Appellees at 15 n.5, Dandridge v. Williams, 397 U.S. 471 (1970) (hereafter "Brief for Appellees").

37. Interview of George Liebmann (April 23, 2013) (hereafter "Liebmann Interview").

38. Appendix at 100–194.

39. These examples of troubling assumptions are available, in the order mentioned, at 200–201, 180, 182, 115, 120, 156, 115, 128, 135.

40. The quotations in this colloquy between Judge Winter and Liebmann appear in the Appendix at 195–96.

41. *Id.* at 196–97.

42. *Id.* at 198–99.

43. *Id.*at 200.

44. *Id.* at 200–201.

45. *Id.*at 214, 238–52.

46. *Id.* at 238–39.

47. The quotations from the court opinion can be found in Appendix at 252–56.

48. For Liebmann's arguments described in these paragraphs, see Brief of Appellants, Dandridge v. Williams, 397 U.S. 471 (1970) (hereafter "Brief of Appellants") at 7, 11, 15, 17, 18, 21–41, 33–36.

49. Brief for the Appellees at 9–17.

50. *Id.* at 16–17. The Court's long record of reviewing the practical, contextual operation of regulation under rational basis review is analyzed in Julie A. Nice, *Whither the Canaries: On the Exclusion of Poor People from Equal Constitutional Protection*, 60 DRAKE L. REV. 1023 (2012).

51. Brief for the Appellees at 20–27.

52. *Id.* at 27–35.

53. *Id.* at 33.

54. *Id.* at 36–63.

55. Reply Brief for the Appellants at 22, Dandridge v. Williams, 397 U.S. 471 (1970).

56. Brief of the State of California Amicus Curiae Supporting Appellants, Dandridge v. Williams, 397 U.S. 471 (1970) (No. 131), 1969 WL 119894 at 2.

57. BUSSIERE, *supra* note 18, at 107, 146.

58. Brief for the Center on Social Welfare Policy and Law, et al. as Amici Curiae Supporting Appellants, Dandridge v. Williams, 397 U.S. 471 (1970), 1969 WL 119897 at 2.

59. See Skinner v. State of Oklahoma, *ex. rel.* Williamson, 316 U.S. 535 (1942).

60. Brief, *supra* note 58, at 16–18.

61. Transcript of oral argument available at http://www.oyez.org.

62. *Id.*

63. *Id.*

64. MARTHA F. DAVIS, BRUTAL NEED: LAWYERS AND THE WELFARE RIGHTS MOVEMENT, 1960–1973 131 (1993). Justice Marshall ended up dissenting, reasoning in part that the maximum grant was so grossly overinclusive and underinclusive that it failed even the minimal rationality test. 397 U.S. at 526–30 (Marshall, J., dissenting).

65. *Dandridge*, 397 U.S. at 472, 478–81.

66. *Id.* at 483–84.

67. *Id.* at 484–85 (quoting from Williamson v. Lee Optical of Oklahoma, Inc., 348 U.S. 483, 488 (1955); Lindsley v. Natural Carbonic Gas Co., 220 U.S. 61, 78 (1911); Metropolis Theater Co v. City of Chicago, 228 U.S. 61, 69–70 (1913); and McGowan v. Maryland, 366 U.S. 420, 426 (1961)).

68. 397 U.S. at 485.

69. *Id.* at 486 n.17.

70. *Id.* at 486.

71. *Id.*

72. *Id.* at 486–87.

73. *Id.* at 487.

74. Liebmann interview.

75. Liebmann interview. Liebmann's assumption misjudged Justice Douglas, who had carefully hewed the line between protecting poor people from governmental discrimination while avoiding interference with business regulation. *See* Nice, *supra* note 50, at 1045–46. Justice Douglas dissented in *Dandridge* on statutory grounds. 397 U.S. at 490–508 (Douglas, J., dissenting).

76. Liebmann interview.

77. LAWRENCE, *supra* note 1, at 50 (quoting interview of Ed Sparer by Jack Greenberg on September 16, 1973).

78. *See* Nice, *supra* note 9, at 655–56, 658 n.117.

79. 397 U.S. at 509 (Marshall, J., dissenting).

80. DAVIS, *supra* note 64, at 133 (quoting from Edward V. Sparer, *The Right to Welfare*, in THE RIGHTS OF AMERICANS 82 (Norman Dorsen ed., 1971).

Privacy as a Luxury Not for the Poor

Wyman v. James • (1971)

MICHELE ESTRIN GILMAN

In the spring of 1969, Barbara James walked into a neighborhood legal services office and spoke to attorney David Gilman.[1] She told him that she received welfare to support herself and her son Maurice. Her caseworker had recently advised her that she had to submit to a home visit as part of the welfare recertification process. In response, James offered to provide documentation to the Department of Social Services (DSS) to demonstrate her eligibility, but she did not want a caseworker coming to her door. She had attended meetings of a welfare rights organization, where she learned that she might be able to fight the home visit policy. James' concerns were widely shared among welfare mothers. At community meetings, welfare recipients regularly told Gilman that caseworkers were searching their homes and "counting toothbrushes to see if there was a man in the house." While some caseworkers were perfunctory in their searches of applicants' homes, others were very aggressive. James asked Gilman to help her fight the city's home visit policy. He took the case, which ultimately ended up in the Supreme Court. In *Wyman v. James*, the Court upheld New York's home visit policy and cemented the differential treatment between the privacy rights of the poor and other Americans, a divide that continues today.

Background: The History of Surveillance of the Poor

Historically, the poor have had less privacy—in their personal information, bodies and homes, and decision making—than their wealthier counterparts.

In colonial America, an "overseer of the poor" tracked the poor and auctioned off them for cheap labor. By the 1900s, the poor were housed in poorhouses, where the "keeper" enforced strict behavioral rules and work requirements. In the late 1900s, the scientific charity movement relied on "friendly visitors" to investigate the homes of the poor and provide them with moral and religious uplift. In each of these forms of poor relief, the lives of the poor were scrutinized and evaluated by outsiders. Then and now, surveillance systems serve to sort the poor into categories of deserving and undeserving, to stigmatize and isolate the poor, and to repress their collective action.[2]

These localized systems gave way to the modern system of welfare benefits in the early twentieth century, when progressive reformers convinced states to adopt mother's pensions. These programs provided aid to "suitable" single women, mostly white widows, so that they could raise their children at home.[3] Mother's pensions were federalized in the New Deal in the form of Aid to Dependent Children (ADC, later renamed Aid to Families with Dependent Children, or AFDC). The New Deal laid the foundations of the modern welfare state, and despite its progressive origins, it reinforced the deserving/undeserving paradigm in poor relief by treating relief for white men differently than relief for minorities and women. Social insurance programs designed for white working men, such as Social Security and unemployment insurance, have carried no stigma, provided generous benefits pursuant to objective criteria, and have been federally administered. By contrast, cash assistance programs such as AFDC, which disproportionately serve women and minorities, became stingy, stigmatized, state-administered, and discretionary. Even today, public programs are grounded in policy that punishes women who do not fit the patriarchal norm of a married, two-parent family with a male breadwinner.[4] Privacy invasions are a primary tactic for stigmatizing welfare and single motherhood.[5]

Indeed, over the decades, states adopted a variety of discretionary and moralistic policies to reduce the welfare rolls and to push black women into the low-wage labor force. These included man-in-the-house and "substitute father" rules that forbade welfare recipients from living with men, "suitable home" requirements that judged the moral fitness of recipients, and midnight raids by social service investigators to catch violators.[6]

The Welfare Rights Movement and the Push for Privacy

In the mid-1960s, a vibrant welfare rights movement flourished in which poor, mostly black, women asserted their political and economic rights and attempted to reform the nation's welfare system.[7] The welfare rights movement addressed economic deprivation in ways that the civil rights and feminist movements failed to do. In 1967, local grassroots welfare organizations from across the country coalesced to form the National Welfare Rights Organization (NWRO) under the leadership of George Wiley, a prominent African American chemistry professor turned social justice activist. Over the following decade, the NWRO fought for adequate income and dignity through sit-ins, demonstrations, protests, rent strikes, and advocacy before Congress and federal agencies. The movement gave voice to welfare mothers as they resisted a dehumanizing welfare system that devalued their work as mothers and their role as citizens. Barbara James was part of this movement.

Simultaneously, poverty lawyers were stretching their own boundaries.[8] Traditionally, legal services lawyers represented individual clients in discrete cases, which they rarely pushed to trial. Yet a group of lawyers lead by Edward Sparer changed this paradigm starting in the mid-1960s, inspired by the legal strategies and successes of the NAACP Legal Defense Fund. At the Mobilization for Youth Legal Office and the Center for Welfare, Social Policy, and the Law, these lawyers wielded litigation to change the law, empower the poor, and eliminate poverty. In a 1965 law review article, Sparer identified the "right to privacy and protection from illegal search" as part of bill of rights for welfare recipients that could be obtained through litigation.[9] His ultimate goal and that of his colleagues was to get the Supreme Court to recognize a right to live, that is, a constitutional right to welfare. Together, the welfare rights movement and their lawyers engaged in organizing and litigation through a planned series of test cases. They challenged a bevy of restrictive welfare policies, such as low benefits amounts, unfair hearings, and limited work opportunities. David Gilman recalls having "about three hours of sleep between 1965 and 1970" as he met with clients and attended fair hearings during the day and engaged in community education and organizing in poor neighborhoods into the wee hours of the morning. As he says, "it was an incredible time." It was during this heady era of social change that Barbara James met with Gilman to challenge the indignity of her scheduled home visit.

The Case Begins: Resistance to Home Visits

As described above, James decided to challenge her caseworker's decision to terminate her welfare benefits if James refused to permit a home visit. On May 13, 1969, DSS sent James a notice of intent to discontinue welfare assistance because she refused to allow a home visit, and her benefits were terminated. On May 16, James retained David Gilman of the Mobilization for Youth Legal Services Unit as her lawyer. On May 27, 1969, James attended a welfare hearing with Gilman, her two-year-old son Maurice, and a representative of the National Welfare Rights Organization. At the hearing, she reiterated that she was willing to cooperate with her caseworker's request for information regarding her eligibility, as long as those discussions did not occur in her home. Gilman stressed that to permit home visits jeopardized James' constitutional right to privacy. Nevertheless, on June 2, 1969, DSS ruled in favor of the caseworker and terminated James' benefits.

The Southern District of New York Enjoins Home Visits

On June 6, 1969, James' legal team filed a complaint in the United States District Court for the Southern District of New York on behalf of a class composed of needy parents and their dependent children residing in the State of New York and eligible to receive AFDC benefits. The complaint alleged that home visits violated the Constitution's privacy protections.

The complaint was accompanied by affidavits from twelve additional welfare recipients, each of whom asserted that she rarely knew when the caseworker was coming until the telltale knock on the door.[10] In boilerplate language, the women stated that "[i]t's very embarrassing to me if the caseworker comes when I have company. Sometimes the worker interviews me in front of my company and sometimes he even asks questions of the people who are visiting me." Moreover, caseworkers often asked questions in front of their children about personal matters. As the affiants asserted, "I'm resentful and embarrassed when a worker looks around my house or asks questions of my children or of people visiting me." Yet each affiant stated that she permitted the caseworkers access to her home "because I feel I have no choice." Not only would denying the home visit result in the termination of benefits, but it could also anger the caseworker, and "I cannot afford to have my caseworker angry at me because I am so dependent on him" for a variety of social services.

In their answers to the complaint, the defendants contended that home visits were not only required by federal law but also limited in scope so as to respect the privacy interests of welfare recipients. As Eleanor Walsh, deputy commissioner of the State Department of Social Services, stated, "the successful administration of a plan of public assistance without home visits is difficult to conceive." For the city, Jack Goldberg, the commissioner of social services of the City of New York, assured the court that "[c]aseworkers are instructed not to enter a home of an applicant or recipient by force, under false pretenses, or without permission, and not to make a search of the home by looking into closets and drawers."

Judge Charles Tenney held a show cause hearing on June 13, 1969. He was a Kennedy appointee who had previously served as corporation counsel for New York City, as well as deputy mayor. Judge Tenney approved the class certification and issued a temporary restraining order that enjoined DSS from denying or terminating AFDC based upon refusal to permit a home visit. Judge Tenney ruled that significant constitutional questions were at stake, irreparable harm would result from a denial of the restraining order, and thus a three-judge district court needed to be convened.[11]

Convincing the Three-Judge Court

The three-judge court was convened on June 30, 1969, consisting of Judges Tenney and Edward McLean of the Southern District of New York District Court, and Judge Wilfred Feinberg of the Second Circuit Court of Appeals. Judge McLean was also a Kennedy appointee with experience in private practice and the district attorney's office. Judge Feinberg was a former district court judge and Kennedy appointee who was elevated to the Second Circuit in 1966 by President Johnson and who was widely admired for his fairness and intelligence.[12] He had previously written the three-judge panel decision that was subsequently affirmed by the Supreme Court in *Goldberg v. Kelly*, holding that termination of welfare benefits without a prior hearing violated due process. In that decision, Judge Feinberg borrowed the phrase "brutal need"—later appropriated by Justice Brennan in *Goldberg*—to describe the importance of welfare for recipients. Moreover, while in law school in the late 1940s, Judge Feinberg had written a law review article surveying the emerging law of privacy.[13] Thus when James appeared before the panel, Judge Feinberg was well steeped in both welfare law and privacy law.

At oral argument, Gilman contended that if a welfare recipient refused to consent to a search, the caseworker "has to go and get a warrant like everyone else has to go and get a warrant who is conducting an administrative search," such as a fire inspector or a health inspector. Indeed, the Supreme Court had previously ruled that health and fire inspectors could not conduct administrative searches without a warrant. Surely the sanctity of the home demanded equal, if not more, protection. Judge McLean pushed Gilman on the warrant requirement, asking, "Why shouldn't they have right to go in and see whether this is a decent home or not without knowledge of what they are going to find before they go there?"

Brenda Soloff argued for the state that home visits were reasonable and necessary; "we want to make sure that is where you are living, we want to make sure that the services that you are getting are sufficient, we want to make sure that the child is all right." Judge Feinberg asked her if the Internal Revenue Service (IRS) "would have a right to send an investigatory into your house to find out if your claim of an exception is a proper one." Soloff responded by emphasizing the need to ensure the health and well-being of the children in welfare families. Judge Tenney commented that it might be easier for DSS to skip obtaining warrants, but "[t]here are a lot of things that can be done easily. The trouble is some of them do infringe on constitutional rights. It would be great if we could do a lot of things that we are circumscribed to doing today, but are circumscribed because we have a Constitution."

On August 18, 1969, the three-judge panel ruled, with Judge McLean dissenting, that the home visit policy was unconstitutional.[14] Writing for the majority, Judge Feinberg held that the home visits were searches, as the Fourth Amendment "governs all intrusions by agents of the public upon personal privacy and security." Further, the court reasoned that even if AFDC grants were privileges rather than rights, the state could not deny "even a gratuitous benefit because of the exercise of a constitutional right." The court returned to the IRS analogy in a footnote, asking, "could it be successfully argued that the right to obtain an income tax exemption for such dependents may lawfully be made dependent upon the taxpayer's consent to the warrantless entry into his home of Internal Revenue Service Agents?" As for the safety of children, there already existed specified procedures for the state to investigate suspected abuse and neglect. The state was thus enjoined from conditioning welfare benefits on consent to a home visit.

In dissent, Judge McLean wrote that home visits were not searches, but rather were essential to assist children. Moreover, warrants would "introduce a hostile arm's length element into the relationship between the welfare worker and the mother of the children, a relationship which can be effective only when it is based upon mutual confidence and trust."

Having lost, the state and City of New York filed a jurisdictional statement for appeal before the Supreme Court, emphasizing the need for home visits in order to carry out AFDC's purposes. Home visits "focus on the child in the home" because "the AFDC child is peculiarly susceptible to the hazards of life, to neglect and even abuse, not necessarily for want of love, but for want of means." The Court granted review.

The Supreme Court Takes the Case

James' legal team was optimistic as they headed to the Supreme Court, given their victories below. Still, Sparer's overall test case strategy was facing mixed success. To be sure, the Court had recently recognized the due process right to a fair hearing before termination of welfare benefits (*Goldberg v. Kelly*, 1970) and had previously struck down rules that discriminated among welfare recipients, such as man-in-the-house rules (*King v. Smith*, 1968) and state residency requirements (*Shapiro v. Thompson*, 1969). Yet *Goldberg* soon proved to be the high-water mark of welfare protection. Subsequent attempts to force states to meet the basic financial needs of welfare recipients failed miserably one month later, on April 6, 1970, when the Court issued *Dandridge v. Williams*, holding that welfare laws were subject to lenient rational basis review. It appeared that the Court was pulling back from the implications of *Goldberg* and its emphasis on the brutal need of welfare recipients. But it was not clear where home visits fit in this shifting picture. Unlike *Dandridge*, a ruling for the welfare recipients in *Wyman v. James* would not require the courts to set or enforce minimum standards of financial need and would thus lessen the specter of judicial activism.

The Briefs before the Supreme Court

The Supreme Court briefs in *Wyman v. James* laid out the arguments offered in the district court, highlighting the tension between privacy and security, a theme that continues to pervade modern discussions of privacy. James' lawyers underscored the sanctity of the home and family, the discriminatory impact of home visits on the poor, and recent case law interpreting the Fourth Amendment warrant requirement for administrative searches.

In response, the city and state argued that "there is no substitute for direct personal observation" and pointed to a "particularly grim but forceful example" in which a caseworker's home visit resulted in the discovery of a dead infant. In light of such facts, they claimed that James and the other plaintiffs were exalting the "'privacy' of the mother over the welfare of the child." James was not in a position to do so. As the appellants asserted:

Appellee has never satisfactorily established her initial eligibility for assistance, she has a serious money management problem, and, most important, she has a child who, in the first year of his life, was in the hospital two times, including once with a skull fracture. Appellee has also had complaints to make about the condition of her apartment, some of which were verifiable, and some of which were not.

To this day, it remains unclear how the appellants were permitted to refer to James' social services file after the lower court placed it under seal.

The attorneys for James conceded that crime would be reduced if the government placed television cameras in every home and had the right to unlimited entry, yet the Constitution forbids such searches.

There were two amicus briefs, both in support of James' position. The Legal Aid Society of San Mateo County argued that the searches violated the Fourth Amendment as well as federal regulations. Interestingly, the Social Service Employees Union Local 371, which represented social service staff working in the Department of Social Services in New York City, argued that "the very utility of the home visit is questionable both in theory and in practice," as well as degrading to welfare recipients.

Lawyers from the Center on Social Welfare Policy and Law drafted, but then decided not to file, an amicus brief on behalf of the National Welfare Rights Organization that made a statutory argument regarding home visits. Based on *King v. Smith*, the brief argued that home visits fell outside the two statutory eligibility factors of need and dependency, and were thus in violation of the law. But the lead attorney on the *Wyman* case, Jonathan Weiss, felt strongly that the case should proceed solely on the constitutional theory, and after extensive debate, the lawyers at the center reluctantly decided to pull the brief.[15] Of course, it is impossible to know if the statutory argument would have changed the outcome.

Oral Argument before the Justices

At oral argument, Jonathan Weiss of MFY argued for appellees, while Brenda Soloff continued to represent the State of New York. Much of the argument explored the boundaries of the right to privacy in hypothetical situations. For instance, Justice White asked Weiss whether DSS has to take clients at their word. Weiss responded, "I would say not, Your Honor. No more than the Internal Revenue Service is required to take the word of the taxpayer." The IRS example came up again when Burger asked Weiss if the IRS could view records and financial documents used to justify deductions, even if the taxpayer feels his papers are private. Weiss pointed out that an intrusion into the home is different than providing information, and of course, the IRS could not deny a deduction based on a taxpayer's refusal to permit entry into the home.

Brennan then asked about how welfare home visits compare to plumbing inspections in a tenement. Weiss distinguished the plumbing situation as involving the public safety of others. Justice Burger queried whether social workers can follow up on the well-being of children placed in foster homes. Weiss explained that these visits are permitted while a family is being established, but not afterward.

Although *Goldberg* rejected the conception of welfare as charity, the comparison still stuck with several justices. For instance, Justice Black stated that if someone makes a charitable contribution to a woman's children, it is reasonable for him to visit her home. Weiss responded that "it's reasonable [to say] my home is my private domain, and I do not want people there . . . and it is my choice." Black pushed him further, asking, "I don't want you there even though you support my children?" Weiss answered, "It is not true they support her children. What is true is they supply money, support requires more than money, she supports her children, she raises them, she talks to them, she clothes, them, she feeds them." Perhaps the writing was on the wall when Justice Blackmun asked, "Soloff, am I not correct that the home visit has been established years and years and years as a social service caseworker's method of operating?"

Justice Blackmun's First Decision

The Supreme Court decision upheld the home visits with a vote of 6–3 in favor of the state.[16] *Wyman* was the first decision authored by newly minted Justice Harry Blackmun. He began the opinion by avowing the sanctity of the home and the Fourth Amendment's warrant requirement. He wrote, however, that such principles were beside the point because a welfare home visit was consensual and thus not a search "in the Fourth Amendment meaning of that term." Moreover, even if the home visits were searches, they were reasonable, given the state's interest in deterring fraud and protecting the public fisc, the need to protect the children of welfare mothers, the rehabilitative purpose of the searches, and the lack of criminal consequences that flowed from the searches. Whereas the *Goldberg* opinion held that welfare benefits were a form of property, the *Wyman* Court compared welfare to a form of charity and that a donor "expects to know how his charitable funds are utilized and put to work."

The Court's opinion also emphasized that the home visits were conducted with advance notice, and that in the home visit policy, "privacy is emphasized" and snooping is forbidden, thereby minimizing any burden on the homeowner's privacy interests. In any event, the opinion went on, "The caseworker is not a sleuth but rather, we trust, is a friend to one in need." This confidence in the caseworker's judgment and ability to respect the recipient's interests was belied in the amicus brief filed by the Social Services Employees Union Local, which stated that "caseworkers are either badly trained or untrained." Yet the Court refused to accredit this admission. Likewise, the Court discounted the affidavits of 12 welfare recipients who asserted that they were subject to unannounced visits and embarrassing searches. Instead, the Court clung to its rosy view that home visits were always rehabilitative in the face of contrary evidence provided by all those involved. To the degree that welfare mothers found personal questions unnecessary and embarrassing, the Court responded that "the same complaint could be made of the census taker's questions."

To further bolster its decision, the Court pulled out information from James' social services case file—the same file the district court had ordered sealed—writing that "the record is revealing as to Mrs. James' failure ever really to satisfy the requirements for eligibility." Based on the case file—and not on any facts adduced at any trial or hearing in the case—the Court went out of its way in footnote 9 to describe James as demanding, reluctant to cooperate, evasive, and belligerent. Moreover, the opinion noted, "[t]here are indications that all was not always well with the infant Maurice (skull fracture, a dent in the head, a possible rat bite). The picture is a sad and unhappy one." The Supreme Court's picture of her completely contradicts the experience of James' lawyers, who remember her as determined, nice, and articulate.[17]

Justice Douglas issued a bitter dissent in *Wyman*, framing "the central question" as "whether the government by force of its largesse has the power to 'buy up' rights guaranteed by the Constitution." He acknowledged, "It may well be that in some tenements one baby will do service to several women and call each one 'Mom,' in order for some women to secure benefits to which they were not entitled." Yet, in his view, the recipients' interest in the right to privacy outweighed any small-scale swindling that might go on by a limited number of recipients. (And notably, there was no evidence in the record about any welfare fraud.) After all, "[i]f the regime under which Barbara James lives were enterprise capitalism as, for example, if she ran a small factory geared into the Pentagon's procurement program, she certainly would have a right to deny inspectors access to her home unless they came with a warrant." In his view, constitutional rights should not hinge on the "poverty or on the affluence of the beneficiary." Instead, "privacy is as important to the lowly as to the mighty."

Justice Marshall also wrote a dissent, joined by Justice Brennan. Marshall disagreed with the majority's characterization of the home visits, pointing out that they were not a "purely benevolent inspection." While caseworkers may be friendly, "they are also required to be sleuths." Indeed, the governments' briefs and oral arguments "emphasized the need to enter AFDC homes to guard against welfare fraud and child abuse, both of which are felonies." He asked:

> Would the majority sanction, in the absence of probable cause, compulsory visits to all American homes for the purpose of discovering child abuse? Or is this Court prepared to hold as a matter of constitutional law that a mother, merely because she is poor, is substantially more likely to injury or exploit her children?

If so, "[s]uch a categorical approach to an entire class of citizens would be dangerously at odds with the tenets of our democracy." As Marshall stated, if the IRS came searching the homes of taxpayers to investigate dependency exemptions, "the cries of constitutional outrage would be unanimous." As for the argument that home visits are not searches, "Surely the majority cannot believe that valid Fourth Amendment consent can be given under the threat of the loss of one's sole means of support."

Reactions in the Court and the Press to the Decision

In later years, Blackmun recalled having "trouble" in writing the decision, and it "took me awhile."[18] Chief Justice Burger wrote to Blackmun after reading the proposed decision: "This is a solid and workmanlike job and an excellent 'opener' for your long season here. More power to the Frankfurter school!" Justice Harlan wrote, "It gives me great pleasure to join your first opinion for the Court, which, if you will allow me to say so, I think is an excellent one."[19] Yet not everyone at the Court admired the decision. Bob Woodward and Scott Armstrong note in *The Brethren*, their behind-the-scenes exposé of the 1970s Supreme Court,[20] that "Stewart was unhappy, but it was Blackmun's first opinion and he wanted to join. Black couldn't understand the opinion, but he too went along. Blackmun 'will learn,' he told his clerks." Tradition was that a justice's first decision would be a unanimous one, but that was obviously not to be. Brennan later apologized to Blackmun for not being able to join the majority.

According to Woodward and Armstrong, the Supreme Court law clerks ridiculed the decision. They report that at a lunch with Blackmun, one of Brennan's clerks said he heard that *Wyman v. James* was going to be used in a law school course titled "Has the Supreme Court Lost Touch with Reality?" The clerk pressed Blackmun on how he could justify the decision. Blackmun explained that James was not even eligible for welfare in the first place. The clerks "were incredulous. Blackmun seemed to think he was still on a lower court, deciding a single case. Didn't he realize that he was creating the law of the land, setting precedent?" Hearing this, "Blackmun's clerks were embarrassed. Clearly if the recipient wasn't eligible for welfare, no precedent-setting decision should have been written."

Martin Spiegel, a lawyer at California Rural Legal Assistance, later wrote a letter to Justice Blackmun assailing footnote 9, the footnote that personally attacked James. He explained that as a legal services lawyer, he regularly faced welfare officials who referred to self-serving welfare case records "in order to find examples of morally reprehensible conduct," which were irrelevant to the legal issues. He feared that footnote 9 would not only encourage future emphasis on morals rather than law, but also decrease the willingness of welfare recipients to fight for their rights, for fear of being embarrassed publicly. He urged that the footnote be deleted.

The *Wyman* decision was widely publicized in the media, and the reaction was mixed. The *New York Times* editorial page supported the decision; the *Washington Post* assailed it. Some viewed the opinion as evidence that Blackmun would fulfill Nixon's desire for a conservative justice; of course, he later emerged as a liberal.

There is some irony in the fact that in *Wyman*, Blackmun wrote that the rights of children outweighed those of their mothers, given that he later authored *Roe v. Wade*, creating a constitutional right to abortion (largely anchored by his deference to the judgment of medical professionals). In *Wyman*, he wrote, "the dependent child's needs are paramount, and only with hesitancy would we relegate those needs, in the scale of comparative values, to a position secondary to what the mother claims as her rights." However, *Wyman* is consistent with Blackmun's often sentimental and emotional response when children were involved. He issued an iconic dissent in *DeShaney v. Winnebago County*, in which the Court majority held that the government has no liability for failing to act to prevent child abuse committed by a parent, even where state officials were aware of the abuse and took steps to assist the child. Blackmun wrote, "Poor Joshua! Victim of repeated attacks by an irresponsible, bullying, cowardly, and intemperate father, and abandoned by respondents, who placed him in a dangerous predicament and who knew or learned what was going on, and yet did essentially nothing." Despite this dissonance, Blackmun later reflected no regret about his decision in *Wyman*, stating he "would vote the same way again. The case served well as a starter."[21]

The Fate of Welfare Privacy Today Under TANF

Starting in the 1950s, the welfare rolls grew tremendously due to successes of the welfare rights movement, changing family structures in society, and economic dislocations that fell disproportionately on minorities. These societal shifts made it harder on states to deny welfare to women of color. In turn, this growth fomented a tremendous backlash that reached a frenzy in the 1980s, as the media and policymakers portrayed welfare mothers as lazy and promiscuous. President Reagan famously stoked stereotypes of AFDC recipients as "welfare queens."[22]

In 1996, AFDC was abolished and replaced with Temporary Assistance for Needy Families (TANF), largely due to the public perception that AFDC was encouraging dependency in welfare mothers and discouraging the formation of two-parent families. Accordingly, TANF abolished the entitlement to welfare, required that welfare recipients work within two years of receiving benefits, and put a five-year lifetime limit on the receipt of welfare benefits.[23]

TANF recipients continue to face the same sorts of stigma and privacy deprivations that were rampant under AFDC, and the advent of new technologies has exacerbated the situation. When a woman applies for and receives TANF, she faces the loss of privacy across multiple dimensions.[24] First, her informational privacy is violated by TANF's extreme verification requirements, which can include demands for highly personal information, such as her sexual relationships. Obviously, a government program must protect the public fisc and ensure that the proper persons are receiving the appropriate levels of benefits, but the data gathered from TANF applicants goes far beyond what is necessary to meet these goals and is often gathered through demeaning techniques.

Second, many jurisdictions invade a welfare applicant's physical privacy through fingerprinting, biometric imaging, DNA testing connected to child support enforcement, drug tests, and of course, home visits. TANF also permits states to invade the decisional privacy of welfare mothers in order to control their behavior in line with middle-class norms. The most controversial of these sexual regulation policies is the imposition of family caps; typically, family caps provide no cash benefit increases for any children conceived while the mother is on welfare.

Low-income Americans experience privacy deprivations in other domains as well, not just in TANF, which is shrinking due to onerous requirements, aggressive sanctioning, and limited state resources. The urban poor live in neighborhoods where cameras track their movements and the police are omnipresent. These realities of geography also mean that poor families are far more likely to become entangled in child welfare and domestic violence investigations. In the workplace, they are more likely than other Americans to be drug tested, psychologically profiled, and videotaped. Poor pregnant patients seeking Medicaid coverage for prenatal health care costs are subject to mandatory interviews that probe the most intimate corners of their lives.[25] The poor face more overt surveillance than their wealthier counterparts.

The Future of *Wyman*

Wyman remains good law, even post-TANF. In *Sanchez v. San Diego*, the plaintiff challenged San Diego's policy of requiring home visits of all welfare applicants who were *not* suspected of fraud or ineligibility.[26] In two unscheduled visits in 2000, an investigator asked plaintiff Sanchez personal questions about her relationship with her husband; they searched her home, including her closets, bathroom cabinets, the bedroom, her dresser drawers, and a trash can; and they questioned her neighbors. Although she was approved for benefits, she was upset by these interrogations and became a plaintiff in a class action lawsuit challenging the constitutionality of home visits.

Ultimately, in *Sanchez v. San Diego*, the Ninth Circuit relied on *Wyman v. James* to uphold the visits, reasoning that "a person's relationship with the state can reduce that person's expectation of privacy, even within the sanctity of the home." The court expressly lumped welfare mothers in with criminals on probation to conclude that neither group has a reasonable expectation of privacy. In holding that *Wyman* was governing precedent, the *Sanchez* court refused to recognize differences between the *Wyman* home visits, which the Supreme Court had characterized as rehabilitative, and San Diego's policy, which was carried out by law enforcement fraud investigators.

Moreover, the *Sanchez* court disregarded thirty years of post-*Wyman* jurisprudence, which has significantly limited suspicionless, administrative searches. The Ninth Circuit also disregarded significant changes to welfare since the 1970s, when it was a means-tested program that came under attack for encouraging welfare dependency. Since 1996, welfare recipients have not only been subject to a five-year lifetime limit on receipt of benefits, but they also must work as a condition of receiving aid. They are fulfilling their part of this new social contract, but the terms still include humiliation and stigma.

In a bitter dissent from the denial of a petition for rehearing en banc, seven Ninth Circuit judges called the case "nothing less than an attack on the poor."[27] As the dissenters stated, most government benefits do not flow to the poor, "yet this is the group we require to sacrifice their dignity and their right to privacy." By contrast, "[t]he government does not search through the closets and medicine cabinets of farmers receiving subsidies. They do not dig through the laundry baskets and garbage pails of real estate developers or radio broadcasters." As the dissenters concluded, "[t]his situation is shameful." The Supreme Court denied certiorari in the case.

The Wider Impact of the *Wyman* Decision

Today, privacy is in the headlines, from National Security Agency surveillance to Facebook privacy settings to Amazon's collection of consumer spending habits. There is a general sense that Orwell's predictions have come to pass and that privacy is dead. Yet the public is conflicted over these privacy deprivations because they trigger competing values. The same people who say they like privacy also value national security, the ability to shop online, and social media. Overall, there is little sustained public outrage over these practices, perhaps because much surveillance is invisible or a minor irritant to most people. Yet this is not necessarily the case for the poor, who face concrete harms from surveillance.

The welfare system of surveillance causes recipients to suffer a myriad of harms. Among them are psychological injuries including stress, fear, and feelings of degradation.[28] Not only is the subject's dignity degraded by surveillance, but society also receives a message that the poor are unworthy. In turn, these stereotypes drive punitive laws directed at the poor. Not surprisingly, the privacy deprivations associated with welfare discourage many needy women from seeking assistance, thus depriving their families of basic goods and services. In addition, welfare receipt today is correlated with lower rates of voting and participation in political affairs, largely because welfare recipients have such negative experiences with the social service bureaucracy, thereby dampening their faith in government responsiveness.[29] In short, privacy matters.

Conclusion

In *Wyman v. James*, the Supreme Court upheld home visits of welfare recipients by the state. In so doing, *Wyman* deemed privacy a luxury for those who can afford it and welfare a form of charity that can be used as a social tool to control the poor. Ironically, the district court's injunction against home visits was never dissolved, and the practice thus ended in New York, a small victory for Ms. James and her fellow welfare mothers. The lawyers who litigated the case remain hopeful that a future generation of poverty lawyers will someday secure the right to privacy for the poor that fell out of their grasp. Until then, welfare recipients remain under the watch of the state.

Notes

1. Interview with David Gilman (June 10, 2013) (transcript on file with author). Much of the narrative outside the case record comes from this interview, which is on file with the author (who is not related to Mr. Gilman).

2. For an excellent overview of the history of privacy and poverty, *see* JOHN GILLIOM, OVERSEERS OF THE POOR: SURVEILLANCE, RESISTANCE, AND THE LIMITS OF PRIVACY 23 (2001).

3. On the gendered nature of AFDC, see MIMI ABRAMOVITZ, REGULATING THE LIVES OF WOMEN: SOCIAL WELFARE POLICY FROM COLONIAL TIMES TO THE PRESENT 313 (1996 rev. ed.); and LINDA GORDON, PITIED BUT NOT ENTITLED: SINGLE MOTHERS AND THE HISTORY OF WELFARE 291 (1994).

4. *See* MARTHA ALBERTSON FINEMAN, THE NEUTERED MOTHER, THE SEXUAL FAMILY AND OTHER TWENTIETH CENTURY TRAGEDIES 106–10 (1995).

5. *See* KAARYN S. GUSTAFSON, CHEATING WELFARE: PUBLIC ASSISTANCE AND THE CRIMINALIZATION OF POVERTY 21 (2011).

6. *See* Charles A. Reich, *Midnight Searches and the Social Security Act*, 72 YALE L.J. 1347 (1963) (describing midnight raids on the homes of welfare recipients, as well as the ensuing criminal consequences).

7. On the welfare rights movement, *see* PREMILLA NADASEN, WELFARE WARRIORS: THE WELFARE RIGHTS MOVEMENT IN THE UNITED STATES (2005); and FELICIA KORNBLUH, THE BATTLE FOR WELFARE RIGHTS: POLITICS AND POVERTY IN MODERN AMERICA (2007).

8. On the history of poverty lawyers in this era, see MARTHA F. DAVIS, BRUTAL NEED: LAWYERS AND THE WELFARE RIGHTS MOVEMENT 1960–1973 (1993).

9. Edward V. Sparer, *Role of the Welfare Client's Lawyer*, 12 UCLA L. REV. 361, 366–67 (1965).

10. The affidavits from which the quotations in these paragraphs are taken were attached to the Complaint, which, along with the other pleadings in the case, are available in the Making of Modern Law research database: APPENDIX. File Date: 5/5/1970, 145 pp., *U.S. Supreme Court Records and Briefs, 1832–1978*, Gale, Cengage Learning, Harvard University.

11. James v. Goldberg, 302 F. Supp. 478, 481 (1969).

12. *See* Maurice Rosenberg, *Chief Judge Wilfred Feinberg: A Twenty-Fifth Year Tribute*, 86 COLUM. L. REV. 1505 (1986).

13. Wilfred Feinberg, *Recent Developments in the Law of Privacy*, 48 COLUM. L. REV. 713 (1948).

14. James v. Goldberg, 303 F. Supp. 935, 943–945 (1969).

15. Interview with Henry Freedman, executive director, National Center for Law and Economic Justice (Sept. 23, 2013) (transcript on file with author).

16. 400 U.S. 309 (1971).

17. Gilman interview, *supra* note 1, and Jonathan Weiss interview, September 25, 2013 (transcript on file with author).

18. The justice's recollections about the opinion are contained in the Justice Harry A. Blackmun Oral History Project: Interviews with Justice Blackmun conducted by Harold Hongju Koh, Yale Law School, July 6, 1994–December 13, 1995, Oral History Transcript, pp. 175–77, http://lcweb2.loc.gov/diglib/blackmun-public/page.html?FOLDERID=D0901&SERIESID=D09.

19. The justices comments on the draft are available at Paul J. Wahlbeck, et al., *The Burger Court Opinion Writing Database, Wyman v. James, 400 U.S. 309 (1971)*, http://supremecourtopinions.wustl.edu/files/opinion_pdfs/1970/70-69.pdf.

20. BOB WOODWARD & SCOTT ARMSTRONG, THE BRETHREN: INSIDE THE SUPREME COURT 141–44 (1979).

21. *See* LINDA GREENHOUSE, BECOMING JUSTICE BLACKMUN 61–63 (2005).

22. On the stereotype of the "welfare queen," *see* Michele E. Gilman, *The Return of the Welfare Queen*, 22 AM. U. J. GENDER& SOC. POL'Y & L. 247 (2014).

23. TANF was created by the Personal Responsibility and Work Opportunity Reconciliation Act of 1996, Pub. L. No. 104-193, 110 Stat. 2105 (1996) (codified at 42 U.S.C. § 604(a) (2000)).

24. For more detail on the nature of these privacy intrusions and the harms caused, see Michele Estrin Gilman, *The Class Differential in Privacy Law*, 77 BROOK. L. REV. 1389 (2012).

25. *See* Khiara Bridges, *Privacy Rights and Public Families*, 34 HARV. J. L. & GENDER 113, 113–14 (2011).

26. Sanchez v. San Diego, 464 F.3d 916, 927 (9th Cir. 2006).

27. Sanchez v. San Diego, 483 F.3d 965, 969 (9th Cir. 2007), *denying pet. reh'g en banc* (Pregerson, J., dissenting).

28. *See* GILLIOM, *supra* note 2, at 66–67, 78 (summarizing interviews with welfare recipients in Appalachia in the early 1990s).

29. JOE SOSS, UNWANTED CLAIMS: THE POLITICS OF PARTICIPATION IN THE U.S. WELFARE SYSTEM 187 (2002).

A Tragedy of Two Americas

Jefferson v. Hackney • (1972)

MARIE A. FAILINGER

The year 1969 was a year of hope and worry for poverty advocates. President Johnson's War on Poverty, declared only five years earlier on January 8, 1964, had produced a flurry of programs to alleviate the tragic conditions of American poverty, among them Medicare, Medicaid, the Food Stamp Act, the Job Corps, and Head Start. Idealistic young professionals and volunteers led community-based efforts funded by the Office of Economic Opportunity's (OEO) Community Action Program, Legal Services program, and Volunteers in Service to America (VISTA) to attack the problems of poverty in depressed neighborhoods in cities throughout the United States. Lawyers in organizations like the Center on Social Welfare Policy and Law (the "Center") were preparing lawsuits to constitutionalize basic welfare rights, such as the right to the necessities of life.

These efforts were joined in some cities by local chapters of the National Welfare Rights Organization, which at its August 1967 inaugural convention adopted a set of four goals: an adequate income "for all Americans to live dignified lives above the level of poverty," a system guaranteeing "freedoms, rights and respect" for all, a system of constitutional protection and justice, and "direct participation in the decisions under which they must live."[1]

And yet the demands of fighting, in reality, three wars—one in Vietnam, one against poverty, and one to achieve civil rights for African Americans—were heavy. And there were plenty of portents of trouble for the poverty fighters in the previous year of 1968: the imposition of mandatory work requirements for welfare recipients; the assassinations of Dr. Martin Luther

King and Sen. Robert Kennedy, two visible leaders for national change on poverty; and the election of Richard Nixon.

The story of *Jefferson v. Hackney* is a microcosm of this period in history. It recounts the efforts of Texas welfare rights recipients to demand an income necessary for dignified existence as well as the right to be recognized as participants in their own destiny. It recalls the optimism and realism with which poverty lawyers and advocates approached their work. Yet it also reflects the way the problems of race and class in America not only intertwine but struggle against each other for recognition, and it serves as a cautionary tale about the grave social consequences of "two Americas," one rich and one poor, one white and one minority.

Background

It was a Wednesday in early 1969, and lawyers at the OEO-funded Bexar County Legal Aid offices were worried.[2] Frank Christian, head of the Legal Aid office, had just received a phone call that the San Antonio welfare rights organization was starting a sleep-in at the local welfare office on Santa Rosa Avenue, protesting the state's July 1968 decision to cut their Aid to Families with Dependent Children (AFDC) benefits. Christian, a blue-blooded San Antonian hailing from Alamo Heights, had a strong reputation and city connections that were a boon to the low-income people he worked with. The Alazan-Apache Homes Welfare Rights Organization, headed by a peppery and outspoken mother, Jo Ann Gutierrez, was out in force;[3] it had been trained by the National Welfare Rights Organization for just such a protest. The new Guadalupe Street OEO office, opened in a crime-ridden area of East San Antonio, had been working with Gutierrez because, under Texas law, she was receiving the family maximum and couldn't receive additional AFDC benefits for her last child.

Although the office was young, by the time of the protest, lawyers at San Antonio's OEO were already involved in filing class action lawsuits. Among other things, they challenged the Texas welfare residency rule and the state's failure to provide pretermination due process hearings to disability recipients.[4] In the due process case, Burton Hackney, the Texas commissioner of welfare, had himself come to testify in federal court before "old school" federal judge Adrian Spears, chief of the Northern District of Texas. In front of the press at the courthouse, Hackney confronted an embarrassed OEO lawyer Lonnie Duke and said, "What are you trying to do? Wreck the welfare department? We're trying to pay the poorest of the poor and you're trying to stop us?"

But in this protest, the welfare mothers were demanding that funds be made available to buy food stamps on an emergency basis because of the crisis caused by the state's decision to reduce their AFDC benefits. Christian dispatched Mel Eichelbaum, a lawyer at the Houston Street office in a largely African American neighborhood, and Duke, who worked at the Guadalupe Street office in the heart of the Latino community, to see what they could do to calm matters down.

Duke had moved into San Antonio after working for the gas company and practicing law for two years in a small town called Post, named after its founder, W. C. Post of "Post Toasties" fame. He had a family and needed to make a better living, so he applied at the San Antonio D.A's office and to OEO, which paid better. Fellow OEO lawyer Jim Lerman got him involved in filing welfare litigation, but Duke was left to pursue these cases on his own when Lerman was tragically killed in a glider plane accident in California.

Eichelbaum had recently been discharged from the Army National Guard. He was saved from being sent to Vietnam to parachute out of airplanes because his superiors recognized that he was well-educated and assigned him stateside to train a promising African American whom the Army was interested in promoting to first sergeant. When Eichelbaum applied for the OEO job, Christian asked, "Are you prejudiced? Do you have any problems with blacks as we're going to put you in the East Houston Street office on the east side of town?" He said, "That's no problem with me, I don't have a prejudiced bone in my body." Christian called with a job offer just as Eichelbaum was headed out the door to take a job with a private law firm. His choice to go with OEO was confirmed when one night the opposing party in a divorce case threw a rock through the Houston Street office window. When Eichelbaum and his wife went down to secure the office at 4 a.m., he found the office ringed with clients and neighbors who had come to protect the office from vandalism. He was "moved to the core" by their loyalty.

Christian dispatched his lawyers to the welfare rights protest because he was afraid that the mothers might be arrested or even blamed for damage to the welfare office. Eichelbaum and Duke had strict instructions to observe but not to participate in the protest. When they arrived, representatives from the Mexican American Legal Defense Fund (MALDEF) were on the scene, so Duke called Christian to see if OEO was going to represent the women, or whether they should defer to MALDEF. Although he was fielding phone calls from members of the bar suggesting that the office should not represent these women who were "breaking the law," Christian said that OEO would take the women's case.

Eichelbaum and Duke found about 25 to 30 mothers and their small children sitting in the hot, airless welfare office, surrounded by police officers. Eichelbaum assured protest leader Jo Ann Gutierrez that OEO would file a lawsuit to overturn the benefit reduction policy, and he tried to convince her that it would be best if the women went home. They were not ready to go, however, so Duke helped the women carry mattresses into the welfare office so they could sleep there overnight. The next day, a photo carried in the San Antonio newspaper prominently featured the two lawyers at the scene,[5] publicity that would later sour Duke's relationship with Christian.

Although the Santa Rosa welfare office was closed on Thursday after consultation with Austin state welfare officials, protesters came and went outside the building from Wednesday to Friday, as many as 100 at a time, mostly Mexican Americans.[6] The police were ordered not to disturb the protesters as long as they were peaceful and stayed outside the building.[7]

By that Friday, the OEO lawyers were successful in arranging a meeting for the next Monday with a group of San Antonio businessmen, city officials, and representatives of the welfare rights organization to respond to the protesters' demands. The organization agreed to call off its protest that evening, but promised in a statement that "[w]e intend to return Monday morning unless our demands are met."[8] Besides seeking emergency food assistance to make up for their AFDC benefit cuts, the mothers were also demanding that welfare appeal hearings for benefit cuts be held in recipients' homes because they could not afford to pay for babysitters or transportation to attend hearings. They also wanted appeal forms to be printed in Spanish because many mothers could not read or write English.[9]

At the Monday meeting, the OEO lawyers stressed how bad it would look for San Antonio if the AFDC children went starving because of the benefit cuts. By the next day, the city had secured a commitment from the Washington OEO office to provide $40,000 to $50,000 in emergency aid to buy food stamps, which the San Antonio city and county, the Council of Churches, and social services programs matched with another $50,000. On Monday, about 50 protesters made one last vigil outside the Santa Rosa office but finally left when they heard about the emergency food aid.[10]

At the time of these protests, Texas was considering a constitutional amendment that would provide more funding for welfare programs, including AFDC. At the Monday summit to resolve the protesters' grievances, San Antonio councilman Felix Trevino expressed concern that "an adverse public reaction" to the sit-in might cause voters to reject the amendment in the August 5 election.[11] Eichelbaum was also concerned that the protest might cause OEO's clients to lose their case and the prospect of a constitutional amendment raising their benefits.

A few weeks earlier than the San Antonio protest, Doug Larson and Ed J. Polk at the Dallas Legal Services Project filed a federal lawsuit in the Northern District of Texas on behalf of a class of welfare recipients challenging the benefit reduction policy. This case, which became known as *Jefferson v. Hackney*, challenged the decision of Texas to reduce AFDC payments to 50 percent of the newly adjusted standard of need. It also attempted to require Texas to count nonexempt outside income against the recipients' actual standard of need in determining benefits, rather than first reducing that standard by 50 percent and then deducting family income from the 50 percent.

The Dallas class action was headed by Ruth Jefferson, a divorced mother of five children aged 9 to 13. Her grant was cut from $135 to $123 because of the policy. Jefferson's ex-husband had stopped paying his child support five months after their divorce. She was joined by named plaintiffs Emma Gipson and Jose Apolinor Vasquez. Gipson, like Jefferson, was African American and depended solely on her $102 monthly AFDC check and food stamps for her three children, aged 2 to 6. Vasquez, with eight children, including two sets of twins, was on AFDC because of family tragedy: a migrant farm worker, he became disabled after his neck was broken in a car accident and he had not been able to get Social Security disability benefits. His wife had wrestled with serious illness, including a heart attack, which left her unable to work more than occasionally, and then not enough even to feed the family.[12]

Within days of the Dallas lawsuit, the San Antonio OEO lawyers filed suit against the grant reduction policy in the Western District of Texas. Besides Hackney, they named as defendants the San Antonio regional director, Raymond Cheeves, and members of the State Board of Public Welfare. For the first named plaintiff in the San Antonio case, the lawyers chose Maria Davila, a pretty and sweet but determined AFDC recipient whose $54 AFDC grant for her three children was being terminated even though her need had increased under the new formula. While Jo Ann Gutierrez, the head of the welfare rights organization, was well-respected by local AFDC recipients because she was unafraid of standing up to welfare officials and telling them why they were wrong, Davila did not have quite the welfare advocacy baggage of Gutierrez, and the lawyers thought her good looks would play well in court.

Because they raised questions of federal statutory and constitutional law, the Dallas and San Antonio class actions were consolidated before a three-judge court that included two Johnson appointees, Circuit Court of Appeals judge Irving L. Goldberg and federal district judge W. M. Taylor, as well as district judge Sarah T. Hughes. At the time, Hughes was well-known nationally as the judge who swore in President Lyndon Johnson on Air Force One after John F. Kennedy's assassination. She was Texas's first woman state district judge, served in the Texas legislature, and was briefly nominated for vice president at the Democratic convention of 1952.

The budget for the State of Texas was doing well in 1969 due to the national demand for oil and gas. The AFDC program, however, had been politically unpopular in the state for a long time, a fact the state agency conceded in the course of the lawsuit. In fact, Article III, section 5 of the original Texas constitution provided that the state legislature would have no power to make "any grant of public moneys to any individual, association of individuals, municipal or other corporations whatsoever."[13] When that section was amended so that Texas could participate in New Deal programs for aged, blind, and disabled residents and "destitute children under the age of fourteen years," a constitutional cap was placed on the amount of money Texas was allowed to spend on these programs. The original cap was $52 million, which was raised to $60 million in 1963, but an attempt to further raise the cap in 1968 to $75 million was defeated at the polls. As a result of the cap, the legislature had to split up a limited pot of money and readjust that amount every few years. In the year beginning September 1, 1968, $48 million of that capped appropriation went to the state's 229,654 elderly, followed by $6.15 million for 138,942 AFDC recipients, $4.25 million for Texas's 15,962 disabled, and $1.4 million for its 4,154 blind citizens.

By 1968, however, AFDC rolls were growing in Texas. And Texas had to do something to implement Congress's directive in the 1967 Social Security Act amendments taking effect on January 2, 1968, in 42 U.S.C. § 601(a)(23) that required:

> by July 1, 1969, the amounts used by the state to determine the needs of individuals will have been adjusted to reflect fully changes in living costs since such amounts were established, and any maximums that the state imposes on the amount of aid paid to families will have been proportionately adjusted.

The law gave the states a generous 18 months to study the best way to update need and payment limits and come up with adequate appropriations. This mandate was necessary because many states, including Texas, had not changed this "standard of need"—for food, clothing, shelter, and other basic living expenses—in many years despite inflation. Most states did not even pay this stagnant standard of need, but rather a maximum amount per family based on family size or some percentage of the standard of need (termed a ratable reduction.)

The difference between true family need, the state's calculation of need, and its actual AFDC payment was stark. In Texas in 1968, before the benefit cut went into place, the federal poverty level for a family of four was $3,944, much less than the 1970 Bureau of Labor Statistics "Lower Living Budget" for a Dallas family of four, or $6,683. Yet the state's AFDC standard of need was a mere $2,184 per year, and the most that the state would pay that family was $114 per month, or $1,368 per year.[14]

To keep its federal Social Security allotment, which funded about three-quarters of the AFDC program, the state of Texas agreed to adjust the standard of need after the 1967 Social Security Act amendments. To deal with the constitutional cap on welfare expenditures, however, the Texas Department of Public Welfare decided to ratably reduce the standard of need that it would use to pay welfare recipients. Old age recipients, a large majority of whom were "Anglo," were held harmless. Disabled recipients, 57 percent Anglo, and blind recipients, 44 percent Anglo, would be paid 95 percent of their standard of need. But AFDC recipients, of whom only 15.4 percent were Anglo, had the updated standard of need reduced by 50 percent as the maximum payment. More than 25,000 Texas AFDC families would have their grants reduced or terminated under this plan.[15]

To compound matters, if an AFDC recipient had other income, that income was deducted not from the actual standard of need, but from the 50 percent cap. Thus if a welfare family's standard of need was $2,184 per year and they had an income of $1,092, they would lose their welfare assistance altogether, because their $1,092 income would be deducted from 50 percent of their standard of need, $1,092.[16] Moreover, they would lose the other benefits that came with AFDC, including job training, social services, and Medicaid.

The San Antonio lawyers favored the federal statutory claims, which they argued at the hearing on the preliminary injunction in Dallas when the cases were consolidated. They claimed that Texas had violated the Social Security Act by raising the standard of need in 1969 but then lowering the amount to be paid under that standard, in violation of Congress's clear mandate that the standard of need be updated and payments adjusted accordingly. They also claimed that Texas's practice of deducting other income from 50 percent of the standard of need before determining eligibility violated 42 U.S.C. § 402(a)(23).[17]

The Dallas lawyers preferred to argue the constitutional claims in the hearing. Their main argument was based on racial discrimination, though in their complaint and memos they also threw in claims that the severe reduction in AFDC benefits was arbitrary and capricious, that state officials discriminated because of some AFDC children's illegitimacy, and that the state's action was a unconstitutional "taking" of the recipients' property.[18] They argued that the Texas scheme constituted racial discrimination because the benefit cuts were visited most heavily on the AFDC program, whose recipients were largely African and Latino Americans. While the San Antonio lawyers thought it was common knowledge that the AFDC program recipients were minorities, they believed it would be difficult to prove that the state had intentionally singled out the AFDC minorities in order to harm them based on race. At least some of the Dallas OEO attorneys, however, believed that they might win the argument that the racially disproportionate impact of the state's action violated the Equal Protection Clause. Not long before, the Supreme Court had decided *Griggs v. Duke Power*, 401 U.S. 424 (1971), holding that under Title VII of the Civil Rights Act, a policy that had a disparate impact on racial minorities could violate the act even if the plaintiffs could not prove intentional discrimination.

At the hearing on the preliminary injunction, shortly after the San Antonio sit-in, the federal judicial panel expressed some exasperation with the racial discrimination claims, but the questions Judge Hughes and Judge Taylor asked suggested sympathy with the federal statutory claim that the 50 percent ratable reduction violated Congress's intention to raise both the standard of need and the amounts paid. After a largely stipulated record, the three-judge court ruled on July 31, 1969, that defendants had violated the "intent and purpose" of Social Security Act 42 U.S.C. § 402(a)(23) by raising the standard of need but lowering the payment levels. The court found that defendants wanted to read the federal mandate as

> a command to make a bookkeeping entry regarding costs of living increases which would be instantly nullified by the payment of a lesser percentage of the book entry. This is a cipher game. We are of the opinion that Congress intended no such academic exercise. We believe instead that Congress desired to increase the size of grants actually reaching AFDC recipients so as to minimize the effect of the rise in the cost of living.[19]

The panel issued an injunction against the policy and gave the state of Texas 60 days to correct its plan.

The plaintiffs were not so successful, however, in convincing the three-judge panel on the merits of their equal protection claim. The panel was unmoved by the argument that past AFDC policies evidenced racial bias by Texas officials. These policies included a "man-in-the house" rule that would terminate assistance to welfare mothers who had male overnight visitors (held unconstitutional in *King v. Smith*, 392 U.S. 307 (1968)) and the "suitable home" policy, which terminated benefits to AFDC children if their mother was deemed unfit. If the state's AFDC policy was racially motivated, the panel reasoned, why would it have raised appropriations for the AFDC program five times between 1943 and 1969? Why would the state raise the standard of need to benefit large families, who were predominantly black and Mexican American? Why would it pay 95 percent of the standard of need in the program for the blind, where over 50 percent of the recipients were minorities?[20]

Moreover, the Texas legislature had submitted proposed constitutional Amendment 5 to the voters in the impending August 1969 election. That initiative would raise the constitutional cap to $80 million, and it was expected that $11.9 million of the new money would go to AFDC, allowing AFDC recipients to be paid 100 percent of their standard of need. These state actions belied the view that Texas was intentionally singling out racial minorities for discriminatory treatment. The panel also noted that the Texas welfare officials had not known of the racial disparities in the programs until after the litigation was filed, suggesting that no intentional discrimination had occurred.[21] The panel admitted that they were "dismayed at the comparative compassion involved in granting 100% of need to adults and 50% to children" and "disconcerted by the apparent insensitivity in being more concerned with self-help for the aged than food and lodging for the young," but that was not enough to find an equal protection violation.[22]

Finally, noting that absent racial or ethnic discrimination or the violation of a fundamental right, the constitutional "rational basis" standard applied, the three-judge panel largely accepted the state's reasoning for lowering the payment levels for AFDC more drastically than for the other programs. Noting that the AFDC program was primarily focused on strengthening family life versus the primary purpose of "self-care" in the other programs, Texas successfully claimed that AFDC children and their mothers were more likely to be able to work than the other categories of recipients, and they could call upon the children's father or their extended family for support.[23]

Texas's claims about possible extra income for AFDC recipients was significantly belied by record evidence, however. The state conceded that about a quarter of all AFDC children in Texas had fathers who were incapacitated, dead, or in prison, and about half of their mothers "are too uneducated or handicapped to hold even the lowest-paying job."[24] Moreover, HEW had concluded that the earnings of AFDC children under the age of 14 were so negligible that they were not even counted as family income for purposes of determining eligibility.[25] As plaintiffs' counsel also reiterated throughout the litigation, those families who actually did have available sources of income like child support or earnings would have their standard of need reduced by that income, so there was no reason to think that the 50 percent rule accounted for available income. Yet the state's argument prevailed.

Despite the loss on the constitutional claim, the San Antonio lawyers were elated. As far as they were concerned, they had won the case. Not only had the three-judge panel ruled in their favor on the Social Security Act claim, but Texas passed Amendment 5 in August, raising the constitutional welfare cap to $80 million in time to comply with the 60-day window set by the three-judge court.[26] The Texas welfare department had responded by raising the percentage reduction for welfare recipients from 50 percent to 75 percent, not quite the full restoration that was expected when the amendment passed but a significant gain for the recipients. The San Antonio lawyers withdrew Davila and went on to other pressing cases.

But the Dallas OEO lawyers were unhappy that they had not prevailed on the equal protection claim. Their requests for retroactive benefits to the class were rebuffed. Determining to appeal, they were joined by lawyers from the Columbia-based Center on Social Welfare Policy and Law under the leadership of Ed Sparer. Sparer had been pursuing a strategy toward getting the Supreme Court to declare that there was a "right to live" and that American citizens deserved a guaranteed annual income. Moreover, Sparer was determined that welfare policies should be reviewed using the "strict scrutiny" standard employed for racial discrimination and other fundamental rights.[27]

As the *Jefferson* appeal moved toward the Supreme Court, the plaintiffs suffered a significant setback. In April, in *Rosado v. Wyman*, 397 U.S. 397 (1970), the United States Supreme Court held that Congress had intended no tie between the requirement to adjust the AFDC standard of need and payment of a higher benefit level. Rather, Justice Harlan announced in *Rosado* that in its 1967 amendments to the Social Security Act, Congress was primarily attempting to assure that states were not obscuring the true standard of recipients' need by failing to update the standard. If they followed the congressional directive to update the standard of need, it was perfectly appropriate to readjust payment levels to something less than the standard of need, whether by using a maximum payment per family, or by paying some percentage (ratable reduction) of the standard of need.

Lawyers from the Center on Social Welfare Policy and Law and in legal services offices were discouraged by the *Rosado* ruling, but they quickly regrouped to continue their constitutional claims and to retool their statutory claims to respond to idiosyncrasies in states' implementation of the congressional directives.

The *Jefferson* case was remanded by the Supreme Court to the three-judge panel on May 4, 1970. That August, the panel, chastened by *Rosado*, found that the Texas scheme was in compliance with the Social Security Act.[28] Even though the constitutional amendment had passed, restoring some of the cuts to AFDC recipients, the *Jefferson* plaintiffs, spurred on by the possibility that they might be able to salvage their lawsuit goals, appealed to the panel to invalidate the rule applying earned income to the 50 percent reduced need rather than the full standard of need. When they were rebuffed in September 1970, they once more appealed to the U.S. Supreme Court.[29]

This time, lawyers from the Center for Social Welfare Policy and Law became lead counsel. Steven J. Cole, a young lawyer with the Center, was assigned the argument because he had been working on other *Rosado*-related litigation arguments. Cole thought this meant that Ed Sparer had decided that the racial discrimination argument in *Jefferson* was not a winner. Cole was on leave from a job offered to him at Hughes Hubbard and Reid before he went to clerk for federal judge Joseph Zavatt. When he saw the notice about a Reginald Heber Smith Fellowship program at Haverford in summer 1969, he thought it would be exciting to make a real difference for poor people and challenge the State of New York's decision to withhold millions in benefits. So he sought, and was granted, an extension of his leave to work at the Center for Social Welfare Policy and Law. Although Cole had a substantial amount of welfare litigation experience by the time *Jefferson* was set for oral argument, he was not sure he was prepared for a Supreme Court hearing.

The *Jefferson* case was originally set for argument in December 1971, but after hours of preparation, Cole got a call from the Supreme Court clerk just days before the argument to notify him that it had been postponed. He later learned that *Jefferson* had been the "extra" case that the Supreme Court often scheduled for argument just in case any of the scheduled cases did not proceed as planned. By the time *Jefferson* reached the Supreme Court for oral argument on February 22, 1972, the composition of the Court had shifted significantly. Both Justice John Harlan and Justice Hugo Black had resigned in September 1971, leaving seven justices on the Court that fall when the case was originally set for oral argument. They were replaced in January 1972 by Nixon's former assistant attorney general William Rehnquist and former ABA president Lewis Powell, respectively. Both would later vote against the plaintiffs in *Jefferson*.

Along with Dallas OEO lawyer Ed Polk, Center lawyers Ed Sparer, Carl Rachlin, Henry Freedman, and Steven Cole led with the racial discrimination claim in their brief, followed by an attack on the 50 percent reduction from the standard of need that Texas had employed. For his part, the state's lawyer, assistant attorney general Pat Bailey, warned the Court of a "virtual torrent of litigation, which is practically inundating the judicial system, and which seeks to challenge practically every legislative and administrative act of the states connected with welfare programs." Plaintiffs' claims were simply "a particular litigant's desire to have the legislative bodies of this country respond to a particular desire in a particular manner."[30]

As the oral argument in the Supreme Court approached, there were discussions among the plaintiffs' lawyers about whether the case had gotten too complex for the justices to understand. Cole found that the oral argument was consumed with explaining how the AFDC program's standard of need and income rules worked, and there was little time to argue the constitutional claim. He wondered if the plaintiffs might have been better off proceeding with only their Social Security claims and leaving the constitutional claims for another day so he could have spent more time talking about how the AFDC children were being harmed by the Texas policy. In fact, Justice Powell, one of the justices who was vacillating, conceded to his clerk that the arguments "were not helpful" and that he had also read *Rosado* "without being greatly enlightened" because it was "too confusing."[31]

William Rehnquist, the junior justice, was the most prolific questioner. Rehnquist, like others, had realized that because of Texas's constitutional cap on welfare expenditures, if the Court ruled favorably on the AFDC recipients' claims, recipients in the old age, blind, and disabled programs would receive fewer benefits. He also saw a potential divergence of class interest between plaintiffs with outside income and those with none, because a plaintiff victory on how earned income should be applied to reduce need would also require readjusting benefits to AFDC recipients without income. But his first challenge was to plaintiffs' harm and their standing, since the remaining named plaintiffs were apparently still on AFDC, while Davila had withdrawn from the appeal. Bailey jumped on this questioning hard with a Texas-style metaphor, "they wanted to change horses here but they haven't got anybody who will fit the saddle of this new horse that they've got."

The first vote of the justices on the *Jefferson* case was inconclusive.[32] Justices Harry Blackmun and William Rehnquist, and Chief Justice Burger were ready to affirm the district panel's ruling that under *Rosado*, the Texas benefit reduction plan was legal under the Social Security Act. While Justice White thought the *Rosado* language "could be construed either way," he was inclined to affirm the state's policy as well. Justice Douglas tentatively voted to reverse without explanation. Justices Brennan and Marshall would reverse on the Social Security Act but thought the Court didn't need to consider the constitutional question. Justice Stewart and Justice Powell both had their doubts about the applicability of *Rosado* to this case, but Stewart was inclined to reverse while Powell was inclined to affirm. Thus, none of the members of the Court were prepared to overturn on equal protection grounds, an abject failure for the lawyers' strategy on the case.

Powell carried on a lengthy correspondence with his clerk Hamilton Fox over whether *Rosado* required affirming the Texas panel's decision that Texas' 50 percent ratable reduction and method of applying earned income to the standard of need did not violate the Social Security Act. While conceding that the plaintiffs had not made out their equal protection case, Fox felt that their Social Security Act claim was correct, if unclear, and he wrote successful memos to Justice Powell trying to clarify how the act worked as the justice wavered about what he should do. Powell was strongly influenced by the fact that HEW had come out in favor of the Texas policy as consistent with the Social Security Act in the lawsuit. He was also clearly bothered by the fact that if the plaintiffs were successful, the poorest of them might be harmed. This conflict between members of the plaintiff class, which the lawyers had recognized from the outset, was troubling. Indeed, Justice Powell said, "this [victory by the plaintiffs] would result in less money for those who need the welfare benefits the most, namely, those with no outside income."[33]

Still, Powell thought, the Texas legislature might have made a policy error. "If I were in the Texas legislature," he mused, "I still think I would prefer the 'alternative system' [deducting income from the full standard of need and not the capped benefit level] in view of its incentive to go to work and earn outside income. But I cannot say that the choice made by the Texas legislature violates the federal statute."[34] Taking a jab at the plaintiff's attorneys for filing a 126-page brief, he concluded that despite Fox's best efforts to educate him, Powell would vote to uphold the Texas scheme.

As the newest justice on the Court, Justice Rehnquist was assigned the opinion. It was his first oral argument and his fourth written opinion on the Court, and it was an opportunity to make his mark both on equal protection law and on Social Security Act interpretations. His selection as opinion writer virtually doomed any chance the plaintiffs may have had to win on racial discrimination. Rehnquist had just survived a confirmation hearing in which *Newsweek* published a memo he had written as a law clerk to Justice Robert Jackson on *Brown v. Board of Education* arguing that "I think Plessy v. Ferguson [upholding the separate but equal doctrine] was right and should be re-affirmed." Rehnquist claimed, dubiously, that the memo was written to express Justice Jackson's views rather than his own, but the memo had hung over the confirmation.[35] Moreover, witnesses in Arizona suggested that after Rehnquist moved there to practice law, he became part of squads of Republican lawyers who harassed black and Latino voters standing in line at the polls, by photographing them and asking them to read from the Constitution or state their qualifications to vote.[36]

In *Jefferson*, Rehnquist not only dismissed the racial discrimination claim but helped to solidify the position that under the equal protection clause, plaintiffs must show not only discriminatory effect but also discriminatory intent, a position later cemented in *Washington v. Davis* in 1976.[37] Calling the plaintiffs' racial claims "unproven allegations," Justice Rehnquist reiterated the three-judge panel's factual conclusions, particularly its conclusion that the defendants did not know the racial makeup of the AFDC and other Texas programs when they proposed the 50 percent rule for AFDC recipients. According to Cole, Rehnquist mistakenly claimed that the plaintiffs had abandoned their claim that the case had evidenced intentional racial discrimination.[38] Rehnquist's circulated draft opinion upset clerks in the other chambers, who thought he had misrepresented the record in his *Jefferson* draft, but he refused to correct his opinion when these errors were pointed out to him.[39]

Justice Rehnquist wrote that finding racial discrimination every time the racial composition of each of the welfare programs was not "identical to each other" would make virtually every government benefits program suspect, "however lacking in racial motivation."[40] In a footnote, he brushed aside the claim that disparate impact on racial groups was enough to trigger heightened constitutional scrutiny after *Griggs*. He also cited Justice Black's opinion in *James v. Valtierra*, 402 U.S. 137 (1971), which dismissed a claim that a California law requiring a referendum for every new public housing project was racially discriminatory, because the law was facially neutral and not provably aimed at racial minorities.

Justice Rehnquist made quick work of the Social Security Act claim, returning to and dismissing the claim made in plaintiffs' first appeal that the

Social Security Act required all four programs to be treated identically. In doing so, he virtually ignored the plaintiffs' argument that Texas had violated the *Rosado* holding by first reducing the standard of need by 50 percent, then applying any family income so as to make many families ineligible even though they were still needy by Texas standards.[41]

Justice Douglas and Justice Marshall both wrote dissents focusing on the Social Security Act claims, though Justice Douglas noted that he would "read the Act against the background of rank discrimination against the blacks and the Chicanos and in light of the fact that Chicanos in Texas fare even more poorly than the blacks."[42] Douglas quoted from a *Rosado* statement that appeared to endorse the plaintiffs' position that income had to be deducted from the actual standard of need, not 50 percent of the standard of need. He noted the importance of that computation in furthering congressional purposes about encouraging welfare recipients to be employed.[43]

Justice Marshall wrote a complex dissent evidencing his grasp of the problem with taking income off the 50 percent standard to determine eligibility. He found this policy to violate the Social Security Act, focusing on both the purposes of the act and congressional history suggesting congressional intent to treat the programs with parity. While he argued that the Social Security Act claim made it unnecessary to reach the question of racial discrimination, he dismissed Rehnquist's treatment of the race claim, noting that there were "numerous statements by state officials to the effect that AFDC is funded at a lower level than other programs because it is not a politically popular program. There is also evidence of a stigma that seemingly attaches to AFDC recipients and no others."[44] The conclusion that such unfavorable treatment had "nothing to do with the racial makeup of the program" was in his view "neither so apparent, nor so correct" as Rehnquist and the three-judge panel made it out to be.[45]

Conclusion

Professor Martha Davis argues that the force of the *Jefferson* loss, the failure of federal legislative efforts to provide a guaranteed minimum income, and the death of National Welfare Rights Organization head George Wiley, spelled the end of the welfare rights movement and the first wave of welfare rights law.[46] While other cases would be filed, the attempt to reform welfare law through litigation was stymied by "the public's perception of the poor as 'undeserving.'"[47] Thus the efforts of the National Welfare Rights Organization to work for a society in which even the poor could "live dignified lives" marked by "freedoms, rights and respect" were only marginally vindicated in the *Jefferson* litigation. As a reminder of that fact, Lonnie Duke recalls that a reporter covering the San Antonio protest and litigation told him that welfare activist Jo Ann Gutierrez "didn't look like she was poor" because she was "too fat to be poor." Duke tried to explain that she was in that condition because of the kind of food that AFDC and food stamps allowed her to buy. To the reporter's remark about his client, Duke said, "that hurt."

Notes

1. The rise of the NWRO and poverty advocacy is recounted in MARTHA F. DAVIS, BRUTAL NEED: LAWYERS AND THE WELFARE RIGHTS MOVEMENT, 1960–1973, see particularly 34–36, 45 (NWRO goals) 56–58, 70–71, 99–100, 128–29 (1993). A good source for information on War on Poverty programs is MICHAEL L. GIL-LETT, LAUNCHING THE WAR ON POVERTY: AN ORAL HISTORY (2010).

2. Except as otherwise noted, the story of the San Antonio litigation in *Jefferson* comes from my interviews with Lonnie Duke on July 17, 2013, and with Mel Eichelbaum on July 11, 2013, and Eichelbaum's e-mail to me dated July 12, 2013. These interviews are on file at the National Equal Justice Library, Georgetown Law School.

3. Clay Robison, *Welfare Recipients Sit In*, SAN ANTONIO EXPRESS, June 19, 1969.

4. Interview with Lonnie Duke, *supra* note 2 (discussing residency and due process cases). For a published opinion, *see Doyle v. Richardson*, 458 F.2d 987 (5th Cir. 1972) (staying federal district court decision to require Texas to provide pre-termination hearings for disability benefits recipients pursuant to *Goldberg v. Kelly*, 397 U.S. 254 (1970) because of new federal regulations). Cases pursued by this office also included *Machado v. Hackney*, 299 F. Supp. 644 (W.D. Tex. 1969) (successfully challenging Texas's substitute father regulation); *Rodriguez v. Vowell*, 472 F.2d 622 (5th Cir. 1973) (in which the OEO lawyers had successfully challenged, on appeal, Texas's policy of denying AFDC to a child who had income over his own standard of need even though the caretaker parent-child unit would still have been eligible because of the caretaker's lack of sufficient income to meet her needs); *Smith v. Vowell*, 379 F. Supp. 139 (W.D. Tex 1974) (successfully challenging Texas's refusal to pay for transportation for certain Medicaid patients).

5. Photo on file with author.

6. Robison, *supra* note 3; *Welfare Protesters Due Back Monday*, LUBBOCK AVALANCHE-JOURNAL, June 21, 1969.

7. *Id.*

8. Robison, *supra* note 3.

9. *Id.*

10. *Id.*

11. *Id.*

12. Complaint at 17–18, Jefferson v. Hackney, 304 F. Supp. 1332 (N.D. Tex. 1969) (No. CA 3-3012-B); Amended Complaint at 36–38, reprinted in Jefferson (Ruth) v. Hackney (Burton), U.S. Supreme Court Transcript of Record with Supporting Pleadings (Gale MoML Print Editions) (hereafter "Transcript").

13. Brief for Appellees at 9–10, Jefferson v. Hackney, 406 U.S. 535 (1972) (No. 70-5064), 1971 WL 135546.

14. Brief for Appellants at 7, Jefferson v. Hackney, 406 U.S. 535 (1972) (No. 70-5064), 1971 WL 133434; Stipulations of Fact at 69, Transcript.

15. Stipulations of Fact at 67–74, Transcript.

16. *Id.* at 90–102. Earned income and unearned income were treated differently by Texas because of Social Security Act requirements. Unearned income was subtracted dollar for dollar. As an incentive to keep their jobs, they could keep the first $30 plus one-third of the remaining gross income if they would still be determined needy without this exemption. They could deduct $28 per month for work expenses such as transportation, lunch, required clothing, but also tax and Social Security withholding, as well as child care costs.

17. Complaint at 20–22, 25–26, Transcript.

18. *Id.* at 23–25.

19. *Jefferson, supra* note 12, at 1344.

20. *Id.* at 1339–40.

21. *Id.*

22. *Id.* at 1345.

23. *Id.* at 1335–38.

24. Stipulations of Fact at 86, Transcript.

25. Brief for Appellants at 61, Jefferson v Hackney, 406 U.S. 535 (1972) (No. 70-5064) (discussing HEW regulation excluding income from children under 14).

26. *Welfare Reversal Announced*, SAN ANTONIO EXPRESS, July 31, 1969; *Welfare Victory Lauded*, BROWNSVILLE HERALD, Aug. 6, 1969.

27. Telephone interview with Steven Cole, attorney, Center on Social Welfare Policy and Law (June 17, 2013). Except as noted, material describing the discussions and strategy of Center lawyers Sparer, Cole, and others and comments made at the oral argument before the Supreme Court are taken from the above referenced interview on file at the National Equal Justice Library.

28. Judgment at 160–62, Transcript.

29. Motion to Amend Judgment at 163–64, Transcript; letter from Ed J. Polk to Hon. Irving Goldberg et al. at 165–68, Transcript.

30. Brief of Appellees at 38, Jefferson v. Hackney, 406 U.S. 535 (1972) (No. 70-5064), 1972 WL 135546.

31. Tentative impressions memo, February 22, 1972; and memorandum from Justice Lewis Powell, U.S. Supreme Court justice, to Hamilton Fox, law clerk, Feb. 22, 1972. See the Lewis Powell Papers in *Jefferson v. Hackney*, Supreme Court Case Files Collection, box 3; Washington & Lee School of Law, Virginia, Lewis F. Powell Jr. Archives, Powell Papers, 18–19, 20–22, available at http://law.wlu.edu/powell archives/page.asp?pageid=1279) (last visited December 2, 2013) (hereafter "Powell papers").

32. This discussion about the internal memos and conversations of the justices about the *Jefferson* case are taken from the Powell papers, *supra* note 31.

33. Memorandum from Justice Lewis Powell, U.S. Supreme Court justice, to Hamilton Fox, law clerk, May 22, 1972, Powell papers, *supra* note 31, at 96.

34. *Id.*

35. For the most recent analysis of this incident, suggesting that Justice Rehnquist was likely not telling the truth about this memo at his confirmation hearings, *see* Brad Snyder and John Q. Barrett, *Rehnquist's Missing Letter: A Former Law Clerk's 1955 Thoughts on Justice Jackson and Brown*, 53 B. C. L. Rev. 631 (2012). *See also* Adam Liptak, *New Look at an Old Memo Casts More Doubt on Rehnquist*, N.Y. Times, Mar. 19, 2012, at A18 (discussing the theft of Rehnquist's letter to Jackson).

36. John W. Dean, The Rehnquist Choice: The Untold Story of the Nixon Appointment that Redefined the Supreme Court 272 (2001).

37. Washington v. Davis, 426 U.S. 229 (1976).

38. *See, e.g.*, Jefferson v. Hackney, 406 U.S. 535, 548 (1972) (noting that "Appellants in their brief in effect abandon any effort to show that these findings of fact [regarding the state's discriminatory intent] were clearly erroneous.")

39. Bob Woodward & Scott Armstrong, The Brethren: Inside the Supreme Court 222 (1979) (noting that Justices Douglas and Marshall objected to Rehnquist's misrepresentation of the legislative history of the federal welfare program).

40. Jefferson v. Hackney, 406 U.S. 535, 548 (1972).

41. *Jefferson*, 406 U.S. at 550–51.

42. *Id.* at 551–52 (Douglas, J., dissenting).

43. *Id.* at 552–53, 55 (quoting Rosado v. Wyman, 397 U.S. 397, 409 n.13 (1970). Douglas also cited *Villa v. Hall*, 6 Cal.3d 227, 490 P.2d 1148 (1971), which invalidated California's statutory maximum scheme under *Rosado*, finding that income should be subtracted from the standard of need and not the maximum to determine eligibility, and suggested that *Townsend v. Swank* and *Dandridge v. Williams* supported plaintiffs' position on income deductions.

44. *Id.* at 575 (Marshall, J., dissenting).

45. *Id.*

46. Davis, *supra* note 1, at 141.

47. *Id.* at 144.

Denying the Poor Access to Court

United States v. Kras • (1973)

HENRY ROSE

Never did I dream that I would live to see the day when a court held that a person could be too poor to get the benefits of bankruptcy.
—*William Douglas*[1]

Robert Kras initially was hoping only for a discharge of his debts in bankruptcy, but he and his lawyers ended up seeking to establish an important constitutional right for poor persons in America: access to court. Kras fell behind in paying his debts when he lost his job and his wife gave birth to a child who suffered from a serious illness. Though he desired to start his economic life anew by seeking a discharge of his debts in bankruptcy, Kras could not afford to pay the bankruptcy court filing fee, and the federal law provided that the debts could not be discharged until the filing fee was paid.

Kras challenged the filing fee requirement, arguing that denying a poor person access to court because he cannot afford to pay such a fee violated the United States Constitution. Though the Supreme Court did not directly address the important constitutional argument he raised, the effect of the Supreme Court's ruling against Kras was that in some cases, the poor can be denied access to court when they cannot afford to pay court filing fees. The case reflects both tensions among the Supreme Court justices over the nature of Kras' claim and, as is sometimes the case in poverty law decisions, the Court's skepticism about Kras' own story.

Background: Misfortune Leads to Bankruptcy[2]

In the 1960s, Robert Kras, his wife, and their daughter lived in New York City. Kras worked as an agent for Metropolitan Life Insurance Company. In 1969, insurance premiums he had collected were stolen from his home by an intruder, and when he could not remit the amount of these premiums to Metropolitan Life, his employment was terminated. Thereafter, Kras had a difficult time obtaining steady employment because Metropolitan Life provided negative references to prospective employers. In 1969 and 1970, he worked odd jobs and earned approximately $300 each year. Kras' wife also worked but she stopped working in March 1970 due to a pregnancy. In late 1970, Kras' wife bore a son who suffered from cystic fibrosis, a medical condition that required hospitalization.

By May 1971, Kras lived in a two-and-a-half-room apartment in New York City with his wife, their two children, his mother, and her six-year-old daughter. They paid $102 per month in rent and subsisted on $366 per month in public assistance benefits from the State of New York. Kras had amassed debts totaling $6,428.69, including a $1,012.64 debt to Metropolitan Life and an unpaid loan from his wife's grandmother. He owned no personal or real property other than $50 worth of household goods and clothing and a couch (of negligible value), for which he owed $6 per month to store.

Kras desired to seek a discharge of his debts in bankruptcy to make a new start in life. He hoped that such a discharge would relieve him and his family of the distress of financial insolvency and creditor harassment and would preclude further negative employment references from Metropolitan Life.

Kras obtained free legal representation from attorneys at the Legal Aid Society in New York City. On May 28, 1971, his attorneys filed a voluntary petition in bankruptcy on his behalf in the federal district court in New York City. The bankruptcy petition was accompanied by Kras' motion requesting that he be allowed to seek discharge in bankruptcy without paying the $50 filing fee because he was unable to pay it and still provide for himself and his family. This filing fee was higher than the initial filing fees for all other types of civil proceedings in the federal courts, and it was the only federal civil filing fee for which the statutory right to seek fee waiver for persons unable to pay was not available.[3]

Kras' Case Goes to Court

Federal district judge Anthony Travia considered Kras' motion to seek discharge in bankruptcy without payment of a filing fee. On September 13, 1971, Judge Travia ruled that the filing fee requirement violated the Fifth Amendment right to due process of law, including the equal protection component of the Fifth Amendment that had been recognized in previous cases. Judge Travia held that Kras' right of access to court, a fundamental constitutional interest, was at stake in his case and the government had not established a compelling interest that justified the statutory requirement that he pay the filing fee before seeking a discharge in bankruptcy. To Judge Travia, the stakes for Kras were far more than receiving the benefits of the bankruptcy law; they involved the "greater significance" of indigent persons being able to gain access to the courts to receive justice.[4]

In holding that access to the courts is a fundamental interest, Judge Travia relied on the opinion of District Judge Alfred Arraj in *In re Smith*, which had also held it was a violation of the equal protection guarantee to require an indigent person to pay a filing fee in order to be discharged in bankruptcy. Judge Arraj had concluded in *Smith* that access to court was a fundamental interest by analogizing it to the interest recognized by the United States Supreme Court in 1966 in *Harper v. Virginia State Board of Elections*,[5] which struck down a $1.50 poll tax on equal protection grounds, finding that voting is a fundamental interest. Reasoning that the right to initiate judicial proceedings is at least as important as the right to participate in the electoral process because it similarly provides a forum for the preservation and vindication of private rights, Judge Arraj concluded that access to court must be similarly protected. Further, Judge Arraj held that the United States had failed to establish a compelling justification for limiting access to court by imposing a bankruptcy filing fee that Ms. Smith could not afford to pay; therefore the fee requirement violated the equal protection guarantee.[6]

The United States government appealed Judge Travia's decision to the United States Supreme Court and the Supreme Court agreed to hear the case. The United States government's appeal of Judge Travia's decision framed an important constitutional issue for the Supreme Court to decide: Is access to court a fundamental interest similar to the right to vote?

The United States government's brief in its appeal to the Supreme Court mischaracterized the nature of the fundamental interest that Judge Travia had found to be at the root of Kras' case. As noted, Judge Travia had explicitly framed the right in Kras' case as access to court,[7] a matter of "greater significance" than an individual's right to a bankruptcy discharge.[8] Yet the government argued that Judge Travia "held that a discharge in bankruptcy was a 'fundamental interest,' which could not be denied unless a 'compelling government interest was shown.'"[9] In his oral argument in the Supreme Court, Edward Korman, the government's attorney, similarly persisted in attempting to limit Kras' interest to a discharge in bankruptcy:

> We are not dealing here with any fundamental constitutional right. Congress could repeal the entire bankruptcy statute tomorrow without raising so much as a constitutional ripple. What we have here is simply a benefit that's provided by Congress and it's clearly improper to hold that Congress must meet a compelling interest standard.[10]

By contrast, Kras' attorney, Kalman Finkel, argued in his brief that Judge Travia properly framed the interest at stake in Kras' case: "We submit that there is only one right at issue in this case and that is the right to access to the courts."[11] In his oral argument to the court, Finkel reiterated this point: "I define access to mean that the individual is in court and the relief he seeks he can obtain without any financial barriers. That is the way I would define initial access to court."[12]

Interplay Among Supreme Court Justices

In conference, tensions emerged among the justices about Kras' case. Some of the justices questioned the bona fides of Kras' case and the urgency of his financial circumstances. Justice Powell noted that in this conference, Justice Blackmun said he considered Kras to be a "phony," and Justice White considered Kras' constitutional claim to be "close to frivolous."[13] Nevertheless, the court noted probable jurisdiction and decided to hear the government's appeal of Judge Travia's decision.

After the oral argument in the case, the justices met in conference and Justice Powell expressed his view that this is "a phony lawsuit" because Kras could afford to pay the filing fee if he made some financial sacrifices.[14] Justice Powell's view resonated with Justice Blackmun, who "suspected that the case had been manufactured by civil rights lawyers in the service of an agenda, an effort to use a sympathetic plaintiff to induce the court to make poverty a basis for special constitutional protection."[15] In the postargument conference, the justices voted 5–4 to overturn Judge Travia's decision, and Justice Blackmun was assigned to write the majority's opinion.

Blackmun circulated a draft majority opinion among the justices concluding that requiring payment of a filing fee in a bankruptcy case as a condition
of discharge was constitutionally permissible.[16] In his draft opinion, Justice
Blackmun also asserted that paying the filing fee in installments would be
within Kras' "able-bodied reach" if he would dispense with the weekly "price
of a movie" or "the cost of a pack or two cigarettes."[17] Justice White informed
Justice Blackmun that he had reservations about joining the draft majority
opinion because of its proposed rationale, and he was considering writing a
concurring opinion that would simply assert that the bankruptcy filing fee
did not amount to invidious discrimination.[18] Justice White's position threatened to deprive Justice Blackmun of a majority rationale for a decision upholding the constitutionality of the bankruptcy filing fee. After Justice White
expressed his reservations to Justice Blackmun, Justice Marshall circulated
a draft dissenting opinion that strongly criticized Blackmun's opinion for
its lack of insight into the financial pressures that the poor face. Soon after
Justice Marshall circulated his draft dissent, Justice White decided to join
Blackmun's majority opinion. Blackmun suspected that Justice Marshall's
stinging draft dissent had "pushed" Justice White into joining his opinion.[19]

The Supreme Court, in a 5–4 decision, ultimately reversed Judge Travia
and found that seeking a discharge in bankruptcy involved no constitutional
interest. The Court held that the government's goal to make the bankruptcy
system financially self-sustaining constituted a rational basis for the required
filing fee.[20] Therefore, the requirement that Kras pay a filing fee before discharge in bankruptcy did not deny him equal protection of the laws. Justice
Harry Blackmun wrote the majority opinion and was joined by Chief Justice
Warren Burger and Justices Lewis Powell, William Rehnquist, and Byron
White. Justices William Brennan, William Douglas, Thurgood Marshall, and
Potter Stewart dissented.

Justice Blackmun began his constitutional analysis in *Kras* by distinguishing *Boddie v. Connecticut*,[21] a 1971 decision of the Supreme Court.[22] In *Boddie*,
indigent persons had been denied the opportunity to pursue divorce actions
against their spouses in Connecticut state courts because they were unable
to pay court filing fees. These Connecticut residents challenged the required
filing fees on due process grounds, and their case reached the Supreme Court.
The Supreme Court held in *Boddie* that since the marital relationship involves interests of basic importance in society, and divorce actions offer the
exclusive means of dissolving marital relationships, due process requires that
indigent persons who cannot afford to pay filing fees must be allowed to

pursue divorce actions without being required to pay the fees. The Supreme Court in *Boddie* specifically limited its decision to filing fees in divorce cases and set aside for another day the question whether access to courts for all individuals in all circumstances was constitutionally guaranteed.[23]

Justice Blackmun distinguished *Boddie* in two ways. First, he found that a bankruptcy petition involves no fundamental interest like a divorce action that affects a marital relationship. Second, he found that a person like Kras who has personal debts has alternative, informal methods available to adjust his legal relationship with his creditors, while a person seeking to terminate a marital relationship must go to court to do so. As a result of these distinguishing factors, Justice Blackmun concluded that the Constitution did not require that filing fees in bankruptcy be waived for indigent petitioners like Kras because the self-sustaining funding goals of the bankruptcy system constituted a rational basis for the fee requirement.[24]

Aftermath: The Justices Spar about the Poor

Justice Blackmun and the other justices in the majority in *Kras* ignored the broader constitutional issue that Kras' case raised. As correctly framed by Judge Travia, Kras' claim involved more than access to bankruptcy discharge. It involved the right of the poor to access court to seek judicial enforcement of their legal rights. As Justice Marshall stated in his dissent in *Kras*:

> I view the case as involving the right of access to the courts, the opportunity to be heard when one claims a legal right, and not just the right to a discharge in bankruptcy. When a person raises a claim of right or entitlement under the laws, the only forum in our legal system empowered to determine that claim is a court. Kras, for example, claims that he has a right under the Bankruptcy Act to be free of any duty to pay his creditors. There is no way to determine whether he has such a right except by adjudicating his claim. Failure to do so denies him access to the courts.
>
> The legal system is, of course, not so pervasive as to preclude private resolution of disputes. But private settlements do not determine the validity of claims of right. Such questions can be authoritatively resolved only in courts. It is in that sense, I believe, that we should consider the emphasis in *Boddie* on the exclusiveness of the judicial forum—and give Kras his day in court.[25]

The final opinions in *United States v. Kras* included a remarkable exchange of views by Justice Blackmun and Justice Marshall about the financial plight of poor persons like Kras. Justice Blackmun, writing for the majority, stated:

> If the $50 filing fees are paid in installments over six months as General Order No. 35 (4) permits on a proper showing, the required average weekly payments is $1.92. If the payment period is extended for the additional three months as the Order permits, the average weekly payment is lowered to $1.28. This is a sum less than the payments Kras makes on his couch of negligible value in storage, and less than the price of a movie and little more than the cost of a pack or two of cigarettes. If, as Kras alleges in his affidavit, a discharge in bankruptcy will afford him that new start he so desires, and the Metropolitan then no longer will charge him with fraud and give him bad references, and if he really needs and desires that discharge, this much available revenue should be within his able-bodied reach when the adjudication in bankruptcy has stayed collection and has brought to a halt whatever harassment, if any, he may have sustained from creditors.[26]

Justice Marshall, in dissent, responded:

> It may be easy for some people to think that weekly savings of less than $2 are no burden. But no one who has had close contact with poor people can fail to understand how close to the margin of survival many of them are. A sudden illness, for example, may destroy whatever savings they may have accumulated, and by eliminating a sense of security may destroy the incentive to save in the future. A pack or two of cigarettes may be, for them, not a routine purchase but a luxury indulged in only rarely. The desperately poor almost never go to see a movie, which the majority seems to believe is an almost weekly activity. They have more important things to do with what little money they have—like attempting to provide some comforts for a gravely ill child, as Kras must do.
>
> It is perfectly proper for judges to disagree about what the Constitution requires. But it is disgraceful for an interpretation of the Constitution to be premised upon unfounded assumptions about how people live.[27]

Justice Blackmun was upset by Justice Marshall's dissent and did not think it was fair. He did not think he was being insensitive to the poor; in his view, he was simply skeptical about whether Kras really could not afford to pay the filing fee.[28] More than a year after *Kras* was decided by the Supreme Court, the government's attorney, Korman, wrote a letter to Justice Blackmun informing him that Kras had paid the $50 filing fee in cash a few weeks after the Supreme Court had ruled against him.[29] Shortly after receiving Korman's letter, Justice Blackmun wrote to Justice Douglas and Justice Stewart:

> It is so seldom that we get a follow-through on cases. Because each of you has given me a hard time on this one (Potter's dissent; Bill's comment on page 175 of his last book), I thought you might be interested in knowing that Kras, within six weeks of the rendition of our decision, paid the $50 filing fee in cash, in full. He was discharged in bankruptcy on March 15, 1973. So it goes.[30]

Justice Blackmun "considered Kras' full payment of the fee vindication of his stance in the case."[31] But payment of the filing fee by Kras did not establish that he was able to pay it initially or that he was even the source of the eventual $50 payment.[32]

Conclusion: Failure to Find a Fundamental Right

Justice Blackmun, writing for the majority, did not acknowledge that Kras' inability to seek discharge of his debts in bankruptcy raised an important constitutional issue: Do the poor have a fundamental interest in being able to access courts to seek judicial resolution of their claims of legal rights? Instead, Justice Blackmun consistently minimized Kras' interest as being to simply seek a discharge in bankruptcy only. The irony of Judge Blackmun's opinion in *Kras* is that by ignoring the key issue, the majority implicitly decided it. The effect of the Supreme Court's rejection of Kras' argument that his fundamental interest in access to court undergirds his right to seek discharge in bankruptcy without prepayment of a filing fee is to establish that there are circumstances in which a poor person, like Kras, can be denied access to court based on the inability to pay a filing fee.

Whether the poor should be allowed to participate in civil litigation if they cannot afford to pay court filing fees is an important constitutional issue. In *Kras*, the Supreme Court implicitly decided that, in some cases, the Constitution allows the poor to be denied access to courts based on an inability to pay filing fees.[33] Kras was entitled to more. He was entitled to a direct decision by the Supreme Court as to whether access to the judiciary, one of the three branches of government, should be constitutionally available to those Americans who cannot afford to pay court filing fees.

Notes

1. William O. Douglas, Go East, Young Man 172 (1974).

2. The factual summary provided here was derived from the affidavit that Kras filed in support of his motion for leave to file a bankruptcy petition without paying required filing fees. *See* U.S. v. Kras, 409 U.S. 434, 437 (1973) (citing the uncontroverted facts presented in Kras' affidavit, which was submitted—alongside his original bankruptcy petition—to the United States District Court for the Eastern District of New York on May 28, 1971).

3. Henry W. Schaeffer, *Proceedings in Bankruptcy In Forma Pauperis*, 69 Colum. L. Rev. 1203, 1203 (1969).

4. In re Kras, 331 F. Supp. 1207, 1212–15 (E.D.N.Y. 1971) (quoting In re Smith, 323 F. Supp. 1082, 1087 (D. Colo. 1971)).

5. 383 U.S. 663 (1966).

6. *See* Judge Travia's opinion in *In re Smith*, 323 F. Supp. 1082, 1086–90 (D. Colo. 1971).

7. 331 F. Supp. at 1214.

8. 331 F. Supp. at 1213–14.

9. Brief for the United States at 3, 409 U.S. 434 (1973).

10. Oral Argument at 15:17, 409 U.S. 434 (1973), *available at* http://www.oyez.org/cases/1970-79/1972/1972_71_749.

11. Brief for Appellee at 16, 409 U.S. 434 (1973).

12. Oral Argument at 46:42, 409 U.S. 434 (1973), *available at* http://www.oyez.org/cases/1970-79/1972/1972_71_749.

13. See Lewis F. Powell Jr. Archives, Washington & Lee School of Law, http://www.law.wlu.edu/deptimages /powell%20archives/71-74USKras.pdf [hereinafter Powell Archives] (preserving Justice Lewis Powell's notes from the conference on February 18, 1972, at which the Supreme Court noted probable jurisdiction of the government's appeal in *Kras*).

14. Linda Greenhouse, Becoming Justice Blackmun: Harry Blackmun's Supreme Court Journey 108 (2007).

15. *Id.*

16. Powell Archives, *supra* note 13, at 23–39.

17. *Id.* at 38–39.

18. Greenhouse, *supra* note 14, at 108.

19. *Id.*

20. 409 U.S. at 445–48.

21. 401 U.S. 371 (1971).

22. 409 U.S. at 441–46.

23. *See* Boddie v. Connecticut, 401 U.S. 372, 376–83 (1971).

24. 409 U.S. at 444–49.

25. *Id.* at 462–63 (Marshall, J., dissenting).

26. 409 U.S. at 449.

27. *Id.* at 459–60.

28. TINSLEY YARBROUGH, HARRY A. BLACKMUN: THE OUTSIDER JUSTICE 187 (2007).

29. *Id.* (citing letter from Edward R. Korman to Harry A. Blackmun (June 17, 1974), Blackmun Papers, Library of Congress, box 156).

30. *Id.* at 188 (citing letter from Harry A. Blackmun to William O. Douglas and Potter Stewart (June 20, 1974), Blackmun Papers, box 156).

31. *Id.*

32. *Id.*

33. Two months after the Supreme Court decided *Kras*, it decided *Ortwein v. Schwab*, 410 U.S. 656 (1973). In *Ortwein*, the majority followed *Kras* and held that indigent welfare recipients who could not afford to pay $25 state court filing fees could be denied their statutory right to seek judicial review of adverse administrative decisions that reduced their welfare benefits. 410 U.S. at 658–60.

"The Poor People Have Lost Again"

San Antonio Independent School District v. Rodriguez • (1973)

CAMILLE WALSH

When he was six years old, Demetrio Rodriguez' farmworker family moved from a Rio Grande agricultural town to San Antonio in search of better schools for him and his siblings. Decades later, he demanded educational opportunity for his own children in a landmark Supreme Court case: *San Antonio Independent School District v. Rodriguez*. Barely a generation after the Supreme Court in *Brown v. Board of Education* had declared the fundamental importance of education, the Court in *Rodriguez* decided that the poor, predominantly Mexican American children receiving substandard education in San Antonio's impoverished Edgewood school district had no fundamental right to equal schooling. In doing so, the Court also halted the nascent trend toward the ability of litigants to claim poverty (or "wealth") as a suspect constitutional classification on par with race or gender.[1]

Background: Fighting for Equal Resources

By the time he signed on as lead plaintiff in the 1968 complaint that led to the case bearing his name, Rodriguez was a 42-year-old veteran who had worked for more than 15 years at Kelly Air Force base outside San Antonio. Three of his four sons attended Edgewood Elementary School in San Antonio, a poorly funded school in a poor neighborhood. It was a school where the "building was crumbling, classrooms lacked basic supplies, and almost half the teachers were not certified and worked on emergency permits."Teacher turnover in the schools was 50 percent annually, while statewide it was only 20 percent. More than 90 percent of Edgewood students were Hispanic and 6 percent were African American. Students in the Edgewood district had one-third as many library books, one-fourth as many guidance counselors, and classes that were 50 percent more crowded than neighboring white districts.[2]

The Edgewood Independent School District was the least affluent district among the seven public school districts in the San Antonio metropolitan area. Twenty-five elementary and secondary schools enrolled approximately 22,000 students in a central city residential neighborhood with minimal commercial or industrial property. The median family income in Edgewood was the lowest in the metropolitan area ($4,686) and the average assessed property value per pupil was also the lowest ($5,960). Yet the Edgewood district taxed itself at the highest equalized tax rate in San Antonio: $1.05 per $100 of property. Despite these taxes, the poverty of the community meant that school funds raised from local property taxes were inadequate to meet the education needs of the students.[3]

Demetrio Rodriguez and a handful of other concerned Mexican American parents took their complaint to Arthur Gochman, a local graduate of the University of Texas Law School. Gochman was a Texan himself, known in the community for his record of defending civil rights and participating in local sit-ins for desegregation of various facilities. Rodriguez had also participated in numerous advocacy organizations for Mexican American rights during the 1960s, such as LULAC and the Mexican American Betterment Association. Gochman told them the central legal issue was the state education financing system that required caps on local taxation. In an area with low property values like Edgewood, voters were flat-out barred from choosing to tax themselves at a higher rate. They did not have the option, under state law, to fund schools at anything close to the same level as other districts in areas with higher property values.[4]

Alamo Heights operated its schools under the same state taxation caps, but they yielded vastly different outcomes. Alamo Heights was a wealthy, overwhelmingly white school district only six miles from Edgewood that frequently served as a counterpoint to Edgewood in the case. Due to the disparities in wealth and property values, and despite the comparatively high tax rate in Edgewood, Edgewood schools were only able to raise $26 per child, while Alamo Heights raised $333. Compared to Edgewood's 22,000 students, Alamo Heights housed 5,000 students. The assessed value per pupil in Alamo

Heights was more than $49,000, more than eight times as much as Edgewood, yet their tax rate was $0.85 per $100 of assessed property while Edgewood's was over $1.00, the highest in the city. A recruiter for Rice University, M. L. Rudee, who routinely visited both Edgewood and Alamo Heights schools, described the visible differences between the two district's resources in a letter to Justice Powell after the eventual Supreme Court ruling. Rudee recalled that Edgewood High School had offices and rooms "lighted by one bare bulb hanging from the ceiling," while Alamo Heights had a large, well-appointed campus. Alamo Heights, according to Rudee, had a huge staff of specialized college preparatory counselors who by themselves had a larger staff of receptionists than Edgewood schools had counselors of any kind. Rudee emphasized that the disparities between the schools were not minor or trivial, but fundamental and "so profound that any person of goodwill would disagree with your decision."[5]

Dr. Jose A. Cardenas, superintendent of the Edgewood Independent School District (the nominal defendant in the case) would later testify in a Senate hearing that state funding was able to do little to equalize resources between the two schools. For example, Texas required at least 26 Spanish-speaking students in a school in order to receive $150,000 for a bilingual education program. Alamo Heights had so few minority students that, as Cardenas noted, it actually had to combine students with another district in order to reach the minimum of 26. This meant that less than 26 students were enrolled in a bilingual program receiving $150,000, while Edgewood had to share the same amount among 22,000 Spanish-speaking students.[6]

The Rodriguez Lawsuit Begins

Based on these disparities and the context of residential segregation that had contributed to them, Gochman filed a class-action lawsuit against local and state officials on behalf of all similarly situated children who were low-income or racial minorities in Texas, making three central legal claims. First, they claimed that poverty constituted a suspect class which meant the finance laws were unconstitutionally discriminatory; second, that education was a constitutionally protected fundamental right infringed by the unequal school financing outcomes; and third, that the plaintiffs were discriminated against on the basis of race due to the overwhelming impact of the school finance inequalities on students of color, in this case Mexican American students.

Gochman's first claim was that poverty should be treated as a suspect class, a status which would trigger heightened constitutional scrutiny and protection against discrimination on the basis of wealth. The question of whether poverty could be analogized to race, the paradigmatic suspect class in twentieth-century jurisprudence, was clearly a current issue before the Court. Cases in the late 1960s and early 1970s indicated that wealth status might be just as irrational a basis for legislative differentiation as race. *Harper v. Virginia State Board of Elections, McDonald v. Board of Election Commissioners,* and other decisions had offered progressively more protections to poor people contesting differential treatment on the basis of income, whether it involved the right to an adequate attorney for criminal defense, the right to access trial transcripts and records for use on appeal, the right to vote, or the right to file for divorce regardless of ability to pay the filing fee.[7]

There was an important strategic reason for the litigants to try to locate wealth or poverty within the rubric of suspect classifications. When courts encountered other suspect classes, for example race or national origin, they approached them with deep suspicion. Unless the government could provide compelling justification, such as national security, for using these suspect categories, legislation containing them was invariably struck down. The alternative and more commonly used standard was the "rational basis" test, in which the government simply had to give a "rational" reason for a court to uphold a law. The two-tiered framework would give way to a three-tiered framework a few years after *Rodriguez,* incorporating a middle tier of scrutiny for "semi-suspect classifications" such as gender. Unfortunately for the *Rodriguez* claimants, their case reached the Court at a moment when it remained unclear if the binary construction of equal protection analysis would be permanent or whether the levels of scrutiny would continue to expand.[8]

Gochman's second claim was that education was a fundamental right. Given the Court's language in *Brown* and high level of attention to education cases during the prior several decades, there was strong precedent supporting the assumption that education was a fundamental right. Warren's brief opinion had asserted that education was "perhaps the most important function of state and local governments . . . the very foundation of good citizenship . . . a right which must be made available to all on equal terms." And if a law impinged on a fundamental right, it could be overturned even if no suspect class was involved. The Court had repeatedly held that actions such as forced sterilization, refusal to allow citizens to travel between states, or even prohibitively high filing fees for marriage or divorce imposed burdens on these fundamental rights that could not be tolerated, even without a clear relationship to a suspect category such as race or national origin.[9]

Finally, the claimants argued that the inequalities prevalent in the school financing scheme constituted discrimination on the basis of race due to their disproportionate effect on Mexican American and African American children. Texas had an especially convoluted legal trajectory with regard to racial discrimination in education and the use of the language of "race." In a 1905 Texas statute, the state required all public school teachers to use only English in school and created separate schools for students with Spanish surnames. Their complex legal position in the Jim Crow era had led many Mexican American advocates to embrace an identity as "other whites," which created difficulties in constructing a unified legal argument encompassing the de jure segregation condemned in *Brown* and the ongoing de facto segregation of Mexican Americans prevalent in Texas. Indeed, the "other white" argument was used by many school boards to avoid or delay the desegregation of all-white schools ordered by *Brown* and its progeny by assigning African American and Mexican American students to the same schools. This action was simplified by the proximity of ghettos and barrios in many urban areas, and it had the effect of allowing school boards to claim that these schools were then technically "desegregated" under *Brown* because Mexican Americans were classified as "other whites."[10]

This type of segregation was not declared illegal until a Texas district court case from 1970 ruled that Mexican Americans in Corpus Christi were entitled to Fourteenth Amendment protections and the protection of the *Brown* line of case precedent. Judge Seals rejected any judicial construction of *Brown* or the Equal Protection Clause that implied that "any other group which is similarly or perhaps equally, disadvantaged politically and economically, and which has been substantially segregated in public schools," should receive less constitutional protection than African Americans, stating that "it is clear . . . that these cases are not limited to race and color alone." While this opinion indicated a willingness to extend equal protection examination to categories outside of race, the Supreme Court would prove less open to a construction of the Fourteenth Amendment that included poverty.[11] The three-judge Texas District Court panel that convened to hear Gochman's complaint needed to find only one of his three arguments valid in order to force the state to provide "compelling justification" for its school financing system. The panel held, however, that the state had failed to "even establish a reasonable basis" for its financing system, without reaching the debate on poverty as a suspect class, education as a fundamental right, or race as an equal protection trigger. The District Court failed Texas on rational basis review, the most deferential judicial standard, and the state appealed.[12]

Going to the Supreme Court on Funding

The attorneys for Texas filed their first jurisdictional brief on April 17, 1972, arguing that any method of funding equalization raised the specter of actually harming public education. Though the brief questioned whether there was a link between funding and quality of education, the attorneys also argued that it was doubtful that parents of children who already enjoyed the best-funded schools would sit by as their district's funding was reduced to equalize educational expenditures. Such a move, the statement claimed, would encourage parents with means to support private schools, particularly with the solid precedent of judicial deference to parental choice in the education of their offspring. The statement finished by arguing that a decision such as the lower court's holding in *Rodriguez* would encourage flight from public schools "at a time when [they] are a principal hope of achieving a society that is not divided by artificial barriers of race or class or wealth."[13]

Perhaps the most important *amicus* brief in determining the form and argument of the eventual majority opinion was from state government representatives of thirty states seeking to overturn the decision, often referred to by Justice Powell as "the Maryland brief." This brief reiterated the earlier argument of the appellants that the *Rodriguez* equality principle would be harmful to poor and minority students. It particularly cited sociologist James Coleman, a citation later repeated by Justice Powell in his notes approving of the brief. Coleman, who had written the foreword to the book *Private Wealth and Public Education*, which was the framework for many school finance suits, was by the 1970s firmly opposed to both school finance reform and busing. Coleman equated revised school financing on the *Rodriguez* model with the exploitative use of schools by "Hitler's Germany . . . Stalin's Russia . . . Mao's China and . . . Castro's Cuba."[14] The brief speculated that implementation of the lower court decision would potentially result in higher taxes for urban areas and a decrease in per-student expenditures in many large city school districts, which, they argued, would harm the educational opportunities of the high percentage of poor students and racial minorities in those cities.[15]

The first *amicus* brief filed in support of the lower court decision was written by the Council of Great City Schools, representing the 23 largest city school districts in the United States, along with various city mayors and councils, the AFL-CIO, the Urban League, and other interest groups. The brief explicitly linked poverty to race in discussing the crises in inner cities, citing the high proportion of African Americans and minorities and high levels of poverty in the Detroit population versus the overwhelmingly white and affluent suburbs surrounding it. The brief also argued that lack of funds for education in heavily populated city school districts contributed to other serious urban problems such as "poverty, crime, unemployment, racial tension, drug abuse, blighted neighborhoods and the flight to the suburbs of business and the white middle class." The authors argued that property tax school financing discriminated against central city school children by creating differential outcomes based on class status.[16] They analyzed the case of Detroit specifically, showing that 65 percent of students in Detroit public schools were black or another minority group, while outlying suburbs like Grosse Pointe weighed in at 0.3 percent minority. Detroit schools were able to spend only three-quarters per pupil (even with federal aid) of what the suburban schools could spend even though the city taxed itself for education at double the statewide average rate.[17]

The NAACP amicus brief, signed by Jack Greenberg, among others, also made a point of linking the race and poverty of the *Rodriguez* plaintiffs as inextricable and tied to the history of racism and educational segregation. The NAACP argued that the disparities in the financing system "make it virtually impossible for Texas school districts of predominantly Mexican-American population to raise sufficient revenues to even begin to meet the educational needs of its children." This brief insisted forcefully that the lower court's decision should be upheld on the grounds of both wealth discrimination and race discrimination since there could be no compelling interest on the state's part to have a financing scheme that came at such a huge cost to poor and minority students.[18]

Professor Charles Alan Wright, a renowned constitutional scholar and veteran Supreme Court advocate, presented oral arguments for the state of Texas before the U.S. Supreme Court on October 12, 1972. He reiterated the claims from his briefs, particularly emphasizing concerns of local control and questioning the linkage of educational quality and financial expenditure. Toward the end of Wright's oral argument, Justice Douglas raised the question of race and its connection to the low-income community for the first time, and Wright admitted that "the racial issue is in this litigation" but argued that racial discrimination need not be part of the court's decision. Wright argued that the correlation between racial composition and poverty in San Antonio was a "happenstance." In addition, Wright referred obliquely to *James v. Valtierra* as an illustration "that this Court is not going to impose a constitutional straightjacket on the states in difficult and intractable questions of social reform, welfare, economics." In describing the arguments of the parents in the *Rodriguez* case, he said they suggested that "the educational needs of the poor are fundamental while their needs for food and for housing are not."

Characterizing this distinction as "untenable," Wright argued that it would be difficult to say "that a higher salaried school teacher is more fundamental to a poor child than food or a sunroof over his head."[19]

Wright also claimed that "Texas is asking this Court to resolve the very vexing questions on the relation of money to quality and education and on whether or not persons who are individually poor are not likely to be found in school districts that are in terms of taxable property, collectively poor." Acknowledging that "[t]he District Court did explicitly find that there is a correlation between poor people and poor school districts," Wright drew upon evidence that in the state of Connecticut, there was at least one community where that relationship was inverse and the poorest people lived in the area where the most was being spent on education while the richest people lived in the area where the least was being spent on education.[20]

Wright finished speaking after the lunch break, and Gochman was called forward to present his argument. Gochman was appearing for the first time in front of the Supreme Court and his strong Texas drawl posed a sharp contrast to Wright's New England propriety. Gochman began by arguing that in Texas, unlike Connecticut, "the poorest people live in the poorest districts and the richest people live in the richest districts," but Justice Brennan quickly interrupted to ask whether or not that was a "necessary correlation."[21] Gochman conceded that it didn't have to be, but that the prevalence of the correlation was the basis of the lawsuit, given that "this kind of discrimination falls most heavily on the poor. The poor have nowhere to go. Edgewood is a barrio district." Justice Blackmun questioned Gochman, referring to an example from his own experience in Minnesota with varied economic areas like the "Iron Range," in which comparatively poor families sometimes lived in a region with highly tax-funded schools due to the presence of industries like steel companies. Gochman acknowledged that some variation took place, but referenced the connection between minority status and segregation along with the poverty of the district, arguing that "the richest districts have the least poor people and the least minorities, and the poorest districts have the most poor people and the most minorities." He concluded that the poor families were "locked in" in the current arrangement, saying that "mobility is a key issue in this litigation—if it was a rich guy in a poor district he could just move. But, the poor have no way out of the present system."[22]

The Justices Deliberate on *Rodriguez*

Justice Lewis Powell was strongly interested in authoring the Court's opinion in the case from the beginning. A former education official on the Richmond

School Board as well as the Virginia Board of Education, Powell felt he had more interest in the functioning of schools than any other justice. He was also strongly suspicious of the claim that the financing system discriminated against the poor, and he was concerned that—having previously pushed back against desegregation during his time in Richmond—he would be perceived as less than committed to equal education. Powell believed that *Rodriguez* was different from *Brown* precisely because the alleged discrimination was based on wealth. For Powell, a remedy for wealth discrimination was a slippery slope toward socialism or worse. He wrote in his conference notes that "in a free enterprise society we could hardly hold that wealth is suspect. This is a communist doctrine but is not even accepted (except in a limited sense) in Soviet countries."[23]

In an early internal memorandum indicating the justices' first impressions of the case, the initial votes hewed closely to the final 5-4 split. Chief Justice Burger cast a straw vote for reversal, stating that he generally agreed with Wright's brief. Justice Stewart also cast an early vote for reversal, arguing that "money is some index, but the [equal protection] clause does not require egalitarianism." Stewart went on to state that "[u]nless there is a specific, identifiable class of people that is being discriminated against, the [equal protection] clause does not apply." According to Stewart, "'[r]ich' and 'poor' are not discrete, specific, and identifiable classes," announcing a concern that would show up again later in Powell's majority opinion. Justice Rehnquist agreed with Stewart's assessment of the case in his vote for reversal. Justice Blackmun's vote for reversal, according to Powell's notes, was based simply on his conclusion that the "Texas system provides adequate basic aid."[24]

Justice Brennan voted to affirm the case, and Powell quoted him verbatim in his conference notes as saying that "[f]ew cases have troubled me more." Brennan argued that "money is important and if a state provides [education] the allocation of money must be substantially equal." Agreeing with the methodology of the district court decision, Brennan stated that the claimants "[d]on't have to show a compelling interest—there is no rational interest." Justice White voted to affirm "with a narrower opinion," agreeing with the district court that in "a district which is 'locked-in,' and where [the] state provides no way to equalize there is a denial of [equal protection]." Douglas also voted to affirm, stating that the case was a "[p]roblem of equality." And in his initial vote to affirm, Justice Marshall argued that the district "can equalize the money even if can't equalize education," since the law created a "geographic distinction."[25]

In an early memo from Justice Powell to J. Harvie Wilkinson III (one of

Powell's law clerks at the time), Powell described the *Rodriguez* case as one in which the district court had "almost slavishly" followed *Serrano*, which Powell claimed "adopted almost literally the 'activist scholarship' theory of Professors Coons and Sugarman in their book *Private Wealth and Public Education.*" The 1970 Coons and Sugarman work was influential in framing public understandings of the effect of property-tax-based financing on low-income school districts and communities. One of Powell's first criticisms of the plaintiff's argument was that the Supreme Court cases the claimants relied upon dealt with wealth classifications that operated against individuals, whereas *Serrano* and *Rodriguez* dealt with the wealth classification of school districts. Thus the case did not fit into the individualized remedies language of constitutional equal protection from previous precedent; in the claim of a collective harm, the injury was further removed from the Court's grasp.[26]

Powell argued that his own experience in public education in Virginia supported the view that the taxable wealth of a school district did not necessarily reflect the wealth of its individual residents. He ventured a guess that "in terms of wealth, the city of Richmond is one of Virginia's wealthiest school districts—largely because of industrial and commercial development within the city." Nonetheless, Powell then speculated that "the wealth per individual or family may be relatively low in view of the large black population." Powell wrote in an early memo that in Virginia, the educational problem of school funding disparities due to differential tax bases was in the rural counties rather than the "urban centers inhabited by the blacks and the poor whites." As an example, Powell cited the case of Giles County, in which there was little or no high-value commercial development or real estate. In Giles County, according to Powell, "[t]he county is poor and the people are poor, but they are not 'ghetto' residents and there are very few blacks."[27]

Rather than follow the standard procedure of crafting an initial bench memo establishing the different issues and questions in the case, Powell asked Larry Hammond, the law clerk he had assigned to the case, to skip that step and just prepare a draft opinion, so certain was he of his position. Hammond chose not to follow this request. Arguing that "the case is clearly the most important one I have participated in since you came to the Court (indeed it is possibly the most important case in recent years)," Hammond instead drafted a bench memo laying out all the potential issues in the case and raising the possibility of affirmance, which Hammond said he "lean[ed] towards" after his review of the complex facts in the litigation. It appears that all three of Powell's law clerks as well as the majority of the other clerks at the time leaned, at least early on, toward affirming the ruling in favor of the Rodriguez family and the other plaintiffs. Hammond attempted to assure Powell at the end of his first memo that the three clerks were not going to "gang up on" him. Indeed, one clerk wrote a law review article three years later critiquing the decision, which prompted Powell to write a slightly affronted letter to all his clerks clarifying the nature of their support for his decision at the time.[28]

Hammond's memo reflected Powell's impulse to shelve the racial component of the case and to question the representativeness of the poverty claim. Early in the bench memo, Hammond argued that "the Court must avoid the temptation to mislabel this case," saying that "[i]t is not a case designed, necessarily, to provide some remedy for the educational ills of racial minorities or of the poor." Though some poor children and some minority children might certainly benefit, Hammond argued, "so will many who cannot claim either status and whose only injury derives from his residence within a property-poor school district." Mentioning the distinction between the wealth of individuals and the wealth of a collection of individuals in a political subdivision, Hammond agreed with Powell and the attorneys for Texas that there was such a distinction, but he argued that "it appears to be a distinction without a difference." Hammond claimed that regardless of the differences in individual wealth versus the wealth of a community, the outcome was what was most relevant, and that "if a state offers a fundamental education to some it must not offer less than tha[t] to others simply because of their lack of wealth."[29]

Powell responded to Hammond's memo a week later, citing the Maryland amicus brief with great support and indicating that he remained strongly in favor of the local fiscal control argument. He also acknowledged that he remained "unconvinced" that the ultimate effect of the case would not be "national control of education." Again citing the Maryland brief and its deployment of Coleman's anticommunist rhetoric, Powell said, "I would abhor such control for all the obvious reasons . . . the irresistible impulse of politicians to manipulate public education for their own power and ideology—e.g. Hitler, Mussolini, and all Communist dictators." By directing the discourse in terms of local control and focusing critique on the quasi-communist specter of potential state or national funding, the Maryland brief held a great degree of sway in Powell's decision about how to formulate the opinion, with many citations to it in his notes, memos, and drafts to his clerks.[30]

Illustrating his desire to distinguish this case from *Brown*, at the bottom of one of the pages of handwritten notes for conference on *Rodriguez*, Powell wrote in large letters that "<u>Brown</u> was based on <u>racial discrimination</u>." Discrimination—or inequality—on the basis of poverty was something he viewed very differently. But some of Powell's clerks remained uneasy with the decision up until the end. In a last set of draft revisions before publication of the opinion, Hammond wrote that he tried to "tone down" one of Powell's footnotes, because "upon rereading it I came away with a sense of inevitability about the status quo." Hammond cited *Baker v. Carr*, a major voting redistricting case that was also cited by the dissents, highlighting its similarities to *Rodriguez* and saying that "[i]f, indeed, no alternative other than what we have today is <u>politically</u> feasible this is the best reason for the Court to intervene." Despite the ongoing questions that seemed to linger in his conferences with his clerks, however, Powell remained set on the same view of the case he had had from the earliest discussion.[31]

The Decision and the Dissent

The final opinion in the case was issued on March 21, 1973, six months after oral arguments. A tight 5-4 vote decided the fate of low-income families, school districts, and public education property taxation schemes nationwide. Justice Powell's majority opinion was joined by Justices Stewart, Blackmun, Rehnquist, and Burger. Justice Stewart filed a concurring opinion, and Justices Brennan, Marshall, and White each wrote dissenting opinions, the latter two of which Justice Douglas joined. The majority reversed the district court ruling, arguing that neither the suspect classification claim nor the fundamental interest claim was convincing. Powell described the wealth discrimination analysis used by the district court as *sui generis*, arguing that the question of whether a local property tax system discriminated on the basis of wealth could not "be so neatly fitted into the conventional mosaic of constitutional analysis."[32] Though the majority opinion never took up the claim of race discrimination, Powell spent the first part of the opinion debating the potential ways in which discrimination could occur on the basis of wealth or poverty. He found three ways that the property tax system could arguably be discriminatory on the basis of wealth: "(1) against 'poor' persons whose incomes fall below some identifiable level of poverty or who might be characterized as functionally 'indigent,' or (2) against those who are relatively poorer than others, or (3) against all those who, irrespective of their personal incomes, happen to reside in relatively poorer school districts."[33]

After creating this framework, he was able to differentiate *Rodriguez* from previous precedents by describing the common thread in prior cases as a complete inability to pay for some desired benefit and an absolute deprivation of a meaningful opportunity to enjoy that benefit. Under this rubric, Powell argued that only the first argument for discrimination in the case could potentially fit the prior precedents, but that there had been no demonstration that the tax system "operates to the peculiar disadvantage of any class fairly definable as indigent, or as composed of persons whose incomes are beneath any designated poverty level." Regardless, Powell concluded, there had not been an absolute deprivation of the desired benefit even if there was a definable category of "poor" people, and thus "the disadvantaged class is not susceptible of identification in traditional terms." Turning finally to the question of a right to education, Powell emphasized "our historic dedication to public education." But, he argued, there was not an absolute deprivation of education in this case, and it was difficult to argue that education was more important than food or shelter, which the Court had not recognized as fundamental in recent welfare cases.[34]

While Justice Brennan's brief dissent focused on the right to education, Justice White's dissent made a forceful argument that there was a clear class subject to discrimination and entitled to the benefits of equal protection. White referenced several recent voter apportionment cases, quoting *Bullock v. Carter* from the year before to argue that regardless of the specificity of the victims of discrimination, "we would ignore reality were we not to recognize that this system falls with unequal weight on voters, as well as candidates, according to their economic status."[35] Similarly, White argued, "we would blink reality to ignore" the differential effect of the financing structure on schools and students with low per-pupil tax bases.[36]

Justice Marshall, in a powerful dissent joined by Justice Douglas, took apart the arguments of the majority point by point. First, he examined the funding variations in the Texas financing scheme and responded to the appellants' argument that there was no correlation between funding levels and educational quality, stating that "[i]t is an inescapable fact that if one district has more funds available per pupil than another district, the former will have greater choice in educational planning than will the latter."[37] Citing the Court's ruling 23 years earlier in *Sweatt v. Painter* for the argument that there was no substantial equality in terms of resources or preference between the segregated law schools, Marshall said that it was "difficult to believe that if the children of Texas had a free choice, they would choose to be educated in districts with fewer resources."[38] He dismissed the majority's interpretation of the appellants' claim that the Equal Protection Clause contained "some theory of constitutional adequacy" in discrimination in the provision of educational opportunity and instead asserted that the question of the case was inequality, not inadequacy. He also dismissed the issue of identification of the class as ultimately irrelevant, stating that "[s]o long as the basis of the discrimination is clearly identified, it is possible to test it against the State's purpose for such discrimination—whatever the standard of equal protection analysis employed."[39] His dissent acknowledged that while previous decisions were largely centered on discrimination on the basis of personal wealth, this case primarily rested on the property wealth of the district where the children reside. Marshall then argued that wealth classifications should be (and had been in previous decisions) suspect, though he paused to note that there were reasons to evaluate wealth discrimination differently than discrimination based on race or ethnicity. He acknowledged that while poverty may entail a social stigma similar to that historically attached to racial and ethnic groups, "personal poverty is not a permanent disability; its shackles may be escaped."[40] Marshall also stated that "most importantly," wealth did not share the "general irrelevance as a basis for legislative action" that race or nationality did, since there could be situations in which social legislation might reasonably be directed toward different income groups. Yet he concluded, given that there was no relationship whatsoever between district wealth and the unchanging and important interest of Texas children in educational opportunity, any form of discrimination that impinged on that interest on the basis of such a broad category should be as constitutionally problematic as any other discrimination on a basis beyond an individual's control.[41]

Conclusion: Educational Equality, Race, and Class Identity

The 1973 *Rodriguez* case, in which plaintiffs linked claims of discrimination based on class and race with the simple claim of a child's right to education, ended up rolling back the possibility of protecting vulnerable economic groups through equal protection. As one equal protection scholar wrote, "in 1973, the Court blinked."[42]

Ultimately, in *Rodriguez*, the Court ruled that there was no constitutional right to education and that property-tax-based school financing did not discriminate on the basis of wealth, despite Edgewood School District's 96 percent minority student population and the fraction of funding they received compared to overwhelmingly white, wealthy school districts nearby. Though financing differences in Texas schools were repeatedly framed as matters of private choice and marketplace decision making, even without the taxation caps, the choice of the local Edgewood community was largely illusory. As one cocounsel who worked with Gochman on the case later said, "Poor districts do not choose to spend less for education. It's like telling a man who makes $50 a week that he has the same right as a millionaire to send his son to Exeter."[43]

Rodriguez illustrates the importance of contesting concepts of poverty as an identity category in the law, whether that identity was framed in terms of personal choice or community accident in the majority opinion or as a historically rooted and clear category in the Marshall dissent. Even as courts throughout the twentieth century found various creative methods to affirm the fixed, supposedly unchanging nature of race and gender—identity categories with much more fluidity than has often been recognized in law—the *Rodriguez* court could not construct a coherent category of class.[44]

Texas continued to serve as a front line in battles over educational equality and access in school financing systems. Litigation based in Edgewood earned victories in state courts years after *Rodriguez* on the basis of state constitutional arguments for minimal adequacy in the provision of education, only to confront the unwillingness of the state legislature to remedy the inequities. The state of Texas passed a law two years after *Rodriguez* that withheld state funds for the education of the children of undocumented immigrants and permitted local districts to exclude them from enrollment. When that case, *Plyler v. Doe*, reached the Supreme Court a decade after *Rodriguez*, Justice Powell, though still committed to his earlier decision, also seemed to feel concerned about where such a ruling had led. He pushed for a heightened level of equal protection scrutiny because he regarded the class at issue as composed of "innocent children" deprived of a minimal education. Of course, the *Rodriguez* complainants were also "innocent" and yet had not been deemed entitled to heightened protection. In the end, Justice Brennan, who wrote the majority opinion in *Plyler v. Doe*, adopted these concerns, arguing that the Texas law would "create and perpetuate a subclass" of children who would be completely excluded from education, which was a violation of equal protection, even if *Rodriguez* would allow their peers to receive an unequal education.[45]

Rodriguez was a case that would not have existed without the intersecting practices of racial segregation, income segregation, and localized education financing rooted in segregated communities. The plaintiffs claimed each of these experiences as a contributing factor in their pursuit of justice for the children in their community, but the legal system mapped its own categorizing process onto their case and rejected each of their arguments. When asked for his reaction to the Supreme Court decision in his case, Demetrio Rodriguez simply said, "The poor people have lost again."[46]

Notes

1. For further discussion of the Rodriguez' family background, see Michael Heise, *The Story of San Antonio Independent School District v. Rodriguez: School Finance, Local Control, and Constitutional Limits*, in EDUCATION LAW STORIES 52 (Michael A. Olivas & Ronna Greff eds., 2008). *See also* San Antonio Indep. School Dist. v. Rodriguez, 411 U.S. 1 (1973).

2. Demetrio Rodriguez' situation at the time of the case is discussed in PETER IRONS, THE COURAGE OF THEIR CONVICTIONS: SIXTEEN AMERICANS WHO FOUGHT THEIR WAY TO THE SUPREME COURT 283–84 (1988); *Rodriguez*, 411 U.S. at 12; brief for ACLU et al. as Amici Curiae Supporting Respondents, 411 U.S. 1 (1973) (No. 71-1332), 1972 WL 136443.

3. *Rodriguez*, 411 U.S. at 12.

4. Richard Schragger, *San Antonio v. Rodriguez and the Legal Geography of School Finance Reform*, in CIVIL RIGHTS STORIES 91 (Myriam G. Gilles & Risa L. Goluboff eds., 2008); RICHARD R. VALENCIA, CHICANO STUDENTS AND THE COURTS 93 (2008); IRONS, *supra* note 2, at 285.

5. Schragger, *supra* note 4, at 86; affidavit of Dr. José A. Cárdenas in *Rodriguez*, http://curiae.law.yale.edu/pdf/411-1/010_3.pdf (on file with author); letter to Powell from M. L. Rudee, March 26, 1973, San Antonio v. Rodriguez, Washington & Lee University School of Law, Lewis F. Powell Jr. Papers, Supreme Court Case Files, series 10.6, box 8-153 [hereinafter Lewis F. Powell Jr. Papers, Supreme Court Case Files].

6. Testimony of Dr. José A. Cárdenas, Hearings before the U.S. Senate Select Committee on Equal Educational Opportunity, *Part 4: Mexican American Education*, 91st Cong., August 1970 (Washington, D.C.: GPO, 1970), 2443.

7. *See, e.g.*, Griffin v. Illinois, 351 U.S. 12 (1956) (establishing the right of criminal defendants to a free transcript for use on appeal regardless of ability to pay); Harper v. Virginia State Board of Elections, 383 U.S. 663 (1966) (outlawing state poll tax); Boddie v. Connecticut, 401 U.S. 371 (1971) (ruling that filing fee for divorce imposed on a fundamental right for indigent people).

8. Korematsu v. United States, 323 U.S. 214 (1944).

9. Brown v. Board of Education, 347 U.S. 483, 493 (1954); Skinner v. Oklahoma, 316 U.S. 535 (1942) (ruling forced sterilization of habitual criminals unconstitutional for impinging on fundamental right to procreate); Edwards v. California, 314 U.S. 160 (1941) (ruling state statute prohibiting bringing an indigent person into the state unconstitutional because interstate travel constituted a fundamental right); Boddie v. Connecticut, 401 U.S. 371 (1971).

10. Steven H. Wilson, *Brown Over "Other White": Mexican Americans' Legal Arguments and Litigation Strategy in School Desegregation Lawsuits*, 21 L. & HIST. REV. 145 (2003); DAVID MONTEJANO, ANGLOS AND MEXICANS IN THE MAKING OF TEXAS, 1836–1986 252 (1987); *see also* NEIL FOLEY, THE WHITE SCOURGE: MEXICANS, BLACKS, AND POOR WHITES IN TEXAS COTTON CULTURE (1997); GUADALUPE SAN MIGUEL JR., "LET ALL OF THEM TAKE HEED": MEXICAN AMERICANS AND THE CAMPAIGN FOR EDUCATIONAL EQUALITY IN TEXAS, 1910–1981 175 (1987).

11. Cisneros v. Corpus Christi Indep. School Dist., 324 F. Supp. 599, 601 (S.D. Tex., 1970), cited in Wilson, *supra* note 10, at 187–88.

12. Rodriguez v. San Antonio Indep. School Dist., 337 F. Supp. 280–282 (W.D. Tex. 1971), *rev'd*, 411 U.S. 1 (1973).

13. Briefs filed in the case were formerly available online at the Yale Law School Curiae Project, curiae.law.yale.edu, which is not currently active, but the briefs are on file with the law school library and with the author. Wright, Jurisdictional Statement for Appellants 8–9, Pierce v. Society of Sisters, 268 U.S. 510 (1925) (cited in the brief and holding that parents have a constitutional privacy right to decide on the manner of education of their children).

14. Brief of Reps. of State Gov'ts as Amici Curiae in Support of Petitioner at 37, San Antonio Indep. Sch. Dist. v. Rodriguez, 411 U.S. 1 (1973) (No. 71-1332) (hereinafter Govt. Amici Brief), *citing* John Coleman, *Foreword*, in JOHN E. COONS ET AL., PRIVATE WEALTH AND PUBLIC EDUCATION (1970).

15. Govt. Amici Brief, supra note 14, at 37, 68, 83–88, 411 U.S. at 12 (1972) (on file with author); JOHN E. COONS ET AL., PRIVATE WEALTH AND PUBLIC EDUCATION (1970).

16. Brief for Council of Great City Schools et al. as Amici Curiae Supporting Respondents at 16–17 (1972) (on file with author).

17. *Id.* at 6–7, 9–12, 16–17.

18. Brief for NAACP Legal Defense Fund et al. as Amici Curiae Supporting Respondents at 3–7 (1972) (on file with author).

19. Oral arguments in *Rodriguez*, Oct. 12, 1972, *available at* http://www.oyez.org/oyez/resource/case/343/audioresources. These oral arguments are also available in edited form in MAY IT PLEASE THE COURT: THE MOST SIGNIFICANT ORAL ARGUMENTS MADE BEFORE THE SUPREME COURT SINCE 1955 321 (Peter Irons & Stephanie Guitton eds., 1993).

20. Oral arguments in *San Antonio v. Rodriguez*, *supra* note 19.

21. This exchange between Gochman and Brennan appears in the oral arguments in *San Antonio v. Rodriguez*, *supra* note 19.

22. *Id.*

23. Paul A. Sracic, *The Brown Decision's Other Legacy: Civic Education and the Rodriguez Case*, 37 PS: POLITICAL SCIENCE & POLITICS 2: 215, 217 (2004).

24. Description and notes on deliberations except where otherwise noted are taken from the Lewis F. Powell Jr. Papers at Washington & Lee University School of Law. Initial Vote Chart, San Antonio v. Rodriguez, Washington & Lee University School of Law, Lewis F. Powell Jr. Papers, Supreme Court Case Files, series 10.6, box 8-153.

25. Initial Vote Chart, *supra* note 23.

26. Memo from Powell to J. Harvie Wilkinson III, August 30, 1972, San Antonio v. Rodriguez, Lewis F. Powell Jr. Papers, Supreme Court Case Files.

27. Bench memo from JWZ on *Rodriguez* to Blackmun, October 4, 1972, Papers of Harry Blackmun, box 161, folder 5, *Rodriguez* file; memo from Powell to J. Harvie Wilkinson III, August 30, 1972, San Antonio v. Rodriguez, Lewis F. Powell Jr. Papers, Supreme Court Case Files.

28. Memo from Larry Hammond to Powell, October 2, 1972, San Antonio v. Rodriguez, Lewis F. Powell Jr. Papers, Supreme Court Case Files; letter from Powell to J. Harvie Wilkinson III, March 11, 1976, San Antonio v. Rodriguez, Lewis F. Powell Jr. Papers, Supreme Court Case Files. The comments from Hammond and Powell in the following paragraphs are taken from these sources. For the later article that spawned the discussion with its critique of the *Rodriguez* opinion, see J. Harvie Wilkinson III, *The Supreme Court, the Equal Protection Clause, and the Three Faces of Constitutional Equality*, 61 VA. L. REV. 945 (1975).

29. Memo from Larry Hammond to Powell, October 2, 1972, San Antonio v. Rodriguez, Lewis F. Powell Jr. Papers, Supreme Court Case Files.

30. Memo from Powell to Hammond, October 9, 1972, San Antonio v. Rodriguez, Lewis F. Powell Jr. Papers, Supreme Court Case Files.

31. Undated conference notes, San Antonio v. Rodriguez, Lewis F. Powell Jr. Papers, Supreme Court Case Files; undated memo from Hammond to Powell, San Antonio v. Rodriguez, Lewis F. Powell Jr. Papers, Supreme Court Case Files.

32. These quotations are taken from *Rodriguez*, 411 U.S. at 54–56.

33. *Rodriguez*, 411 U.S. at 54–56.

34. The quotations in this paragraph are taken from *id.* at 55.

35. *Id.* at 69 (quoting Bullock v. Carter, 405 U.S. 134, 144 (1972).

36. *Id.* at 64–70.

37. *Id.* at 83.

38. *Id.* at 84, quoting Sweatt v. Painter, 339 U.S. 629, 633–34 (1950).

39. *Id.* at 93.

40. *Id.* at 121.

41. *Id.* at 94–95.

42. EVAN GERSTMANN, THE CONSTITUTIONAL UNDERCLASS: GAYS, LESBIANS, AND THE FAILURE OF CLASS-BASED EQUAL PROTECTION 45 (1999).

43. Summary of remarks made at the NCAEW Seminar on School Finance, Oct. 3, 1972, by Mark Yudof, cocounsel for the *Rodriguez* plaintiffs, *Rodriguez* backgrounder from National Council for the Advancement of Education Writing, January 1973, Part I, *available at* Harvard Law School library, Papers of William Brennan, box 297.

44. For an example of the contested and often fluid legal conceptions of race in U.S. history, see ARIELA GROSS, WHAT BLOOD WON'T TELL: A HISTORY OF RACE ON TRIAL IN AMERICA (2008).

45. Edgewood Indep. School Dist. v. Kirby, 777 S.W. 2d 391 (Tex. 1989); Plyler v. Doe, 457 U.S. 202 (1982); memo from Lewis Powell to William Brennan, et al., re *Plyler*, January 30, 1982, Papers of Harry Blackmun, box 154, folder 6, *Plyler* file.

46. IRONS, *supra* note 2, at 292.

Part III

The Modern Era

Reflecting and Foreshadowing

Mathews v. Eldridge • (1976)

JOHN J. CAPOWSKI

Decided in 1976, *Mathews v. Eldridge*[1] was a case about whether a Social Security disability recipient could get benefits while awaiting a hearing challenging the termination of his benefits, but the *Mathews* decision may be more important as a marker for our changed views of public benefits and the poor. *Mathews* is a case that foreshadowed the rightward political movement in this country. This chapter not only tells the story of *Mathews* but also the story of how the economic, social, and political climate influenced the decision in that case.

The 1970s were so unlike the decade that had preceded it. While the 1960s were characterized by great prosperity, by 1976 the economy showed a decline characterized by a marked increase in imported goods (including automobiles and appliances), a sharp drop in the stock market, and the ascendency of the Chicago School of Economics and deregulation. Perhaps because of the economy, the decade became one in which people were concerned about their own well-being rather than that of others. And instead of a divisive and embattled President Nixon in the White House, Gerald Ford, who was more of a caretaker, was sitting in the Oval Office. These events of the early 1970s, while seemingly unrelated to defining procedural due process, were the cultural setting for *Mathews*.

The Issue in *Mathews* and the Social Security
Disability Standard and Process

The vehicle that brought *Mathews v. Eldridge* to the Supreme Court was George Eldridge's claim for Social Security disability benefits. The issue the Court addressed (in the face of the Social Security Administration's decision that he was no longer disabled) was whether he should be able to continue receiving benefits while he awaited a posthearing examiner's decision on his appeal.

The Social Security Administration's definition of disability is not the one people ordinarily use. To be disabled under the Social Security Act, a person, due to physical and/or emotional disabilities, must be "unable to engage in substantial gainful activity."[2] For Social Security Disability (SSD), though not for Supplemental Security Income (SSI), an applicant must have worked long enough to become "insured"[3] under the Social Security Act (the "Act"). In deciding on eligibility, the Social Security Administration (SSA) and a designated state agency examine a claimant's medical history, functional limitations, and the duration of the disability. Whether one would ever actually be hired or whether there are positions available is irrelevant to the decision. The question is whether one would be able to do a job that "exists in significant numbers in the national economy."[4] Many have criticized the disability standard for being highly subjective and incapable of yielding accurate and consistent decisions.[5] While taxpayers may realize that this is a federal program because funding for Social Security comes from federal withholding, Congress structured the program to have state agencies administer portions of it, including initial eligibility decisions. Because state agencies make these initial eligibility decisions but the Social Security Administration sets the standards[6] and federal administrative law judges[7] handle review hearings, the system is one of co-operative federalism.[8]

If the state agency finds a claimant disabled after the initial application, the process for granting benefits is simple and direct. But if the state agency finds that an applicant is not disabled under the Act's definition, a claimant may move through several stages in having the claim reviewed. One may first request "reconsideration" of the denial, and the state agency will assign a different reviewer to look at the claim again. If the agency denies the claim following its reconsideration, a claimant can request a hearing before an administrative law judge (ALJ). A claimant who is denied eligibility after an ALJ hearing can seek review of the ALJ's decision through the Appeals Council of the Social Security Administration. If the Appeals Council affirms the hearing examiner's decision, a claimant may appeal to the United States District Court for the district in which the claimant lives.

Eldridge's Claim and Appeal

Eldridge first applied for benefits in 1967 and was, like so many applicants, initially denied benefits. The hearing officer who eventually heard his claim found him disabled,[9] and in 1968 Eldridge began receiving Social Security disability insurance benefits under Title II of the Social Security Act.[10] His initial disability was based on chronic anxiety and back strain, and he was later diagnosed with diabetes. The case that bought George Eldridge to the Supreme Court began after he had been collecting disability benefits for four years. In 1972, the state agency based in Richmond, Virginia, sent him a questionnaire as part of their review of his disability. In the questionnaire, he stated that his health problems had not improved and listed the health care providers he had recently seen. After obtaining reports from Eldridge's physician and a consulting psychiatrist whom the agency selected, the state agency sent Eldridge a letter telling him that his benefits would be terminated and that he could submit additional information. In his response, Eldridge stated that he had arthritis in his spine (not simply a strained back as described in the agency correspondence) and that the agency had enough evidence to find him disabled. Without any further investigation, the agency found he was no longer disabled. The Social Security Administration accepted the state agency's decision and told Eldridge it was terminating his benefits. The state agency's 1972 decision was not the first time the agency and SSA had found that Eldridge was not disabled. In fact, they had never found him disabled without his having had to seek an evidentiary hearing.

Goldberg v. Kelly and Seeking Pretermination Benefits in Federal Court

While Eldridge requested reconsideration, he and his attorney also went directly to the United States District Court for the Western District of Virginia to obtain benefits for Eldridge while he awaited a hearing examiner's decision.[11] To understand the decision he and his attorney made to go to federal court immediately, one should know that Eldridge was a widower with six children and could not sustain his family's living situation without the disability benefits. One should also know the Supreme Court's decision in the analogous case of *Goldberg v. Kelly*[12] and the decisions in other cases in the early 1970s that expanded procedural due process.[13]

The enigmatic question about the Court's decision in *Mathews* is how the Court decided only six years after *Goldberg* that a Social Security disability recipient was not entitled to a pretermination evidentiary hearing, while in *Goldberg* the Court found that recipients of the federal Aid to Families with Dependent Children (AFDC) program were entitled to continuing benefits while awaiting an evidentiary hearing. One might simply suggest, as the Court's majority did in *Mathews*, that the two cases are distinguishable, but the Court's effort to distinguish the two cases by differentiating AFDC recipients from disability recipients and AFDC determinations from decisions on disability is neither persuasive nor empirically supported.

In *Goldberg*, Justice Brennan, writing for the majority and answering the due process question, balanced the individual's right against the state's interest. He stated:

> [T]he crucial factor in this context—a factor not present in the case of the blacklisted government contractor, the discharged government employee, the taxpayer denied a tax exemption, or virtually anyone else whose governmental entitlements are ended—is that termination of aid pending resolution of a controversy over eligibility may deprive an eligible recipient of the very means by which to live while he waits.[14]

AFDC recipients like John Kelly were entitled to AFDC benefits based upon a showing of financial need. To distinguish Eldridge and other Social Security disability recipients from AFDC recipients, the Court in *Mathews* assumed that a Social Security disability recipient's need is less than that of an AFDC recipient. While this distinction between Social Security recipients and AFDC recipients holds true for some disability recipients, it does not for the great majority of disability recipients. The resources that the Court pointed to as potentially available to Social Security disability beneficiaries included savings, public and private pensions, and other public benefits. Justice Brennan objected, noting that the assumption of additional resources is speculative and "it is also no argument that a worker, who has been placed in the untenable position of having been denied disability benefits, may still seek other forms of public assistance."[15] As he realized, even those who may be eligible for other public benefits are likely to suffer harms from which they and their families will not be able to recover, even if their benefits are reinstated after a positive decision following an evidentiary hearing. Like many others whose benefits are temporarily terminated, Matthew Eldridge's family suffered several losses, including the foreclosure on their home and the repossession of the family's furniture.[16] In addition to losing Social Security benefits, recipients like Eldridge will lose medical coverage that is based on the disability, and the disability recipient who has been receiving benefits is unlikely to be able to work even if she or he can find employment. The disability makes the plight of the recipient whose benefits are being terminated perhaps more difficult than that of some AFDC recipients, who may be able to find work if their benefits are terminated. In addition to the financial harm a beneficiary may suffer while awaiting an administrative law judge decision, the claimant's disability is likely to become more severe. Emotional problems often accompany severe physical disabilities, and for individuals whose disability has an emotional component, the termination of benefits and financial hardship will likely exacerbate the emotional problem.

In addition to distinguishing the cases based on resources Social Security recipients are unlikely to have, Justice Powell wrote that hearings are more important in AFDC eligibility decisions than disability determinations. Quoting *Richardson v. Perales*,[17] he suggested that unlike AFDC hearing decisions, where witness credibility may be critical to the outcome, the decision to discontinue disability benefits in most cases will be based on "routine, standard, and unbiased medical reports by physician specialists."[18] The Court also assumed that disability recipients, unlike AFDC recipients, will be able to effectively make their cases in writing.

There are several problems with the Court's assumptions about disability determinations. First, in many cases, a Social Security claimant's disability will be based on a combination of physical and mental problems that no one medical expert has addressed, and, as the district court found, there may be conflicting reports from medical specialists. An ALJ will be able to question the disability claimant about the effect of these problems on the individual's daily life and, understanding the disability standard, will be able to make a more accurate disability determination than could be made on a paper record. Second, disability often depends on a number of factors that are unlikely to be part of a paper record but are likely to be clear during an evidentiary hearing. Robert G. Dixon observed that "the claimant's personal 'set' in the relation to his handicaps is often really the key factor. This is not specified in the statute, regulations, or disability insurance letters, but an observer at several hearings is immediately struck by its overwhelming nature."[19] Dixon goes on to say that "[t]he claimant's set regarding enduring pain, discomfort, and restricted movement, regarding his willingness to try to learn a new skill, regarding his willingness to adjust his life style to the need for greater off-the-job rest, regarding his residual 'zip' in general and especially his pride, are all relevant."[20] These characteristics are ones that a hearing examiner could observe but are unlikely to be discussed or understood by a decision maker reviewing a case file.

A third key to understanding the Court's holding in *Mathews* is the Court's failure to properly understand the importance of the error rate for claims denied by the state agency. SSA's "open file" approach permits adding documents to the case file at any time between the reconsideration and hearing stages. The Court, without discussing how many cases are affected by SSA's "open file" approach, found that the "open file" approach makes the rate at which hearing examiners reverse state agency decisions unhelpful in determining the actual error rate. Because the parties and amici presented differing reversal rates, one can understand why the Court decided that the claimed error rate is relevant but "not controlling."[21] While the Court limited the importance of the error rate as a factor in assessing the importance of a fact-finding hearing, the 58 percent reversal rate acknowledged in the government's supplemental brief leaves the impression that state agencies in reconsideration decisions are either making inaccurate disability decisions or decisions that are significantly different from those hearing examiners make.[22] The discrepancy between state agency and hearing examiner decisions, despite the "open file" process, supports the importance of an evidentiary hearing. The Court minimized the benefits and importance of an evidentiary hearing by stating that "'[d]ue process,' unlike some legal rules, is not a technical conception with a fixed content unrelated to time, place, and circumstances."[23]

In *Mathews* the Court not only distinguished the case from *Goldberg* but also set out factors for courts to use in deciding procedural due process issues. Those factors are:

> First, the private interest that will be affected by the official action; second, the risk of an erroneous deprivation of such interest through the procedures used, and the probable value, if any, of additional or substitute procedural safeguards; and finally, the Government's interest, including the function involved and the fiscal and administrative burdens that the additional or substitute procedural requirement would entail.[24]

Changes in the Court

The explanations for the different outcomes in *Goldberg* and *Mathews* are specific and concrete as well as general and diffuse. While not a complete explanation, one reason for the difference was the changing membership of the Court, and the changes in the justices in those six years foreshadowed the significant rightward movement of the Court.

In 1975, Justice Douglas, who had joined the majority in *Goldberg*, left the Court. Political conservatives of the day criticized him for the decisions he made in his personal life, including his several marriages, some to much younger women, but were most enraged by his absolute perspective on individual rights. He would have surely voted for continuing disability benefits. Stevens replaced Douglas on the Court and would have likely joined the dissenters in *Mathews*, but Stevens took no part in the *Mathews* decision.

William Rehnquist joined the Court in 1972, and during his term as chief justice led a court that overturned and limited the individual rights decisions of the Warren Court. The addition of Justice Rehnquist foreshadowed a further rightward movement toward great deference to the executive, administrative agencies, and Congress. As one would expect, Justice Rehnquist joined the majority in *Mathews*, and while the justice he replaced, Justice John Harlan, is generally classified as a conservative, Harlan joined the majority in *Goldberg* and might have joined the dissenters in *Mathews*. Of course, it is difficult to predict how Justice Harlan might have voted in *Mathews*. Additionally, Justice White, who supported prehearing benefits for AFDC recipients in *Goldberg*, did not vote in favor of them for Social Security claimants.

Justice Lewis Powell, who wrote the majority opinion in *Mathews*, and Justice Harry Blackmun, who joined the majority, also joined the Court in the years between these decisions. The *Mathews* decision and the changes in the Court evinced not only a rightward shift as the Court moved away from a strong individual rights jurisprudence but also a pragmatic judicial philosophy in which the Court became comfortable in balancing individual rights against governmental interests.

The Changed Economic, Political, and Social Landscape

While the changes in the Court's personnel affected the Court's procedural due process standard set out in *Mathews*, the changed political, cultural, social, and economic context also likely influenced the outcome. This chapter begins with some of those features from 1976, the year of the *Mathews* decision. In contrast, when *Goldberg* was decided in 1970, there was economic prosperity; people whose basic needs were met could afford to be concerned about the welfare of others. The solid economy was in part because of the war in Vietnam, which that year expanded into Cambodia. In part because the war ended and government defense expenditures waned, the 1970 unemployment rate of 3.3 percent rose to 7.7 percent in 1976. At the same time that unemployment was increasing, so was inflation. This combination of increasing unemployment accompanied by inflation, given the portmanteau "stagflation," is an event that is not possible under traditional Keynesian economic theory and is difficult to cure. Stagflation further weakened the economy. Adding to the misery index and the lack of confidence in the economy was the 1973–74 bear market, in which stocks lost more than 45 percent of their value. The market recovered after this dramatic downturn, but confidence in the economy did not.

While the Great Depression heralded the New Deal and the development of public benefit programs, the reaction in the United States in the 1970s to the economically difficult decade was characterized by pressure to limit both public benefit programs and the programs that were part of the War on Poverty. While many of President Johnson's War on Poverty programs, part of his Great Society initiative, survived,[25] by the early 1970s the Nixon administration had abolished the initiative's umbrella organization—the Office of Economic Opportunity—and many of the programs had become more limited in their scope.

Even the changes in popular music may have reflected our decreasing empathy, unwillingness to deal with difficult issues, and increasing self-absorption. In 1970, "Bridge Over Troubled Water" topped the *Billboard* chart and Edwin Starr's "War" was at number five, but by 1976, Paul McCartney's "Silly Love Songs" was the song of the year.

While some members of the Court deny that politics, the economy, or social climate affect their decision making, the changes in these areas between 1970 and 1976 affected us and likely the Court's decision in *Mathews*. Current and past members of the Court suggest that they are simply reading and applying the Constitution and other laws as written. During his confirmation hearing, Chief Justice Roberts testified that a judge's role is analogous to the role of a baseball umpire.[26] If one accepts the aptness of the analogy, one might say that during the hearing he was unwilling to describe his strike zone. Justice Scalia, the Court's current textualist archetype, has spoken about how, for example, his Roman Catholicism does not affect his judicial decision making.[27] While the justices' statements about simply applying the law are great political answers to questions about their judicial philosophies, these answers evince a certain pragmatism and disingenuousness.

In contrast to the statements of Chief Justice Roberts and Justice Scalia, some justices have acknowledged the importance of context in judicial decision making. Justice Breyer, whose judicial-interpretation theory is one of purposive analysis, looks to the reasons behind a provision in interpreting its meaning and considers how a specific interpretation may support a democratic society.[28] Former Justice O'Connor acknowledged the role that context has played in her decisions during her time on the Court.[29] As members of today's Court are influenced in their decisions by the political, economic, and social climate, those factors likely influenced the Court's decision in *Mathews*.

The Majority's Pragmatic View of Individual Rights

In its opinion in *Mathews*, the Court implicitly acknowledged factoring the economic climate into their due process standard; they included in their analysis "[t]he Government's interests, including the fiscal . . . burdens that the additional or substitute procedural requirement would entail" and their balancing of this burden against the claimant's rights.[30] In the case of Social Security disability benefits, the fiscal impact of requiring pretermination benefits is difficult to determine, and the Court decided to avoid the empirical issue. Justice Powell was willing to speculate that "the fact that full benefits would continue until after such hearings would assure the exhaustion in *most* cases of this attractive option."[31] Avoiding an estimate of the financial burden on the Social Security program, the Court simply found "that the ultimate additional cost in terms of money and administrative burden would not be insubstantial. . . . At some point the benefit of an additional safeguard to the individual affected by the administrative action and to society in terms of increased assurance that the action is just, may be outweighed by the cost."[32]

The *Mathews* Standard and Robert Bork

Because the due process framework the Court set out in *Mathews* is troublingly flawed, readers of the case may wonder how the Court crafted the standard. The surprising answer is that the Court adopted the standard set out in the government's brief.[33] The government had cobbled together language from earlier Supreme Court due process opinions on Nebraska's correctional procedures and a Columbus, Ohio, school system's transfer of a student.[34] In addition, a surprising number of the assumptions the Court used to distinguish the AFDC recipient in *Goldberg* from the Social Security disability recipient in *Mathews* and the differences in termination evidentiary hearings came directly from the government's brief. The brief made assumptions about the resources that disability claimants may have and expressed the view that disability determinations are easily and accurately made when they are based solely on medical reports.[35]

Among the subplots in *Mathews* is the role of Robert Bork, who was the solicitor general at the time and argued the case before the Court. Bork's career later included teaching at Yale Law School, being the person who fired Watergate special prosecutor Archibald Cox, and serving on the U. S. Court of Appeals for the District of Columbia Circuit. He is also known for developing and championing originalism, the constitutional interpretation doctrine that focuses on the intent of the drafters in deciding a provision's meaning. This view has become a standard interpretive tool of conservative judges and was the view of Justice Rehnquist, who joined the majority in *Mathews*.[36]

Though he had a distinguished career, Robert Bork may be best known for the Senate's rejection of his nomination by Ronald Reagan to the Supreme Court. The Senate used his paper trail of conservative articles and decisions in rejecting his appointment, but for progressives, his oral argument in *Mathews* would have been enough.

During the argument, Bork was callous toward those whose disability benefits were terminated, and he stated that terminated claimants lacking resources could obtain "welfare," a claim that for many would not be true. After he suggested that those awaiting an evidentiary hearing could become welfare recipients, he ignored the principles underlying an individual's due process rights when he made the purely economic argument that "the dollar amounts are real proxy for the interests that go into the due process balance."[37]

While he argued that due process could be defined solely by the monetary interests, he also expressed concern that continuing benefits until an evidentiary hearing "imposes a social cost independent of money on the erosion of individual character."[38] At one point in the argument, possibly because of either confusion or disingenuousness, he suggested that the Court look to the reconsideration stage in accessing error rate and with mathematical legerdemain obtained a "harmful error rate of 7/10 of 1%."[39] He later acknowledged this percentage was not the reversal rate following the hearing examiners' review of reconsideration decisions.

Conclusion

While it is not a positive case in the development of poverty law or protection of the poor, *Mathews v. Eldridge* both reflected the change in our society during the early 1970s and foreshadowed the conservative judicial movement. Decided during a time of high unemployment and general economic downturn, *Mathews* reflected a turn away from President Johnson's goal of the Great Society, one in which poverty would be eliminated, and toward an end to the War on Poverty and an emphasis on fiscal pragmatism. The case also signaled the Court's move toward pragmatism and away from the individual rights emphasis of the Warren Court.

Although the reasoning of *Mathews* is flawed, some have suggested the test the Court adopted has worked reasonably well,[40] but many have criticized the factors the Court adopted for balancing an individual's procedural due process rights against the government's interest. In a takeoff on Pirandello's play "Six Characters in Search of an Author," Yale law professor Jerry Mashaw titled his major article on the case "The Supreme Court's Due Process Calculus for Administrative Adjudication: Three Factors in Search of a Theory of Value." From the title, the reader immediately knows Professor Mashaw's general view of the Court's procedural due process standard; his major criticism is that the Court's standard maximizes social justice but fails to address the values that support due process, including the dignity of the individual whose benefits are being terminated.[41] Professor Mashaw also chastises the Court for a standard that is subjective, impressionistic, and overly generalized.[42] A reader of *Mathews* can easily criticize the Court's standard, the assumptions it uses in giving weight to the factors, and its inability to effectively distinguish *Goldberg v. Kelly*. At the same time, one must acknowledge that any due process standard, including one that is based on the values underpinning due process, is likely to be amorphous and will require the exercise of discretion.

Because of the current makeup of the Court, we are unlikely to see a progressive and positive trend in poverty law decisions, but, just as we have become a more conservative country, we may become more progressive in the coming years.

Notes

1. 424 U.S. 319 (1976).
2. 42 U.S.C. § 423 (2004).
3. SSA Federal Old-Age, Survivors and Disability Insurance, 20 C.F.R. §§

404.130–146 (2013). Also, applicants must meet certain earnings requirements. 20 C.F.R. §§ 404.801–831 (2013).

4. 20 C.F.R. § 416.960 (2013).

5. Jerry Mashaw et al., Social Security Hearings and Appeals: A Study of the Social Security Administration Hearings System xxi (1978).

6. 20 C.F.R. § 405.1 (2013).

7. When Eldridge initially received disability benefits and when his case moved through the federal courts, hearing examiners handled the evidentiary hearings. Today those hearings are conducted by administrative law judges.

8. Frank S. Bloch, *Cooperative Federalism and the Role of Litigation in Development of Federal AFDC Eligibility Policy*, 1979 Wis. L. Rev. 1, 1–8 (discussing the contours of "cooperative federalism" in the development of Social Security and in the AFDC process).

9. For a discussion of the disability process, *see* John J. Capowski, *Accuracy and Consistency in Categorical Decision-Making: A Study of Social Security's Medical-Vocational Guidelines—Two Birds with One Stone or Pigeon-Holing Claimants?*, 42 Md. L. Rev. 329 (1983).

10. 424 U.S. at 319–20.

11. Eldridge v. Weinberger, 361 F. Supp. 520 (W.D. Va. 1973).

12. 397 U.S. 254 (1970).

13. *See, e.g.*, Gagnon v. Scarpelli, 411 U.S. 778 (1973) (holding that the state must hold a hearing before revoking an individual's probation); Bell v. Burson, 402 U.S. 535 (1971) (holding that a state statute that postponed a hearing to determine automobile accident liability until after the uninsured motorist's driver's license was suspended violated due process).

14. *Goldberg*, 397 U.S. at 264.

15. *Id.* at 350 (Brennan, J., dissenting).

16. *Mathews*, 424 U.S. at 350 (Brennan, J., dissenting) (citing Transcript of Oral Argument at 39, 47–48, Mathews v. Eldridge, 424 U.S. 319 (1976) (No. 74-204).

17. 402 U.S. 389, 404 (1971).

18. *Mathews*, 424 U.S. at 322.

19. Robert G. Dixon Jr., Social Security Disability And Mass Justice 61 (1973). While Dixon limits his view to "borderline cases," he describes those cases broadly as those in which no listed impairment has been found and which do not involve "'individuals with a marginal education and long work experience (e.g., 35–40 years or more) limited to the performance of arduous unskilled labor' who 'is not working and is no longer able to perform such labor because of a significant impairment or impairments and, considering his age, education, and vocational background is unable to engage in lighter work.'" *Id.* at 54–56.

20. *Id.* at 61.

21. Mathews v. Eldridge, 424 U.S. 319, 347 (1976). *See* Cynthia R. Farina, *Due Process at Rashomon Gate: The Stories of Mathews v. Eldridge, in* Administrative Law Stories 229, 241–47 (Peter L. Strauss ed., 2006) (discussing the parties' and amici's claimed error rates).

22. In its supplemental brief, the government acknowledges that 58.6 percent of

the cases that go to an evidentiary hearing are reversed. Supplemental Brief for the Petitioner at 14, *Mathews*, 424 U.S. 319 (No. 74-204). *See also Mathews*, 424 U.S. at 346 (stating that "[d]epending upon the base selected and the line of analysis followed, the relevant reversal rates urged by the contending parties vary from a high of 58.6% for appealed reconsideration decisions to an overall reversal rate of only 3.3%.").

23. *Id.* at 334 (citing Cafeteria Workers v. McElroy, 367 U.S. 886, 895 (1961)).

24. *Mathews*, 424 U.S. at 335.

25. These programs are now part of other federal agencies.

26. *Confirmation Hearing on the Nomination of John G. Roberts, Jr. to Be Chief Justice of the United States: Hearing Before the S. Comm. on the Judiciary*, 109th Cong. 56 (2005), *available at* http://abcnews.go.com/Archives/video/john-roberts-base ball-analogy-10628259 (stating that "judges are like umpires. Umpires don't make the rules; they apply them.").

27. *Justice Scalia on Life Part 2*, at 4:20 (CBS News *60 Minutes* broadcast Sept. 14, 2008), *available at* http://www.cbsnews.com/video/watch/?id=4448193n.

28. Linda Greenhouse, *Judicial Intent: Competing Visions of the Role of the Court*, N.Y. TIMES, July 7, 2002.

29. *See, e.g.*, JEFFREY TOOBIN, THE NINE: INSIDE THE SECRET WORLD OF THE SUPREME COURT 66 (2007).

30. 424 U.S. at 321.

31. *Id.* at 347 (emphasis added).

32. *Id.* at 347–48.

33. Brief for the Petitioner at 36, 424 U.S. 319 (No. 74-204).

34. Goss v. Lopez, 419 U.S. 565 (1975) (cited in brief as No. 73-898); Wolff v. McDonnell, 418 U.S. 539 (1974) (cited in brief as No. 73-679); *see also* GARY LAWSON, FEDERAL ADMINISTRATIVE LAW TEACHER'S MANUAL 201 (5th ed. 2009). Professor Lawson states not only that the three-factor framework came from the government's brief but also that the framework was crafted to maximize the government's "chances of winning on the specific issues involved in *Mathews*." *Id.*

35. Brief for the Petitioner at 40–41, 44, 424 U.S. 319 (No. 74-204).

36. The member of the current Court who most champions this view is Justice Scalia, who knows the intent of the drafters in a way that others do not.

37. Transcript of Oral Argument at 39, 47–48, 424 U.S. 319 (No. 74-204).

38. *Id.*

39. Transcript of Oral Argument at 19–20, 424 U.S. 319 (No. 74-204). For a summary of this portion of the argument, *see* Farina, *supra* note 21, at 245.

40. *Id.* at 256–57 (stating that the Court "emerge[d] with . . . a solution that has worked for nearly 30 years . . . but 'worked' is used here in a very modest sense."). In the criminal justice area, the Court's solution has worked more favorably for individuals. *See, e.g.*, Ake v. Oklahoma, 470 U.S. 68 (1985) (granting the assistance of a psychiatric expert to an indigent criminal defendant).

41. *See, e.g.*, Jerry L. Mashaw, *The Supreme Court's Due Process Calculus for Administrative Adjudication: Three Factors in Search of a Theory of Value*, 44 U. CHI. L. REV. 28, 46–57 (1976).

42. *Id.* at 39.

Chronicle of a Debt Foretold
Zablocki v. Red Hail • (1978)

TONYA L. BRITO, R. KIRK ANDERSON,
AND MONICA WEDGEWOOD

Zablocki v. Red Hail[1] is a canonical case in family law jurisprudence. One of the few Supreme Court decisions addressing the fundamental right to marry, it is typically located in family law textbooks immediately after *Loving v. Virginia*. Positioning *Zablocki v. Red Hail* in this line of cases makes sense; after all, the case involves a successful challenge to Wisconsin's "permission to marry" statute. The conventional understanding of the case, however, addresses only part of the story. The narrative threads uncovered as part of our oral history research study of *Zablocki v. Red Hail* reveal a more multifaceted and complicated story than has been previously appreciated. Unexpectedly, it is also an ongoing story.

The story behind *Zablocki v. Red Hail* spans the 1970s in Milwaukee, a period of great inequality and dynamic social change. It was a unique moment in time: inadequate government responses to disparities between the city's white and nonwhite populations in poverty rates, employment, housing, and education produced a range of overlapping and intersecting social movements. Both Roger Red Hail and Milwaukee Legal Services—the advocates that successfully represented him in challenging Wisconsin's permission-to-marry law—were situated within the crosscurrents of these social movements.

The story behind *Zablocki v. Red Hail* also engages the American Indian[2] experience in the United States, particularly the experience of urban Indians who have been uprooted from their native lands and disconnected from their heritage and history. One doesn't learn that Roger Red Hail is

Oneida from reading any of the case briefs or opinions in *Zablocki v. Red Hail*. In the view of his attorneys, it just didn't matter to the case. And while the constitutionality of the permission-to-marry statute did not turn on Red Hail's Indian heritage, his being an Oneida matters. It matters not only for the unique social and historical background of this story but also because Red Hail's dual citizenship—as both a citizen of Oneida and the United States—offers parallel, alternative legal systems and possibilities. And while the Oneida option did not supply Red Hail with an avenue to get around his marriage problem back in 1978, it holds promise for resolving his (still) pending child support problem.

Roger Red Hail, Marriage, and Poverty

Roger Red Hail still cannot get married. At 60, he lives with his fiancée Colleen in a suburban community outside Milwaukee. Framed family photographs decorate the tabletops, shelves, and walls in their cozy and welcoming home. Roger and Colleen have been together for 19 years and would like to get married. But, just as it did 40 years ago, child support debt stands in the way.

In 1974, Wisconsin's permission-to-marry law created the bar. Then 19-year-old Roger and his fianceé, Terry, went to the county clerk's office for a marriage license. Several months into a pregnancy, they wanted to tie the knot before the child's birth. They were surprised when the county clerk turned them away, citing Roger's child support debt as the reason. The law required Wisconsin residents under an order of child support to seek judicial permission to marry. Under the terms of the statute, permission would only be granted if the petitioner could demonstrate both that he was current in his child support payments and that his children were not then nor were likely in the future to be on public assistance.

At the time, Roger and Terry were unaware of the statutory requirement that child support be paid in full as a precondition of obtaining a marriage license. Red Hail's child support order had been entered in 1972, not long after the 1971 birth of the daughter he fathered at age 16 with his high school girlfriend, Donna. Red Hail came from a very poor family and could not afford the $109 per month in child support he had been ordered to pay. The child support debt he owed had ballooned to nearly $4,000 by the time he sought a marriage license two years later. Red Hail still lacked the money to pay the debt, and even if he could somehow get caught up on the debt, his daughter would still be on welfare. Under these circumstances, seeking permission to marry from the court seemed futile.

Poverty was a stark reality of Red Hail's childhood, as it was for many of Milwaukee's Indians. Many of the neighborhoods occupied by the city's nonwhite residents were centers of poverty and unemployment. The 1970 federal census determined that the poverty rate for Milwaukee County was 6.4 percent, but those numbers hide the racial disparities: 24.8 percent for black families and 13.5 percent for "other race" families. Among American Indians, estimates for the time put 33.1 percent of the community under the poverty line.

Red Hail grew up in a close-knit but poor Indian family of seven boys and two girls.[3] The family knew what it was like to go without and to be hungry. Things improved somewhat when his mother, Lorraine Red Hail, got a job as a cook at the Guadalupe Center, a local Head Start facility, and was able to bring leftovers home to feed her children. The children did what they could to help out, with some of the boys shining shoes for a quarter in the neighborhood bars in order to buy food and candy. Nonetheless, Lorraine struggled to keep the family together, and for a time she lost custody of six of her children. Roger was around seven years old when they were taken by Milwaukee County Social Services.

The breakup of Indian families was a common occurrence in the United States at that time. Across the country, white child welfare caseworkers routinely removed Indian children from their homes. As in the case of the Red Hail family, conditions of poverty provided the justification for state intrusion. Lorraine Red Hail was told by her caseworker that in order to regain custody of her children, she had to find a larger home with more bedrooms and suitable furniture. Meeting that requirement was no small feat, but she somehow managed, even pulling dressers into the house in the winter with a wagon. When the caseworker later visited to inspect the home, he became visibly angry and told her, "You need one more bed, you know." Lorraine promptly got the bed and reclaimed her children. The family occupied that home on Third and Orchard on the near-South Side of Milwaukee for the next 45 years.

The Red Hail experience with Milwaukee's child welfare system fits within a larger and longstanding national story involving the systematic removal of Indian children from their homes. A 1976 study by the Association on American Indian Affairs found that 25 to 35 percent of all Indian children were being placed in out-of-home care, with 85 percent of those children being placed in non-Indian homes or institutions. Lorraine Red Hail was not supposed to get her children back. As in the case of the Relocation Act, government practice here was aimed at the disruption of Indian communities and families with the goal that Indians would assimilate into American society and leave their culture behind. And, indeed, most of the removed children never returned home and instead were adopted by white families, forever disconnected from their Indian identity and communities. Indian activism forced the federal government to take action to put a stop to the alarmingly high number of Indian children being removed from their homes by nontribal agencies. Congress eventually responded by passing the Indian Child Welfare Act of 1978.

The Indian Experience in Milwaukee

To better understand the social and historical contexts of Red Hail's life as a young Oneida man in Milwaukee, we must also consider the history of American Indians in the city and how the realities of Indian life there paralleled the experiences of other communities of color. Milwaukee has a long tradition of ethnic and racial diversity in the city. The presence of Indians in the region stretches back to before Milwaukee was formed. The city's white and Indian residents were joined by black migrants, who began moving to the city during the late 1800s. It would not be until much later—the 1920s—when Latinos began trickling into the city as a result of the job opportunities available in the city's tanneries. Other American Indian groups, such as the Oneida, began migrating to the city around the same time. These communities generally concentrated around the Menominee River Valley, with the black community largely situated on the near-North Side and the city's Latino/a population clustered on the near-South Side. By 1971, the year Roger Red Hail's daughter was born, 15.6 percent of Milwaukee's total population of 717,372 was nonwhite.

Histories of American Indians in urban centers often begin with the federal relocation policy of the 1950s, which sought to push Indians from reservations to urban areas in order to foster social and cultural assimilation. The story of Indians in Milwaukee neither begins with, nor is adequately explained by, relocation, given that a noticeable migratory trend had been established decades before. Migration in the early half of the twentieth century significantly altered the composition of Milwaukee's Indian community; the Oneida tribe quickly became the largest tribal group in the city.

The Oneida Tribe of Indians of Wisconsin is located just outside the city of Green Bay, roughly two hours north of Milwaukee. The growth, decline, and resurgence of jobs in the war industries during the World Wars and the Great Depression drew the Oneida back and forth between the reservation and the city. These patterns are indicative of larger trends of continuous migration between the reservation and the city that led to a unique relationship between Oneida and Milwaukee. Since much of the migration was driven by jobs, Milwaukee became something of an extension of, or "economic outpost" for, the Oneida reservation in the tribe's struggle for financial stability.

Red Hail's maternal grandparents settled on the near-North Side of Milwaukee when they moved from the reservation to the city with their nine children, including his mother Lorraine. As did many other Oneida, they came looking for work. Though Lorraine Red Hail grew up on the near-North Side of the city, her family later moved to the near-South Side and remained connected to that area for decades to follow.

While many of Milwaukee's Indians were embedded within other communities of color, Roger Red Hail described the near South-Side neighborhood he grew up in as predominantly white. Latinos were just starting to move into the area. There were just a few Indians. Their friends, who were predominantly white, accepted the Red Hail boys and did not see them as different. Perhaps because of the group's proportionally small size, American Indians were generally unrecognized by the city's white population and were often misrecognized as vaguely or generally nonwhite. In any event, the Red Hail boys were thoroughly absorbed into mainstream white culture and enjoyed doing all of the same things their majority friends did: hanging out, dating white girls, and playing sports. One family member, in describing their experience growing up, stated, "We grew up, like I said, the majority of my friends were white . . . [b]ut I knew I was different, and I had no identity, you know, at that time, but I blended into white culture."[4]

Red Hail's extended family also resided on the near-South Side, and he grew up surrounded by a large and close-knit family. When describing his family, Red Hail said, "My aunt had 15 kids. My other aunt had 10 kids, and my uncle had nine kids. My other uncle had one, two, three, four, five, six kids, so, yeah, pretty big family." For Red Hail, home life was defined more by his large family than by being Indian or Oneida. Visits to the Oneida tribe were so rare that one family member, when describing a trip there in about 1972 to bury their grandfather, recalled feeling culture shock at seeing dirt roads and rural poverty.[5] Loretta Metoxen, historian for the Oneida Tribe of Wisconsin, explained that "the tribes were very, very poor, our tribe included, at that time. . . . [I]n the 1970s, it was very difficult to live here."[6] According to Metoxen, the living conditions were challenging and work was hard to find:

The roads were all gravel. . . . Many of our homes here did not have bathroom facilities, I mean, indoor bathroom facilities[.] Most of them had electricity by that time, but I would say that 50% of them did not have water installed in their homes. And . . . obtaining income was very, very difficult at that time.[7]

Rather than make frequent visits back to the Oneida reservation, the Red Hail family would at most sometimes go to a powwow in Franklin, Wisconsin. More likely, they would just spend time visiting at their grandparents' home or with their many cousins and neighborhood friends. On any given night, there might be 30 of his first cousins gathered together in a bar just hanging out together. Despite growing up amidst a large American Indian family, during the 1970s Roger and his siblings did not have a strong identity as Oneida or as Indians. Like many urban Indians of that time period, the Red Hail family was not involved in the city's Indian social and cultural groups or with the broader Indian political movement.

Educational Inequality and Social Movements in 1970s Milwaukee

American Indians made up an even smaller proportion of the student population than they did the population at large. While exact figures are unavailable for Milwaukee Public Schools (MPS) in 1970, a report a decade later would estimate that 1,466 of MPS's 95,000 students were Indian. It is well-documented that these students experienced significant challenges in public schools. Newspaper articles from the time highlight discriminatory attitudes and practices among teaching staff, and a government report from the time notes a statewide lack of awareness by administrative and teaching staff of the unique needs of Indian students.

Among Red Hail's generation of young urban Indians in Wisconsin, there were significant educational disparities. At the time, as many as a quarter of Indian students were not in school, and the dropout rate among men aged 15–29 was estimated to be one-third. Education was a serious challenge for several of Red Hail's siblings as well. His older brothers did not make it through Milwaukee's public schools. He himself left school at 17 but returned after a year to attend an alternative high school and earn a diploma.

Conditions of poverty, discrimination, and a lack of sufficient social services would eventually culminate in a range of social movements in the city. Poverty and "urban decay" on the city's North Side became a central issue in city politics. Tensions over how to address these issues helped to launch the city's civil rights movement. Racial tensions between the white and nonwhite communities and economic tensions culminated in a riot in the summer of 1967, resulting in greater urban segregation and increased white flight from the North Side. Two years after the riots, in another important landmark in the Milwaukee civil rights struggle, Welfare Mothers March participants walked the 90 miles from Milwaukee to Madison to protest proposed cuts to social services.

Around the same time, Indian groups in the city also began to organize and agitate for social change in the city, and their movements would intersect with the larger civil rights struggle in the city. Indians in Milwaukee have a long tradition of organizing to meet the social and cultural needs within their community. The city's Indian population began to organize as early as 1929 with the formation of the Council Fire of American Indians, although the Consolidated Tribes of American Indians, formed in 1937, became the first real hub within the community. This organization, which sought to address the social, cultural, economic, and educational needs of the community, was dominated by members of the Oneida tribe and was viewed as something of an Oneida club. By 1973, there were more than 10 different organizations in the city, which engaged in a host of activities, from sponsoring social events and powwows to political activism and providing social services to members of the community. Many of these organizations were located on North 27th Street in the Midtown neighborhood. The last of these functions was especially important as public social services were generally seen as inadequate to the needs of the Indian American population. Outside these organizations, local churches and "Indian bars" would also serve as informal pillars of the city's Indian community.

By the beginning of the 1970s, the Indian struggle for social change was under way. The American Indian Information and Action Group (AIIAG) was formed in March of 1969 with a small grant from the Methodist Church to address the lack of an Indian voice in local government, the inadequacy of social services, and federal paternalism and "disregard for Indian Civil Rights." AIIAG advocated for welfare rights for Indians and protested the lack of adequate housing to the city's development office. AIIAG also took other causes related to employment and discrimination. They conducted an independent census of the Milwaukee Indian community in an attempt to respond forcefully to what they saw as an inaccurate 1970 federal census that undercounted their community. As a member organization of the Indian Urban Affairs Council (IUAC), AIIAG maintained ties with other politically and socially active groups in the Indian community. The group produced a Milwaukee Indian Resource Handbook, which provided local Indians with information about their rights and how to access available services, including legal assistance from Milwaukee Legal Services (MLS), which later represented Roger Red Hail in court.

An outside observer might easily portray the Milwaukee Indian community as relatively united or cohesive, but in reality there were often sharp divisions, and political and social activism was one such dividing line. Those involved in cultural organizations, like the Consolidated Tribes, often disapproved of the actions of the political organizations like the American Indian Movement (AIM) or the American Indian Information and Action Group (AIIAG). Political activism was seen by many as inappropriate for Indians. For them, fighting for equal rights was what other marginalized communities did; Indians were instead supposed to be interested in restoring what they had lost (i.e., tribal sovereignty), not agitating for equal rights.

Tribal leaders also rejected the political activism of groups like AIM in favor of an emphasis on tribal sovereignty. Oneida tribal historian Loretta Metoxen recalled that tribal leaders wanted to hold the tribe together on the reservation and argued that rather than demonstrate in the cities, Indians should be living on sovereign land and under tribal authority. By this time, more Oneida lived in the cities than on the reservation. Thus there were many urban Indians like the Red Hail family who were disconnected from the tribe and relatively uninvolved in Indian culture or organizations. Metoxen, however, rejected the criticism directed at Indians who lived in the cities. She reminded leaders of federal practices, such as the Indian Boarding School Movement, that took Indian children from the reservations with the goal of assimilating them and making them "non-Indian":

> They said, well, you should be, you should have lived on the reservation. I said, well, I, historically, it's not their fault that they're living in town . . . or that they had two or three generations [off the reservation.] They didn't do that on their own. It was a whole lot of political push from the government that did it.[8]

Notwithstanding the position of tribal leaders, the activism of urban Indians flourished throughout the 1970s. And while the activities described here provide a snapshot of the political and social changes in the Indian community and the city as a whole, it is impossible to do justice in this chapter to all the Indian activists and organizations that were engaged in Milwaukee. The

picture this history paints is that the 1970s were an exciting time both cultur-
ally and politically for Indians in Milwaukee. Indians developed a sense that
they were taking control. They felt optimistic about their future, some for the
first time, and a deepening pride in being Indian.

Red Hail's Child Support Case

On July 5, 1971, 16-year-old Roger Red Hail fathered a daughter, Angela, out
of wedlock. Following the birth of their child, his teenage girlfriend, Donna,
applied for welfare benefits under the Aid to Families with Dependent Children program (AFDC). A year and a half later, in January 1973, Milwaukee
County filed a paternity action against Red Hail. Red Hail appeared at the
hearing on February 23, 1972, and admitted that he was the father of the child.
The case was continued until May 12, and because Red Hail was himself a
minor, a guardian ad litem (GAL) was appointed to represent him.

A May 12, 1972, hearing was held before Judge Robert J. Miech. Neither
of the teenage parents appeared at the hearing. Assistant corporation counsel
Karl M. Dunst appeared on behalf of the state, and appearing on behalf of
Red Hail was his GAL, John Malinowski. The court adjudged Red Hail to
be the father of the child and ordered that he pay $109 per month in child
support until his daughter turned 18. The court order also imposed $120 in
legal fees for his representation by the GAL and an additional $466 for birth
expenses and other fees.

Child support awards like Red Hail's, during the pre-child-support guidelines legal regime, were made under a Wisconsin statute that authorized the
court to set an amount it considered "just and reasonable."[9] The determination of the amount of the child support award was within the sole discretion
of the trial court. Unlike current Wisconsin law, there was no legislative guidance as to the amount or the factors to be included in determining whether
an amount was "just and reasonable." Exercising their unfettered discretion,
judges set child support orders at amounts that lacked consistency or predict-
ability. Litigants and law reformers complained that the awards were often
far too low or far too high.

Red Hail's order of $109 per month was shockingly high, even considering
that during the 1970s the Wisconsin family law system was a highly discretionary system. To put the amount in its proper context, in 1972 Wisconsin's
minimum wage for minors was $1.45 per hour. A child support order of $109/
month was equivalent to 50 percent of gross wages for someone like Red Hail
working a full-time (35 hours/week) minimum wage job. Under Wisconsin's

current percentage of income child support guidelines, a child support order for someone in similar circumstances would be 17 percent of gross wages, or $37 per month. Thus, the child support order imposed on Red Hail in 1972 was nearly three times what a young man in his situation would likely be ordered to pay today.

The exorbitant size of Red Hail's child support order was especially problematic given his youth, poverty, and employment prospects. Unemployment data for the early 1970s reveal other staggering disparities between Milwaukee's white and nonwhite populations. In 1971, white unemployment was 5.1 percent compared to 13.6 percent for nonwhite Milwaukee residents. The struggle for adequate resources and employment generated conditions of poverty that had a long-standing impact on members of the Oneida Tribe. Statewide, 78.8 percent of young Indian men between the ages of 20 and 29 participated in the labor force, with an unemployment rate of 18.5 percent. For those without a high school diploma, labor participation was much worse, only 49.8 percent. The employment experiences of Red Hail and his siblings are consistent with the statistics: they only had access to jobs consisting primarily of summer Youth Corp jobs and intermittent part-time low-wage positions. Unsurprisingly, Red Hail was unable to pay the child support ordered by the court, and as a result he was one of many Wisconsinites that were adversely affected by Wisconsin's permission-to-marry statute.

Wisconsin's Permission-to-Marry Law

The permission-to-marry law dates back to 1957, when the Wisconsin legislature ordered a review of the state's marriage and divorce statutes. To help assist the legislature in this effort, Governor Walter J. Kohler appointed a family law committee composed of persons representing the bar, the bench, the clergy, welfare agencies, and the general public to study and revise the state laws.

The family law committee recommended, among other things, that divorced persons who had support obligations to children of a former marriage must obtain judicial consent to remarry. The committee wanted the process of entering marriage to reflect the seriousness of marriage itself. They reasoned that the requirement of judicial consent provided an opportunity to counsel parents with child support obligations, and that it was especially important to do so when they were behind in paying support. Additionally, the judicial hearing would make the person's intended partner aware of these financial obligations before the marriage. The committee clarified, however, that the provision "was not designed to preclude the contemplated marriage, but merely assure that there was an awareness of the situation."[10]

Based on the family law committee's recommendation, the following version of Section 245.10 was drafted in Assembly Bill 151A:

> 245.10 Approval of Judge required in certain cases. When it appears that either applicant has minor issue of a prior marriage not in his custody and which he is under obligation to support by court order or judgment, no license shall be issued without the approval of a judge of a court having divorce jurisdiction in the County of application.[11]

This new provision was designed "to cover a situation where a person who is about to assume new marital responsibilities has failed to fulfill the obligation of a prior marriage."[12] In such a case, the legislature determined, "judicial approval must be obtained" in order to give "the judge and the family court commissioner an opportunity to emphasize the responsibilities of support of the present family before new obligations are incurred."[13]

The permission-to-marry statue was later revised, with subsequent amendments expanding both the scope of its application and the requirements needed for permission. Its scope was extended to cover unmarried as well as divorced persons under an order of support, and the statutory requirements for issuance of a marriage license were increased. In addition to demonstrating compliance with his child support order, the petitioner was required to show that his children were not receiving public benefits and were not likely to be recipients in the future.

There were many Wisconsin residents who, like Red Hail, could not get a marriage license because they couldn't satisfy the requirements of Section 245.10. Though most counties did not keep track of the number of couples they turned away, Milwaukee County did. In 1974, in Milwaukee County alone, the county clerk refused to issue a marriage license to 660 applicants. Some of those individuals found their way to a lawyer's office, hoping to get a judge's permission to marry. Milwaukee Legal Services (MLS) handled many of these "right to marry" cases. Initially, legal aid lawyers sought permission on behalf of individual clients. Robert Blondis, managing attorney of the family law unit of MLS at the time, recalled that the selection of the judge was very important in permission-to-marry cases. Some judges, likely feeling that the statute was just wrong, were receptive to MLS attorneys' arguments that the balance of equities favored granting permission to marry even in cases where the statutory terms weren't met. Arguments that sometimes persuaded judges included demonstrations that the father was doing his best to comply with the support order, that the original support order was set ridiculously high, and that there had been a significant change in circumstances since the order was established which warranted granting permission to marry. Judges were sometimes receptive to situations like Red Hail's, where the prospective spouse was pregnant or had given birth, because they saw a denial of the petition to remarry as primarily harming the child.

In situations where the case was before a judge who was known to strictly apply the statute, MLS attorneys would attempt to get a more flexible judge assigned by filing a motion for substitution of the judge. Blondis decided the practice of bringing individual cases, while effective for some clients, was a Band-Aid approach that would not resolve the underlying problem of the statute's impact on the community. MLS would instead attempt to get the law changed by challenging the constitutionality of the statute in federal court. In their eyes, Red Hail was the ideal plaintiff for the case because he did not have any chance of being able to marry as long as the statute remained good law.

Initiating law reform efforts to improve the lives of low-income Milwaukee residents was an essential part of MLS's mission. Formed in 1968, MLS's work was guided by three central precepts: "rapport with the client community, house counsel for community organizations, and the achievement of fundamental changes in the law for the benefit of low-income persons." MLS took its commitment to law reform seriously and implemented an innovative approach in which new hires were immediately expected to take on such cases, working in collaboration with more experienced lawyers. Georgia Ressmeyer recalled that when she joined MLS in 1974, shortly after graduating from Yale Law School, she was immediately slotted onto the Red Hail case. Along with Ressmeyer, the family law section added two other recent graduates that year: Patricia Nelson, a Marquette Law School graduate, and Tom Donegan, a New York University Law School graduate. At the time, new MLS lawyers were instructed to spend half their time on law reform work and half their time on individual cases. As a result, Ressmeyer and Nelson worked alongside supervising attorney Blondis to research and prepare Red Hail's case for trial.

It was an exciting time to be a legal services lawyer in Milwaukee. In the late 1960s, MLS was becoming more active in the community, and by the 1970s there was an explosion of legal action. MLS was growing exponentially, adding 11 new attorneys in 1974 and nearly as many the following year. These resources helped sustain MLS's commitment to community engagement. MLS lawyers provided legal representation to many community organizations, operated satellite offices in low-income neighborhoods on both the near-North and near-South Side of Milwaukee, and engaged in community outreach in an effort to identify possible legal claims to press. The young legal aid attorneys threw themselves into their work, routinely putting in twelve-hour days and working through the weekend. Ressmeyer recalled the idealism and shared commitment of those times: "So much was going on in the community. There was so much excitement about changing things and we were all sort of infused with a desire to change the world and right every injustice."

The individual suits brought by MLS attorneys were as transformational to the legal system as were the "Don Quixote types of actions" that they intentionally brought for law reform purposes. Blondis, who started with Legal Action in 1969 directly out of Marquette Law School, talked of how difficult it was for the legal culture in Milwaukee to adapt to the presence of legal services lawyers. He said they were in court every day representing their clients. They were in small claims courts. They were in eviction court. They were in family court. And they were in children's court. They were there every day, but the private bar did not welcome them. These lawyers didn't like the legal services program. They'd had their way for a long while and now they had to contend with legal services lawyers on the other side. At that time, he recalled, "it was a whole new concept . . . that poor people would be represented."

As an example, Blondis explained how the system operated in the collection court. "[I]n the collection court, for instance, the collection lawyers would be up at the bench with the stamps, with the clerk's stamps, and would just call out the case and cha-ching, cha-ching, cha-ching, judgment, judgment, judgment, judgment. It was automatic." The children's court was also resistant to the efforts legal services lawyers made on behalf of their clients. Blondis initially practiced in children's court, handling detention cases, and the judges there resented his presence. Detention decisions were automatic, and when he challenged the judges' decisions—whether it was a decision to detain a child who stole a bicycle or a decision to incarcerate a minor for truancy—the judges didn't like it. At the time, poverty lawyers were not welcome in the system. The view was that they just slowed everything down and made problems. That was the culture at the time and it took a long time for practices like those to change.

A Companion Case: *Vernon Leipzig and*
Veralyn Randall v. Ruth Pallamolla

The reach of the permission-to-marry statute extended beyond the indigent community in Milwaukee. Throughout Wisconsin, moderate-income residents similarly felt its effect. Some of those individuals hired local attorneys to represent them in judicial petitions for permission to marry. Kenosha attorney Terry Rose handled many such cases.

Rose's law firm, Rose and Rose, is located in downtown Kenosha, a small Wisconsin city with a population of approximately 100,000 people. The street is lined with shops and other small businesses, most housed in retail storefronts. Terry has been practicing law in these offices for 45 years, with a general practice of criminal and civil matters and primarily courtroom litigation. Three generations of Rose men have practiced law at the firm. After graduating from law school in 1967, Terry clerked on the federal court of appeals in Chicago and then joined his father's law practice. Today he practices law with his son, Christopher Rose, who joined the family practice in 1998. His family has deep roots in Kenosha and in his law practice.

Like MLS, Rose handled a steady stream of permission-to-marry cases. The law was well-known in his community. The general public was aware that if you had a child support order in place and wanted to marry, then you needed to file a petition with the court seeking permission to marry. If you were successful, you would bring the court order to the county clerk. It was standard procedure and people simply understood that this is what you did in Wisconsin.

The permission-to-marry hearings were fairly simple, routine proceedings that often were held in the court's chambers or conference room. They were typically 5 or 10 minutes long. Though the petitioner had to give notice to the family court commissioner and the first spouse, no opposition would be mounted. Other than providing the petitioner's child support payment history, the state generally took no position in the cases. The courts in Kenosha treated permission-to-marry cases as open and shut. If the statutory criteria were established, the petition would be granted. And if the criteria were not established, the petition would be denied. Unlike in Milwaukee's courts, appeals to the balance of equity in a particular petitioner's case fell on deaf ears.

Rose found the law to be personally offensive and felt strongly that it was characteristic of a paternalistic state government. The proceedings themselves were, in his view, equally offensive. During hearings, trial judges directly addressed the prospective wife (as it was always noncustodial fathers who owed child support and had to get the court's permission if they wanted to remarry) to admonish her that the petitioner—the man she was about to marry—had a financial duty to support the children from his prior marriage first. Rose thought it was out of line for the court to speak that way to the parties as it was a private matter between the spouses.

Like MLS attorney Blondis, Rose was interested in challenging the permission-to-marry statute on constitutional grounds. He found his ideal plaintiffs in Vernon Leipzig and his fianceé, Veralyn Randall. Rose had represented Leipzig in his recent divorce action, in which he was granted a divorce from former wife Theresa Leipzig in December 1973. The court granted primary custody of the couple's four children, Kim (age nine), Karla (five), Keith (four) and Kelly (three), to Theresa Leipzig and required Vernon Leipzig to pay $60 per week ($15 per child) in child support. Leipzig contacted Rose because he wanted to remarry and needed a court order to obtain a marriage license.

Rose asked Leipzig if he'd be interested in filing suit to challenge the statute if his petition to remarry was denied. Leipzig was, in Rose's view, the ideal plaintiff. Leipzig was a deputy county sheriff, he was regularly paying his court-ordered child support, and yet his four children were nonetheless receiving AFDC. From Rose's perspective, the facts were as good as they get. He warned Vernon, however, that he expected the trial court to deny the petition because his former wife was receiving $355 per month in AFDC for the children. As expected, Kenosha County judge Crosetto denied the petition following a hearing on December 13, 1974. Strictly applying the statute, the judge refused to grant Leipzig permission to marry because Leipzig's minor children received welfare. With Leipzig lending his name, Rose set out to file suit challenging the statute on constitutional grounds. The lawsuit was sponsored by the Wisconsin Civil Liberties Union (WCLU), an affiliate of the American Civil Liberties Union (ACLU). WCLU executive director William Lynch advised Rose that MLS was planning to bring a similar legal challenge to the permission-to-marry statute.

Zablocki v. Red Hail Procedural History in the Eastern District

On Christmas Eve in 1974, Blondis and Rose simultaneously filed their cases in federal district court in Milwaukee. They chose federal court because at the time the federal courts were more receptive than state courts to constitutional arguments. The Red Hail complaint sought declaratory and injunctive relief under the Civil Rights Act, 42 U.S.C. § 1983 on behalf of Red Hail and others similarly situated. His case was pursued as a dual class action; it was brought on behalf of a plaintiff class of all Wisconsin residents subject to the permission-to-marry statue and against a defendant class of the 72 Wisconsin county clerks who were responsible for applying the statute.

The actions required a three-judge district court because plaintiffs sought a permanent injunction restraining the enforcement of a state statute. The chief judge of the Seventh Circuit entered an order assigning District Judges John W. Reynolds, Robert W. Warren, and Philip W. Tone of the Seventh District of the U.S. Court of Appeals to the three-judge court.

In their briefs, the state argued that the interests they sought to promote by Section 245.10 were those articulated by the statute's legislative history. According to the state, it had a compelling interest in preventing children from becoming public charges, enforcing the parent's duty to support his child or children, and preventing parents from assuming new legal obligations that they may not be able to meet or that might disable them from meeting the pre-existing child support obligations.

The plaintiffs countered that none of these interests justified the state's infringement on the fundamental right to marry, and the statute was not rationally related to the ends the state sought to promote, particularly as it applied to poor people. Denying the right to marry to someone who was too poor to meet the requirements of the statute would not help the state to compel support. Indeed, the plaintiffs argued, it may even work against the state's interest, because marriage does not necessarily diminish the ability to discharge prior obligations but may in fact increase it. Furthermore, denying the right to marry would not guarantee that the person denied permission would not have children anyway, as was clearly demonstrated by Red Hail's situation. Moreover, the statute condemned to illegitimacy later children born to persons who were denied permission to marry.

Both Red Hail and Leipzig married their fiancés while the case was pending before the three-judge panel. It was common for couples who were turned down by the court to go out of state to get married. Cohabitation, still fairly uncommon in the 1970s, was not the preferred response. Leipzig and Veralyn married in Antioch, Illinois, on December 28, 1974, days after their district court complaint was filed. Red Hail and his fiancé Terry likewise traveled to Illinois to get around the state ban. They married in Waukegan, Illinois, on February 20, 1976. Despite their efforts to avoid the application of Wisconsin's permission-to-marry statute, the Red Hail and Leipzig marriages were void in Wisconsin.[14] According to Rose, such marriage could be and sometimes were annulled.

On August 31, 1976, the district court issued its unanimous decision, finding the statute unconstitutional and granting the requested injunctive and declaratory relief. Because the court decided that Leipzig and Randall were members of the plaintiff class in *Red Hail*, their separate action was dismissed as moot. With the case finally decided by the court, Vern and Veralyn Leipzig remarried in Kenosha.

Wisconsin Passes a Fallback Permission-to-Marry Law

Immediately after the decision of the three-court panel was handed down, Milwaukee County officials began to take steps to preserve the statute. The Milwaukee County Commission on Family Relations considered whether the Wisconsin legislature could enact another permission-to-marry statute to replace Section 245.10. Emphasizing that time was of the essence because of the impending Supreme Court ruling, Assistant Attorney General John Devitt urged that a replacement statute be passed as a precautionary measure. Devitt proposed that the substitute law be framed more narrowly than Section 245.10 so that it might withstand any subsequent constitutional challenge. He suggested first that the replacement permission-to-marry law apply only to remarriages (rather than first marriages) so as to distinguish it from the *Red Hail* case. Devitt reasoned that although the Supreme Court had held that marriage is a fundamental right, it had not yet ruled that there is a fundamental right to *remarry*. Second, Devitt suggested that the replacement law require courts to grant permission to marry to parents who are up to date with their support payments, regardless of whether their children are receiving welfare payments. The County Commission on Family Resources later submitted this legislative proposal as Section 245.105 to the Milwaukee County Board of Supervisors and requested that the board sponsor the law with the legislature.

On January 27, 1977, George Rice, corporation counsel of Milwaukee County, submitted a drafting request to the Legislative Reference Bureau ("LRB"). Over the next few months, Linda Roberson, senior legislative attorney with the LRB, prepared numerous drafts in consultation with attorney Devitt. In her drafter's notes, Roberson raised concerns about the proposed law's differential treatment of children from first marriages (who received preferential treatment) and any subsequent born children (who might be both marital and nonmarital), and noted that an equal protection challenge might be brought on behalf of children in the nonpriority class. To solve this problem, she suggested that the proposed legislation give courts discretion to grant petitions to remarry even in cases where the petitioner had not complied with the support order.

On April 12, 1977, by request of Thomas Zablocki, Wisconsin representatives Tesmer, Tuczynski, Snyder, and Thompson introduced Assembly Amendment 1 to Assembly Bill 100, which created Section 245.105 "Permission of the Court Required for Certain Remarriages." Section 245.105 was narrower than the earlier statute. It affected a smaller group of people and applied different standards for the granting or withholding of permission to marry. This bill created a temporary statute applying only to parents whose children result from a prior marriage and permitting them to remarry if they are in compliance with support obligations regardless of whether their children receive public assistance. The bill also established a rebuttable presumption that remarriage may affect a child's right of support, but the presumption can be overcome by contrary proof. Finally, the bill allowed the court to grant permission to remarry to a parent who for reasonable cause was not able to comply with a court obligation for child support. The new statute was to be effective until July 1, 1979.

In the United States Supreme Court

Red Hail's attorneys did not expect the case to reach the United States Supreme Court. Wisconsin's permission-to-marry statute was one of a kind. Red Hail's legal team researched the issue and could not locate similar laws in other states. There was thus no split among the federal circuits regarding the constitutionality of permission-to-marry statutes that warranted resolution by the Supreme Court. Consequently, it was doubtful that if an appeal were filed, the Supreme Court would take the case.

Additionally, it seemed unlikely that an appeal would ever be filed. After appearing opposite each other on so many cases, Blondis was a friend of government lawyers Ward Johnson and George Rice. They informed him that the state and county weren't interested in pursuing an appeal. Ultimately, however, the state filed a notice of appeal in October of 1976. Assistant corporation counsel John Devitt had become active in the case and lobbied the attorney general hard to appeal the case.

On October 4, 1977, Bob Blondis, the senior MLS attorney working on Red Hail's case, appeared before the Supreme Court to argue the case.[15] He was 31 years old at the time and this was his first appearance before the Supreme Court.

Eleven days after the oral argument, the Wisconsin legislature passed Assembly Bill 100, which enacted Section 245.105, an alternative permission-to-marry statute. Because Section 245.105 was intended to be a fallback law, it did not become effective automatically. Instead, the effect of the new law was contingent on the Supreme Court's ruling in the *Red Hail* case. Under the terms of Section 245.105, it was to "be enforced only when the provisions of Section 245.10 and the utilization of the procedures thereunder are stayed or enjoined by the order of any court." Thus if the Supreme Court affirmed the lower court ruling striking down Section 245.10, Wisconsin would fall back section 245.105.

On January 18, 1978, the Supreme Court affirmed the ruling of the district court, holding Section 245.10 unconstitutional under the Equal Protection Clause and enjoining its enforcement. In an 8-1 decision, the majority opinion by Justice Thurgood Marshall found that the right to marry is of "fundamental importance" and held that the statute significantly interfered with that right. Justice William Rehnquist dissented from the majority opinion. Following the decision in *Red Hail*, the Wisconsin legislature acted. On February 9, 1978, the assembly passed a provision that repealed both permission-to-marry laws, Section 245.10, the original law struck down by the Supreme Court, and Section 245.105, the alternative backup legislation enacted by the Wisconsin legislature after the oral argument before the Supreme Court.

Red Hail's lawyers were not surprised by the outcome. They all believed strongly that the Supreme Court would not uphold a statute that so fundamentally restricted a person's right to marry. Moreover, MLS had been on a winning streak. In their view the state's attorneys did not put up a vigorous defense. Blondis thought that the other side simply wasn't ready for them.

The Tribal Marriage Alternative Then and Now

Right to Marry Under Tribal Law

Red Hail has a unique political status as a member of a sovereign tribal government. As a member of the Oneida tribe, and thus a dual citizen, Red Hail could have pursued another option. He could have sought to marry his fiancée Terry under the tribal law and customs of the Oneida Tribe of Indians of Wisconsin. Red Hail stated that "it never crossed his mind" to marry under tribal law. Given his distance from the tribe at that time (both literally and figuratively), it is not surprising that he never considered the alternative of a tribal marriage.

A tribal marriage carried its own risks, however. Even though historically,

Indian American tribes have had their own social and religious mechanisms for recognizing marriage, it has only been recently that states have begun to recognize and give legal significance to these processes. In the 1970s, the tribe and its members would have likely recognized a marriage that took place on the Oneida reservation, but it was common even for tribal members to seek a marriage sanctioned under Wisconsin state law. It is questionable whether the state would have recognized a tribal marriage as valid. While states such as Oklahoma, Montana, and Nevada had developed case law stating that all marriages valid under tribal customs would be recognized by the state, Wisconsin had not addressed the issue at the time Red Hail was faced with his dilemma. Indeed, it is likely that Wisconsin would not have recognized any marriage (tribal or out-of-state) of a man who was prohibited from marrying under Wisconsin law.

Today, however, an Oneida marriage is a more viable option for those who can't obtain a Wisconsin-sanctioned marriage. Wisconsin law gives the "public acts, records, and judicial proceedings of any Indian tribe" full faith and credit.[16] In 2002, the Supreme Court of Wisconsin held in *Teague v. Bad River Band* that state courts are required to give tribal court judgments full faith and credit. The court's decision endorsed Wisconsin tribal courts, giving them the standing that they did not have in the 1970s. While the relationship between state courts and tribal courts continues to evolve, the *Teague* decision signals that a tribal marriage would be recognized by Wisconsin today.

Transfer of Child Support Cases from State to Tribal Courts

Although *Zablocki v. Red Hail* was a significant victory, the ruling did not secure justice for Roger Red Hail. *Zablocki v. Red Hail* is not solely or even mostly about the permission-to-marry law that restricted Red Hail's access to a Wisconsin marriage license. While undoubtedly the statute unlawfully barred access to marriage, in actuality it was a child support enforcement law in the guise of a marriage law. Like many other child support enforcement laws, it sought to condition access to state-issued licenses on compliance with court orders of child support. The primary difference between Wisconsin's permission-to-marry law and the enforcement measures impacting access to other licenses—such as drivers' licenses, hunting and fishing licenses, and professional licenses—is that the permission-to-marry statute intruded into a fundamental constitutional right and for that reason it was struck down. Striking down the law, however, did not resolve the injustice inherent in Red Hail's child support order.

We did not expect to learn that Red Hail is still paying on the child support debt that brought about the 1978 Supreme Court decision. The exorbitant $109 per month child support order that was entered in 1972 and prevented him from marrying in Wisconsin in 1974 is still pending *40 years later*. Roger Red Hail owes about $10,000 in child support for his daughter Angela, who is now 42 years old. Moreover, Red Hail owes child support in the tens of thousands of dollars for the three children—Dawn, Jennifer, and Roger—he and his wife Terry had together. They divorced after a seven-year marriage and Red Hail was faced with another child support order.

Red Hail's total child support debt now exceeds $63,000, and, pursuant to court order, he continues to pay the debt on a monthly basis. Each month $50 is garnished from his paycheck by the state of Wisconsin. The monthly payment, however, will never satisfy the staggering accumulated child support arrearage. It would take 1,260 monthly payments of $50 (or 105 years) for Red Hail to pay his debt, assuming no interest on the debt. But there is interest on the child support debt. Indeed, because the interest that accumulates on the debt annually—currently at 6 percent but previously as high as 18 percent— far exceeds Red Hail's annual court-ordered payments, the debt has grown and will continue to grow to unimaginable proportions.[17]

Even though Red Hail pays his child support order on a monthly basis, the large outstanding debt is an inhibiting and intimidating burden. One the one hand, the debt prevents Roger and his fianceé Colleen from marrying. Though they have been together for nearly twenty years and live together in Colleen's home, they have been putting off marriage out of fear that the state's pursuit of Red Hail's child support arrears will impair Colleen's financial security. In particular, they have heard stories that the state has put liens on the homes of women who marry men with child support debt, and they fear that if they marry, the same thing will happen to Colleen. Red Hail also worries that even though he pays his child support on a monthly basis as required, he will be imprisoned for the debt.

At the time we interviewed Red Hail, he was waiting to hear when his pending child support cases under the jurisdiction of Milwaukee County would be transferred to the Oneida Tribal Judicial System. A notable impact of *Teague*, which has opened a new possibility for the resolution of Red Hail's child support cases, has been Wisconsin's transfer of child support cases from state to tribal courts. Concurrent with the *Teague* decision, Wisconsin tribes received a grant of federal funding to administer child support cases of their members. Because Red Hail is a tribal member, he is now eligible to have his cases transferred from the state to the tribe.

The Wisconsin Department of Children and Families (DCF) took on the task of creating the processes to transfer all existing tribal child support cases. Once the transfer of a postjudgment case is initiated, tribal members whose cases are eligible for transfer will receive a letter from the tribe introducing itself and explaining that their case can be transferred. After that, the state will send the party notice that their case will be transferred. So far about 2,000 state child support cases have been transferred to tribes, and beginning with Brown County, the transfers are taking place on a county-by-county basis. The process is under way for Milwaukee County cases to be transferred.

Tribes and the State Department of Children and Families believe that the transfer of tribal cases is beneficial to tribal members because of the greater time, flexibility, and resources the tribe can invest in resolving the cases. It would be within the tribal court's sovereign discretion to waive the interest that has accumulated on the debt, reach a settlement with Red Hail, or even assess an in-kind order if the tribe determined it was appropriate. The transfer of Red Hail's case from Milwaukee County to Oneida may very well open the door to a reassessment on what was and still is an impossibly high child support burden.

Return to Oneida

The Red Hail family now has a strong sense of pride in being Indian. The family began to embrace their Indian heritage in earnest following the 1987 death of one of Red Hail's brothers due to substance abuse and what Red Hail referred to as "street life." It was a pivotal event for the family. Lorraine Red Hail, Red Hail's mother, was devastated and told her children that she didn't want to have to bury any more of her sons, several of whom were at the time struggling with alcoholism and other addictions. One by one, the Red Hail sons entered treatment and eventually sobered up. Roger Red Hail has been sober for 11 years.

The process of sobering up took many of them on a spiritual path and brought them closer to their Indian heritage and identity, with each Red Hail brother pulling the next along with him on this journey. The turnaround has been dramatic. Each year the Red Hails make a pilgrimage to South Dakota, their father's homeland, to visit Wounded Knee, and on a weekly basis they participate in Sioux rituals, like sun dances and sweat lodges. Most of the family now speaks the Oneida language fluently. A pattern of reverse migration brought the family from Milwaukee to the Oneida reservation, where most of the family now lives. The Red Hails' relocation to the reservation is part of a broader social trend. As tribal historian Loretta Metoxen explained, there has been an influx of 1,500 to 2,000 Oneida to the reservation, largely because of the availability of jobs resulting from gaming operation revenues.

Unlike the rest of the Red Hail family, who have reclaimed their Oneida identity and moved to the reservation, Roger Red Hail's roots are still in Milwaukee. Roger has been slower to embrace Indian cultural rituals and spiritual practices. He doesn't travel with them to Wounded Knee. He said that when he goes to a powwow today, "I can feel like I want to get up there, but, no, but, you know, it's like it's still in me, but . . ." Though his brothers have encouraged him, Roger Red Hail has not yet completed the journey. According to Roger, "So me, I'm still outside looking in, and I will eventually."

Notes

This oral history research study would not have been possible without the contributions of Diane Amour, Robert Blondis, Dr. Nancy Lurie, Loretta Metoxen, Roger Red Hail, Georgia Ressmeyer, Terry Rose, and Reneé Zakhar, who graciously agreed to participate in interviews. The authors also would like to thank Reneé Zakhar for her enthusiastic support of this project, her assistance in archival research, and her generosity in sharing her extensive knowledge of and contacts in the Oneida community in Wisconsin. The authors are also grateful to Doug Kiel for being our guide through the history of the Oneida Tribe in Wisconsin. The project also greatly benefited from assistance from Dr. Nancy Lurie, who shared both her rich memories and her collection at the Milwaukee Public Museum, and Bonnie Shucha, who provided valuable library assistance with legal research, and from conversations with Richard Monette, who shared his expertise on Indian law, history, and politics, and Connie Chesnik, who shared expertise in the area of Wisconsin child support law and practice. And, finally, we are deeply grateful to Roger Red Hail for sharing his personal story with us. Professor Brito would also like to acknowledge the Jefferson Burrus-Bascom Professorship awarded to her by the University of Wisconsin, which provided funding for research-related travel and transcription expenses.

1. Roger Red Hail's last name is misspelled as Redhail in the *Zablocki v. Redhail* judicial opinion. He mentioned that after his mother learned the true spelling of the family name, she insisted that family members use the correct spelling and that others do so as well. Interview with Roger Red Hail (Sept. 26, 2013).

2. The individuals interviewed in our study expressed a preference for "Indian" or "American Indian" over "Native American." As one individual put it, "'Indian' is the noun; 'Native' is the adjective."

3. Red Hail's parents had 10 children but one of his older sisters passed away when she was a toddler before Roger was born.

4. Confidential Interview (Sept. 5, 2013).

5. *Id.*

6. Interview with Loretta Metoxen (Sept. 5, 2013).

7. *Id.*

8. *Id.*

9. Wis. Stat. § 247.26 (1975).

10. Defendants' Brief in Opposition to Plaintiffs' Prayer for Final Declaratory and Injunctive Relief at 8, Red Hail v. Zablocki, 418 F. Supp. 1061 (1976) (No. 74-C-624).

11. *Id.*

12. *Id.*

13. *Id.*

14. Wis. Stat. § 245.10(5) (1971).

15. Defendants' Brief in Opposition to Plaintiffs' Prayer for Final Declaratory and Injunctive Relief, *supra* note 10, at 14 (citing Note to Proposed Draft of Bill 151A).

16. Wis. Stat. § 806.245.

17. The imposition of high statutory interest rates on child support debt is only one of several factors that contribute to the development of large arrearages by low-income child support obligors. *See* Tonya L. Brito, *Fathers Behind Bars: Rethinking Child Support Policy Toward Low-Income Noncustodial Fathers and Their Families*, 15 J. Gender Race & Just. 617 (2012).

The Movement for a Right to Counsel in Civil Cases

Turner v. Rogers • (2011)

KELLY TERRY

Background: Support, Contempt, and Michael Turner

In 1996, a daughter, identified in subsequent court proceedings only as B.L.P., was born to teenage parents Rebecca Rogers and Michael Turner in Oconee County, South Carolina.[1] Oconee County is a rural county located in the northwest corner of the state, on the edge of the Blue Ridge Mountains. When B.L.P. was born, Turner was 19 years old, and Rogers was 17. Turner and Rogers were not married, and they drifted apart shortly after their daughter's birth.

Rogers assumed custody of B.L.P., and in 2003 she sought public assistance from the South Carolina Department of Social Services through the federal Temporary Assistance to Needy Families program. To receive federal assistance, she was required to aid the state in determining the paternity of her child, which she did. The South Carolina Department of Social Services subsequently established that Turner was B.L.P.'s father and notified him of his duty to support her. The department then asked the Oconee County Family Court to determine the amount of his financial responsibility. In an order entered on June 18, 2003, the court recorded Turner's employment status as "unemployed," but it nonetheless imputed a monthly gross income of $1,386 to him and ordered him to pay $51.73 per week in child support.

Imputing income to a noncustodial parent is not uncommon in child support proceedings.[2] The rationale for imputing income, rather than basing the support amount on the parent's actual income, is to address situations in which parents either underreport income or are intentionally underemployed. Imputing income, however, can produce unrealistic support amounts, as courts typically will impute the ability to earn minimum wage and will assume the parent has a full-time, 40-hour-a-week job, which overestimates income for low-income parents who lack stable employment and often work less than 40 hours a week. In Turner's case, the family court imputed a weekly income of approximately $350, despite the absence of any evidence that he had underreported his income or was intentionally unemployed.

Turner and Rogers consented to and signed the support order, which made Turner's support obligation retroactive to the beginning of the child support proceedings. Thus he immediately fell more than $200 behind in child support the moment the order was entered. In addition, the order imposed weekly costs of $7.99 for court fees and payments toward his arrearage.

Turner subsequently struggled to maintain employment and pay his child support. Court records show that he worked intermittently and held a series of jobs with various employers, including stints with construction contractors, auto-repair shops, and a painting company. In August 2003, the clerk of the family court issued an order for Turner to appear and show cause why he should not be held in civil contempt for failing to pay his support. The order was issued pursuant to a South Carolina court rule that authorizes the clerk to automatically issue a show-cause order when a parent falls five days behind on payments. In September 2003, the family court held Turner in civil contempt for nonpayment and sentenced him to 90 days in the county jail unless he paid the entire arrearage within a month. This proceeding initiated a vicious cycle in which Turner repeatedly fell behind on his support payments, the family court held him in civil contempt, and each time he either paid some amount toward his balance or was sentenced to jail.

It is not uncommon for parents to fall into arrears on their child support. According to the federal Office of Child Support Enforcement, delinquent parents across the country owed a total of $114,558,969,584 in child support arrears in 2012. Most of the arrears are owed by parents with no or low reported income. While the number of parents jailed nationwide for failure to pay child support is not tracked, a 2005 survey of South Carolina jails revealed that at any given time, they average more than 1,500 child support contemnors like Turner.[3]

Between 2003 and 2006, the family court found Turner in civil contempt five times. The first four times, the family court sentenced him to 90 days' imprisonment, but he ultimately paid the amount due either without being jailed or after spending two or three days in jail. The fifth time, Turner did not make a payment and spent six months in the county jail. Turner was not represented by a lawyer during any of these contempt proceedings, and his unpaid child support continued to accumulate while he was incarcerated.

After his release from imprisonment on the fifth contempt citation, Turner remained behind on his child support, and in March 2006 the court clerk issued another order for him to show cause why he should not be held in contempt. The family court held a hearing in January 2008, at which Turner and Rogers both appeared pro se. By this time, Turner owed $5,728.76 in unpaid child support. The hearing was brief; after swearing Turner in to testify, the trial judge simply asked him, "Is there anything you want to say?" Representing himself, Turner replied:

> Well, when I first got out, I got back on dope. I done meth, smoked pot and everything else, and I paid a little bit here and there. And, when I finally did get to working, I broke my back, back in September. I filed for disability and SSI. And, I didn't get straightened out off the dope until I broke my back and laid up for two months. And, now I'm off the dope and everything. I just hope that you give me a chance. I don't know what else to say. I mean, I know I done wrong, and I should have been paying and helping her, and I'm sorry. I mean, dope had a hold to me.[4]

The judge did not respond to Turner's testimony, and he did not inquire about Turner's job status, his ability to work in light of his broken back and drug problems, his support obligations to his other children, his educational level, his attempts to find work, or the jobs available in the community. In January of 2008, the United States was entering into the greatest economic recession since the Great Depression, and the statewide unemployment rate for South Carolina was 5.5 percent.[5] By the end of 2008, the annual unemployment rate for Oconee County was 7.3 percent. Most of the jobs in Oconee County are in the fields of manufacturing, health care, and social assistance, and more than 60 percent of the employers in the county employ fewer than five employees. Only 33.47 percent of the residents of the county are high-school graduates.

Instead of weighing any of these factors in Turner's case, the judge simply found him in civil contempt and sentenced him to a year in jail, stating that he could purge himself of the contempt if he paid his outstanding balance in full. Turner could not pay, so he served the entire one-year sentence in jail.

While he was in jail, Derek Enderlin, the chief public defender for Oconee County, agreed to represent him pro bono and appeal his case in the South Carolina appellate courts.[6]

While this appeal was proceeding, Turner was cited for contempt again in March 2009 for not paying child support for B.L.P. The family court held a hearing on April 29, 2009, at which Turner again appeared pro se. By this time, Turner owed $9,251.84 in unpaid support. At the hearing, the judge simply asked Turner, "Anything you want to say?" Turner replied:

> No, sir. I just got out—I done a year '07 to '08, got out for like four months. I've tried to find a job. I, honest to God, have tried this time. There's no work out there hardly for carpenters. I couldn't find any-thing, so I been putting in applications in grocery stores, you name it. I've got in applications. I have tried. I've honestly tried this time. That's all I can say. I can't find no work.[7]

Just as in the previous hearing, the trial judge did not ask Turner any questions about his ability to work, his ability to pay his child support debt, or his efforts to find a job. In 2009, the annual unemployment rate in Oconee County had risen to 13.6 percent. The judge sentenced Turner to six months in the county jail, with the condition that he could avoid going to jail if he paid $2,500 toward his child support debt.

Turner's Appeal: The Right to an Attorney

In the appeal to the South Carolina Supreme Court, Turner argued that un-der the Sixth and Fourteenth Amendments to the U.S. Constitution, an at-torney should have been appointed to represent him at the contempt hearing and that sentencing him to a year in jail in the absence of counsel violated his constitutional rights. The South Carolina Supreme Court rejected this argument, ruling that Turner did not have a right to counsel at the contempt hearing because he had been charged with civil contempt and not criminal contempt. According to the court, this distinction between civil and criminal contempt was dispositive, because constitutional safeguards like the right to counsel, the right to a jury trial, and the standard of proof beyond a reason-able doubt apply only in criminal proceedings. Thus, the court ruled that Turner had no right to appointed counsel at the hearing—even though he faced the possibility of a year in jail—because his contempt citation was des-ignated as a civil proceeding and not a criminal one.

Moreover, while the purpose of criminal contempt is to punish someone for disobeying a court order, the ostensible purpose of civil contempt is only to coerce a person to comply with a court order. Thus courts in civil contempt proceedings often invoke the notion that defendants "hold the keys" to their prison cells because all they must do to obtain release is comply with the underlying court order. The South Carolina Supreme Court reiterated this notion in Turner's case, concluding that all he had to do to gain his freedom was pay the child support that he owed. The court did not consider, however, whether Turner actually had the money to pay his support debt.

While these appellate proceedings were taking place, Rebecca Rogers became financially unable to support B.L.P., and she relinquished custody of B.L.P. to her parents, Larry and Judy Price. The family court then directed that Turner's child support payments be paid to Judy Price. Rebecca found a job as a waitress, walking five miles to and from work because she could not afford a car, and began paying weekly support for her children. Judy Price subsequently died, and B.L.P. remained in the care of Larry, who worked intermittently as a roofer and was close to retirement age. Larry Price also had assumed responsibility for caring for three of Rebecca's other children.

After losing at the South Carolina Supreme Court, Turner petitioned the U.S. Supreme Court to grant a writ of certiorari to hear his case. In his petition, Turner was represented not only by his previous attorney, Derek Enderlin, but also by Seth Waxman, a former solicitor general of the United States, Paul R. Q. Wolfson, who also had served in the solicitor general's office, and their Washington, D.C., law firm, Wilmer Cutler Pickering Hale and Dorr LLP. Turner's petition framed the question before the Supreme Court as "[w]hether the Supreme Court of South Carolina erred in holding—in conflict with twenty-two federal courts of appeals and state courts of last resort—that an indigent defendant has no constitutional right to appointed counsel at a civil contempt proceeding that results in his incarceration."[8]

Recognizing the significance of Turner's case, many organizations filed amicus briefs supporting his petition, including the Constitution Project, the National Association of Criminal Defense Lawyers, the Brennan Center for Justice, the National Legal Aid & Defender Association, the Center for Family Policy and Practice, the South Carolina Appleseed Legal Justice Center, and the South Carolina Center for Fathers and Families. Representing Rebecca Rogers, law professor Stephanos Bibas of the University of Pennsylvania Law School Supreme Court Clinic and Stephen Kinnaird of the Washington, D.C., law firm of Paul, Hastings, Janofsky & Walker LLP filed a response opposing the certiorari petition.

On November 1, 2010, the U.S. Supreme Court agreed to hear Turner's appeal from his 2008 contempt sentence. The granting of his petition set the stage for the Court to consider—for the first time in 30 years—whether indigent litigants have a federal right to appointed counsel in civil proceedings.

The Movement for a Federal Right to Appointed Counsel in Civil Cases

Michael Turner's case did not arise in a vacuum.[9] As early as 1923, Harvard law professor John MacArthur Maguire advocated for establishing a comprehensive *in forma pauperis* system that included a right to counsel in certain civil cases.[10] In 1963, the Supreme Court issued its landmark decision in *Gideon v. Wainwright*,[11] holding that the Sixth Amendment to the federal Constitution guarantees all indigent criminal defendants facing felony charges a right to appointed counsel. According to law professor Russell Engler, the "ink was barely dry" in *Gideon* "before advocates sought to expand the right to counsel to the civil context."[12] Indeed, attorney general Robert F. Kennedy emphasized the importance of legal representation for those in poverty in a Law Day address on May 1, 1964, lamenting that the legal profession had "secured the acquittal of an indigent person—but only to abandon him to eviction notices, wage attachments, repossession of goods and termination of welfare benefits."[13]

Efforts to obtain recognition of a federal right to counsel for indigent civil litigants occurred against the backdrop of, and are intertwined with, the creation of federally funded legal services during President Lyndon Johnson's "War on Poverty." In 1964, Congress passed the Economic Opportunity Act, which established the Office of Economic Opportunity (OEO) to administer Johnson's antipoverty programs, which included, for the first time, a federal program to provide legal services for the poor. Led by Sargent Shriver, the OEO recruited a cadre of legal services lawyers whose mission was to use the law to challenge and remedy the causes and effects of poverty. The primary focus of these early antipoverty lawyers was not on providing representation in individual cases, but on generating impact litigation to reform political processes and legal procedures that disadvantaged low-income Americans. Their initial efforts were successful, as they won important victories for the poor on issues such as residency requirements for government benefits, access to the courts, and due process rights in welfare determinations.[14]

While legal services lawyers engaged in systemic reform, advocates for a right to counsel for indigent civil litigants also pressed their cause through litigation. Their efforts reached a high-water mark in 1967 with the Supreme Court's decision in *In re Gault*.[15] In *Gault*, the Supreme Court held that due process requires the appointment of counsel for juvenile defendants in delinquency proceedings that may result in their commitment to a detention facility. After *Gault*, however, the movement for a federal right to counsel in civil cases suffered serious setbacks, as the Supreme Court rejected categorical rights to appointed counsel in probation revocation hearings, school disciplinary proceedings, summary court-martial proceedings, and involuntary transfers of prison inmates to mental hospitals.[16]

As the movement for a civil right to counsel met resistance in the courts, the broader legal services movement encountered intense political opposition that resulted in significant restructuring of federally funded legal services for the poor. After Richard Nixon was elected president in 1968, he proposed dismantling the OEO and transferring its legal services program into a private, nonprofit organization. He accomplished this goal in 1974 with passage of legislation creating the Legal Services Corporation (LSC), which is a private, nonprofit corporation that receives funds appropriated by Congress and distributes them via grants to local legal services agencies.

The subsequent decade of the 1980s was a pivotal time for both federally funded legal services and the movement for a right to counsel in civil cases. After Ronald Reagan became president in 1981, he sought to eliminate the LSC altogether and replace it with law student clinical programs and block grants funding a judicare system. In response to this pressure from the White House, Congress cut LSC funding by 25 percent, reducing its appropriation from $321 million in fiscal year 1981 to $241 million in 1982. This drastic cut forced LSC-funded legal services programs to lay off staff, close offices, and dramatically reduce their level of services. In the meantime, on October 6, 1980, the Supreme Court granted certiorari in *Lassiter v. Department of Social Services of Durham County*, which presented the question of whether an indigent mother had a federal right to appointed counsel in a civil proceeding to terminate her parental rights.[17]

In 1975, a district court in Durham County, North Carolina, adjudicated Abby Gail Lassiter's infant son, William, a neglected child based on evidence that she had not properly cared for him, and the court placed him in the custody of the Department of Social Services. Lassiter was subsequently convicted of second-degree murder in 1976 and sentenced to prison, and the department petitioned the court to terminate her parental rights. Lassiter was brought from prison to attend the hearing on the termination petition, and she represented herself without the assistance of an attorney. After hearing testimony from a social worker, Lassiter's mother, and Lassiter, the court found that Lassiter had not expressed concern for William's welfare and had made no efforts to plan for his future, so it terminated her status as his parent.

On appeal, Ms. Lassiter argued that because she was indigent, the Due Process Clause of the Fourteenth Amendment had entitled her to the assistance of counsel at the termination hearing. In a 5-4 decision, a slim majority of the Court rejected her claim to a categorical right to counsel and held instead that its precedents had established a presumption that due process requires appointed counsel for indigent litigants only if the litigants may lose their physical liberty if they lose the litigation. The majority then weighed Ms. Lassiter's claim to counsel against this presumption using the three-part balancing test it had articulated in *Mathews v. Eldridge*[18] for evaluating due process requirements. Applying the *Mathews* calculus assessing the private interests at stake, the government's interest, and the risk that the procedures used will lead to erroneous decisions, the Court concluded that due process does not require the appointment of counsel for indigent litigants in all parental termination proceedings. Rather, the Court held that trial courts should evaluate on a case-by-case basis whether due process requires the assistance of counsel in any given proceeding.

Pursuing the Right to Counsel after the *Lassiter* Loss

Lassiter was a devastating blow to the movement for recognition of a federal right to counsel for indigent civil litigants, and the movement essentially went dormant after the decision. Advocates shifted their efforts to the states, pursuing litigation to recognize rights to counsel under state constitutions and legislation to enact statutory rights to counsel. These efforts achieved some success in state courts and legislatures. After *Lassiter*, courts in at least thirteen states held that their respective state constitutions granted a right to appointed counsel in proceedings to terminate parental rights. States also created statutory rights to counsel or recognized rights to counsel under their state constitutions for poor litigants facing proceedings for involuntary civil commitment or guardianship, domestic violence proceedings, paternity or child custody proceedings, divorce and annulment proceedings, or proceedings to remove children due to allegations of abuse or neglect.

In the meantime, after a brief resurgence during the first Bush administration and the early years of the Clinton administration, the legal services movement faced devastating blows of its own. In the 1994 congressional elections, the Republican Party won control of the House of Representatives, and under the leadership of House Speaker Newt Gingrich, conservatives committed themselves to eliminating the LSC and ending federal funding for legal services. Supporters of legal services and the LSC fought for their preservation, and a significant political battle ensued. In the end, LSC and legal services survived, but in a much altered and diminished state. Congress cut LSC funding by 30 percent, reducing its appropriation from $400 million in 1995 to $278 million in 1996. In the year following these cuts, the number of LSC-funded attorneys nationwide dropped by 900, 300 local program offices closed, and the number of cases closed fell by 300,000.

In addition to these severe budget cuts, Congress imposed significant restrictions on LSC's legal work as a condition of continuing its existence. It prohibited LSC grantees from representing certain kinds of clients, including prisoners, certain undocumented aliens, and public housing residents evicted for drug-related charges. Congress also restricted the types of legal work that LSC grantees could perform, banning them from participating in class-action lawsuits, welfare-reform advocacy, abortion litigation, redistricting challenges, lobbying, and administrative rulemaking processes. These restrictions forced a paradigm shift in federally funded legal services, transforming their focus from systemic reform and poverty reduction to providing representation in individual cases involving clients' day-to-day legal problems.

As a result of this congressionally mandated shift in LSC priorities, the legal services movement and the movement for a right to counsel in civil cases essentially converged, as both focused on providing representation for litigants in individual cases. In response to the drastic cuts in LSC funding, legal services providers looked for new funding sources, and states restructured their systems for providing legal services to the poor. Many states created "access to justice" commissions to develop new strategies for providing legal services to the poor, including increased pro bono involvement from private attorneys, needs assessments, training for judges and court administrators, increased state funding, and self-help assistance for pro se litigants, such as forms, fact sheets, hotlines, and online services.

While these efforts undoubtedly have provided access for many Americans, they have not been sufficient to satisfy the overwhelming demand for legal services. According to an LSC study conducted in 2009, there is only one lawyer for every 6,415 low-income people, and more than 80 percent of the legal needs of the poor go unmet.[19] Many of these needs involve housing, family, and consumer issues, but for every client served by an LSC-funded program, another eligible client who seeks help is turned down due to insufficient resources.

In 2003, the 40th anniversary of the *Gideon* decision was celebrated and brought new energy to the movement for recognition of a right to counsel for indigent litigants in civil cases. The years that followed saw a marked increase in activity supporting a civil right to counsel. Scholars published numerous articles proposing strategies for implementing a right to counsel, and several law schools sponsored academic conferences on the topic. In 2004, advocates formed the National Coalition for a Civil Right to Counsel, with the mission of encouraging, supporting, and coordinating advocacy efforts to expand recognition and implementation of a right to counsel in civil cases. In particular, the coalition provides assistance, such as model laws, research strategies, legal experts, and litigation support, to advocates pursuing civil right-to-counsel initiatives. Advocates also created the National Center for Access to Justice at Cardozo Law School, which describes itself as "the single academically affiliated non-partisan law and policy organization dedicated exclusively to assuring access to our civil and criminal justice systems."[20]

In 2006, the movement took a significant step forward when the American Bar Association (ABA) House of Delegates unanimously approved a resolution calling on governments to create and implement a right to counsel in civil cases. The resolution urges

> federal, state, and territorial governments to provide legal counsel as a matter of right at public expense to low income persons in those categories of adversarial proceedings where basic human needs are at stake, such as those involving shelter, sustenance, safety, health or child custody, as determined by each jurisdiction.[21]

The resolution had many cosponsors, including the National Legal Aid and Defender Association, and the bar associations of New York, Maine, Colorado, Washington, Minnesota, Connecticut, New York City, Los Angeles, Boston, Philadelphia, the District of Columbia, New York County, and King County, Washington. In addition to the resolution, the ABA created a Resource Center for Access to Justice Initiatives that organizes state access to justice commissions and other efforts to provide assistance and support for state funding of civil legal services.

The ABA resolution generated renewed activity at the state level for a right to counsel in civil cases. Advocates in New York, for example, held a day-long symposium to design a blueprint for a civil right to counsel in the state. Chief Judge Lippman of New York called for implementation of a right to counsel in civil cases and appointed a Task Force to Expand Access to

Legal Services. In California, advocates drafted two model statutes establishing an expanded civil right to counsel. California went even further in 2009, enacting the Sargent Shriver Civil Counsel Act. This act created a six-year pilot program, which began in 2011 with annual funding of $9.5 million, to assess the effects and feasibility of providing counsel to low-income litigants in cases involving housing, domestic violence restraining orders, elder abuse, child custody, and conservatorships and guardianships.

In March 2010, the U.S. Justice Department established an Access to Justice Initiative, the mission of which is to help the justice system efficiently deliver fair and accessible outcomes to all people, regardless of their wealth or status. The initiative's staff works with federal agencies and with state, local, and tribal justice systems to increase access to counsel and to improve the justice delivery systems that serve people who cannot afford lawyers. Shortly thereafter, in August 2010, the ABA adopted a Model Access Act, which provides a model statute for states to use in creating and implementing a civil right to counsel. The act establishes a right to counsel in only the five categories of cases listed in the 2006 ABA resolution, rather than all civil cases, sets income eligibility at 125 percent of the federal poverty level or below, and includes merits tests to decide whether full representation by a lawyer should be provided. For example, to receive full representation, a plaintiff must have a "reasonable possibility of achieving a successful outcome," and a defendant must have a "non-frivolous defense."

The Supreme Court's Decision in Michael Turner's Case

Michael Turner's appeal reached the Supreme Court against the backdrop of this resurgence of energy in the movement to create a federal right to counsel for indigent civil litigants. In addition, by the time the Supreme Court heard Turner's case, 7 federal circuit courts, 15 state courts of last resort, and 8 state intermediate appellate courts had held that indigent defendants in civil contempt proceedings have a right to counsel if they face incarceration. In light of these decisions, state access to justice efforts, and the growing consensus among government, judicial, and bar leaders about the need for counsel, advocates were optimistic that a civil right to counsel was finally within reach and that the Court would recognize that right in *Turner*. The Court, however, did not take that step.

Proponents of a right to counsel were hopeful about what the Supreme Court would decide in *Turner* in part because the Court had said in *Lassiter* that its precedents established a "presumption that an indigent litigant has a right to appointed counsel only when, if he loses, he may be deprived of his physical liberty." Turner's attorneys argued that this language meant that the Court had recognized that a person is entitled to appointed counsel when he or she faces the risk of incarceration, as Turner had. The Court, however, rejected that argument and immediately distinguished the language in *Lassiter*. Writing for the majority, Justice Breyer stated that the language meant only that "the Court previously had found a right to counsel '*only*' in cases involving incarceration, not that a right to counsel exists in *all* such cases."

After rejecting the claim that there was a presumed right to counsel in cases involving incarceration, the Court turned to the balancing test from *Mathews v. Eldridge* to determine whether the Due Process Clause requires appointed counsel in civil contempt proceedings involving a risk of imprisonment. Under that test, a court must evaluate three factors to determine the specific safeguards the Due Process Clause requires for a civil proceeding to be fundamentally fair. Those three factors are "(1) the nature of 'the private interest that will be affected,' (2) the comparative 'risk' of an 'erroneous deprivation' of that interest with and without 'additional or substitute procedural safeguards,' and (3) the nature and magnitude of any countervailing interest in not providing 'additional or substitute procedural requirement[s].'"

Applying the first factor, the Court found that the private interest at stake—Turner's loss of liberty—was strong and weighed heavily in his favor. Indeed, it pointed out that freedom from bodily restraint lies "at the core of the liberty protected by the Due Process Clause." Turner did not fare so well on the other two *Mathews* factors, however.

The Court next analyzed the comparative risk of an erroneous deprivation of a delinquent parent's liberty if the parent is not appointed counsel in a contempt proceeding. The Court concluded that the risk is low because the critical issue in the proceeding—the parent's ability to pay—is a straightforward determination when the right procedures are in place. In addition, the Court found that a state can significantly reduce the risk of an erroneous deprivation of liberty by following a set of substitute procedural safeguards that the solicitor general had proposed as an alternative to appointing counsel. Those recommended procedures, which the solicitor general had suggested in an amicus brief filed at the merits stage of the case, include:

> (1) notice to the defendant that his "ability to pay" is a critical issue in the contempt proceeding; (2) the use of a form (or the equivalent) to elicit relevant financial information; (3) an opportunity at the hearing for the defendant to respond to statements and questions about his

financial status, (*e.g.*, those triggered by his responses on the form); and (4) an express finding by the court that the defendant has the ability to pay.

On the third *Mathews* factor—the nature and magnitude of any counter-vailing interest in not providing additional safeguards—the Court reasoned that requiring a state to provide counsel to the delinquent parent could make the proceeding less fair overall. The Court pointed out that the opposing party in child support proceedings is sometimes the custodial parent who is not represented by counsel, which was the situation in Turner's case. In that circumstance, appointing counsel for the delinquent parent could create an "asymmetry of representation" that would significantly alter the nature of the proceeding. The Court also expressed concern that providing counsel for the delinquent parent would inject formality or delay into the proceedings, which would slow payments to families in need and deprive them of the support to which they are entitled.

After considering all these factors, the Court concluded that the simplic-ity of the ability-to-pay question, the availability of alternative procedural safeguards, and concerns about asymmetry of representation weighed against mandating appointed counsel. Thus the Court ruled that the Due Process Clause "does not *automatically* require the provision of counsel at civil con-tempt proceedings to an indigent individual who is subject to a child support order, even if that individual faces incarceration (for up to a year)." However, the Court expressly left undecided the questions of whether due process re-quires appointing counsel in contempt proceedings in which the underlying child support debt is owed to a state, if the other parent or the state is repre-sented by an attorney, or if unusually complex issues are present. Finally, in a hollow victory for Turner, the Court ruled that his incarceration violated due process because South Carolina had not provided him with an attorney or al-ternative procedural safeguards in lieu of an attorney. Accordingly, the Court vacated the contempt judgment against him, after he had already served a year in prison for it.

The Right to Counsel Movement After *Turner*

The *Turner* decision generated a tremendous amount of discussion about the movement for a civil right to counsel and access to justice generally.[22] On the day the Court issued the decision, scholars and advocates launched an online symposium on the Concurring Opinions blog in which they discussed its implications at length. Proponents of a federal right to counsel in civil cases expressed their deep disappointment with the decision's rejection of a categorical right to counsel. Peter Edelman, a law professor at Georgetown and a recognized expert on access to justice issues, commented that the decision demonstrates the Court's misunderstanding of "the world of trying to navigate the court system without a lawyer." Norman Reimer, executive director of the National Association of Criminal Defense Lawyers, said the decision "betrays naïve simplicity and a breathtaking disconnect from the real world."

Others, such as law professor Marty Guggenheim, found grounds for optimism in the fact that *Turner* suggests that appointed counsel would be constitutionally required in other cases, such as when the government is the opposing party seeking the contempt order and is represented by an attorney. He opined that *Turner* will come to stand for an important new right to counsel for indigent litigants in these circumstances. Others found a positive aspect in the Court's recognition that procedures are required to protect the due process rights of pro se litigants and that trial courts have an obligation to ensure that such procedures are in place. Richard Zorza, for example, called the decision a landmark because it is the Supreme Court's first statement regarding "trial court judges' access to justice due process responsibilities (beyond criminal cases) to unrepresented persons." In a similar vein, Laura Abel commented that the decision, if fully and effectively implemented, "could be a force for making the court system more user friendly" for people who cannot afford a lawyer. Indeed, in response to *Turner*, the Self-Represented Litigation Network issued guidelines for judges to follow to achieve compliance with the decision's mandate regarding pro se litigants.

Others, however, such as law professors Benjamin Barton and Stephanos Bibas, have asserted that *Turner* "got it right" and is the "death blow" to the movement for a federal right to counsel in civil cases. Bibas represented Ms. Rogers in *Turner* and argued the case before the Supreme Court, while Barton filed an amicus brief supporting Ms. Rogers' position. They assert that appointing counsel in civil cases is not financially feasible and that the Court's refusal to recognize a federal right to counsel will steer future developments toward more affordable court reforms for pro se litigants. John Pollock and Michael Greco, long-time proponents of a civil right to counsel, dispute the characterization of *Turner* as a "death blow." They contend that *Turner* will be viewed more as a footnote in the movement, because, after *Lassiter*, the battleground for recognition of a civil right to counsel shifted from the federal courts to the state courts.

Conclusion: Deciding Next Steps for Right-to-Counsel Advocates

Given this divergence of opinions, *Turner*'s impact on the movement for a right to counsel in civil cases remains to be seen. Advocates for such a right now must decide the path they wish to take. Should they focus on ensuring that trial courts follow *Turner*'s mandate to develop meaningful procedures to protect the due process rights of pro se litigants? Should they focus on lobbying state legislatures to enact statutes providing counsel at state expense in civil cases involving basic human needs, such as the ABA Model Access Act? Or should they continue to bring test cases seeking court recognition of a right to counsel under state constitutions and in the situations left open by *Turner*?

While proponents of a civil right to counsel did not achieve the victory they had hoped for in *Turner*, it is doubtful that *Turner* will put an end to the movement. Proponents of the right to counsel are committed to the cause, and there remains an overwhelming demand for legal services in this country. While in the future the movement may stake its claim on a foundation other than the federal Constitution, advocates will continue to press for meaningful access to justice in all its forms and for all people. In a country that enshrines the notion of "equal justice under law," the quality of justice that a person receives cannot depend on one's wealth or status.

Notes

1. This narrative of Turner's case is based on the Supreme Court's opinion in *Turner v. Rogers*, 131 U.S. 2507 (2011), and the following pleadings in the case: the Brief of Respondents, the Joint Appendix, the Petitioner's Appendix, and the Petition for a Writ of Certiorari.

2. This discussion of imputed income is based on Tonya L. Brito, *Fathers Behind Bars: Rethinking Child Support Policy Toward Low-Income Noncustodial Fathers and Their Families*, 15 J. GENDER RACE & JUST. 617 (2012).

3. This information about child support arrearages and imprisonment for civil contempt is based on Elizabeth G. Patterson, *Civil Contempt and the Indigent Child-Support Obligor: The Silent Return of Debtor's Prison*, 18 CORNELL J. L. & PUB. POL'Y 95 (2008) (citing Elizabeth G. Patterson, Child Support Detainees by County 2009); U.S. DEP'T OF HEALTH AND HUMAN SERVS., OFFICE OF CHILD SUPPORT ENFORCEMENT, THE STORY BEHIND THE NUMBERS: UNDERSTANDING AND MANAGING CHILD SUPPORT DEBT (2008), *available at* http://www.acf.hhs.gov/programs/css/resource/story-behind-the-numbers-understanding-managing-child-support-debt; U.S. DEP'T OF HEALTH AND HUMAN SERVS., OFFICE OF

Child Support Enforcement, FY 2012 Preliminary Report, Table P-18: Total Amount of Arrearages Due for All Fiscal Years for Five Consecutive Fiscal Years, *available at* http://www.acf.hhs.gov/programs/css/resource/fy2012-preliminary-report-table-p-18 (last visited Nov. 2013).

 4. *Turner, supra* note 1, at 2513.

 5. Economic and employment data are based on the following sources: South Carolina Dep't of Commerce, Community Profile: Oconee County (2012), *available at* http://maps.sccommerce.com/community/ComProReport/04000073.pdf; U.S. Dep't of Labor, Bureau of Labor Statistics, South Carolina Statewide Data, *available at* http://data.bls.gov/timeseries/LASST45000003.

 6. Discussion of the South Carolina appeal is based on *Price v. Turner*, 691 S.E.2d 470 (S.C. 2010).

 7. Joint Appendix, *supra* note 1, at 90a.

 8. Petition for Certiorari, *supra* note 1, at i.

 9. This discussion of the history of legal services and the movement for a right to appointed counsel in civil cases is based on the following sources: Laura K. Abel & Max Rettig, *State Statutes Providing for a Right to Counsel in Civil Cases*, 40 Clearinghouse Rev. 245 (July–Aug. 2006); American Bar Association, House of Delegates Resolution 112A (2006), *available at* http://www.americanbar.org/content/dam/aba/administrative/legal_aid_indigent_defendants/ls_sclaid_06A112A.authcheckdam.pdf; American Bar Association, Report to the House of Delegates, Resolution 104 (2010), *available at* http://www.americanbar.org/content/dam/aba/administrative/legal_aid_indigent_defendants/ls_sclaid_104_revised_final_aug_2010.authcheckdam.pdf; Cal. Gov't Code §§ 68650–68651; Jeanne Charn, *Celebrating the "Null" Finding: Finding Evidence-Based Strategies for Improving Access to Legal Services*, 122 Yale L. J. 2206 (2013); Jeanne Charn, *Symposium Foreword: Toward a Civil Gideon: The Future of American Legal Services*, 7 Harv. L. & Pol'y Rev. 1 (2013); David J. Dreyer, *Déjà vu All Over Again: Turner v. Rogers and the Civil Right to Counsel*, 61 Drake L. Rev. 639 (2013); Russell Engler, *Reflections on a Civil Right to Counsel and Drawing Lines: When Does Access to Justice Mean Full Representation By Counsel, and When Might Less Assistance Suffice?*, 9 Seattle J. Soc. Just. 97 (2010); Alan W. Houseman & Linda E. Perle, Center for Law and Social Policy, Securing Equal Justice for All: A Brief History of Civil Legal Assistance in the United States (2007); Judicial Council of California, Fact Sheet on Sargent Shriver Civil Counsel Act, *available at* http://www.courts.ca.gov/documents/AB-590.pdf (2012); Paul Marvy, *Advocacy for a Civil Right to Counsel: An Update*, 41 Clearinghouse Rev. 644 (Mar.–Apr. 2008); Paul Marvy, *Thinking About a Civil Right to Counsel Since 1923*, 40 Clearinghouse Rev. 170 (July–Aug. 2006); Clare Pastore, *A Civil Right to Counsel: Closer to Reality?*, 42 Loy. L.A. L. Rev. 1065 (2009); John Pollock & Michael S. Greco, *It's Not Triage If The Patient Bleeds Out*, 161 U. Pa. L. Rev. PENNumbra 40 (2012); Deborah Rhode, *Whatever Happened to Access to Justice?*, 42 Loy. L.A. L. Rev. 869 (2009); Louis S. Rulli, *On the Road to Civil Gideon: Five Lessons From the Enactment of a Right to Counsel for Indigent Home-*

owners in Federal Civil Forfeiture Proceedings, 19 J. L. & POL'Y 683 (2011); Steven D. Schwinn, *Faces of Open Courts and the Civil Right to Counsel*, 37 U. BALT. L. REV. 21 (2007); Gary F. Smith, *Poverty Warriors: A Historical Perspective on the Mission of Legal Services*, 45 CLEARINGHOUSE REV. 34 (May–June 2011); DAVID UDELL & LAURA ABEL, NATIONAL COALITION FOR A CIVIL RIGHT TO COUNSEL, INFORMATION FOR CIVIL JUSTICE SYSTEMS ABOUT CIVIL RIGHT TO COUNSEL INITIATIVES, http://www.civilrighttocounsel.org/pdfs/NCCRC%20Informational%20Memo.pdf; U.S. DEP'T OF JUSTICE, THE ACCESS TO JUSTICE INITIATIVE, http://www.justice.gov/atj.

10. John MacArthur Maguire, *Poverty and Civil Litigation*, 36 HARV. L. REV. 361 (1923).

11. 372 U.S. 335 (1963). In 1972, the Court extended the right to appointed counsel to criminal defendants charged with misdemeanors who faced the risk of imprisonment. Argersinger v. Hamlin, 407 U.S. 25 (1972).

12. Engler, *supra* note 9, at 102.

13. Attorney General Robert F. Kennedy, Law Day Address at the University of Chicago Law School (May 1, 1964), *available at* http://www.justice.gov/ag/rfk-speeches/1964/05-01-1964.pdf. In addition, legal scholars at the time advanced the concept of a right to counsel in civil cases. *See, e.g.*, Note, *The Indigent's Right to Counsel in Civil Cases*, 76 YALE L. J. 545 (1967); Francis William O'Brien, *Why Not Appointed Counsel in Civil Cases? The Swiss Approach*, 28 OHIO ST. L. J. 1, 9 (1967); Alan Jay Stein, *Note, The Indigent's "Right" to Counsel in Civil Cases*, 43 FORDHAM L. REV. 989 (1975).

14. *See* Fuentes v. Shevin, 407 U.S. 67 (1972) (due process requirements for prejudgment replevin statutes); Boddie v. Connecticut, 401 U.S. 371 (1971) (due process requirements for access to courts); Goldberg v. Kelly, 397 U.S. 254 (1970) (due process requirements for termination of welfare benefits); Shapiro v. Thompson, 394 U.S. 618 (1969) (residency requirements for welfare assistance); King v. Smith, 392 U.S. 309 (1968) (legality of state "substitute father" regulation applied in eligibility determination for welfare benefits).

15. 387 U.S. 1 (1967).

16. Vitek v. Jones, 445 U.S. 480 (1980) (involuntary transfer of prison inmate to mental hospital); Middendorf v. Henry, 425 U.S. 25 (1976) (summary courts martial); Goss v. Lopez, 419 U.S. 565 (1975) (school disciplinary proceedings); Gagnon v. Scarpelli, 411 U.S. 778 (1973) (probation revocation hearings). Interestingly, four of the justices in *Vitek* were in favor of a right to appointed counsel for prison inmates facing involuntary transfers to mental hospitals.

17. 452 U.S. 18 (1981).

18. 424 U.S. 319 (1976).

19. LEGAL SERVICES CORPORATION, DOCUMENTING THE JUSTICE GAP IN AMERICA: THE CURRENT UNMET CIVIL LEGAL NEEDS OF LOW-INCOME AMERICANS (2009), *available at* http://www.lsc.gov/sites/default/files/LSC/pdfs/documenting_the_justice_gap_in_america_2009.pdf. The study found that there is one lawyer for every 429 people in the general population. *Id.* In addition, the number of LSC-funded programs dropped from more than 325 to 138 between 1995 and 2006, and the geographic areas served by many existing programs increased significantly.

20. http://ncforaj.files.wordpress.com/2012/11/overview-of-ncaj-11-2-12. pdf.

21. ABA House of Delegates Resolution 112A, *supra* note 9, at 1.

22. This discussion of *Turner*'s implications relies on the following sources: Benjamin H. Barton & Stephanos Bibas, *Triaging Appointed-Counsel Funding and Pro Se Access to Justice*, 160 U. Pa. L. Rev. 967 (2012); Russell Engler, *Turner v. Rogers and the Essential Role of the Courts in Delivering Access to Justice*, 7 Harv. L. & Pol'y Rev. 31 (2013); Pollock & Greco, *supra* note 9; Rulli, *supra* note 9; The Turner Symposium, Concurring Opinions Blog, http://www.concurringopinions.com/archives/category/symposium-turner-v-rogers/page/2; Richard Zorza, *A New Day for Judges and the Self-Represented: The Implications of Turner v. Rogers*, 50 No. 4 Judges' J. 16 (Fall 2011); Richard Zorza, *A New Day for Judges and the Self-Represented: Toward Best Practices in Complex Self-Represented Cases*, 51, no. 1 Judges' J. 36 (Winter 2012).

Public Housing as Housing of Last Resort

Department of Housing and Urban Development v. Rucker • (2002)

NESTOR M. DAVIDSON

On December 31, 1997, in the depths of a typically damp and chilly northern California winter, the Oakland Housing Authority filed an unlawful detainer action in the Alameda County Municipal Court to evict Pearlie Rucker, a 63-year-old great-grandmother, from the apartment she had lived in since 1985. According to the complaint against her, Rucker's mentally disabled daughter Gelinda had been arrested for public drunkenness three blocks from Rucker's apartment the previous March. A search of Gelinda at the time turned up a rock that police suspected was cocaine as well as a pipe for smoking crack cocaine.[1] As grounds for the eviction, the housing authority invoked paragraph 9(m) of Rucker's lease, which required her to "assure that . . . any member of the household, or another person under the tenant's control, shall not engage in . . . [a]ny drug related criminal activity on or near the premise[s]."[2] Pearlie Rucker insisted that she was not aware of any drug use by Gelinda and had, in fact, searched Gelinda's room every week for years, fruitlessly trying to find signs to alert her to any drug problems.

The attempted eviction of Pearlie Rucker—and similar attempts that same winter by the housing authority to evict three other elderly residents, Willie Lee, Barbara Hill, and Herman Walker, for alleged drug-related criminal activity by family members and others—began a fight that would eventually reach the United States Supreme Court. On a technical level, the case that re-

274

sulted, *Department of Housing and Urban Development (HUD) v. Rucker*, posed a deceptively simple question of statutory interpretation. The housing authority leases at issue were drafted in response a federal statute, 42 U.S.C. § 1437d(*l*)(6), that mandated that such leases contain a clause that "any drug-related criminal activity on or off [the] premises engaged in by a public housing tenant, any member of the tenant's household, or any guest or other person under the tenant's control, shall be cause for termination of tenancy." Rucker and her fellow plaintiffs argued that the word "any" in this provision should not be read to authorize the eviction of tenants who did not know of or control the relevant activity of others. If it were so interpreted, they further argued, the provision would raise serious due process concerns. The Supreme Court disagreed, reading the statute to permit the eviction of tenants regardless of whether they knew or had control over the person involved in drug-related criminal activity. The Court batted aside due process concerns by finding such evictions merely to be the work of a landlord enforcing a lease term on property it owns, rather than the acts of a governmental entity imbued with constitutional significance.

Rucker crystallizes dilemmas that have long plagued public housing and the vulnerable residents who make up most of its population. One dilemma is doctrinal and has to do with ambiguities over the *public* nature of public housing. Housing authorities and HUD often assert legal defenses grounded in the fact that housing authorities are governmental entities. This is most evident in claims of pre-emption and sovereign immunity, but it also extends to other legal issues. Courts have grappled with whether providing public housing is a governmental function or whether the government is simply acting as a private landlord. This doctrinal puzzle has significant constitutional and practical consequences, and the Court took a decidedly privatized view of public housing in *Rucker*.

A related but more fundamental dilemma highlighted by *Rucker* is that in the nearly 80 years since its inception, public housing has become the housing of last resort in many communities. Public housing often shelters residents with significant personal challenges, and, particularly for large, urban authorities, it can concentrate those residents in places with few opportunities or community resources. Despite this, because so few options exist for the lowest-income individuals and families, public housing has long had significant waiting lists for even the most severely underfunded developments. *Rucker* thus involves not only four elderly tenants facing the loss of their homes for activities they were never directly involved in, but also echoes the struggles within housing policy that have left public housing authorities in a position to reach for such dire measures.

Public Housing, the War on Drugs, and the One-Strike Policy

Understanding the stakes in *Rucker* and the Supreme Court's avoidance of any serious engagement with the constitutional issues the case raised requires some grounding in the history and nature of public housing. *Rucker* must also be understood in light of the decades-long struggle many larger, urban public housing authorities have faced with drug-related crime and the policy responses that emerged from that struggle.

Public Housing: From New Deal Urban Renewal to Clinton-Era Concentrated Poverty

The federal public housing program was prefigured by a series of New Deal responses to severe housing problems during the Great Depression. From 1933 through 1935, the Roosevelt administration began experimenting with directly developing housing, something that had been tried previously on the state level and on an emergency basis during World War I.[3] Under the National Industrial Recovery Act,[4] the Public Works Administration's Housing Division built nearly 22,000 homes.[5] But in the wake of a Sixth Circuit decision holding that the federal government could not exercise the power of eminent domain to assemble land for this purpose, New Deal policymakers began working on a model of federal funding for state and local efforts.[6]

This effort culminated in the United States Housing Act of 1937, establishing the federal public housing program.[7] Housing activists at the time like Catherine Bauer envisioned the 1937 act primarily as a tool to attack problems of housing quality and remediate urban "slum" conditions and less as a means of addressing housing affordability.[8] Public housing was also seen by many primarily as an economic stimulus program, drawing the support of the labor movement and policymakers focused on recovery at a time when building activity had ground almost to a halt nationwide.[9]

In terms of the population that would occupy this new public housing, the original vision was akin to public transportation or public libraries: a service available to the general public but not particularly targeted toward low-income populations. Initially, public housing "was designed to serve the needs of the 'submerged middle class,' who were temporarily outside of the labor market during the Depression,"[10] and in the early years of the program, many local authorities aggressively screened tenants to maintain what they saw as appropriate community standards. As one historian of public housing has noted, "[u]nwed pregnant women could be evicted and large fines for property damage were imposed. Other criteria were that families have two parents, the head of the household hold a job, and that families have some record of good housekeeping skills."[11]

The funding model introduced in the 1937 act, which is not entirely dissimilar to the model that still prevails, involved long-term annual contribution contracts between the federal government and local public housing authorities created by state law. These public housing agencies (PHAs) would borrow through bond issuances and pay reduced interest rates on that debt, providing a modest subsidy. As originally conceived, operating costs would largely be covered by tenant rents, which was another incentive for housing authorities to seek a resident population with at least some financial capacity.

Several forces coalesced in the program's early decades to change the trajectory of public housing from its original vision, both in terms of who occupied public housing and the environment in which that housing existed. First, and perhaps foremost, public housing never received the funding necessary for long-term capital needs. As the tenant population became progressively less able to contribute to operations, a long-term vicious cycle of underinvestment set in. Exacerbating this cycle, in response to ongoing opposition to public housing from significant sectors of the real estate industry, Congress in 1949 mandated that public housing must be built in a simple, pared-down fashion, that PHAs rent levels be at least 20 percent below the lowest prevailing market rents, and that tenant incomes be capped.[12] Moreover, a 1969 statutory change known as the Brooke Amendment, after its sponsor, Massachusetts senator Edward Brooke, unintentionally concentrated poverty in public housing even further. The Brooke Amendment capped public housing rent levels at 25 percent of tenant income (a limit that was raised in 1981 to 30 percent, where it remains),[13] which effectively meant that public housing came to serve some of the lowest-income populations among housing programs. At the time the *Rucker* controversy erupted, the national average annual income for public housing residents was roughly $8,500, with many living on Social Security or other public benefits.[14]

In terms of the context for public housing, particularly for larger, urban housing authorities, the initial promise of replacing slums with model housing often gave way to a reality of concentrated poverty and racial segregation. Built into the decentralized model of federal financing of local housing authorities was deference to local political dynamics for siting and tenanting. With this HUD deference, public housing was often disproportionately built in African American and other minority neighborhoods.[15] At the same time, after World War II, suburbanization and "white flight" from traditional urban cores contributed to the economic and social isolation of the communities where public housing was located. As early as the 1950s, advocates present at the creation of the federal housing program were already decrying, in Bauer's oft-cited words, the program's "dreary deadlock."[16]

The "One Strike and You're Out" Policy

Too often, public housing has been defined in the public imagination by its most egregious failures rather than by its quiet successes. Most public housing at the time of *Rucker*—and throughout its history—has provided decent shelter for vulnerable populations and draws long waiting lists. And most public housing, including the apartments in which the *Rucker* tenants lived, is in scatter-site developments rather than in massive, high-rise projects such as the infamous (if perhaps unfairly maligned) Pruitt-Igoe complex in St. Louis and Chicago's notorious Cabrini-Green.

That said, there is little dispute that by the 1980s and into the 1990s, violent crime in and around larger, urban public housing developments had become a serious problem.[17] Throughout this period, housing authorities struggled through a number of policies to combat crime. Among the more prominent strategies were architectural changes based on Oscar Newman's idea of defensible space, an approach designed to prevent crime by empowering residents to take control of public commons. Many housing authorities also turned to intensive policing and security initiatives, such as "clean sweeps" and hot-spot targeting. These tactics consistently raised civil liberties concerns, and even where successful they faced problems with sporadic funding, with gains often reversed. And for the most severely distressed public housing, desperate policymakers eventually turned to large-scale demolition in part as a crime-prevention strategy, reinventing large swaths of public housing along a low-rise, scatter-site, mixed-income model.[18]

In 1988, Congress responded to broader national concerns about drug-related crime with a sprawling statute called the Anti–Drug Abuse Act.[19] The act is perhaps best known for having established the Office of National Drug Control Policy (and the so-called "drug czar" to head it), but its 10 titles and numerous subtitles covered everything from international narcotics control to imposing a federal death penalty for certain drug-related crimes. Tucked away in Title V, Subtitle C of the act was a provision that required public housing authorities to include language in leases that would

> provide that a public housing tenant, any member of the tenant's household, or a guest or other person under the tenant's control shall

not engage in criminal activity, including drug related criminal activity, on or near public housing premises, while the tenant is a tenant in public housing, and such criminal activity shall be cause for termination of tenancy.[20]

Congress amended this language twice before the *Rucker* case erupted, each time broadening its reach. In 1990, Congress expanded the bases for eviction to include any criminal activity that threatens the health, safety, or right to peaceful enjoyment of the premises by other tenants and at the same time rephrased the operative clause to cover "any" drug-related criminal activity on or near the premises.[21] Congress in 1996 then expanded this final clause to cover activities "on or off such premises,"[22] freeing the provision's coverage from its previous link to the proximity of the criminal activity at issue to public housing.

The legislative framework was in place, then, for a national policy that would incentivize PHAs to evict tenants as a core strategy for responding to drug-related criminal activity in public housing.[23] On January 23, 1996, President Bill Clinton used the occasion of his final State of the Union speech before his 1996 re-election campaign to announce what became known as "One Strike and You're Out." In a statement that HUD would soon adopt as a rallying cry around the policy, the president said, "I challenge local housing authorities and tenant associations: Criminal gang members and drug dealers are destroying the lives of decent tenants. From now on, the rule for residents who commit crime and peddle drugs should be one strike and you're out."[24]

Because the statutory authority merely vested discretion in housing authorities but did not mandate that any actions actually be taken at the local level, HUD took several steps to implement the one-strike policy. In a formal notice, and less-formal guidance, HUD made clear that PHAs should have in place one-strike policies. HUD also modified what was called the Public Housing Management Assessment Program, a numerical grading system HUD was using at the time for PHA oversight, indicating that one basis on which PHAs would be evaluated was "adopting and implementing effective applicant screening and tenant eviction policies and procedures."[25] Higher-scoring PHAs would be subject to lighter oversight and be eligible for additional funding.[26] And HUD offered a series of recommendations to PHAs for implementing one-strike policies, including spelling out eviction policies in the lease, marshalling evidence before eviction, and, most broadly, making "tenants responsible for the conduct of everyone in their households."[27] PHAs across the country quickly began to implement this policy.[28]

The Sins of the Daughter?

Into this mix of national politics and local challenges stepped the Oakland Housing Authority (OHA) in the winter of 1997 and 1998. By any measure, Oakland in the mid-1990s was experiencing significant crime and violence. A report by the Alameda County Public Health Department called the situation a public health crisis, noting that although the violent crime rate was dropping in this period, even by the early 2000s the city's homicide rate was four times as high as the statewide and national rate.[29] OHA managed a sprawling portfolio of more than 3,300 units housing roughly 8,000 residents,[30] and crime had become such a significant issue in OHA housing that a coalition of tenants sued the housing authority in 1994 for failing to provide adequate security against drug dealers.[31]

After HUD formalized the one-strike policy, OHA quickly began to implement it, evicting 18 families in 1997 alone.[32] One-strike was thus beginning to loom large by the time OHA attempted to evict Pearlie Rucker for the alleged activities of her daughter Gelinda. At the time, Rucker was living in an apartment in a small, two-story building on East 21st Street in Oakland, in a struggling neighborhood called Highland Terrace. In addition to Rucker's daughter Gelinda, the apartment was also home to Gelinda's two daughters and one granddaughter, bringing four generations under one roof.

Pearlie Rucker's New Year's Eve Day notice was only one of four that formed the eventual basis for *Rucker*. Willie Lee and Barbara Hill, two neighbors in a small apartment building on Shafter Avenue north of downtown Oakland, were likewise targeted for eviction. In the case of Lee and Hill, the ground for eviction was that their grandsons, Robert Lee and Donte McPherson, had allegedly been found smoking marijuana in the parking lot outside their apartment the previous November 6th.[33] Lee was 71 years old at the time and had been living in the apartment for roughly 25 years; Hill was 63 and had been a tenant there for roughly 30 years.

The final plaintiff in the *Rucker* case, Herman Walker, was 75 years old and had lived in public housing for eight years at the time OHA first served him with a three-day notice of termination. Walker was disabled, and he required the help of an in-home caregiver. The eviction notice against Walker alleged that on three occasions, OHA officers had searched Walker's apartment and had found evidence that Walker's caregiver and guests had been storing cocaine and crack pipes. All four of these elderly residents asserted that they did not have any knowledge of the relevant activity and would not have permitted it had they known.[34]

One by one, first Walker, then Lee and Hill, and finally Rucker all sought the help of an organization called the Eviction Defense Center, a unit of a small legal defense nonprofit in Oakland called Collective Legal Services. Their cases were taken up by a young attorney named Anne Omura, who was then only a little more than a year out of Boalt Law School. With pro bono assistance, Omura and a team of attorneys crossed the East Bay to file suit on February 27, 1998, challenging the evictions in federal district court in San Francisco.[35]

On June 19, 1998, District court judge Charles Breyer issued an injunction to halt the eviction. Judge Breyer found the relevant provision of § 1437d to be "silent as to whether a tenant must have knowledge of, or the ability to control, the drug-related criminal activity of a household member, guest or other person in order for that other person's conduct to be cause for terminating the tenant's lease."[36] To Judge Breyer, the central question was whether the lease provision was rationally related to a legitimate housing purpose, and on that, Judge Breyer concluded that the authority to evict innocent tenants "on its face appears irrational because evicting the tenant will not reduce drug-related criminal activity since the tenant has not engaged in any such activity or knowingly allowed such activity to occur."[37]

On appeal, a three-judge panel of the Ninth Circuit, over a vigorous dissent by Judge Fletcher, initially overturned the injunction. However, the Ninth Circuit agreed to hear the case *en banc* and reversed itself, holding that "if a tenant has taken reasonable steps to prevent criminal drug activity from occurring, but, for a lack of knowledge or other reason, could not realistically exercise control over the conduct of a household member or guest, § 1437d(*l*) (6) does not authorize the eviction of such a tenant."[38] To the *en banc* panel, any other reading would raise significant due process concerns on the ground that an innocent party should not be deprived of a property interest through this kind of forfeiture without fault.[39]

The Supreme Court granted certiorari and in a unanimous, cursory opinion typical of Chief Justice Rehnquist's style toward the end of his time on the bench, unanimously reversed the Ninth Circuit. To the Court, the unadorned word "any" in the phrase "any drug-related criminal activity" precluded the conclusion that innocent tenants should be excluded from the statute's reach.[40] As to the constitutional consequences of this kind of strict liability, the Court cursorily batted aside the issue of forfeiture by concluding that the Oakland Housing Authority was "not attempting to criminally punish or civilly regulate respondents as members of the general populace," but was "instead acting as a landlord of property that it owns."[41] With that, the one-strike policy was validated.

Although the Oakland Housing Authority fought all the way to the Supreme Court for the right to evict Pearlie Rucker, the housing authority ultimately allowed her, as well as Willie Lee and Barbara Hill, to remain; only Herman Walker was ultimately forced out.[42]

Two Dilemmas of Public Housing as Housing of Last Resort

The Court's decision in *Rucker* may have turned on a relatively narrow question of statutory interpretation, indeed on the meaning of the single word "any." But in both its doctrinal analysis and the deep challenges facing public housing that gave it birth, *Rucker* highlights two fundamental dilemmas that have always been central to public housing. The first is that while public housing is undeniably provided by a governmental entity, the line between public and private when the state acts as a landlord has long been contested. The second dilemma is more fundamental: the one-strike policy challenged in *Rucker* underscores the reality that public housing has become the housing of last resort for its extremely vulnerable residents, and a very scarce resource at that. This heightens the power of the kind of exile that eviction represents as well as the incentives that housing authorities, facing long waiting lists of deserving residents, can have to use that power. *Rucker* resolved neither of these tensions, but, as one of the highest-profile judicial pronouncements on public housing, it validated both a privatized vision of public housing and the broad discretion to manage such housing that that vision carries.

A Doctrinal Dilemma: The Public in Public Housing

When *Rucker* reached the Supreme Court, the potential was there for the Court to grapple seriously with a number of questions involving individual property rights and the due process implications of forfeiture for innocent tenants, as well as other constitutional concerns with excessive fines and associational rights. The Supreme Court, however, took a dismissive approach to these constitutional concerns, as noted, likening the Oakland Housing Authority to a private landlord for the purposes of eviction.

Public housing is one end of spectrum that ranges from purely private to purely public provision of affordable housing. The largest stock of housing available for people living in poverty is not directly subsidized by the government, but consists of private rental housing in neighborhoods that for reasons of poverty, isolation, or otherwise, have sufficiently low rents to be affordable.[43] Within the portfolio of housing that does receive direct government subsidies, however, there are a range of approaches to the balance between public and private. Most new affordable housing construction, for example, is funded today through Low-Income Housing Tax Credits, a program that provides tax credits for private investors in exchange for providing equity to housing owned by for-profit and nonprofit developers. Various smaller grant programs likewise subsidize private owners to provide below-market-rent housing, and since the early 1970s, much of the subsidy stream from HUD has gone to vouchers that tenants can use in the private market.

Given that range of approaches, the fact that public housing remains relatively distinctive in its model of public ownership has done little to resolve the many doctrinal questions that arise from the government being a housing provider. On one level, the fact of public ownership is inescapable. As the D.C. Circuit famously noted in *Rudder v. United States*, a McCarthy-era case that barred a requirement that tenants certify that they were not members of a subversive organization, the "government as landlord is still the government. It must not act arbitrarily, for, unlike private landlords, it is subject to the requirements of due process of law."[44] The fact that PHAs act with a certain amount of delegated sovereignty arises in cases involving pre-emption[45] and is a leitmotif in cases involving tort liability, where both the issue of housing as a government function as well as the scope of waivers of sovereign immunity are frequently litigated.[46] And basic procedural due process applies to both the subsidy and the actual tenure for public housing residents, even if the exact scope of that protection is contested.[47]

All this reflects a basic tension: there is no doubt that public housing authorities are state actors, but they are state actors charged with providing housing that requires authorities to take on the responsibilities of a landlord. One of the primary fault lines in larger policy discussions of public housing has always been conflict over privatization; clashes over recent efforts to reform public-housing subsidies along a more private-finance-oriented model are only the most recent flare-up.[48]

The Supreme Court did not question the public nature of public housing at a fundamental level in *Rucker*, but the question was what flowed from this recognition. In *Rucker*, functionally nothing did. The Court's casual dismissal of concerns about the forfeiture of property interests of innocent tenants—after all, a leasehold is property—with the declaration that the eviction of tenants under § 1437d(*l*)(6) was no different from an action taken by a private landlord validates a privatized vision of public housing. *Rucker* did not, and could not have, resolved basic tensions about the nature of public housing, and housing authorities remain bound up in a web of important public obligations. But *Rucker* did bolster the conception of public housing as indistinguishable from other low-income housing, indeed indistinguishable from private housing at the very juncture—the rights of tenants to retain the housing benefit—where the public nature of public housing would seem to be most important.

Scholars have argued that living in public housing is profoundly stigmatizing. As Lawrence Vale has noted, as "public housing resources became increasingly targeted to those with the fewest alternatives, the admissions pipeline served to consolidate and channel the victims of all the nation's most virulent prejudices into a single program."[49] But as the fight the *Rucker* tenants waged makes clear, residents of public housing—even of the most distressed public housing—have a deep attachment to their homes. This fact does not resolve the appropriate standard for eviction—and each of the tenants in *Rucker* had signed leases and further assurances reflecting the one-strike policy—but it does underscore how striking was the casual nature of the Court's dismissal not only of the tenants' due process concerns but of the serious dignitary interests underlying those concerns.

The Last Resort

Public housing occupies a distinctive and important niche. Of all subsidized housing, public housing has come to serve people who would otherwise truly be on the margins, including a large number of residents whose sole source of income is public benefits, such as disabled and elderly tenants.[50] These are among the hardest populations to house, and they tend to have few other supports. This means that the imperative to protect vulnerable residents with extremely limited resources is perhaps the most acute in public housing of all of mainstream housing programs. And it also means that the impact of an eviction-based policy is that much more significant. Many residents of public housing—and the plaintiffs in *Rucker* are emblematic of this—have few, if any, other viable options.[51]

At the same time, however, public housing's status as housing of last resort can underscore the power of an eviction-based response to crime within the community. Public housing is a very scarce resource. Unlike other measures to relieve core aspects of poverty, no affordable housing program reaches nearly the range of recipients who qualify for the assistance. If a family in poverty qualifies for Supplemental Nutrition Assistance Program (SNAP) payments, they obtain the benefit as of right; similarly, if someone qualifies for Medicaid, he or she is admitted to the program without having to endure any kind of wait-list or policy lottery for scarce slots. This is simply not true for subsidized housing, and especially so for public housing. What the Seventh Circuit said of Section 8 in *Eidson v. Pierce* applies equally to public housing: "the fact [is] that there are not enough . . . housing units to accommodate all who are eligible" and at issue "are the rights not only of those . . . who were denied . . . benefits but also of those who received those benefits in the[ir] stead."[52] Indeed, the Oakland Housing Authority noted in its argument before the Supreme Court that, at the time, "for every unit of public housing in existence, three low-income families are on waiting lists, sometimes waiting years for selection."[53]

This very scarcity and overwhelming need means that incentivizing residents to control drug-related activities in this housing of last resort becomes a tempting strategy for public housing managers who may not have sufficient resources for other options. And, given the concentrated poverty that defines much of public housing, the policy draws much support when it does not involve innocent tenants.[54] This does not detract from the pain that eviction brings to families who lose their homes, but it does underscore that public housing, like any support of last resort, is going to be all the more valuable—and contested—for the overwhelming need that it serves.

Conclusion

Rucker resonated well beyond the lives of the tenants involved. On the one hand, the case affirmed the broad discretion of housing authorities to evict tenants, with all the consequences that brings, marking a significant turn in conceptions of public housing on the public-private spectrum. In the wake of *Rucker*, however, there was a public outcry, given the circumstances of the four tenants who brought the case. Shortly after the Court announced *Rucker*, then HUD Secretary Mel Martinez advised public housing directors to be "guided by compassion and common sense" in their enforcement of the one-strike policy and consider eviction "as the last option . . . after all others have been exhausted."[55] This was followed by a formal HUD notice seeking to temper the exercise of the one-strike policy by admonishing PHAs to consider all circumstances before evicting, most notably the effect of the eviction on innocent family members.[56]

These HUD responses have by no means stopped the practice of evicting tenants for the drug-related criminal activities of family members or caretakers, although tenant advocates have developed new ways to defend these cases since *Rucker*.[57] But it does signal a waning, if nothing else, in the ardor with which national policymakers emphasize eviction as a primary tool for responding to crime in public housing. The story of *Rucker*, then, may ultimately be a story of four elderly public housing tenants losing a legal fight that, by highlighting the harsh consequences of eviction from public housing, may have served as a reminder of the importance of such housing.

Notes

1. Joint Appendix at *43aa, U.S. Dep't of Hous. & Urb. Dev. v. Rucker, 535 U.S. 125 (2002) (Nos. 00-1770, 00-1781), 2001 WL 34093958 (Declaration of Pearlie Rucker). The eviction also alleged that Pearlie Rucker's adult son, Michael, had been arrested the previous September and found with cocaine. When arrested, Michael gave his mother's address as his residence, but Pearlie Rucker denied that Michael had lived with her.

2. Dep't of Hous. & Urb. Dev. v. Rucker, 535 U.S. 125, 128 (2002).

3. The history of efforts to provide housing for the poor includes a variety of public and private approaches, stretching back to the colonial era, that included the establishment of state and local housing authorities before the federal program, as well as a long tradition of almshouses, "houses of industry," settlement houses, model tenements, and similar efforts. *See* LAWRENCE J. VALE, FROM THE PURITANS TO THE PROJECTS: PUBLIC HOUSING AND PUBLIC NEIGHBORS 19–91 (2000).

4. Act of June 16, 1933, ch. 90, 48 Stat. 195 (formerly codified at 15 U.S.C. § 703).

5. Fenna Pit & Willem van Vliet, *Public Housing in the United States, in* HANDBOOK OF HOUSING AND THE BUILT ENVIRONMENT IN THE UNITED STATES 199, 205 (Elizabeth Huttman & Willem van Vliet eds., 1988).

6. See Roberta L. Rubin, *Public Housing Development—Mixed Finance in the Context of Historical Trends, in* NAVIGATING HUD PROGRAMS: A PRACTITIONER'S GUIDE TO THE LABYRINTH 231, 232 (George Weidenfeller & Julie McGovern eds., 2012) (citing United States v. Certain Lands in the City of Louisville, Jefferson County, 78 F.2d 684 (6th Cir. 1935)).

7. Pub. L. No. 75-412, 50 Stat. 888 (1937) (codified as amended at 42 U.S.C. § 1437 et seq.).

8. *See* Lawrence M. Friedman, *Public Housing and the Poor: An Overview*, 54 CAL. L. REV. 642, 642 (1966) (quoting N.Y. TIMES, Sept. 3, 1937, at 1).

9. See Rubin, supra note 6, at 233.

10. Jennifer A. Stoloff, U.S. Dep't of Hous. & Urb. Dev., Office of Policy Development and Research, A Brief History of Public Housing 1 (paper presented at the Annual Meeting of the American Sociological Association, Aug. 14, 2004) (on file with author).

11. *Id.* at 4.

12. Housing Act of 1949, Pub. L. 81-338, §§ 301, 303, 63 Stat. 413 (1949).

13. Housing and Urban Development Act of 1969, Pub. L. 91-152, 83 Stat. 379 (1969).

14. *See* PAUL BURKE, OFFICE OF POLICY DEV. & RESEARCH, U.S. DEP'T OF HOUS. & URBAN DEV., A PICTURE OF SUBSIDIZED HOUSEHOLDS, VOLUME II, UNITED STATES: LARGE PROJECTS & AGENCIES 8 (1996).

15. *See, e.g,* Hills v. Gautreaux, 425 U.S. 284, 286–89 (1976) (recounting the history of HUD-facilitated local discrimination in the siting of Chicago public housing).

16. Catherine Bauer, *The Dreary Deadlock of Public Housing*, 106 ARCHITECTURAL FORUM 5 (May 1957), at 140.

17. *See, e.g.*, TERENCE DUNWORTH & AARON SAIGER, NATIONAL INSTITUTE OF JUSTICE, DRUGS AND CRIME IN PUBLIC HOUSING: A THREE-CITY ANALYSIS (1994) (discussing national trends and examining crime rates in public housing in Los Angeles, Phoenix, and Washington, D.C.).

18. For an overview and evaluation of these waves of public housing criminal-justice efforts, *see* SUSAN J. POPKIN ET AL., THE HIDDEN WAR: CRIME AND THE TRAGEDY OF PUBLIC HOUSING IN CHICAGO 27–37 (2000).

19. Pub. L. 100-690, 102 Stat. 4181 (1988). The 1988 statute was a follow-up to the Anti-Drug Control Act of 1986, Pub. L. No. 99-570, 100 Stat. 3207 (1986) (codified as amended at 21 U.S.C. § 841 (1986)).

20. 42 U.S.C. § 1437d(*l*)(5) (1989). In 1991, HUD issued regulations implementing this provision, tracking the language of the statute. 24 C.F.R. § 966.4(f)(12)(i) (B); *see also id.* § 966.4(l)(2)(ii)(B). In the Federal Register notice promulgating the 1991 regulations, HUD specifically addressed the question whether knowledge or control were required for evictions under § 966.4(f)(12)(i). Commentators on the proposed rule had argued that tenants should not be evicted if they did not know of or reasonably foresee or took reasonable steps to prevent criminal activity. Public Housing Lease and Grievance Procedures, Final Rule, 56 Fed. Reg. 51560–1, 51563–64, 51566 (Oct. 11, 1991). HUD rejected these comments, emphasizing the administrability of a no-fault standard and the incentives HUD believed it would create. *Id.* at 51566–67.

21. The Cranston–Gonzalez National Affordable Housing Act of 1990, Pub. L. No. 101-625, § 504, 104 Stat. 4079, 4185 (1990).

22. The Housing Opportunity Program Extension Act, Pub. L. No. 104-120, § 9(a)(1), 110 Stat. 834 (1996) (codified as amended in scattered sections of 42 U.S.C. and 12 U.S.C.). The 1996 amendments also facilitated PHA criminal background screening for admissions, 42 U.S.C. § 1437d(q), and barred those evicted for drug-related crimes for three years, *id.* § 1437d(r). In 1998, Congress redesignated the language as subsection (*l*)(6). Quality Housing and Work Responsibility Act, Pub. L. No. 105-276, § 575(a), 112 Stat. 2461, 2634 (1998).

23. Public housing evictions for crime-related activities of family members and guests long predated the Anti-Drug Abuse Act, *see* Nelson H. Mock, Note, *Punishing the Innocent: No-Fault Eviction of Public Housing Tenants for the Actions of Third Parties,* 76 TEX. L. REV. 1495, 1502 (1998), but the act and its subsequent amendments sought to make the authorization for such evictions nationally uniform.

24. State of the Union Address by the President of the United States, 142 Cong. Rec. H768, H770 (daily ed. Jan. 23, 1996). The formal policy was announced two months later, on March 28, 1996. *See* Memorandum from President William J. Clinton to the Secretary of Housing and Urban Development (Mar. 28, 1996) (*available at* 1996 WL 139528).

25. U.S. Dep't of Hous. & Urb. Dev., "One Strike and You're Out" Policy in Public Housing 4 (1996).

26. *See* U.S. Dep't of Hous. & Urb. Dev., "One Strike and You're Out" Screening and Eviction Guidelines for Public Housing Authorities (HAs), Notice PIH 96-16 (HA), at 2 (1996).

27. *Id.* at 6–7.

28. At the time of the *Rucker* case, there were more than 3,100 local public housing authorities overseeing more than 1.3 million units that housed more than three million people nationwide. *See* Rucker v. Davis, 203 F.3d 627, 631 (9th Cir. 2000).

29. *See* Sandra Witt et al., Alameda County Public Health Department, A Public Health Crisis: Alameda County Violent Death Reporting System 2002–2004 9 (2006).

30. Brief for Petitioners at *6, Oakland Housing Authority v. Rucker, 534 U.S. 813 (2001) (No. 00-1781), 2001 WL 1548770, at *5.

31. *Id.*

32. *See* Henry K. Lee, *Oakland Seniors Sue To Block Evictions / Housing Authority's '1-strike' Policy*, S.F. Chron., Mar. 6, 1998.

33. Joint Appendix at *30aa–*35aa, *supra* note 1, at *1aa.

34. *See* Joint Appendix at *20aa, *supra* note 1.

35. In addition to statutory and constitutional claims under the Administrative Procedure Act and Section 1983, the plaintiffs' complaint also alleged violations of the Americans with Disabilities Act, 42 U.S.C. Ch. 126, based on the fact that Pearlie Rucker's daughter was disabled as was Herman Walker. *See* Joint Appendix, *Rucker*, 535 U.S. 125 (Nos. 00-1770, 00-1781). The district court cited Walker's ADA claim as part of the rationale for its injunction while dismissing Rucker's claim on behalf of her daughter, but neither of these disability challenges reached the Supreme Court.

36. Rucker v. Davis (No. C 98-00781 CRB), 1998 WL 345403, at *5 (N.D. Calif. Jun. 19, 1998). Judge Breyer is the brother of Supreme Court Justice Stephen Breyer, who accordingly recused himself when the Court heard *Rucker*.

37. *Id.* at *11.

38. Rucker v. Davis, 237 F.3d 1113, 1126 (9th Cir. 2001).

39. *Id.* at 1124–25.

40. *Rucker*, 535 U.S. at 130–31 (invoking the first step of the framework established in Chevron U.S.A. Inc. v. Natural Res. Def. Council, Inc., 467 U.S. 837, 842–43 (1984)). The Court quickly dispatched arguments based on comparisons to other statutes and the interaction with a related forfeiture provision, as well as resorts to legislative history (in a footnote) and consequentialist policy arguments, noting that the statute does not require, but merely authorizes, evictions, while accepting the claim that "no fault" evictions create appropriate incentives for tenants.

41. *Rucker*, 535 U.S. at 135.

42. *See* Jim Herron Zamora, *'One Strike' Tenants Keep Apartments in Oakland / 3 of 4 Evictions Dropped Although Law Upheld*, S.F. Chron., Apr. 5, 2002. OHA had dismissed the eviction action against Rucker in February 1998, after Gelinda was incarcerated. *See Rucker*, 535 U.S. at 128 n.1.

43. In 2009, the stock of unsubsidized affordable rental housing, at just over 10 million units, was roughly three times the size of the subsidized portfolio. *See* Harvard Joint Center for Housing Studies, America's Rental Housing: Meeting Challenges, Building on Opportunities 22 (2011).

44. 226 F.2d 51, 52 (D.C. Cir. 1955).

45. *See, e.g.*, Ayers v. Philadelphia Housing Authority, 908 F.2d 1184, 1191–93 (3d Cir. 1990) (public-housing-related regulations of eviction proceedings pre-empt state law). Indeed, in its *Rucker* briefing, HUD argued that any state-law-based limitation on a no-fault interpretation of the eviction standard under § 1437d(*l*)(6) would be pre-empted. *See* Reply Brief for the U.S. Dept. of Hous. & Urb. Dev. at *15, *Rucker*, 535 U.S. 125 (2002) (Nos. 00-1770, 00-1781).

46. *Compare, e.g.*, Moore v. Lorain Metro. Hous. Auth., 905 N.E.2d 606, 609 (Ohio 2009) *with* Moore v. Wilmington Hous. Auth., 619 A.2d 1166 (Del. 1993).

47. *See* Thorpe v. Hous. Auth. of Durham, 393 U.S. 268, 274 (1969).

48. *See* George Lakoff, *HUD Is Trying to Privatize and Mortgage Off All of America's Public Housing*, Huff. Post, May 21, 2010, http://www.huffingtonpost.com/george-lakoff/hud-is-trying-to-privatiz_b_585069.html.

49. Lawrence J. Vale, Reclaiming Public Housing: A Half Century of Struggle in Three Public Neighborhoods 13 (2002).

50. *See supra* text accompanying note 14. At the time of the *Rucker* evictions, one-third of public housing heads of households or their spouses were over 62, and somewhere between a fifth and a third of all residents were disabled. *See* Burke, *supra* note 14, at 8–9.

51. Public housing tenancies, absent eviction for good cause and similar requirements, are automatically renewed, 42 U.S.C. § 1437d(*l*)(1), which makes eviction an even more severe sanction.

52. 745 F.2d 453, 457 (1984).

53. Brief for Petitioners at 2–3, *Rucker*, 535 U.S. 125 (2002) (No. 00-178).

54. *See* Adam P. Hellegers, Comment, *Reforming HUD's "One-Strike" Public Housing Evictions Through Tenant Participation*, 90 J. Crim. L. & Criminology 323, 324–25 (1999) (noting evidence of a bifurcation in support amongst public housing residents between tenant criminal-activity-related evictions and evictions for third-party criminal activity).

55. Letter from Mel Martinez, secretary of U.S. Department of Housing & Urban Development, to public housing directors, Apr. 16, 2002.

56. Letter from Michael M. Liu, assistant secretary, Public and Indian Housing, U.S. Department of Housing and Urban Development, to public housing directors, June 6, 2002.

57. *See* Robert Hornstein, Article, *Litigating Around the Long Shadow of Department of Housing and Urban Development v. Rucker: The Availability of Abuse of Discretion and Implied Duty of Good Faith Affirmative Defense in Public Housing Criminal Activity Evictions*, 43 U. Tol. L. Rev. 1 (2011) (discussing post-*Rucker* practices and tenant defenses based on abuse of discretion and other theories).

Contributors

Melanie B. Abbott is Professor of Law Emeritus at Quinnipiac University School of Law, where she continues to teach Poverty Law and acts as an informal advisor to student groups working in public interest. She graduated from the University of Bridgeport School of Law and clerked for a federal appellate judge before practicing corporate law. She taught for 27 years, most often Civil Procedure and Administrative Law.

R. Kirk Anderson is a PhD candidate in Educational Policy Studies at the University of Wisconsin–Madison. He holds an MA in Educational Policy Studies from UW–Madison and a BA in English literature from Texas A&M University.

Wendy A. Bach is Associate Professor at the University of Tennessee College of Law, where she teaches Poverty, Race, Gender and Law, and the Advocacy Clinic, and writes on poverty and law. She practiced welfare law in New York City at the Legal Aid Society and was the director of the Homelessness Outreach and Prevention Project at the Urban Justice Center.

Tonya L. Brito is the Jefferson Burrus-Bascom Professor of Law at the University of Wisconsin Law School. She also serves as the director of the Institute for Legal Studies and as a faculty affiliate with the Institute for Research on Poverty, University of Wisconsin. She holds a JD from Harvard Law School and an AB from Barnard College.

John Capowski has been a full-time faculty member at Cornell, Maryland, and Widener Commonwealth. A former director of the clinic at Cornell, he currently writes on evidence law. He has worked as a Legal Services attorney in New York, and as the first director of attorney training at the Maryland Office of the Attorney General.

Nestor Davidson directs the Fordham Law School Urban Law Center and writes on property, land use, local government law, and affordable housing law and policy. He served as Special Counsel and Principal Deputy General Counsel at the U.S. Department of Housing and Urban Development and practiced in commercial real estate and affordable housing at Latham & Watkins.

Marie A. Failinger is Professor of Law at Mitchell Hamline School of Law, where she writes on poverty law and Legal Services practice. She is a former Legal Services attorney and is a board member of Central Minnesota Legal Services and the National Equal Justice Library. She earned her JD at Valparaiso University School of Law and her LLM at Yale Law School.

Anne Fleming is an Associate Professor of Law at Georgetown University Law Center. She holds a JD from Harvard Law School and a PhD from the University of Pennsylvania.

Henry Freedman was executive director of National Center on Law and Economic Justice from 1971 until 2014. Over the years he has also taught in law and social work schools at Catholic, Columbia, and New York University. A graduate of Amherst College and Yale Law School, he chaired the Committee on Legal Assistance of the Association of the Bar of the City of New York and has received numerous public interest awards.

Michele Gilman is Venable Professor of Law and director of the Civil Advocacy Clinic at the University of Baltimore School of Law, representing low-income individuals and community groups. She writes about social welfare issues and is a codirector of the Center on Applied Feminism, which works to apply insights of feminist legal theory to legal practice and policy.

Elisa Minoff is Assistant Professor of History at the University of South Florida. She was Visiting Research Fellow in Economic and Social History for 2013–2014 at the German Historical Institute in Washington, D.C. A political and legal historian of the United States in the twentieth century, she received her PhD from Harvard University.

Julie Nice is the Herbst Foundation Professor of Law at University of San Francisco School of Law. Author of *Poverty Law: Theory and Practice* and numerous poverty law works, she has also taught at the University of Denver and Northwestern, where she received her BS and JD. She was formerly a public interest litigator at the Legal Assistance Foundation of Chicago.

Clare Pastore is Professor of the Practice of Law at the University of Southern California Gould School of Law, where she teaches poverty law, nonprofit ethics, and an access to justice practicum. She is coauthor of a poverty law textbook and is a former staff attorney at the Western Center on Law and Poverty and the ACLU. She holds a BA from Colgate University and a JD from Yale Law School.

Henry Rose is Professor of Law at Loyola–Chicago and formerly directed the Loyola University Community Law Center. After receiving his BA from Northwestern and his JD from IIT–Chicago Kent, Rose practiced law for Cook County Legal Assistance and was a Legal Services Corporation management consultant. He focuses on civil law affecting low-income persons and property.

Ezra Rosser is Professor of Law at American University Washington College of Law, where he teaches poverty law, housing law, property law, and federal Indian law. He has an MPhil from Cambridge, a JD from Harvard, and a BA from Yale.

Kelly S. Terry is Associate Professor of Law and Director of the Public Service Externship Program and Pro Bono Opportunities at the University of Arkansas, Little Rock. She also serves as a co-director of the Institute for Law Teaching and Learning. She has practiced at the Department of Justice, in the Arkansas Attorney General's Office, and as a partner at Williams & Anderson PLC. She has a BA from Hendrix College and a JD from the University of Arkansas at Fayetteville.

Camille Walsh is Assistant Professor of American and Ethnic Studies and Law, Economics and Public Policy in the School of Interdisciplinary Arts and Sciences at University of Washington Bothell. She has a BA from New York University, a JD from Harvard Law School and a PhD in U.S. history from University of Oregon.

Monica Wedgewood practices law with von Briesen & Roper, SC, in Madison, Wisconsin. She holds a JD and MPA from the University of Wisconsin–Madison, where she served as a managing editor of the *Wisconsin Law Review* and as a member of the Moot Court Board. She holds a BA in history from the University of Illinois Urbana–Champaign.

Index